THEORY AND INTERPRETATION OF NARRATIVE
JAMES PHELAN AND PETER J. RABINOWITZ, SERIES EDITORS

Postclassical Narratology

Approaches and Analyses

EDITED BY
JAN ALBER AND MONIKA FLUDERNIK

 THE OHIO STATE UNIVERSITY PRESS / COLUMBUS

Copyright © 2010 by The Ohio State University.
All rights reserved

Library of Congress Cataloging-in-Publication Data
Postclassical narratology : approaches and analyses / edited by Jan Alber and Monika Fludernik.
    p. cm. — (Theory and interpretation of narrative)
Includes bibliographical references and index.
ISBN-13: 978-0-8142-5175-1 (pbk. : alk. paper)
ISBN-10: 0-8142-5175-7 (pbk. : alk. paper)
ISBN-13: 978-0-8142-1142-7 (cloth : alk. paper)
ISBN-10: 0-8142-1142-9 (cloth : alk. paper)
[etc.]
1. Narration (Rhetoric) I. Alber, Jan, 1973– II. Fludernik, Monika. III. Series: Theory and interpretation of narrative series.
PN212.P67 2010
808—dc22
                    2010009305
This book is available in the following editions:

Cloth (ISBN 978-0-8142-1142-7)
Paper (ISBN 978-0-8142-5175-1)
CD-ROM (ISBN 978-0-8142-9241-9)

Cover design by Laurence J. Nozik
Type set in Adobe Sabon

∞ The paper used in this publication meets the minimum requirements of the American National Standard for Information Sciences—Permanence of Paper for Printed Library Materials. ANSI Z39.48-1992.

9 8 7 6 5 4 3 2 1

Contents

Acknowledgments   vii

Introduction
    JAN ALBER AND MONIKA FLUDERNIK   1

PART I.
Extensions and Reconfigurations of Classical Narratology

1. Person, Level, Voice: A Rhetorical Reconsideration
   RICHARD WALSH   35

2. *Mise en Cadre*—A Neglected Counterpart to *Mise en Abyme*: A Frame-Theoretical and Intermedial Complement to Classical Narratology
   WERNER WOLF   58

3. Large Intermental Units in *Middlemarch*
   ALAN PALMER   83

4. Mediacy, Mediation, and Focalization: The Squaring of Terminological Circles
   MONIKA FLUDERNIK   105

PART II.
Transdisciplinarities

5. Directions in Cognitive Narratology: Triangulating Stories, Media, and the Mind
   DAVID HERMAN   137

6 Hypothetical Intentionalism: Cinematic Narration Reconsidered
   JAN ALBER   163

7 Sapphic Dialogics: Historical Narratology and the Sexuality of Form
   SUSAN S. LANSER   186

8 Narrators, Narratees, and Mimetic Desire
   AMIT MARCUS   206

9 Narratology and the Social Sciences
   JARMILA MILDORF   234

10 Postclassical Narratology and the Theory of Autobiography
   MARTIN LÖSCHNIGG   255

11 Natural Authors, Unnatural Narration
   HENRIK SKOV NIELSEN   275

Contributors   303
Author Index   307
Subject Index   315

Acknowledgments

This book has benefited greatly from the advice and support by a number of people. First of all, we would like to thank Sandy Crooms from The Ohio State University Press for guiding this volume so expertly to its finishing line. Our gratitude extends also to Jim Phelan, Peter Rabinowitz, and the anonymous external reader for their hard work on the manuscript as well as their extensive and perceptive comments on it. We have tried to incorporate their insights into the final version of the volume, but any remaining infelicities are of course our own responsibility. Finally, for editorial assistance and help with the proofreading, we would like to thank Ramona Früh, Moritz Gansen, Theresa Hamilton, Carolin Krauße, Luise Lohmann, and Rebecca Reichl.

An earlier version of Susan S. Lanser's contribution appeared as "Novel (Lesbian) Subjects: The Sexual History of Form," in *Novel: A Forum on Fiction* 42.3 (2009): 497–503.

JAN ALBER AND
MONIKA FLUDERNIK

Introduction

The title of this collection of recent narratological work, *Postclassical Narratology: Approaches and Analyses,* openly alludes to David Herman's seminal bimillennial volume *Narratologies: New Perspectives on Narrative Analysis* (1999b), in which he introduced the term postclassical narratology[1] and defined it as follows:

> Postclassical narratology (which should not be conflated with poststructuralist theories of narrative) contains classical narratology as one of its "moments" but is marked by a profusion of new methodologies and research hypotheses: the result is a host of new perspectives on the forms and functions of narrative itself. Further, in its postclassical phase, research on narrative does not just expose the limits but also exploits the possibilities of the older, structuralist models. In much the same way, postclassical physics does not simply discard classical Newtonian models, but rather rethinks their conceptual underpinnings and reassesses their scope of applicability. (1999a: 2–3)

As Herman here indicates, recent postclassical narratology has to be contrasted with what he calls classical narratology. What is subsumed under classical narratology primarily embraces the work of the French structural-

---

1. David Herman originally coined the term "postclassical narratology" in an essay called "Scripts, Sequences, and Stories: Elements of a Postclassical Narratology" (1997).

ists (Roland Barthes, Claude Bremond, Tzvetan Todorov, A. J. Greimas, and Gérard Genette), but also the German tradition in narrative theory (Eberhard Lämmert and Franz Karl Stanzel). Herman, in turn, refers back to Shlomith Rimmon-Kenan's classic study *Narrative Fiction: Contemporary Poetics* (1983) (Herman 1999a: 1), which—together with Seymour Chatman's *Story and Discourse* (1978) and Gerald Prince's work (e.g., 1982, 1987)—most clearly shaped the image of what narratology is for a wide readership of students and academics. Other influential spokespersons at first seen to fit the same groove were Meir Sternberg (1978), Thomas Pavel (1986), and Susan Lanser (1981).[2] Yet, one could argue that these representatives of classical narratology already started to drift away from the structuralist model, if ever so slightly and imperceptibly. Where Rimmon-Kenan felt she had to cling to the "geometric imaginary" of narratology (Gibson 1996) in order to ward off deconstruction (Herman 1999a: 1), Lanser began to incorporate questions of gender and ideology (see her debate with Diengott—Lanser 1986, 1988; Diengott 1988), Sternberg went beyond mere chronology to focus on the dynamics of narrative design, Thomas Pavel founded possible-worlds theory, and Seymour Chatman started to analyze film narrative.

Herman uses the term narratology "quite broadly, in a way that makes it more or less interchangeable with *narrative studies*" (1999a: 27, n1; original emphasis). In fact, it is more or less synonymous with the phrase "narrative analysis" in his subtitle and in the final sentence of the "Introduction," which provides an outlook for "narrative analysis at the threshold of the millennium" (27).[3] In order to understand how Herman conceives of the originary quality of classical narratology, it is therefore useful to contrast it with its postclassical progeny. As Herman sketches the distinction in the passage cited above, postclassical narratology introduces elaborations of classical narratology that both consolidate and diversify the basic theoretical core of narratology. Such work is exemplified by the essays in the first section of the volume. Moreover, postclassical narratology proposes extensions of the classical model that open the fairly focused and restricted realm of narratology to *methodological, thematic,* and *contextual influences from outside.* These reorientations reflect the impact of literary theory on academia in the 1980s and 1990s. Herman in this second area notes three major lines of

---

2. All of these scholars have groundings in Russian Formalism and linguistics-based narrative semiotics. The term narratology was coined by Todorov in *Grammaire du Décameron* (1969), where he writes: "Cet ouvrage relève d'une science qui n'existe pas encore, disons la NARRATOLOGIE, la science du récit" (1969: 10).

3. For a critique of this broad usage see Nünning (2003: 257–62) and Meister's more radical suggestions concerning a narratological fundamentalism (2003).

development which reflect sections two to four of the collection: the rise of "new technologies and emergent methodologies"; the move "beyond literary narrative"; and the extension of narratology into new media and "narrative logics." (Compare the table of contents and 1999a: 14–26 in the "Introduction.")

With some historical hindsight one could now perhaps regroup these developments slightly differently and focus on four types of interactions. The first category is roughly equivalent to Herman's revisions of classical problems. It includes work that extends the classical paradigm intradisciplinarily by focusing on theoretical blind spots, gaps, or indeterminacies within the standard paradigm. *Methodological* extensions of the classical model, secondly, absorb theoretical and/or methodological insights and import them, producing, for instance, narratological speech act theory (Pratt 1977), psychoanalytic approaches to narrative (Brooks 1984, Chambers 1984, 1991), or deconstructive narratology (O'Neill 1994, Gibson 1996, Currie 1998). The third orientation integrates *thematic* and therefore variable emphases into the classical model, whose core had consisted of invariable, i.e., universal, categories. Examples are feminist, queer, ethnic or minority-related, and postcolonial approaches to narrative (see Nünning's diagram listing the many new versions of narratology [2003: 249–51]). Contextual versions of postclassical narratology, constituting the fourth trend, extend narratological analysis to literature outside the novel. Narratology now includes a consideration of various media (films, cartoons, etc.), the performative arts as well as non-literary narratives. Conversely, the narrative turn (Kreiswirth 2005, Phelan 2008b)[4] in the (social) sciences and humanities has resulted in an awareness of the centrality of narrative in many areas of culture, from autobiography and history to psychology, the natural sciences, banking or even sports (Nash 1990).[5]

Thus, while some scholars continue to work within the classical paradigm by adding analytical categories to the original base of structuralist concepts, others attempt to instantiate a more or less radical break with the tradition by transcending the assumptions and categorical axioms of the classical paradigm. The motives for such a reconceptualization of the theoretical models and even the discipline of narratology often relate to the consequences of the narrative turn. Put differently, it is because narrative theory can now service

---

4. See also, for current relevance, the ESRC seminar "The Narrative Turn: Revisioning Theory" at the Centre for Narrative and Auto/Biographical Studies at the University of Edinburgh (2007–2008). www. sps.ed.uk/NABS/AbstractsSem1.htm.

5. For extensive surveys see Fludernik (2000), Nünning (2000), Nünning/Nünning (2002), Ryan (2004), and Phelan/Rabinowitz (2005).

many different sciences (or serve quite diverse masters) that an adaptation of its theoretical bases becomes necessary. In this way new light tends to be shed on hitherto unquestioned axioms which had been developed in relation to literary narrative, most often the novel, and which are therefore not ideally suited to their new contexts of application.

The present volume abides by Herman's dual focus on what one could call a critical but frame-abiding and a more radical frame-transcending or frame-shattering handling of the classical paradigm. The first part of this book deals with extensions of classical narratology that take the achievements of structuralism as a starting point for close scrutiny and then suggest revisions of the traditional paradigm. Here the emphasis is on adding new distinctions, questioning unacknowledged presuppositions, and on radically revising the standard concepts and typologies, redesigning the conceptual underpinnings of structuralist approaches. The second part, on the other hand, focuses on narrative analyses that move beyond the classical framework by extending their focus to a variety of medial and thematic contexts, from the visual realm to the generic (e.g., autobiography), the queer, and the non-literary (e.g., medical interviews). Some contributions also arrive at radical revisions of the classical model because the intermedial or thematic applications they have in hand require such trimming or redesigning.

The essays in this volume moreover address potential overlaps between the various postclassical approaches. For instance, they link ethnic concerns with those of gender, visual narration with reader response, the autobiographical mode and psychoanalysis with issues of gender and sexual orientation, formal concerns with sociological analysis, or the rhetorical approach with the unnatural. More generally, this collection presents new perspectives on the question of what narratives are and of how they function in their different media. We also wish to suggest that, as the first decade of the third millennium draws to a close, we are now perhaps beginning to see a second phase of postclassical narratology. David Herman's volume *Narratologies* could be argued to represent the first adult phase in a *Bildungsroman*-like story of narratology. In this reading, Shklovsky and the Russian Formalists figure as narratology's infancy and the structuralist models of the 1960s and 1970s as its adolescence. This

> [. . .] adolescence of narratology was followed by a reorientation and diversification of narrative theories, producing a series of subdisciplines that arose in reaction to post-structuralism and the paradigm shift to cultural studies. [. . .] Out of the diversity of approaches and their exogamous unions with critical theory have now emerged several budding narratologies which beto-

ken that the discipline is in the process of a major revival. (Fludernik 2005: 37)

Herman's narratologies would therefore correspond to a phase of diversification. In postclassical narratology's second phase, which is one of both consolidation and continued diversification, one now has to address the question of how these various narratologies overlap and interrelate (see also Herman/Biwu, 2009). Narratology, to continue our metaphor, in settling down, will now have to align with one another the numerous centrifugal models that arose in the first phase of postclassicism; it will now have to determine how these thematic and contextual inflections of narratology can be linked to the structuralist core in methodologically sound ways. This is not a call for a prescriptive unity of methods and models but an attempt to align the many disparate ways of doing postclassical narratology (phase one) and to check out their moments of overlap as well as the extent of their incompatibilities. Newer developments also focus on the no doubt fuzzy boundary line between a general literary study of narratives and more specifically narratological analysis of the same texts. No one overarching model is envisaged here, but in our opinion considerable consolidation despite continuing diversity is called for at this moment. By taking phase-one developments seriously, postclassical narratology will moreover subject its structuralist core to severe critical scrutiny, lopping, modifying, revising, or redesigning the foundations of the discipline. In what follows, we will first discuss the diversity of current narratological research and then turn to developments that suggest a more centripetal tendency in the process of establishment.

POSTCLASSICAL NARRATOLOGY: PHASE ONE
Multiplicities, Interdisciplinarities, Transmedialities

As Luc Herman and Bart Vervaeck put it, the differences between the classical structuralist paradigm and the new postclassical research program can be characterized as follows: "Whereas structuralism was intent on coming up with a general theory of narrative, postclassical narratology prefers to consider the circumstances that make every act of reading different. [. . .] From cognition to ethics to ideology: all aspects related to reading assume pride of place in the research on narrative" (2005: 450).

Ansgar Nünning has captured the extent and variety of new approaches in a useful diagram (2003: 243–44) that provides a visual map for what he considers to be the most important distinctions between classical and postclassical narratologies.[6] He contrasts (1) classical text-centeredness with postclassical context orientation and (2) the treatment of narrative as a *langue* with the pragmatic focus on the *parole* of individual (use of) narratives in postclassical approaches.[7] As in the syntax vs. pragmatics dichotomy, Nünning also (3) sees classical narratology as a closed system and postclassical narratologies as emphasizing the dynamics of narration. He moreover (4) subsumes the shift from the functional analysis of features to a reader-oriented focus on strategies and applications in the dichotomy and (5) contrasts classical bottom-up analysis with postclassical top-down inferencing. Nünning's table next opposes (6) "(reductive) binarism" with a "preference for holistic cultural interpretation" and (7) structuralist taxonomy with thematically and ideologically directed analysis. As a consequence, (8) where classical narratology remained shy of moral grounding, postclassical narratologies open themselves to moral issues, analogously causing (10) a shift from descriptive to interpretative and evaluative paradigms. Thus, (9) classical narratology's aim to provide a "poetics of fiction" (in alignment with the semiological thrust of narratology) is superseded by "putting the analytical toolbox to interpretative use." Nünning also sees the rise of diachronic or historical narratology as a postclassical phenomenon (11). His summary in the diagram of the dichotomy classical vs. postclassical consists in the contrasts of (12) universalism vs. particularism (which is equivalent to contextualism), and (13) the opposition between a relatively unified discipline vs. "an interdisciplinary project consisting of heterogeneous approaches" (all 243–4). Paradoxically, Nünning's rhetorical strategy of establishing open, non-taxonomic postclassical narratologies actually involves the dualism of a before and after and therefore relies on a structural binarism of the very kind that it is trying to transcend.

Generally speaking, then, postclassical narratologies along the lines sketched by Nünning seem to move toward a grand contextual, historical, pragmatic and reader-oriented effort. Such integration and synthesis allows researchers to recontextualize the classical paradigm and to enrich narrative theory with ideas developed after its structuralist phase. While classical narratology was a relatively unified discipline or field, postclassical narratologies are part of a large transdisciplinary project that consists of various heterogeneous approaches (see also Herman 2007).

---

6. The numbering in what follows corresponds to Nünning's order in the diagram.

7. To put this slightly differently, the chief concern of structuralist narratologists was "with transtextual semiotic principles according to which basic structural units (characters, states, events, etc.) are combined, permuted, and transformed to yield specific narrative texts" (D. Herman 2005: 19–20).

Feminist narratology can serve as a good example of the types of strategies and extensions of the classical model that are being practiced in postclassical narratologies. Feminst narratologists such as Robyn Warhol or Susan Lanser have highlighted the fact that narratives are always determined "by complex and changing conventions that are themselves produced in and by the relations of power that implicate writer, reader, and text" (Lanser 1992: 5). Much feminist narratology studies elements of story and/or discourse against the foil of gender differences. Such a deployment of narratological models places narratives in their historical and cultural contexts, highlighting the central significance of gender stereotypes. As a consequence, some feminist narratologists like Susan Lanser (1986, 1988) and Ruth Page (2006) have proposed that one take the gender of authors, authorial audiences, actual readers, narrators, narratees, and characters into consideration, thus initiating a rewriting of classical models. The question of a narrator's properties needs to incorporate their sex and gender; the explicit naming of narrator figures, their external appearances, and actions often yield information on the basis of implied genderization by means of dress codes, behavioral patterns, and cultural presuppositions. Feminist narratologists moreover supplement classical theories about actants by sociocultural roles. Under the heading of "the engaging narrator," Robyn Warhol has postulated the existence of different types of narratorial discourse in texts by nineteenth-century male and female authors (1989), adding a consideration of popular literature to this field of inquiry (2003). Kathy Mezei (1996) and Ruth Page (2003), on the other hand, look at "male" and "female" plot structures (e.g., one climax vs. several climaxes or no climax at all).

It is also worth noting that Judith Roof (1996) and Lanser (1995, 1999, this volume) have extended feminist narratology into queer studies. For example, in *Come As You Are,* Judith Roof looks at the reciprocal relation between narrative and sexuality. Queer narratology should disclose the traces of heterosexuality in narratives, pointing out "the production of sexual categories whose existence and constitution depend upon a specific reproductive narrative heteroideology" (1996: xxvii). Thus, narrative analysis should uncover "the preservation of literal and metaphorical heterosexuality as (re)productive (and hence valuable)." At the same time, Roof pleads for a "constitution of narrative that includes both heterosexuality and homosexuality as categories necessary to its dynamic" (xxvii). This raises the following narratological problem: In what way do feminist and queer approaches go beyond the thematic highlighting of male (patriarchal and heteronormative) dominance in literature and beyond an analysis of counterhegemonic and subversive discourse in general? One way of answering this question is to describe feminist/queer (or postcolonial) strategies by resorting to narratological categories. Thus, the use of second-person fiction in Edmund White's *Nocturnes for the King of Naples* (1978) allows the author to inveigle the heteronormative reader into sympathizing with a love relationship, which only later emerges as homosexual (cp. Fludernik 1994b: 471).

Analogously, postcolonial narratologists centrally address the question of how the narrative text is imbued with colonial or neocolonial discourse that correlates with the oppression of native populations and how the discourse simultaneously manages to undermine this very ideology (Pratt 1992, Spurr 1993, Doyle 1994, Aldama 2003). Brian Richardson (2001a, 2006, 2007b), for instance, has suggested that we-narration occurs strategically in postcolonial fiction, reflecting the anti-individual conception of traditional cultures.[8] While these two examples focused on the use of a prominent experimental form of narrative for the purposes of conveying non-normative or counterhegemonic messages, other narratologists have tried to argue that the categories of narratology need to be modified or extended in order to accommodate the concerns of race, power, gender, ethnicity, or sexual orientation. In a recent MLA panel on "Race and Narrative Theory," Dorothy M. Hale proposed that narratology could not adequately deal with postcolonial writing since its categories were imbued with colonial logocentrism (Hale 2008). Though we do not share this viewpoint, we do agree that colonial, sexist, or racist literature often uses narrative devices and strategies that through their use in these ideologically loaded texts may seem to acquire phallogocentric and discriminatory overtones. Yet postcolonial, queer or antihegemonic narratives may be using the same writing strategies for quite subversive ends. Such a technique of "double-voicing" can be fruitfully compared with Henry Louis Gates's category of "signifying" (Gates 1988) and of course with Mikhail Bakhtin's characterizations of heteroglossia (Bakhtin 1981). Narrative devices by themselves do not carry any ideological freight; often they are neutral modes of focusing attention that only acquire normative or critical meanings in their various contexts of use.

Another important feature of postclassical narratologies already noted in Herman (1999a) is their emphasis on new media. While traditional narratologists such as Stanzel and Genette primarily focused on the eighteenth-century to early twentieth-century novel, transmedial approaches seek to rebuild narratology so that it can handle new genres and storytelling practices across a wide spectrum of media. An interesting issue in this context is the question of how narrative practices are shaped by the capacities of the medium in which the story is presented. In their attempts to determine the different lan-

---

8. For work in the area of cultural narratology see also Nünning (1997 and 2000).

guages of storytelling, proponents of transmedial narratology look at plays, films, narrative poems, conversational storytelling, hyperfictions, cartoons, ballets, video clips, paintings, statues, advertisements, historiography, news stories, narrative representations in medical or legal contexts, and so forth.[9] For instance, much attention has recently been paid to the analysis of drama (Richardson 1987, 1988, 2001b, 2007a, Fludernik 2008, Nünning/Sommer 2008) as a narrative genre. Thus, the question of whether it makes sense to posit a dramatic narrator (Jahn 2001)[10] or whether one will need to introduce a level of performance into narratology (Fludernik 2008) has been raised. Work on drama as narrative has highlighted the numerous narrator figures in plays (Richardson 1988, 2001b; Nünning/Sommer 2008). Analogously, film studies have underlined narrator-like elements in film such as voice-over narration (Bordwell 1985, Kozloff 1988, Branigan 1992). The concept of a dramatic narrator as the instance that tells the story of the play similarly echoes discussions about the existence of a "cinematic narrator" in film; both resort to the narrator category from novels or short stories (Chatman 1990: 127).[11]

Other transmediality narratologists such as Marie-Laure Ryan, Jörg Helbig, and Werner Wolf have studied the potential narrativity of hyperfictions (Ryan 1999, 2001; Helbig 2001, 2003). They also focus on possible narratives in paintings, poetry, and even musical pieces (Wolf 1999, 2002, 2003; Ryan 2004). Transgeneric extensions of narratology (see especially Ryan 2008), in addition to the analysis of drama and poetry (Müller-Zettelmann 2002, in progress), target autobiography, historiography, legal narrative, documentaries, and conversational storytelling (see also Nünning and Nünning 2002).

Besides the theoretical and medial extensions just outlined, some forms of postclassical narratology ground themselves in a rhetorical framework. For both Genette and Booth, rhetoric served as a mastertrope for their textual analyses. Rhetorical narratology moreover integrates findings from reader-response theory. Rhetorical theorists such as Wayne C. Booth, James Phelan, and Peter Rabinowitz are particularly interested in the contexts of narra-

---

9. For instance, Jarmila Mildorf's essay in this collection addresses the potential usefulness of narratology in the social sciences, while Martin Löschnigg looks at autobiographies from the perspective of cognitive narratology.

10. Manfred Jahn argues that "all narrative genres are structurally mediated by a first-degree narrative agency which, in a performance, may either take the totally unmetaphorical shape of a vocally and bodily present narrator figure (a scenario that is unavailable in written epic narrative), or be a disembodied 'voice' in a printed text, or remain an anonymous and impersonal narrative function in charge of selection, arrangement, and focalization" (2001: 674).

11. For a detailed discussion of the concept of the cinematic narrator see Jan Alber's essay in this volume.

tive production and reception. More specifically, they see narrative as an act of communication between the real author and the flesh-and-blood reader, but also between the implied author and the authorial audience (or implied reader), and, finally, between the narrator and the narrative audience (or narratee). In short, the rhetorical approach attempts to ascertain the purpose of stories and storytelling.

Thus, Wayne C. Booth, in the context of the neo-Aristotelianism of the Chicago School, introduced the term *implied author* as a heuristic tool. The "implied author" denotes the real author's "second self," and as such satisfies "the reader's need to know where, in the world of values, he stands, that is, to know where the author wants him to stand" (1983: 73). Booth argues that analyses along the lines of the implied author enable us "to come as close as possible to sitting in the author's chair and making this text, becoming able to remake it, employing the author's 'reason-of-art'" (1982: 21). Similarly, James Phelan defines the implied author as "a streamlined version of the real author," and this version is "responsible for the choices that create the narrative text as 'these words in this order' and that imbue the text with his or her values" (2005: 45; 216).[12] The ultimate goal of narrative criticism is to asymptotically approximate the condition of "the authorial audience," i.e., the ideal audience for whom the author constructs the text and who understands it perfectly (Rabinowitz 1977: 121–41; see also Rabinowitz 1998; Phelan 1996: 135–53). According to Phelan, "the rhetorical model assumes that the flesh and blood reader seeks to enter the authorial audience in order to understand the invitations for engagement that the narrative offers" (Phelan 2007b: 210).

Furthermore, rhetorical theorists argue that narrative texts permanently invite us to make ethical judgments—about characters, narrators, and implied authors (Phelan 2007a: 6). Phelan thus discriminates between four ethical positions. The first involves (1) the ethics of the told (character-character relations); the second and third concern the ethics of the telling, namely (2) the narrator's relation to the characters, the task of narrating, and the audience, and (3) the implied author's relation to these things. The fourth ethical position relates to (4) the flesh-and-blood audience's responses to the first three positions (Phelan 2005; 2007a: 11).

12. For discussions of the implied author see Kindt and Müller (2006) and the contributions by Jan Alber and Henrik Skov Nielsen in this collection. In *The Rhetoric of Fictionality*, Richard Walsh reintroduces the actual author. More specifically, he suggests eradicating extra- and heterodiegetic narrators in narrative fiction: "Extradiegetic heterodiegetic narrators (that is, 'impersonal' and 'authorial' narrators), who cannot be represented without thereby being rendered homodiegetic or intradiegetic, are in no way distinguishable from authors." He therefore concludes that "the narrator is always either a character who narrates, or the author" (2007: 84; 78).

Finally, it is worth noting that a narrative's development from beginning to end is governed by a textual and a readerly dynamics (along the pattern of instability—complication—resolution) (Phelan 2007a: 15–22), and understanding their interaction provides a good means for recognizing the purpose of the narrative. Recent rhetorical narratology can therefore be seen as a continuation and deepening of the rhetorical framework of Boothian theory and as an underlining of discourse narratology's rhetorical foundations. At the same time, it can be regarded as an important contextualizing venture that opens the text to the real-world interaction of author and reader, and hence provides a perfect model for discussing the ethics of reading and the treatment of ethical problems in narrative fiction.

So far, we have listed several extensions of narratology that tried to take into account theoretical developments in academia since the 1970s—reader response theory, feminism, gender and queer studies, postcolonialism, the ethical turn. We would now like to turn to developments in narratology that are not linked to external stimuli but have arisen from inside the discipline and in reaction to extensive analysis of the theoretical models, their gaps, inconsistencies, even contradictions. However, it should be noted that this distinction is not a watertight binary opposition but rather a convenient way of highlighting intrinsic and extrinsic developments that are both affecting postclassical narratologies, sometimes in combination with each other. Generally speaking, we feel that this contest between different positions is healthy for narratology because it generates different kinds of valuable knowledge about narratives.

Besides accommodating many diverse intellectual currents, postclassical narratology also seeks to address and potentially remedy some of the shortcomings of traditional narratology. For example, structuralist narratology did not pay much attention to the referential or world-creating dimension of narratives (perhaps because structuralism's precursor, the Swiss linguist Ferdinand de Saussure, excluded the referent from his theory of the sign and instead favored the dichotomy signifier vs. signified) (see also Herman/ Biwu, forthcoming). Cognitive narratologists, like Monika Fludernik (1996, 2003b), David Herman (2002, 2003), Manfred Jahn (1997, 1999b, 2003), and Ralf Schneider (2000), on the other hand, show that the recipient uses his or her world knowledge to project fictional worlds, and this knowledge is stored in cognitive schemata called frames and scripts.[13] The basic assumption of cognitive narratology is that readers evoke fictional worlds (or story-

---

13. "Frames basically deal with situations such as seeing a room or making a promise while scripts cover standard action sequences such as playing a game of football, going to a birthday party, or eating in a restaurant" (Jahn 2005: 69).

worlds) on the basis of their real-world knowledge; cognitive narratology seeks to describe the range of cognitive processes that are involved. Alan Palmer (2004) and Lisa Zunshine (2006), for instance, argue that the way in which we attempt to make sense of fictional narratives is similar to the way in which we try to make sense of other people. They argue that we understand narratives by understanding the minds of the characters and narrators, that is, their intentions and motivations. Most importantly, cognitive approaches are based on a constructivist theory of reading, arguing that what we read into texts is not necessarily "there" as a pre-given fact. This emphasis ties in with non-essentialist, pluralist, and generally pragmatic concerns and preoccupations, thereby establishing connections with recent developments in linguistics, where the direction of research has also moved from syntax to pragmatics and on to cognitive approaches. Cognitive narratology can thus be argued to affect the status of categories of narratological analysis; it shifts the emphasis from an essentialist, universal, and static understanding of narratological concepts to seeing them as fluid, context-determined, prototypical, and recipient-constituted.

Possible-worlds theory is an area of narratological study which links with postclassical narratology in interesting ways. The basic assumption of possible-worlds theory is that reality is a universe composed of a plurality of distinct elements. The actual world (AW) is the central element, and it is surrounded by various alternative possible worlds (APWs), such as dreams, fantasies, hallucinations, and the worlds of literary fiction. For a world to be possible it must be linked to the center by "accessibility relations." Important possible-worlds theorists are Lubomír Doležel (1998), Marie-Laure Ryan (1991, 1999, 2001, 2005, and 2006), and Ruth Ronen (1994). It could be argued that Marie-Laure Ryan's more recent research (1999, 2001, and 2004) constitutes an interesting postclassical development over Doležel's and her own earlier work (Ryan 1991). Her forays into media studies highlight the way in which the underlying cognitivist and transmedial aspects of her 1991 model have been extended and explicated in the last fifteen years. Furthermore, Ryan has recently shown that postmodern narratives have found in the concepts of possible-worlds theory "a productive plaything for [their] games of subversion and self-reflexivity" (2005: 449). She also looks at potential analogies between parallel universes in physics on the one hand and possible worlds in narrative fiction on the other (esp. Ryan 2006). Ryan's concept of immersion (Ryan 2001), moreover, builds a bridge to cognitive studies of narration.

We just referred to the pragmatic revolution in linguistics with the development of context-oriented models in text linguistics, speech act theory, sociolinguistics, and conversation analysis. For narratology, the analyses of conversational narrative by William Labov (1972), Deborah Tannen (1984), and Wallace Chafe (1994) have been seminal. Discourse analysis has had a major impact on the postclassical narratological work of David Herman (1997, 1999c, 2002) and Monika Fludernik (1991, 1993, 1996). In the wake of linguistic pragmatics, narrative analysis has started to include nonfictional narrative in its analyses. Conversation analysis in narratology has largely fed into cognitive strands of narratology. In Fludernik's work (1996, 2003a) it has moreover impacted diachronic narratology. This trend is complemented by extensive interest in narratology on the part of conversation analysts. Linguists and psychologists like Michael Bamberg (2007; Bamberg et al. 2007), Brigitte Boothe (2004), Anna de Fina (2003), Mark Freeman (1999), Alexandra Georgakopoulou (1997) and others are doing research on narrative identity, performance and empathy. A true interdisciplinary field has here been emerging.

A fourth development that rewrites the classic design of narratology concerns the discovery of narrative's evolution over time. This comes in two forms, as a study of how narrative changes through the centuries and, in conjunction with this descriptive focus, a revision of narratological categories as a response to the different aspects and textual features that one finds in earlier texts. Thus, Fludernik's diachronic study of narrative structure (1996, 2003a) provides a functional re-analysis of patterns from earlier narrative at later stages of literary storytelling besides discussing the move from oral to written forms of narrative. Another diachronically focused study is Werner Wolf's analysis of anti-illusionism (1993). Nünning's volume *Unreliable Narration* (1998) not only produces a new extensively outlined model of the signals of unreliability in the introduction but also includes a series of essays illustrating the historical development of this narrative strategy (see also Zerweck 2001). David Herman's volume *The Emergence of Mind* (2011) is probably the most perfect example of the diachronic approach. It includes essays on the representation of consciousness which systematically cover all periods of English literature from the Middle Ages to the present time.

In recent years, a number of radical critiques and suggestions for rewriting the classical model have been proposed. Besides suggesting specific extensions or supplements to the classical paradigm, this type of research has additionally aimed at restructuring the basic setup of Genettean typology. The categories that have so far come in for most critical attention include focalization, voice, person, the status of the narrator and the implied author, and the story-discourse distinction. Thus, focalization figures in the already classical rewrite of Genette by Mieke Bal (1983, 1985/1997), but has been the focus of further revision by, among others, Chatman (1990), Edmiston (1991) and Jahn (1996, 1999a). Voice has been targeted in Aczel (1998, 2001), Fludernik (2001), and in Walsh (2007, this volume). Walsh (2007) moreover queries the story-discourse distinction (see also Fludernik 1994b, this volume) and the existence of a heterodiegetic extradiegetic narrator (see also this volume), in continuation of Ann Banfield's theses in *Unspeakable Sentences* (1982; see also Fludernik 1993). Massive attention has recently been given to the implied author and the issue of unreliability, and even a return of the author into narrative studies is being promoted in clear violation of what has almost become a taboo in literary studies.[14] The list could be extended to include many more issues and critics and a large variety of supplementary proposals and critical restructurings.

A final postclassical area of research is the study of unnatural narratives, that is, anti-mimetic narratives that challenge and move beyond real-world understandings of identity, time, and space by representing scenarios and events that would be impossible in the actual world.[15] Brian Richardson (1987, 1997, 2000, 2002, 2006) is the most important representative of this type of postclassical narratology that looks at anti-mimeticism, but recently a number of younger scholars such as Jan Alber (2002, 2009a, 2009b, in progress), Henrik Skov Nielsen (2004), and Rüdiger Heinze (2008) have also begun to look at the ways in which some (primarily postmodernist) narratives challenge our real-world parameters.[16] Even before the invention of the term "unnatural," Brian McHale (1987, 1992) and Werner Wolf (1993) devoted themselves to the range of specific techniques employed in postmodern or anti-illusionist narrative texts. McHale lists a substantial number of metafictional strategies, all of which are designed to foreground the inventedness of the narrative discourse. Wolf's study attempts an exhaustive description of anti-illusionistic techniques which are meant to cover all anti-illusionistic writing, not just the specific kind of anti-illusionism practiced in postmodernist texts. Unnatural narratology, in a sense, is a combination of postmodernist narratology and cognitive narratology. It could also be argued to constitute an answer to poststructuralist critiques of narratology as guilty

---

14. On the implied author debate see Nünning (1998, 2005, and 2008) as well as Phelan/Martin (1999), Phelan (2008a), and Kindt/Müller (2006); on unreliability see also Yacobi (1981).

15. Alber argues that unnatural narratives confront us with physically or logically impossible scenarios or events (2009a; 2009b; in progress; Alber/Heinze in progress; see also Tammi 2008: 43–47 and Alber/Iversen/Nielsen/Richardson 2010). Alber's *Habilitation* (in progress) also contains a historical analysis of the development of unnaturalness in English literary history.

16. See also the essays by Jan Alber and Henrik Skov Nielsen in this volume.

of logocentrism and displaying a "geometrical imaginary" (Gibson 1996; see also Currie 1998). However, rather than deconstructing narratology's constitutive binaries, unnatural narratology (as a development from Fludernik's "natural" narratology and cognitive narratology in general) tries to set up a narratological model for experimental texts that complements classical narratology and also connects with it by means of a cognitive framework.

PHASE TWO: CONSOLIDATION AND CONTINUED DIVERSIFICATION
Essays in this Volume

The essays collected here typically combine the resources of various disciplinary traditions of postclassical narratology. They also reach back to concerns and theories already current in the heyday of classical narratology, though not usually discussed as "narratological," like the work of Girard, Bakhtin, and David Lodge.[17] All Anglo-American work on narrative moreover takes its reference point in the seminal thought of Henry James and E. M. Forster, which proved to be of continuing relevance even during the heyday of structuralist narratology. In our summary of the essays, we will foreground their potential as indices of where narratology may be heading at the moment. In our view, the research that follows seems to suggest that we have reached a new stage at which one has to ponder the overlaps and potential areas of cross-fertilization between the numerous flourishing narratologies.

The volume divides into two parts. A shorter first part deals with a number of extensions and criticisms of classical narratology. It includes creative additions to the standard model by Werner Wolf and Alan Palmer and a radical critique of the category of voice (as well as other cherished staples of narratology) by Richard Walsh, and an analytical essay on mediacy versus mediation by Monika Fludernik. Part II, called "Transdisciplinarities," documents a number of innovative blendings of narratological issues with generic, medial, gender-related, psycho-analytic, and nonfictional contexts.

Richard Walsh opens the volume by radically questioning key axioms of narratology. His *point de repère* is the question of voice. In development of his 2007 book *The Rhetoric of Fictionality,* Walsh here proceeds to link his questioning of the category voice with his reservations about the communicative model of narratology, i.e. the assumption that every text must have a narrator figure. He conceptualizes narrative representation as rhetorical in

---

17. We owe this point to James Phelan (personal communication).

mode, and as semiotic (rather than narrowly linguistic) in scope. The rhetorical orientation of his argument appropriates Plato's emphasis upon the act of narrative representation as diegesis or mimesis. Walsh draws out the recursiveness implicit in that formulation, and discriminates between its legitimate scope as a model of agency and the rather different issue of rhetorical effect. The semiotic nature of narrative representation is asserted through the metaphorical nature of the concept of voice, and through Walsh's efforts to take the full measure of that fact with respect to other narrative media (principally film, but also the cognitive medium of mental representation).

Werner Wolf's is the first of two essays that attempt to close gaps in the traditional narratological model. Noting that the concept of *mise en abyme* has no conceptual counterpart relating to its frame, he proposes the concept of *mise en cadre* for this lacuna. Wolf outlines how the addition of this concept can help to describe a number of textual features and how it can also be applied to medial contexts. Wolf's contribution aims at bridging the gulf between classical and postclassical narratology by proposing a "neo-classical" variant. He suggests that the concepts devised by classical narratology have not lost their relevance. On the contrary, they are open to a fruitful development and supplementation and can be adapted to recent approaches.

Alan Palmer contributes to the extension of narratological categories by proposing a theory of *intermental thought*. Such thinking is joint, shared, or collective and community-based, as opposed to intramental, individual, or private thought. It can also be described as *socially distributed, situated,* or *extended cognition,* or as *intersubjectivity*. Intermental thought is a crucially important component of fictional narrative because much of the mental functioning depicted in novels occurs in large organizations, small groups, work colleagues, friends, families, couples and other intermental units. It could plausibly be argued that a large amount of the subject matter of novels is the formation, development and breakdown of these intermental systems. So far this aspect of narrative has been neglected by traditional theoretical approaches and fails to be considered in discussions of focalization, characterization, story analysis, and the representation of speech and thought. Palmer therefore crucially contributes to closing this gap in the traditional narratological paradigm.

Monika Fludernik in her contribution returns to a both historical and critical analysis of the relationship between the terms *mediacy, mediation,* and *focalization*. Following on from earlier work on drama as narrative, Fludernik considers the status of mediality for narrativity and contrasts Stanzel's and Genette's complex negotiations with the story-discourse dichotomy, the status of the narrator as mediator, and with the placing of focalization or perspective in relation to the story-discourse binary. The essay revisits the exchange between Chatman and Barbara Hernstein Smith on the notion of narrative transmission. It also engages extensively with Richard Walsh's no-mediation thesis (Walsh 2007) and places the mediacy and (re)mediation debate within the framework of her own narratological model. Like Walsh's paper in this volume, this essay queries some long-held beliefs or basic axioms of narratology.

David Herman opens Part II of the volume by looking at William Blake's poem "A Poison Tree" (1794), a text which operates across various communicative media. Herman inquires into "(1) the structure and dynamics of storytelling practices; (2) the multiple semiotic systems in which those practices take shape, including but not limited to verbal language; and (3) mind-relevant dimensions of the practices themselves—as they play out in a given medium for storytelling." According to Herman, Blake's poem articulates and enacts a model according to which a more effective engagement with the world is premised on the ability to take up the perspectives of others. And, according to Herman, this is one of the most important features of narrative in general: narrative is centrally concerned with *qualia,* i.e., the sense of "what it is like" for someone or something to have a particular experience, and hence narrative is uniquely suited to capturing what the world is like from the situated perspective of an experiencing mind. Herman's contribution merges cognitive and transmedial narratology; he sees his essay as a first step toward an investigation of the potential overlaps between different postclassical approaches. His contribution also has an openly ethical slant, thus linking to the paper of Amit Marcus.

Jan Alber's essay can be situated at the crossroads of transmedial narratology, the rhetorical approach to narrative, and unnatural narratology. He reconsiders the process of cinematic narration from the perspective of hypothetical intentionalism, a cognitive approach in which "a narrative's meaning is established by hypothesizing intentions authors might have had, given the context of creation, rather than relying on, or trying to seek out, the author's subjective intentions" (Gibbs 2005: 248). Alber argues that when we make sense of a film, we always speculate about the potential intentions and motivations behind the movie, without ever knowing whether our speculations are correct. In a second step, Alber shows that there is a convergence between the functions of the cinematic narrator, that is, "the organizational and sending agency" (Chatman 1990: 127) behind the film, and those of the implied filmmaker, who mediates the film as a whole and guides us through it (Gaut 2004: 248). Replacing the filmic narrator and the implied filmmaker (analogous to the "implied author" [Booth 1982: 21; Phelan 2005: 45]) with the "hypothetical filmmaker," Alber integrates the viewers' speculations about the conscious or unconscious motivations of the professionals responsible for the making of the film into the analysis. He thus combines the views on intentionality provided in Herman (2008) with a cognitive and reader-response oriented model. Alber applies this new theoretical framework to an experimental narrative, namely David Lynch's film *Lost Highway* (1996).

Susan Lanser sketches the ways in which a particular topos, namely lesbian desire, may be linked with historically variable narrative parameters, thus combining feminist/queer narratology with a diachronic outlook on narrative. More specifically, Lanser explores what she calls the "sapphic dialogic," a form of narrative intersubjectivity in which erotic content is filtered through the relationship between a (typically intradiegetic) female pairing of narrator and narratee. Reaching back to the sixteenth century, Lanser uncovers the history of a typical scenario in which female narrators tell other women about heterosexual congress in a context in which the telling becomes yet another erotic experience. Hence, Lanser identifies sapphic form as an underpinning of the eighteenth-century novel's domestic agenda. Linking these analyses to the rise of the novel, Lanser is able to demonstrate that the eighteenth-century novel female protagonist is not only swept up in the consolidation of the heterosexual subject; but further, the novel preserves within its heterosexual frame the secret of domesticity's dependence on the structural deployment of lesbian desire. Lanser's contribution therefore uses the communicative scenario of text-internal dialogue and storytelling to figure an underlying sexual subtext. The paper combines a gender approach with a framework of reader response and the concerns (if not the model) of rhetorical narratology.

Our next contributor, Amit Marcus, merges narratology with psychoanalysis by looking at René Girard's notion of mimetic (or triangular) desire (Girard 1965) and setting this in correlation with the story-discourse distinction. For Girard, the subject does not desire the object in and for itself. Rather, the desire is mediated through another subject, who possesses or pursues the object. This third figure (the mediator or rival) is admired by the subject but also despised as an obstacle in achieving the object. In his contribution, Marcus looks at narratives in which the narrator is both one of the main characters in the story and the desiring subject. He shows that the narratives he analyzes present several ways in which narration can be linked with mimetic desire. While in two of the narratives he analyzes (Grass's *Cat and Mouse* and Genet's *The Thief's Journal*) mimetic desire only motivates the narration and the narrator's appeal to a narratee, without there existing a story on that level, in Camus's *The Fall* the story at the level of narration is woven into the story of the past life of the narrator. In sum, Marcus argues that if mimetic desire is the basis of the relation between the narrator and the narratee, then narratorial authority seems to be motivated by the anxiety that the loss of the narratee will cause unbearable pain to the narrator, whose mediator and rival will no longer provide him with the (fragile) existential security that he needs. The essay illustrates how the narrator-narratee relationship interacts with the story-discourse level of narrative in ways which, incidentally, are also notable in second-person narratives (Fludernik 1993, 1994a).

In her contribution, Jarmila Mildorf follows David Herman's suggestions concerning the development of a "socionarratology" (1999b) and shows that narratology, if suitably adapted to social science requirements, can add further insights into the particularly "narrative" features of oral stories. More specifically, she analyzes two oral narratives from the database of personal experience of health and illness (DIPEx) with a view to identifying possible points of convergence between narratology and the social sciences. Mildorf uses narratological terms such as the "experiencing I," the "narrating I," "focalization," "slant," "filter," and "double deixis" in you-narratives and illustrates that frequently-evoked concepts in the social science literature such as "social positioning," "identity," and the marking of "in-group" and "out-group" relations can be further illuminated if reconsidered through a narratological lens. Her contribution is therefore a test case for narratology's ability to connect with work on storytelling outside the humanities. In particular, it provides a useful model for cooperation between narratologists and sociologists or psychologists who have so far been using different models and terminology. By showing that these models may be compatible with the narratological paradigms, Mildorf sketches an optimistic horizon for narratology's involvement with its neighbor disciplines in the social sciences.

Martin Löschnigg discusses models and categories of cognitive narratology that may be relevant for a narratologically grounded analysis of autobiographical discourse. More specifically, he merges cognitive and transmedial narratology and, using Fludernik's model of "natural" narratology, deals with the discursive representation of experientiality in autobiography. He focuses on the role of narrative in the formation of identity; the role of frames and scripts in the textual representation of memory; and finally, on the question of the fictionality of autobiography. Löschnigg argues that the new frame-oriented models of cognitive narratology provide criteria for describing one's life as (re)lived, allowing one to emphasize the continuity of narration and experience. This puts the binary narrator-experiencer model of classical narratology on a different and more flexible basis. He suggests that narrativity is a determinant of autobiography; "narrativized" understandings of identity are based on lived experience and on the capacity of narrative to impose order and coherence on what is otherwise a jumble of disconnected fragments of experiences and memories. Löschnigg also demonstrates that the frames, scripts, and schemata of cognitive narratology can help us grasp autobiography's temporal complexity by identifying processes of segmentation and of creating coherence, which are especially important in memory-based narratives. The essay closes with a consideration of the question of fictionality in autobiography, which can now be approached in a more differentiated manner. If narratology cannot provide criteria to distinguish between "fact" and "fiction" in autobiographical writing, provided such a distinction is possible at all, it can at least, according to Löschnigg, provide the theoretical basis for describing the fictional as an integral element of life-writing. Löschnigg's paper is therefore located at the borderline of fictionality and in this way reaches out from classical literary narratology to the wider area of real-life storytelling practices.

Finally, Henrik Skov Nielsen discusses hybrid narrative texts which cannot easily be categorized as either fiction or non-fiction. More specifically, he looks at two types of texts. On the one hand, he considers what he calls "underdetermined texts," such as James Frey's *A Million Little Pieces* (2003), i.e., texts that present themselves as neither fiction nor non-fiction. On the other hand, he analyzes "overdetermined texts," such as Bret Easton Ellis's *Lunar Park* (2005), that present themselves as *both fiction and non-fiction*. Frey's book was published as non-fiction but turned out to represent the experiences of James Frey in an exaggerated and partly inaccurate way; Ellis's was published as fiction but is in many (though definitely not all) respects a factually accurate rendering of Bret Easton Ellis's life. Nielsen notes that, interestingly, both kinds of texts use techniques of fictionalization. He moves beyond the fiction/non-fiction boundary by arguing that invention is a resource of fictionality available as a rhetorical strategy in the real-world discourse of the author. Nielsen therefore combines a rhetorical slant on narrative with a reconsideration of the fiction/non-fiction divide and with a focus on the curious status of autobiography. He also proposes some radical revisions of the classical paradigm of narratology, thereby linking back to Part I of the volume.

As this summary illustrates, one can observe many synergetic effects between the diverse essays collected in this volume. Some of these connections arise from a common focus on a specific genre (autobiography in the essays by Löschnigg and Nielsen); the history of narratology (Walsh, Fludernik); questions of fictionality (in Walsh and Löschnigg); the central role of cognition in narrative (in Palmer, Herman, and Alber); questions of authorship, responsibility or authority (in Walsh, Wolf, Alber, and Nielsen); as well as the issues of gender and queering (Lanser, Marcus).

Theoretically speaking, what is even more interesting is the fact that these very different approaches document that the field of narratology has now reached a phase which is dominated by partial consolidation without any undue reaching after singularity. At the same time, the trends towards commonality are offset by the diversity of approaches, a multiplicity of co-operations with partner disciplines, and the general theoretical "promiscuity" typical of postmodernity. All of the contributors to the volume are critical of traditional theories, but not one of them wants to eliminate the classic model as a whole. Rewriting the traditional paradigm in its various typological manifestations instead takes the form of querying one particular element (voice, mediacy, the narrator) or of adding one more distinction to the paradigm (Wolf, Palmer, Lanser), extending the model to cover new generic applications (poetry, film) or linking it with new thematic foci (collectivities in Palmer, sexuality and queerness in Lanser and Marcus, ethics in Marcus and Nielsen). Some contributors also try to extend narratology theoretically by adopting research questions, concepts, or frameworks from outside structuralism: cognitive studies (Fludernik, Herman, Alber, Löschnigg), painting (Wolf), Girard's psychoanalysis (Marcus), and media studies (Walsh, Alber). One could summarize these tendencies by saying that there is a consensus on narratology as a *transgeneric, transdisciplinary,* and *transmedial* undertaking, to echo Nünning and Nünning's 2002 title.

Secondly, all contributors on the whole agree that narratology should cover more than the classical genre of the novel. Postclassical narratology, one could therefore argue, has a much wider conception of what counts as narrative than just the traditional novel (Genette, Stanzel, Chatman, Rimmon-Kenan). The debate on extending narratology to other genres has resulted in a general consensus of crediting film as a narrative genre and a wide acceptance of drama, cartoons, and much performance art, as well as some painting, under the description of narrative genres. The borderline is now located in the gray area made up of poetry, music, and science. One can therefore claim that narratology's *object of analysis* has shifted since the 1980s—narrative now includes a much wider spectrum of "texts." This change requires a reworking of narratological concepts since the traditional model was based on a very restrictive corpus of (generically) rather uniform verbal narratives.

Third, the extension of narrative into a variety of different media has been accompanied by a shift from text-internal close analysis to context-relative cultural studies, particularly foregrounding the question of narrative's function in social, historical, ideological, or psychological contexts. Rather than merely analyzing how texts work, and which of their elements are responsible for which meaning or design effects, the current emphasis lies on what these narratives achieve in communication, which ideological or identity-related messages they convey, what 'cultural work' (Tompkins 1986, Beck 2003) they perform, and what possible effects they may engender in the real world. One could, therefore, argue that all narratology nowadays is *context-sensitive*.

Fourth, we would like to propose that the *cognitive model*, which is one of the many ongoing projects in the field,[18] is slowly establishing itself as a new basis for ever-increasing areas of narratological research. The cognitive model provides a useful explanatory framework which offers a potentially empirical grounding for dealing with textual features. It has also introduced to narrative studies some new terminology and concepts which are perhaps apt to replace more traditional elements in the paradigm. Among such new concepts one can point first and foremost to the notion of the frame, which has now been generally absorbed into narratology much in the same way that linguistic terminology (e.g., of deixis and temporal modes) was in classical narratology. A second major adoption from cognitive science is prototype theory, which is becoming more widely accepted in narrative studies and is beginning to replace the former insistence on clear distinctions between narratological categories. Deconstructive treatments of the binary oppositions of classical narratology have helped to popularize a more relaxed attitude towards classification. One could also count experientiality, originally proposed by Fludernik in 1991 (see also 1996), as a cognitively based concept that has meanwhile been adopted by a number of researchers such as Wolf (2002) and Löschnigg (2006). A reliance on cognitivist and constructivist principles is now common in postclassical narratology, for instance in recent work by Ansgar Nünning (1998), Ralf Schneider (2000), Alan Palmer (2004), Richard Walsh (2007), and Jochen Petzold (2008).[19] This emphasis on cognitive issues is linked to the medial extension of narratology since the classical model was unable to deal with many of the newer types of narrative, and the cognitive approach offers a model which can accommodate linguistic storytelling besides a host of other forms of narrative.

What we are arguing here is that, although there is no unified new methodology in sight for postclassical narratology (nor do we plead for such a

18. So-called cognitive narratology is usually associated with Monika Fludernik, David Herman, Manfred Jahn, and Lisa Zunshine.
19. See also Fludernik (2001) as well as Alber (2002, 2009a, 2009b, and forthcoming) and Aldama (2003).

development), there is sufficient justification for referring to current narratological work in the singular as postclassical narratology; one does not necessarily have to foreground the existing diversity in a plural label—postclassical narratolog*ies*. Our reason for emphasizing an incipient move toward congruence, compatibility, and consolidation is our perception of recurrent strategies of patchwork and blending as illustrated in the essays in this volume. We are not saying that *all* future narratology will be based on cognitive theory, or that all research in narrative will necessarily be transmedial and function-oriented. What we are noting is a confluence of the various approaches that David Herman so magisterially outlined in his 1999 volume. Almost none of the essays printed in this book abides by any one single approach. The papers all combine and creatively blend different approaches, cognitive or otherwise, to achieve a synthesis that looks different in every individual essay but is a synthesis nevertheless. We do not maintain that there is a unified postclassical model on the horizon—nor would we want to invent one—but we are arguing that narratologists nowadays see the object of their research as more variegated than was the case twenty years ago; that they resort to very different methods in combination when approaching a problem; and that they will tend to ground their analyses in a rich contextual framework. To this extent, and to this extent only, do we see postclassical narratology not as continuing to proliferate into numerous new directions, but as beginning to sediment and crystallize into a new *modus vivendi.*

REFERENCES

Aczel, Richard (1998) "Hearing Voices in Narrative Texts." *New Literary History* 29: 467–500.
——— (2001) "Understanding as Over-Hearing: Towards a Dialogics of Voice." *New Literary History* 32: 597–617.
Alber, Jan (2002) "The 'Moreness' or 'Lessness' of 'Natural' Narratology: Samuel Beckett's "Lessness" Reconsidered." *Style* 36.1: 54–75. Reprinted in *Short Story Criticism* 74 (2004): 113–24.
——— (2007) *Narrating the Prison: Role and Representation in Charles Dickens' Novels, Twentieth-Century Fiction, and Film.* Youngstown, NY: Cambria Press.
——— (2009a) "Impossible Storyworlds—and What to Do with Them." *Storyworlds: A Journal of Narrative Studies* 1.1: 79–96.
——— (2009b) "Unnatural Narratives." *The Literary Encyclopedia.* www.litencyc.com.
——— (forthcoming) "Cinematic Carcerality: Prison Metaphors in Film." *The Journal of Popular Culture.*
——— (in progress) "Unnatural Narrative: Impossible Worlds in Fiction and Drama." Habilitation, University of Freiburg, Germany.
Alber, Jan, Stefan Iversen, Henrik Skov Nielsen, and Brian Richardson (2010) "Unnatural Narratives, Unnatural Narratology: Beyond Mimetic Models." *Narrative* 18.2: 113–36.
Alber, Jan, and Rüdiger Heinze (forthcoming) Eds. *Unnatural Narratology.* Berlin and New York: de Gruyter.
Aldama, Frederick Luis (2003) *Postethnic Narrative Criticism: Magicorealism in Oscar "Zeta" Acosta, Ana Castillo, Julie Dash, Hanif Kureishi, and Salman Rushdie.* Austin, TX: University of Texas Press.
Allen, Robert Clyde (1987) "Reader-Oriented Criticism and Television." *Channels of Discourse: Television and Contemporary Criticism.* Ed. Robert C. Allen. London: Methuen. 74–112.
Bakhtin, Mikhail (1981) *The Dialogic Imagination: Four Essays.* Ed. Michael Holquist. Austin: The University of Texas Press.
Bal, Mieke (1983) "The Narrating and the Focalizing: A Theory of the Agents in Narrative." *Style* 17.2: 234–269.
——— (1997) *Narratology. Introduction to the Theory of Narrative* [1985]. Toronto, ON: University of Toronto Press.
Bamberg, Michael (2007) Ed. *Narrative, State of the Art.* Amsterdam: John Benjamins.
Bamberg, Michael, Anna de Fina, and Deborah Schiffrin (2007) Eds. *Selves and Identities in Narrative Discourse.* Amsterdam: John Benjamins.
Banfield, Anne (1982) *Unspeakable Sentences: Narration and Representation in the Language of Fiction.* Boston: Routledge.
Beck, Andrew (2003) Ed. *Cultural Work: Understanding the Cultural Industries.* London: Routledge.
Booth, Wayne C. (1982) "Between Two Generations: The Heritage of the Chicago School." *Profession* 82: 19–26.
——— (1983) *The Rhetoric of Fiction* [1961]. Chicago: University of Chicago Press.
Boothe, Brigitte (2004) *Der Patient als Erzähler in der Psychotherapie* [1994]. Gießen: Psychosozial-Verlag.

Bordwell, David (1985) *Narration in the Fiction Film*. London: Routledge.
Branigan, Edward (1992) *Narrative Comprehension and Film*. London and New York: Routledge.
Brooks, Peter (1984) *Reading for the Plot: Design and Intention in Narrative*. New York: Vintage.
Chafe, Wallace L. (1994) *Discourse, Consciousness, and Time: The Flow and Displacement of Conscious Experience in Speaking and Writing*. Chicago: University of Chicago Press.
Chambers, Ross (1984) *Story and Situation: Narrative Seduction and the Power of Fiction*. Minneapolis: University of Minnesota Press.
—— (1991) *Room for Maneuver: Reading (the) Oppositional (in) Narrative*. Chicago: University of Chicago Press.
Chatman, Seymour (1978) *Story and Discourse: Narrative Structure in Fiction and Film*. Ithaca, NY: Cornell University Press.
—— (1990) *Coming to Terms: The Rhetoric of Narrative in Fiction and Film*. Ithaca, NY and London: Cornell University Press.
Currie, Mark (1998) *Postmodern Narrative Theory*. New York: St. Martin's Press.
de Fina, Anna (2003) *Identity in Narrative: A Study of Immigrant Discourse*. Amsterdam: John Benjamins.
Diengott, Nilli (1988) "Narratology and Feminism." *Style* 22.1: 44–50.
Doležel, Lubomír (1998) *Heterocosmica: Fiction and Possible Worlds*. Baltimore and London: The Johns Hopkins University Press.
Doyle, Laura (1994) *Bordering on the Body: The Racial Matrix of Modern Fiction and Culture*. New York: Oxford University Press.
Edmiston, W. F. (1991) *Hindsight and Insight: Focalization in Four Eighteenth-Century French Novels*. University Park: Pennsylvania State University Press.
Eco, Umberto (1979) *The Role of the Reader: Explorations in the Semiotics of Texts*. Bloomington: Indiana University Press.
Ellis, Bret Easton (2005) *Lunar Park*. London: Picador.
Fludernik, Monika (1991) "The Historical Present Tense Yet Again: Tense Switching and Narrative Dynamics in Oral and Quasi-Oral Storytelling." *Text* 11.3: 365–97.
—— (1993) *The Fictions of Language and the Languages of Fiction. The Linguistic Representation of Speech and Consciousness*. London: Routledge.
—— (1994a) "Introduction: Second-Person Narrative and Related Issues." *Style* 28.3: 281–311.
—— (1994b) "Second-Person Narrative As a Test Case for Narratology: The Limits of Realism." *Style* 28.3: 445–79.
—— (1996) *Towards a 'Natural' Narratology*. London and New York: Routledge.
—— (2000) "Beyond Structuralism in Narratology: Recent Developments and New Horizons in Narrative Theory." *Anglistik* 11.1: 83–96.
—— (2001) "New Wine in Old Bottles? Voice, Focalization and New Writing." *New Literary History* 32.3: 619–38.
—— (2003a) "The Diachronization of Narratology." *Narrative* 11.3: 331–48.
—— (2003b) "Natural Narratology and Cognitive Parameters." *Narrative Theory and the Cognitive Sciences*. Ed. David Herman. Stanford, CA: CSLI. 243–67.
—— (2005) "Histories of Narrative Theory (II): From Structuralism to the Present." *A*

Companion to Narrative Theory. Ed. James Phelan and Peter J. Rabinowitz. Malden, MA: Blackwell. 36–59.

—— (2008) "Narrative and Drama." *Theorizing Narrativity.* Ed. John Pier and José Ángel Garcia Landa. Narratologia, 12. Berlin and New York: de Gruyter. 355–83.

Freeman, Mark (1999) "Culture, Narrative, and the Poetic Construction of Selfhood." *Journal of Constructivist Psychology* 12: 99–116.

Frey, James (2003) *A Million Little Pieces.* New York: Random House.

Gates, Henry Louis (1988) *The Signifying Monkey: A Theory of African-American Literary Criticism.* New York: Oxford University Press.

Gaut, Berys (2004) "The Philosophy of the Movies: Cinematic Narration." *The Blackwell Guide to Aesthetics.* Ed. Peter Kivy. Malden, MA: Blackwell. 230–53.

Georgakopoulou, Alexandra (1997) "Self-Presentation and Interactional Alliances in E-mail Discourse: The Style- and Code-Switches of Greek Messages." *International Journal of Applied Linguistics* 7: 141–64.

Gibbs, Raymond W. (2005) "Intentionality." *Routledge Encyclopedia of Narrative Theory.* Ed. David Herman, Manfred Jahn, and Marie-Laure Ryan. London: Routledge. 247–49.

Gibson, Andrew (1996) *Towards a Postmodern Theory of Narrative.* Edinburgh: Edinburgh University Press.

Girard, René (1965) *Deceit, Desire, and the Novel: Self and Other in Literary Structure.* Trans. Yvonne Freccero. Baltimore: The Johns Hopkins University Press.

Hale, Dorothy (2008) "Narrative Theory/Narrative in Critical Theory." Paper given at the panel on "Race and Narrative Theory," MLA Conference 2008.

Heinze, Rüdiger (2008) "Violations of Mimetic Epistemology in First-Person Narrative Fiction." *Narrative* 16.3: 279–97.

Helbig, Jörg (2001) *Intermedialität: Eine Einführung.* Frankfurt/Main: Suhrkamp.

—— (2003) "Wie postmodern ist Hyperfiction? Formen der Rezeptionslenkung in fiktionalen Hypertexten." *Moderne/Postmoderne.* Ed. Jan Alber and Monika Fludernik. Trier: Wissenschaftlicher Verlag Trier. 299–313.

Herman, David (1997) "Scripts, Sequences, and Stories: Elements of a Postclassical Narratology." *PMLA* 12.5: 1046–59.

—— (1999a) "Introduction." *Narratologies: New Perspectives on Narrative Analysis.* Ed. David Herman. Columbus: The Ohio State University Press. 1–30.

—— (1999b) Ed. *Narratologies: New Perspectives on Narrative Analysis.* Columbus: The Ohio State University Press.

—— (1999c) "Toward a Socionarratology: New Ways of Analyzing Natural-Language Narratives." *Narratologies: New Perspectives on Narrative Analysis.* Ed. David Herman. Columbus: The Ohio State University Press. 218–46.

—— (2002) *Story Logic: Problems and Possibilities of Narrative.* Lincoln: University of Nebraska Press.

—— (2003) Ed. *Narrative Theory and the Cognitive Sciences.* Stanford, CA: CSLI.

—— (2005) "Histories of Narrative Theory (I): A Genealogy of Early Developments." *A Companion to Narrative Theory.* Ed. James Phelan and Peter J. Rabinowitz. Malden, MA: Blackwell. 19–35.

—— (2006) "Genette Meets Vygotsky: Narrative Embedding and Distributed Intelligence." *Language and Literature* 15.4: 357–80.

—— (2007) Ed. *The Cambridge Companion to Narrative*. Cambridge: Cambridge University Press.
—— (2008) "Narrative Theory and the Intentional Stance." *Partial Answers* 6.2: 233–60.
—— (2011) Ed. *The Emergence of Mind*. Lincoln: University of Nebraska Press.
Herman, David, and Shang Biwu (2009) "New Developments in the Study of Narrative: An Interview with David Herman." Translated into Chinese by Shang Biwu. *Foreign Literature* 5: 97–105.
Herman, Luc, and Bart Vervaeck (2005) "Postclassical Narratology." *The Routledge Encyclopedia of Narrative Theory*. Ed. David Herman, Manfred Jahn, and Marie-Laure Ryan. London: Routledge. 450–51.
Jahn, Manfred (1996) "Windows of Focalization: Deconstructing and Reconstructing a Narratological Concept." *Style* 30.2: 241–67.
—— (1997) "Frames, Preferences, and the Reading of Third-Person Narratives: Towards a Cognitive Narratology." *Poetics Today* 18.4: 441–68.
—— (1999a) "More Aspects of Focalization: Refinements and Applications." *Recent Trends in Narratological Research: Papers from the Narratology Round Table. GRAAT 21: ESSE 4, Debrecen, September 1997*. Ed. John Pier. Tours: Publications des Groupes de Recherches Anglo-Américaines de l'Université François Rabelais de Tours. 85–110.
—— (1999b) "'Speak, Friend, and Enter': Garden Paths, Artificial Intelligence, and Cognitive Narratology." *Narratologies: New Perspectives on Narrative Analysis*. Ed. David Herman. Columbus: The Ohio State University Press. 167–94.
—— (2001) "Narrative Voice and Agency in Drama: Aspects of a Narratology of Drama." *New Literary History* 32: 659–79.
—— (2003) "'Awake! Open Your Eyes!' The Cognitive Logic of External and Internal Stories." *Narrative Theory and the Cognitive Sciences*. Stanford, CA: CSLI. 195–213.
—— (2005) "Cognitive Narratology." *The Routledge Encyclopedia of Narrative Theory*. Ed. David Herman, Manfred Jahn, and Marie-Laure Ryan. London: Routledge. 67–71.
Kindt, Tom, and Hans-Harald Müller (2006) Ed. *The Implied Author: Concept and Controversy*. Berlin: de Gruyter.
Kozloff, Sarah (1988) *Invisible Storytellers: Voice-Over Narration in American Fiction Film*. Berkeley: University of California Press.
Kreiswirth, Martin (2005) "Narrative Turn in the Humanities." *Routledge Encyclopedia of Narrative Theory*. Ed. David Herman, Manfred Jahn, and Marie-Laure Ryan. London/New York: Routledge. 377–82.
Labov, William (1972) *Language in the Inner City: Studies in the Black English Vernacular*. Philadelphia: University of Pennsylvania Press.
Lämmert, Eberhard (1993) *Bauformen des Erzählens* [1955]. Stuttgart: Metzler.
Lanser, Susan (1981) *The Narrative Act: Point of View in Prose Fiction*. Princeton, NJ: Princeton University Press.
—— (1986) "Toward a Feminist Narratology." *Style* 20.3: 341–63.
—— (1988) "Shifting the Paradigm: Feminism and Narratology." *Style* 22: 52–60.
—— (1992) *Fictions of Authority: Women Writers and Narrative Voice*. Ithaca, NY: Cornell University Press.
—— (1995) "Sexing the Narrative: Propriety, Desire, and the Engendering of Narratology." *Narrative* 3.1: 85–94.

—— (1999) "Sexing Narratology: Toward a Gendered Poetics of Narrative Voice." *Grenzüberschreitungen: Narratologie im Kontext/Transcending Boundaries: Narratology in Context.* Ed. Walter Grünzweig and Andreas Solbach. Tübingen: Narr. 167–84.

Löschnigg, Martin (2006) *Die englische fiktionale Autobiographie. Erzähltheoretische Grundlagen und historische Prägnanzformen von den Anfängen bis zur Mitte des 19. Jahrhunderts.* Studies in English Literary and Cultural History, 21. Trier: Wissenschaftlicher Verlag Trier.

Margolin, Uri (2000a) "Telling in the Plural: From Grammar to Ideology." *Poetics Today* 21.3: 591–618.

—— (2000b) "Telling Our Story: On 'We' Literary Narratives." *Language and Literature* 5: 115–33.

McHale, Brian (1987) *Postmodernist Fiction.* New York and London: Methuen & Co. Ltd.

—— (1992) *Constructing Postmodernism.* London and New York: Routledge.

Meister, Jan Christoph (2003) "Narratology as Discipline: A Case for Conceptual Fundamentalism." *What is Narratology?* Ed. Tom Kindt and Hans-Harald Müller. Berlin: de Gruyter. 55–71.

Mezei, Kathy (1996) Ed. *Ambiguous Discourse: Feminist Narratology and British Women Writers.* Chapel Hill: University of North Carolina Press.

Müller-Zettelmann, Eva (2002) "Lyrik und Narratologie." *Erzähltheorie transgenerisch, intermedial, interdisziplinär.* Ed. Ansgar Nünning and Vera Nünning. Trier: WVT. 129–53.

—— (in progress) "Poetry and Narratology." *Current Trends in Narratology.* Ed. Greta Olson.

Nash, Christopher (1990) Ed. *Narrative in Culture: The Use of Storytelling in the Sciences, Philosophy, and Literature.* London: Routledge.

Nielsen, Henrik Skov (2004) "The Impersonal Voice in First-Person Narrative Fiction." *Narrative* 12.2: 133–50.

Nünning, Ansgar (1995) *Von historischer Fiktion zu historiographischer Metafiktion.* 2 vols. Trier: WVT.

—— (1997) "But Why Will You Say That I Am Mad? On the Theory, History, and Signals of Unreliable Narration in British Fiction." *Arbeiten aus Anglistik und Amerikanistik* 22.1: 83–105.

—— (1998) Ed. *'Unreliable Narration': Studien zur Theorie und Praxis unglaubwürdigen Erzählens in der englischsprachigen Erzählliteratur.* Trier: WVT.

—— (2000) "Towards a Cultural and Historical Narratology: A Survey of Diachronic Approaches, Concept, and Research Projects." *Anglistentag 1999 Mainz: Proceedings.* Ed. Bernhard Reitz and Sigrid Rieuwerts. Trier: WVT. 345–73.

—— (2003) "Narratology or Narratologies? Taking Stock of Recent Developments, Critique and Modest Proposals for Future Usages of the Term." *What is Narratology?* Ed. Tom Kindt and Hans-Harald Müller. Berlin: de Gruyter. 239–75.

—— (2005) "Reconceptualizing Unreliable Narration: Synthesizing Cognitive and Rhetorical Approaches." *A Companion to Narrative Theory.* Ed. James Phelan and Peter J. Rabinowitz. Malden, MA: Blackwell. 89–107.

—— (2008) "Reconcepualizing the Theory, History and Generic Scope of Unreliable

Narration: Towards a Synthesis of Cognitive and Rhetorical Approaches." *Narrative Unreliability in the Twentieth-Century First-Person Novel*. Ed. Elke D'hoker and Gunther Martens. Narratologia, 14. Berlin: de Gruyter. 29–76.

Nünning, Ansgar, and Vera Nünning (2002) Eds. *Erzähltheorie transgenerisch, intermedial, interdisziplinär*. Trier: WVT.

Nünning, Ansgar, and Roy Sommer (2008) "Diegetic and Mimetic Narrativity: Some Further Steps Towards a Transgeneric Narratology of Drama." *Theorizing Narrativity*. Ed. John Pier and José Ángel Garcia Landa. Narratologia, 12. Berlin and New York: de Gruyter. 331–53.

O'Neill, Patrick (1994) *Fictions of Discourse: Reading Narrative Theory*. Toronto: University of Toronto Press.

Page, Ruth (2003) "Feminist Narratology? Literary and Linguistic Perspectives on Gender and Narrativity." *Language and Literature* 12: 43–56.

—— (2006) *Literary and Linguistic Approaches to Feminist Narratology*. Basingstoke: Palgrave Macmillan.

Palmer, Alan (2004) *Fictional Minds*. Lincoln: University of Nebraska Press.

Pavel, Thomas (1986) *Fictional Worlds*. Cambridge, MA: Harvard University Press.

Petzold, Jochen (2008) "Sprechsituationen lyrischer Dichtung: Ein schematheoretischer Beitrag zur Gattungstypologie." Habilitation, University of Freiburg, Germany.

Phelan, James (1996) *Narrative as Rhetoric: Technique, Audiences, Ethics, Ideology*. Columbus: The Ohio State University Press.

—— (2005) *Living to Tell about It: A Rhetoric and Ethics of Character Narration*. Ithaca, NY: Cornell University Press.

—— (2007a) *Experiencing Fiction: Judgments, Progressions, and the Rhetorical Theory of Narrative*. Columbus: The Ohio State University Press.

—— (2007b) "Rhetoric/Ethics." *The Cambridge Companion to Narrative*. Ed. David Herman. Cambridge: Cambridge University Press. 203–16.

—— (2008a) "Estranging Unreliability, Bonding Unreliability, and the Ethics of *Lolita*." *Narrative Unreliability in the Twentieth-Century First-Person Novel*. Ed. Elke D'hoker and Gunther Martens. Berlin: de Gruyter. 7–28.

—— (2008b) "Narratives in Contest; or, Another Twist in the Narrative Turn." *PMLA* 123: 166–75.

Phelan, James, and Mary Patricia Martin (1999) "The Lessons of 'Weymouth': Homodiegesis, Unreliability, Ethics, and The Remains of the Day." *Narratologies: New Perspectives on Narrative Analysis*. Ed. David Herman. Columbus: The Ohio State University Press. 88–109.

Phelan, James, and Peter J. Rabinowitz (2005) Eds. *A Companion to Narrative Theory*. Malden, MA: Blackwell.

Pier, John, and José Ángel García Landa (2008) Eds. *Theorizing Narrativity*. Narratologia, 12. Berlin: de Gruyter.

Pratt, Mary Louise (1977) *Toward a Speech Act Theory of Literary Discourse*. Bloomington: Indiana University Press.

—— (1992) *Imperial Eyes: Travel Writing and Transculturation*. London: Routledge.

Prince, Gerald (1982) *Narratology: The Form and Functioning of Narrative*. Berlin: Mouton.

—— (1987) *A Dictionary of Narratology*. Lincoln: University of Nebraska Press.
Rabinowitz, Peter J. (1977) "Truth in Fiction: A Re-examination of Audiences." *Critical Inquiry* 4: 121–41.
—— (1998) *Before Reading: Narrative Conventions and the Politics of Interpretation* [1987]. Columbus: The Ohio State University Press.
Richardson, Brian (1987) "'Time is Out of Joint': Narrative Models and the Temporality of Drama." *Poetics Today* 8.2: 299–310.
—— (1988) "Point of View in Drama: Diegetic Monologue, Unreliable Narrators, and the Author's Voice on Stage." *Comparative Drama* 22.3: 193–214.
—— (1997) "Beyond Poststructuralism: Theory of Character, the Personae of Modern Drama, and the Antinomies of Critical Theory." *Modern Drama* 40: 86–99.
—— (2000) "Narrative Poetics and Postmodern Transgression: Theorizing the Collapse of Time, Voice, and Frame." *Narrative* 8.1: 23–42.
—— (2001a) "Construing Conrad's *The Secret Sharer*: Suppressed Narratives, Subaltern Reception, and the Act of Interpretation." *Studies in the Novel* 33.3: 306–21.
—— (2001b) "Voice and Narration in Postmodern Drama." *New Literary History* 32: 681–94.
—— (2002) "Beyond Story and Discourse: Narrative Time in Postmodern and Nonmimetic Fiction." *Narrative Dynamics: Essays on Time, Plot, Closure, and Frames*. Ed. Brian Richardson. Columbus: The Ohio State University Press. 47–63.
—— (2006) *Unnatural Voices: Extreme Narration in Modern and Contemporary Fiction*. Columbus: The Ohio State University Press.
—— (2007a) "Drama and Narrative." *The Cambridge Companion to Narrative*. Ed. David Herman. Cambridge: Cambridge University Press. 142–55.
—— (2007b) "Singular Text, Multiple Implied Readers." *Style* 41: 259–74.
Rimmon-Kenan, Shlomith (1983) *Narrative Fiction: Contemporary Poetics*. London: Methuen.
Ronen, Ruth (1994) *Possible Worlds in Literary Theory*. Cambridge: Cambridge University Press.
Roof, Judith (1996) *Come As You Are: Sexuality and Narrative*. New York: Columbia University Press.
Ryan, Marie-Laure (1991) *Possible Worlds, Artificial Intelligence, and Narrative Theory*. Bloomington: Indiana University Press.
—— (1999) Ed. *Cyberspace Textuality: Computer Technology and Literary Theory*. Indianapolis: Indiana University Press.
—— (2001) *Narrative as Virtual Reality: Immersion and Interactivity in Literature and the Electronic Media*. Baltimore, MD: Johns Hopkins University Press.
—— (2004) Ed. *Narrative Across Media: The Language of Storytelling*. Lincoln: University of Nebraska Press.
—— (2005) "Possible-Worlds Theory." *Routledge Encyclopedia of Narrative Theory*. Ed. David Herman, Manfred Jahn and Marie-Laure Ryan. London/New York: Routledge. 446–50.
—— (2006) "From Parallel Universes to Possible Worlds: Ontological Pluralism in Physics, Narratology, and Narrative." *Poetics Today* 27.4: 633–74.
—— (2008) "Transfictionality across Media." *Theorizing Narrativity*. Ed. John Pier and José Ángel García Landa. Berlin: de Gruyter. 385–417.

Schneider, Ralf (2000) *Grundriß zur kognitiven Theorie der Figurenrezeption am Beispiel des viktorianischen Romans*. Tübingen: Stauffenburg.

Spurr, David (1993) *The Rhetoric of Empire: Colonial Discourse in Journalism, Travel Writing, and Imperial Administration*. Durham: Duke University Press.

Stanzel, Franz Karl (1984) *A Theory of Narrative* [1979] Transl. Charlotte Goedsche, with a Preface by Paul Hernadi. Cambridge: Cambridge University Press.

Sternberg, Meir (1978) *Expositional Modes and Temporal Ordering in Fiction*. Baltimore, MD: Johns Hopkins University Press.

Tammi, Pekka (2008) "Against 'Against' Narrative." *Narrativity, Fictionality, and Literariness: The Narrative Turn and the Study of Literary Fiction*. Ed. Lars-Åke Skalin. Örebro: Örebro University Press. 37–55.

Tannen, Deborah (1984) *Conversational Style: Analyzing Talk Among Friends*. Norwood, NJ: Ablex.

Todorov, Tzvetan (1969) *Grammaire du Décameron*. The Hague: Mouton.

Tompkins, Jane P. (1986) *Sensational Designs: The Cultural Work of American Fiction 1790–1860* [1985]. New York: Oxford University Press.

Walsh, Richard (2007) *The Rhetoric of Fictionality: Narrative Theory and the Idea of Fiction*. Columbus: The Ohio State University Press.

Warhol, Robyn (1989) *Gendered Interventions: Narrative Discourse in the Victorian Novel*. New Brunswick, NJ: Rutgers University Press.

——— (2003) *Having a Good Cry: Effeminate Feelings and Pop-Culture Forms*. Columbus: The Ohio State University Press.

White, Edmund (1978) *Nocturnes for the King of Naples*. Stonewall Inn Editions. New York: St. Martin's Press.

Wolf, Werner (1993) *Ästhetische Illusion und Illusionsdurchbrechung in der Erzählkunst. Theorie und Geschichte mit Schwerpunkt auf englischem illusionsstörenden Erzählen*. Tübingen: Max Niemeyer Verlag.

——— (1999) *The Musicalization of Fiction: A Study in the Theory and History of Intermediality*. Amsterdam: Rodopi.

——— (2002) "Das Problem der Narrativität in Literatur, bildender Kunst und Musik: Ein Beitrag zu einer intermedialen Erzähltheorie." *Erzähltheorie transgenerisch, intermedial, interdisziplinär*. Ed. Ansgar Nünning and Vera Nünning. Trier: WVT. 23–104.

——— (2003) "Narrative and Narrativity: A Narratological Reconceptualization and its Applicability to the Visual Arts." *Word & Image* 19.3: 180–97.

Yacobi, Tamar (1981) "Fictional Reliability as a Communicative Problem." *Poetics Today* 2.2: 113–26.

Zerweck, Bruno (2001) "Historicizing Unreliable Narration: Unreliability and Cultural Discourse in Narrative Fiction." *Style* 35.1: 151–78.

Zunshine, Lisa (2006) *Why We Read Fiction: Theory of Mind and the Novel*. Columbus: The Ohio State University Press.

Extensions and Reconfigurations of Classical Narratology

1

RICHARD WALSH

Person, Level, Voice

A Rhetorical Reconsideration

My purpose in this essay is to critique the concept of narrative voice from the vantage point of a rhetorical model of fictive representation. In its core sense, narrative voice is concerned with the narrating instance, the various manifestations of which are usually categorized in terms of person and level. These distinctions provide for a typology of narrating instances which is conventionally understood within a communicative model of narration—a model in which the narrating instance is situated within the structure of narrative representation, as a literal communicative act (that is, as a discursive event that forms part of a chain of narrative transmission). By adopting a rhetorical approach to voice, I am proposing to invert the hierarchy of that relationship between structure and act. From a rhetorical standpoint, narrative representation is not conceived as a *structure* within which a communicative model of narrative acts is implied, but as an act itself, the performance of a real-world communicative gesture—which, in the case of fictional narrative, is offered as fictive rather than informative, and creates, rather than transmits, all subordinate levels of narration. Such a perspective upon narrative representation exposes the fundamental incoherence of the standard communicative model, and establishes the need for some basic distinctions between different senses of voice in narrative theory.

My argument, then, begins by demonstrating the incoherence of the representational typology of narrative voice as embodied in the communicative model of the narrating instance. This demonstration focuses upon the elementary categories of person and level that articulate this typology; its claim is that it is not possible to sustain the distinction between these two categories in representational terms, and their collision results in contradiction. I go on to show that a rhetorical model of instance, reverting to Plato's distinction between diegesis and mimesis and the recursive principle it embodies, can accommodate the range of narrative possibilities more coherently and simply. By elaborating upon the principle of recursiveness in representation I demonstrate the need for a distinction between narrative voice as instance and as idiom; closer attention to the function of voice in free indirect discourse and focalization establishes a further distinction between idiom and a third sense of voice I term interpellation; finally, a return to my overarching rhetorical frame of reference clarifies the distinction between this third sense and the sense of voice as instance with which I began.

The key premises for the whole discussion, for which I have argued elsewhere, are the conception of narrative representation as rhetorical in mode, and as semiotic (rather than narrowly linguistic) in scope.[1] I comment further upon these issues in the discussion that follows, so here I will only indicate the forms in which they arise. The rhetorical orientation of my argument straightforwardly appropriates Plato's emphasis upon the act of narrative representation as either diegesis or mimesis (the poet either speaking in his own voice, or imitating the voice of a character); I merely draw out the recursiveness implicit in that formulation, and discriminate between its legitimate scope as a model of agency and the rather different issue of rhetorical effect. The semiotic nature of narrative representation is asserted here in my insistence upon the (generally acknowledged) metaphorical nature of the concept of voice, and my efforts to take the full measure of that fact in respect of other narrative media (principally film, but also the cognitive medium of mental representation). These two premises share the common definitional assumption that stories, of whatever kind, do not merely appear, but are told.

Stories do not emerge circumstantially out of phenomena: they exist as stories by virtue of being articulated (always admitting that this may be a private, internal act of representation as well as a public, social one). The immediate implication is that narration in its primary sense is never merely narrative transmission but narrative representation—that is, the semiotic use of its medium. Narrative transmission applies not to the telling of a story (as if it pre-existed as such), but to the merely reproductive mediation of a prior discourse. In fiction, transmission is an element of the rhetoric of *represented telling*—that is, representing an intra-fictional narrative discourse as if you were transmitting an extant discourse. Acts of narrative representation, in

---

1. See especially chapters 1 and 6 of *The Rhetoric of Fictionality* (Walsh 2007).

other words, are themselves among the possible objects of narrative representation: one of the things a story may be about is the telling of a story. The crucial point, however, is that this recursive possibility, however prominent in fiction, does not account for fictionality itself: the *effect* of narrative transmission is a subordinate and contingent product of the rhetoric of narrative representation.

The dominant narratological sense of voice, that which bears upon the narrating instance, is Gérard Genette's. One of the main sources of confusion around the concept of voice is that Genette's version of the metaphor does not draw upon the sense of voice as vocalization, but upon its grammatical sense (active or passive voice): "'the mode of action [. . .] of the verb considered for its relation to the subject'—the subject here being not only the person who carries out or submits to the action, but also the person (the same one or another) who reports it" (1980: 213). It is no less metaphorical for that—indeed, Genette acknowledges that his appropriation of linguistic terminology throughout *Narrative Discourse* shows most figurative strain at just this point (31–32). But the range of Genette's metaphorical vehicle is quite distinct from that of the more general, or more intuitive, usage; a major consequence being that many of the concerns that fall naturally under voice for other theorists are addressed separately by Genette. So free indirect discourse, for many the key issue in discussions of voice, is treated under mood in Genette's scheme. The chapter on mood is also where he presents the crucial concept of focalization, which for theorists following Franz Karl Stanzel is inextricable from the broader notion of mediacy—that is to say voice in Genette's own sense, as narrating instance. Given these terminological and taxonomical discrepancies, it is perhaps all the more striking that both theorists explicitly privilege language as the paradigmatic, if not intrinsic, medium of narrative instanciation. Genette makes this axiomatic: he refers to media such as film and the comic strip as extranarrative, "if one defines narrative *stricto sensu,* as I do, as a *verbal* transmission" (1988: 16).

I am suggesting instead that a narrating instance may be considered as any particular use of any medium for narrative purposes. Narration, on this view, is essentially a representational act, not just a verbal one. Voice in Genette's sense, as instance, is a figure for agency in narration: I take that to be as inherently a part of film and drama as it is of the novel, and as crucial to understanding the rhetorical import of narratives in those media. Seen in this light the voice metaphor is in no way specific to language, and neither are the main concerns that Genette addresses under this heading: person and level. (Tense, Genette's other concern under the heading of voice, is clearly specific to language unless taken more broadly as an index of the temporal relation between represented narrations and the events they narrate; but see the following discussion of his comments upon the intrinsic "homodiegeticity" of present-tense narration.) Genette is himself quick to point out the strict irrelevance of the linguistic category of person in the traditional distinction between first- and third-person narration: the basis for his own distinction between homo- and heterodiegetic narration, as well as the distinction of level between extra- and intradiegetic narration, is the relation between the narration and the represented world of the story (I am leaving aside autodiegetic, which is just a subset of homodiegetic; and metadiegetic, which is just second-degree intradiegetic). I want to suggest, however, that even these distinctions, whilst undeniably useful, are not finally well founded in terms of their own theoretical premises.[2] This points us towards a somewhat different paradigm in which the salient fact is simply the recursive possibility that a narrating instance may represent another narrating instance; or in Plato's terms, that narrative diegesis may give way to narrative mimesis.

It is clear that any narration, whether first-person or third-person (as these terms are generally understood) may incorporate the event of another act of narration, at a second level. Conversely, any narration, at whatever level, may equally well be first-person narration or third-person narration. The categories of person and level appear to be clear and distinct; the classification of a narrative discourse in either respect is not determined by its classification in the other. Whence the possibility of such four-part typologies of narrators as Genette's (Figure 1.1), in which the categories of level and person respectively define the horizontal and vertical axes (person, here, is "relationship," since Genette rejects the traditional terminology). Genette's more analytic terminology makes it clear that the category of person is not really about the choice of personal pronouns, but rather a matter of the status of the narrative act. The dominant issue for the "relationship" distinction seems to be an epistemological one: with what kind of authority does the narrator speak? That of omniscient or impersonal detachment from the events related? Or that of an interested witness to those events? With regard to level, on the other hand, the dominant issue seems to be ontological: from which world does the narrator speak? Ours? Or the world of another narrative—the world of the *Arabian Nights,* or of the *Odyssey*? What Genette's terminol-

---

2. To clarify the scope and purpose of my argument here, it is worth noting that I do not want to suggest that Genette's typology lacks analytical value, or to diminish its significance to narrative theory ever since the publication of *Narrative Discourse.* My claim is simply that it is *logically* incoherent, and therefore should not finally be taken as an account of the representational logic of fictional narrative, but as a testament to the fictive rhetoric that produces and frames the *appearance* of such a logic.

LEVEL: RELATIONSHIP:	Extradiegetic	Intradiegetic
Heterodiegetic	Homer	Scheherazade
Homodiegetic	Marcel	Ulysses

Figure 1.1. from *Narrative Discourse* 248 (simplified)

ogy also implies, however, is that the categories of person and level do share a common frame of reference, with respect to which all four of his terms are defined: that is, the notion of *diégèse*, or story world.

Genette's term *diégèse* does not relate to the Platonic term, diegesis, but to a distinction originating in film theory between the diegetic universe (domain of the signified) and the screen universe (domain of the signifier). So a *diégèse* is the universe of the events represented by a given narration. Despite this subordination of *diégèse* to narration, Genette's classification of narrative levels assigns each narrating instance to the diegetic level that includes it, so that the first level of any narrative is necessarily extradiegetic.[3] Well then, is the extradiegetic a diegetic level? Genette needs it to be such, because the primary narrating instance may be fictional, and so represented (as with Marcel's narration, or Pip's, or Huck's). At the same time he also needs it not to be diegetic, because the primary narrating instance is directly addressed, he says, to "you and me" (1980: 229).[4] The equivocal status of the extradiegetic level serves to evade the infinite regress of diegetic levels that must result from the assumption, fundamental to the communicative model, that every narrating instance is literal with respect to the events represented—that it is ontologically continuous with the world on which it reports (this is simply a precondition for narrative transmission). Such an assumption dictates that if the events are fictional, the report is fictional, and therefore must itself be represented; but the representation of *that* fictional event must then also be fictional—and so we face the prospect of an endless series of implicit narrators. This conception of narrative mediacy as literal (irrespective of whether

    3. Note that extradiegetic narration is defined in relation to the most inclusive, or first-level, *diégèse*, not in relation to the main action of the narrative. So Marlow relates the main action of *Heart of Darkness*, but his narration is intradiegetic, represented as taking place during a long night on the sea-reach of the Thames, waiting for the tide to turn. The point is that Genette's taxonomy of narration is a structural one, rather than a rhetorical one.
    4. Richardson mentions a number of canonical modern texts for which it is unhelpful to take this literalistic view of the extradiegetic narrative situation (2001b: 700–1); many more examples could be added.

or not the narrative is fictive) means that each act of narration, and the *diégèse* to which it belongs, must be part of one continuous line of narrative transmission through which that narration is channeled. If narrative mediacy is always transmission, the communicative model of narrative levels allows for no point of ontological discontinuity.[5]

The category of person, as re-articulated in Genette's distinction between homodiegetic and heterodiegetic narration, also has a problematic relation to *diégèse*. In *Narrative Discourse Revisited,* Genette notes two circumstances in which the apparently heterodiegetic status of a narration can be compromised by a degree of "homodiegeticity" (1988: 80). The effect occurs in present-tense narration and the narration of historical fiction. Present-tense narration, by foregrounding the narration's contemporaneity to diegetic events, pulls towards a sense of the narratorial perspective as that of a witness, who would therefore be part of the *diégèse* (Genette cites the last chapter of *Tom Jones* among his examples). The narration of a historical novel, on the other hand, by virtue of its claims to historicity, undermines our sense of the narrative's discrete diegetic universe and consequently the narrator comes to figure as a quasi-homodiegetic "subsequent witness," in Genette's phrase (1988: 80). As these examples make clear, in the communicative model *diégèse* is not conceived of merely as an effect of signification, but as an ontological notion; and the category of person comes down to a relation of identity or non-identity between the narrator and some member of the story universe, the complete set of states of affairs posited by the narrative. Accordingly, the category of person has no place except within the ontology of fiction: non-fictional heterodiegetic narration becomes meaningless. That is to say, the distinction of narrative person depends upon ontological discontinuity (cp. Genette 1993: 54–84; Cohn 1999: 109–31).

---

5. Genette, of course, does not believe that fictions are true. He offers his own account of the ontological break between author and narrator required by his model, in an essay on John Searle's pretended speech act account of fiction (Genette 1993: 30–53). The thrust of his argument is that the authorial act of pretending to assert is also an indirect speech act instituting a fictional world, the world within which those same pretended assertions are the true assertions of a narrator. Genette's appeal to indirect speech acts is a good move, I think (because it is a move towards a rhetorical model); his retention of Searle's pretence account is not. The essential feature of Searle's account is that a pretended assertion has no illocutionary force (that is what, for Searle, renders the falsehood of fictions unproblematic). The occasion for an indirect authorial speech act, therefore, does not even arise; no speech act at all, direct or indirect, is seriously performed. Yet Genette requires the pretence formula, as a basis for the structural role of extradiegetic narration. Accordingly the only serious speech act available, and the only candidate for the indirect institution of a fictional world, is the narrator's—which is within the world in question. This is the same logical paradox as I have been describing, recast in a different form. See Walsh (2007: 74–78).

So, within the communicative model, the concept of level disallows ontological discontinuity, because it is understood as a chain of literally transmitted narratives; but the concept of person depends upon ontological discontinuity, because otherwise there can only be homodiegetic narration. The crunch comes when these contradictory implications of person and level meet in the extradiegetic heterodiegetic narrator. Genette's example in Figure 1.1 is Homer, which is rather evasive; elsewhere he also offers the narrator of *Père Goriot*. This narrator, he says, unlike Balzac himself, "knows" (with scare quotes) the events of the narrative as fact (1980: 214). If we take the claim literally, it aligns with the logic of narrative levels and the principle of ontological continuity, but contradicts the designation of this narrator as heterodiegetic. If we do not take it literally, Genette forfeits his rationale for distinguishing between this narrator and Balzac; and in terms of the communicative model such a heterodiegetic narrator would have to mediate the narration of a further narrator who does indeed know the events of the narrative as fact—and so we founder upon an infinite regress of narrative levels. The collision between person and level, as I have articulated it here, follows from the communicative model's ontological notion of *diégèse* as story world and its literal model of narrative transmission. And it should be clear that the problem of ontological discontinuity is simply the problem, in this model's terms, of fictionality itself. The problem arises in the first place, then, because of the logical priority the communicative model grants to the *products* of fictive representation.

This is a mistake avoided by the most venerable alternative to the communicative account of person and level, Plato's distinction between diegesis (the poet speaking in his own voice) and mimesis (the poet imitating the voice of a character). Such a distinction characterizes the *act* of fictive representation, and taken as a typology of narration it identifies a single salient feature: the recursive possibility that a narration may represent another narration. It makes the cut, in other words, between Genette's extradiegetic heterodiegetic category (diegesis) and all the others (mimesis). A typology of narration based upon Plato's distinction, then, recognizes two hierarchical modes of fictive representation, which may be a matter of information (diegesis) or of imitation (mimesis). In fictive diegesis, the information is offered and/or interpreted under the real-world communicative regime of fictionality, in which an awareness of its fictive orientation is integral to its rhetoric. In mimesis the imitation is specifically of an act of narration, so accordingly the informative function of diegesis is performed at one remove. The rhetorical gesture of fictionality, however, remains attached to the act of imitation itself. Note that this act is an imitation of a discursive form of narration, not of a

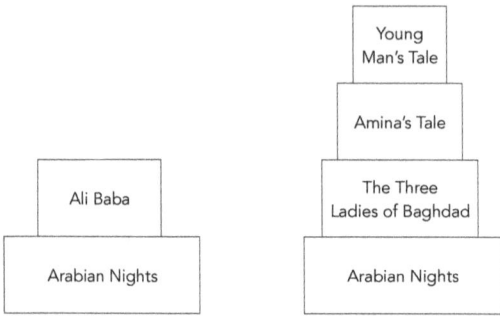

Figure 1.2. from "Stacks, Frames and Boundaries," 880 (simplified)

specific, notionally prior narrative act—it is a representational rather than reproductive use of the medium. The non-fictional version of this recursive structure would indeed be the transmission of an extant narrative; that is quotation, not mimesis. The two features of this model of fictive narration that I want to emphasize, then, are first that the fictive rhetorical gesture is always present, and always attached to the actual communicative act; and second that the recursive capacity of the model is subordinate to this fictive rhetoric, but also defined in terms of communicative acts. The permutations of this relation between fictionality and narrative information can accommodate the range of narratorial possibilities identified by Genette's typology in Figure 1.1, whether the diegesis mediates a mimesis of non-fictive narration (Ulysses), or of fictive narration (Scheherazade); or whether the mimesis is coextensive with the narrative itself (Marcel).

In order to draw out the implications of this view of fictive communication and its capacity for recursiveness, I shall invoke Marie-Laure Ryan's interesting alternative to the narrative-level model of recursiveness, which is the concept (borrowed from computer science) of the stack. The metaphor, she explains, refers to a stack of trays in a cafeteria: "The stack is supported by a spring, and the top tray is always level with the counter. When a customer puts a tray on the top of the stack, the structure must be pushed down in order to make the top tray even with the counter; when a tray is removed, the structure pops up, and the next tray on the stack is lifted to counter level. Being on top of the stack and level with the counter makes a tray the 'current tray'" (1990: 878). She illustrates the idea with an example representing the tales within tales of the *Arabian Nights*, as in Figure 1.2.

These are snapshots of the stack at two different points in the narrative—the "Tale of Ali Baba" and the "Young Man's Tale." The diagram is offered as a representation of distinct ontological realms within the narrative, but it

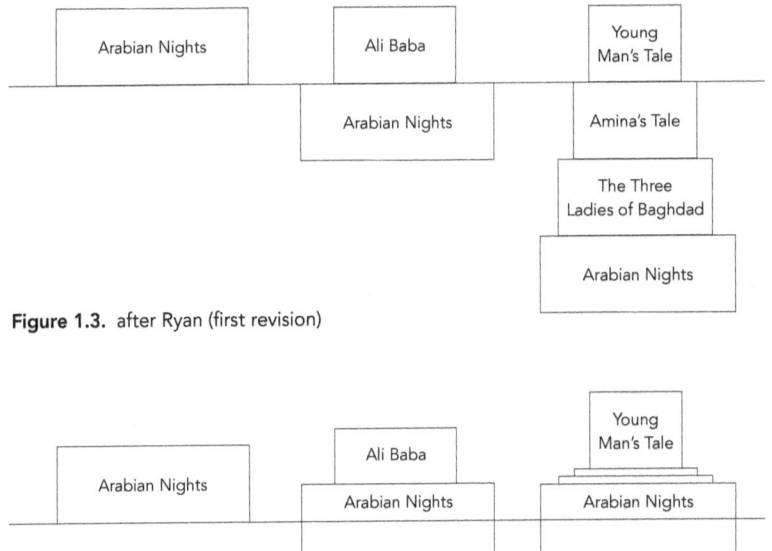

Figure 1.3. after Ryan (first revision)

Figure 1.4. after Ryan (second revision)

works equally well as a representation of distinct narrative acts; and as a diagram of recursive narration it is something we can work with. But first of all, as drawn it does not really capture the most suggestive feature of the stack metaphor as Ryan herself glosses it, which is the notion of the "current tray" at counter level. That would suggest the arrangement in Figure 1.3, in which anything below counter level is beneath our threshold of attention at a given point (I have added a snapshot of pure diegesis to clarify the idea).

But now I want to revise the model, because although intermediate layers of narration may be occluded while we attend to the current narration, I have argued that the fictive rhetorical gesture of the diegesis is not. So we need to adjust the counter level, and represent the buoyancy of the stack as in Figure 1.4.

The actual communicative act here, *The Arabian Nights,* has a fictive orientation that is necessarily apparent at all times, even when it is not the direct focus of our attention; whereas any narrative levels (or degrees of recursion) in between the diegesis and the current narration are virtually effaced. Not absolutely effaced, because it is open to us at any moment to wonder, for example, whether the current story is likely to interest King Shariah as much as Sheherazade needs it to (which refers us, even during the "Young Man's Tale," to the telling of "The Three Ladies of Baghdad"). So these levels are collapsed, latent contexts of the current narrative situation. This is as true of recursive narrative structures in which the intermediate levels of narration are all non-fictive with respect to each other. So, in *Frankenstein*, we attend to the monster's narration in its own right, not as Walton's written record of Victor's oral relation of that narration. This is not at all to say that we do not cross-reference between the monster's narration and information gleaned from our attention to these framing narrative acts when they are current; nor does it exclude our response to thematic connections between levels, which is provided for by our continual awareness of Mary Shelley's fictive rhetoric.[6]

The collapsed intermediate levels in this diagram are a mark of the insubstantiality of narrative transmission as conceived in the communicative model. One of the merits of the most prominent alternative to Genette's typology of narration, Stanzel's typological circle, is that it registers this insubstantiality (Figure 1.5). The category of figural narrative treats the perspectival mode Genette called internal focalization as integral to narrative mediacy, which implies a salutary disregard for the communicative model's commitment to a literal mode of transmission. Internal focalization is inherently an imaginative alignment of the narration with a character perspective: its assimilation, under the heading of mediacy, within the same typology as diegesis (the authorial situation) and mimesis (the first-person situation) implies the equally imaginative status of the latter's recursive structure. Both are contingent devices of the rhetoric of fictive narration, and neither entails a commitment to the literal logic of narrative transmission that leads the communicative model astray. On the other hand, the figural narrative situation cannot be homologous with Stanzel's other two categories in the sense that they are with each other, precisely because the character perspective is not part of any communication. Unlike first-person narrative, figural narrative is not a recursive representational doubling of the narrative act that characterizes authorial narrative. The same blurring of conceptual boundaries occurs within a different paradigm when Mieke Bal proposes to incorporate focalization into the recursive hierarchy of embedded narration. She notes that, as a criterion of recursiveness, "the two units must belong to the same class" (43), but then defines the relevant class, too broadly, as "subject-object relations" (45), which effaces the key difference between narration and focalization—that is, communication. So too with the figural narrative situation: its assimilation to the same class as diegesis and mimesis disregards the intrinsically communicative nature of narration. The figural narrative situation cannot be reconciled with communication, not even self-communication, since it definitionally involves a disjunction between narration and character perspec-

---

6. The concept of voice as idiom is also illuminated by this characteristic strategy, in the Gothic novel, of embedding multiple layers of narration—as we shall see below.

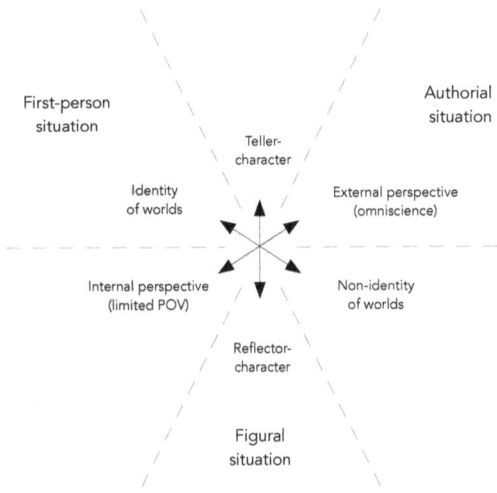

Figure 1.5. from *A Theory of Narrative* xvi (simplified)

tive. Monika Fludernik aptly describes the figural narrative situation as "non-communicative narrative" (1994: 445), which captures its incompatibility with the literal logic of the communicative model. But from a more inclusive rhetorical point of view, non-communicative narrative is a contradiction in terms; and it is only from a rhetorical point of view that any parity between (represented) narrative transmission and character perception can be countenanced in the first place. Figural narration, from this perspective, is simply a rhetorical option available to diegesis; one that exploits fiction's imaginative freedom from the literalism of the communicative model just as some features of first-person narration do, but without the recursive structure of mimesis.

The categories of person and level, as conceived in the communicative model, are logically incompatible with each other, then, and we can only make sense of fictive narratives (and narratives within narratives) in terms of a rhetorical paradigm more akin to Plato's distinction between diegesis and mimesis and the recursive options it accommodates. This rhetorical paradigm involves awareness of fictionality at all times as an integral part of our interpretation of fictions, so that recursive narratives do not at any point harden into discrete ontological facts with logical implications beyond the rhetorical focus of the particular case. Fictionality is a rhetorical gesture: as rhetoric it is necessarily communicative; as a gesture it is semiotic, but not intrinsically linguistic. This is important for two reasons. Firstly it accounts for a problem that exercises Genette in his discussion of *La Chute*, which (because of its resemblance to dramatic monologue) he is tempted to say has no extradiegetic level (1988: 89); as well as the analogous issue of the status of *interior* monologue, over which Stanzel and Dorrit Cohn disagree—Cohn sees it as direct discourse, Stanzel as pure reflector mode (Cohn 1981: 169–70). These problems arise because of an assumption that the fictive diegesis, to be diegesis at all, must be a linguistic act—so that if there is no overt narration to the reader, there is no diegesis. But communication is the semiotic use of media: as long as the character discourse is understood as represented, not transmitted, the fictive act of the diegesis is manifest. The second reason for insisting upon a semiotic frame of reference is already apparent from the way these two problem cases border upon drama: it is that a rhetorical model of fictionality as a communicative gesture recognizes no categorical boundary between fictions in language and fictions in other media. So whereas the model of mediacy presented by Stanzel embodies a tradition in which mediacy is an indirect form of representation, and its antithesis is the direct, immediate presentation of drama, or film, I am claiming instead that mediacy is a property of media; and that the distinction between, for instance, fiction and drama is not a distinction between indirect and direct form, but between different semiotic means of representation: in one case symbolic (language), in the other iconic (mise en scène, performance, etc.).[7]

There is an inherent possibility for any representational medium to represent an instance of its own use: for example, a film that represents the filming of a series of events (e.g. *The Blair Witch Project,* in which the whole film takes the form of documentary footage shot by the hapless characters; or *The French Lieutenant's Woman,* in which a relationship between two actors parallels that of their characters in the film they are making). Such recursive possibilities are rarely realized in the extradiegetic instance of a film, though the film-within-a-film is common enough. By contrast, the equivalent in linguistic fiction encompasses the whole range and history of homodiegetic narration, as well as intradiegetic narration (whether homo- or hetero-); that is to say, the whole order of narrative mimesis in Plato's sense. The reason, presumably, is that verbal narration is a native human faculty, whereas cinematic narration is a sophisticated technological extension of human narrative powers. On the other hand, the private, internal faculty of narrative articulation (that is, self-communication) may as readily be cognitively perceptual as lin-

---

7. Note that the language within dramatic performance is itself represented, and subordinate to the iconic function of the medium. My position here takes up the possibility of a trans-media model of narrative raised by Manfred Jahn (2001: 675–76) and Brian Richardson (2001a: 691), though emphatically not by postulating the agency of a dramatic (or filmic) narrator, for the reasons I first set out in "Who Is the Narrator?" (1997).

guistic—as, for example, in dreams or memories. Techniques of literary narration that strive to represent this mental faculty (interior monologue, stream of consciousness) can be seen as straining at the limits of their medium, and depend upon the establishment of certain representational conventions; their filmic equivalents—representations of dream narratives, for example—are accommodated more straightforwardly by the medium (it is notable that dreams figure prominently in the early history of film).[8] The prominence, in verbal fictions, of the mimetic paradigm (that is, of the narrating instance as a product of representation) may account for a *non sequitur* that seems to underlie the communicative model. Represented narrations are theorized (modeled) in terms of actual narrations—a perfectly appropriate interpretative strategy (though theory often extends it well beyond its legitimately rhetorical scope by insisting upon a systematic logical equivalence that is by no means inherent in the analogy, and sometimes obfuscatory); then, by a kind of back-formation, actual narrations of fiction are themselves modeled as represented narrations—a move that requires some such hypothesis as a default narrator and a dummy representational frame. A trans-media sense of narrating instance can be a helpful corrective here if we reflect upon the redundancy of treating film in that way; as if there were any theoretical dividend to be gained from regarding the discourse of every fiction film not as the film itself, but as something ontologically framed and mediated by the film (the discourse of a filmic narrator, communicating as fact the narrative of the film, through the medium of film, yet being only a formal inference from the fictionality of the film).[9]

By viewing the narrating instance as a representational act, then, I am affirming two things. Firstly, that the most elementary and irreducible distinction among narrating instances is not symmetrical but hierarchical, corresponding to Plato's distinction between diegesis and mimesis as, on the one

---

8. Richardson's discussion of memory plays (2001a: 682–83) provides further support for this observation.

9. This is essentially David Bordwell's point in *Narration in the Fiction Film* (1985), where he argues for a view of filmic narration as the set of cues from which the viewer constructs the fabula, but denies that narration implies a narrator (1985: 62). His emphasis upon the viewer's understanding of the representational product inevitably slights the communicative process, however, and arises from problems with the notion of fictionality that Bordwell does not explore, despite the prominence of "fiction" in his title. Edward Branigan does discuss communication in the context of fictionality, though preferring to "remain neutral" (1992: 107) on the merits of communication models. He finds himself caught between, on the one hand, a sense of agency in narration—he himself speaks of "an implicit extra-fictional narration [. . .] the 'voice' of an 'implied author'" (91)—and, on the other hand, the "anthropomorphic fiction" of a narrator (108–10). On this question, see also Jan Alber's contribution in this volume.

hand, a first-degree act of narrative representation (Genette's extra-heterodiegetic narration), and on the other hand, a second-degree narrative representation of a narrative representation (extra-homodiegetic narration, and all intradiegetic narration, homo- or hetero-). Second-degree narrative representation is more prevalent in linguistic media than others, but in any case encompasses all circumstances in which the need arises for a second sense of voice, as represented idiom, in conjunction with the sense of voice as narrating instance, because such narrative mimesis encompasses all circumstances in which the instance is itself an object of representation. Secondly, I am affirming the importance of a distinction between narrative representation and narrative transmission. Properly speaking, media cease to function transmissively (i.e. as technological conduits for independently semiotic content) as soon as they themselves become semiotic—which is to say, here, representational. So it is possible in non-fiction for a narrating instance to be transmitted within a framing instance (for example when a historian quotes an eye-witness account, or when a literary biography quotes from the work of its subject), but within fiction the appearance of such hierarchies of transmission is itself a product of representational rhetoric. The various transgressions of level that Genette classifies as metalepsis, whether foregrounded or incidental, are answerable only to that rhetoric: their significance is to be evaluated in relation to the discernible import of the representational discourse, rather than to the iron law of non-contradiction. Apart from the pragmatic, contextual circumstances of actual communication (including actual fictive communication), the structure of narrative instanciation does not exist except as a product of representation, and the logic of represented narrative transmission has no priority over the rhetorical emphases of the representational act itself. Narrative theory and interpretation, then, must avoid the temptation to impose the coherence of a systematic logical structure upon the process of narrative representation, which is contingent and inherently protean in its rhetorical emphasis and focus, direction and misdirection. In reading through the *represented* structure of narrative transmission, narratologists should take care not to mistake interpretative strategies for theoretical paradigms.

Where voice is used as a metaphor of idiom in narrative theory, it is a way of bringing to the fore the mimetic dimension of the narrative discourse; its capacity for representing the discourse of another. The represented discourse concerned may itself be a narrating instance, or it may be a discursive act of another kind; it may imply a particular discursive subject, or it may be a generic representation. The defining feature of voice in the sense of idiom is that it is always objectified, as the product of a representational rhetoric; and in this respect it is crucial to keep it distinct from voice as instance. The temptation is to apply the sense of voice as idiom equally to represented discourses and first-degree narrative discourse, or diegesis, because intuitively, narrative language does not only represent voices, but also exhibits voice. In rhetorical terms, however, the function of voice in these two discursive contexts—diegesis and mimesis—is quite different. It is true that we are likely to focus upon a similar range of phenomena whether we attend to qualities of voice in narrative diegesis or in a represented discourse; but the significance of these phenomena for narrative interpretation is radically distinct in each case. When attending to voice in diegesis we are attending to rhetorical means (which may or may not be intentional, but are certainly authorial); whereas in attending to voice in represented discourses we are attending to rhetorical effects—even where these take the form of represented rhetorical means, as for example in the case of a represented narrating instance (Humbert Humbert's, say). So in diegesis, questions of voice bear upon the significance we attribute to the represented events, the narrative object; whereas mimetic voice (which I am calling idiom) invites evaluation of the character whose discourse it represents—the discursive or narrative subject. It is easy to see why the notion of voice as idiom might seem applicable to all discourse, but it is also apparent, I think, that such usage strains the range of a single concept, given this disparity of rhetorical emphasis. In fact, the case in which both senses of voice are applicable (that of a represented narrating instance) does not obscure the difference between them, but highlights it. A narrative told by a character, considered as idiom, contributes to the job of characterization; considered as instance, it contributes to the job of narration. In *Moby-Dick*, Ishmael's narration considered as idiom tells us about Ishmael; as instance it tells us about Ahab and the white whale. Most of the time there is no incompatibility between these two functions, though the emphasis varies widely from case to case; but fictions can include embedded narratives for reasons that have nothing to do with characterization, and in fact the latter may be an undesirable distraction. In such cases idiom defers to instance: this is commonplace in film, where a character's narration typically progresses in quick succession from diegetic verbal discourse to voice-over, to impersonal filmic narration (*Citizen Kane*, for example, provides several variations on this technique); but consider also the Gothic novel, where the function of elaborate narrative embedding often has much less to do with the narrating characters than with a generic strategy for bridging the gap between the reader's quotidian norms and the novel's extreme, imaginatively remote subject matter (a similar strategy, in fact, to the "friend of a friend" framework typical of urban legend). Perhaps the most extreme example is *Melmoth the Wanderer*, the story of which is in part relayed via a Shropshire clergyman,

Melmoth the Wanderer himself, the ancient Jew Adonijah and the Spaniard Monçada to the student John Melmoth. Furthermore, these various narrating instances span about 150 years; yet there is little attempt to distinguish the idiom of any of them.

Even within narratives in linguistic media, voice is used in senses ranging from the almost literal, for representations of oral discourse, to metaphorical applications so far abstracted from orality that the term becomes virtually interchangeable with vision: but throughout this spectrum the notion of voice enshrines an assumption that the distinctive features of a discourse afford an insight into an enunciating subject—that voice is expression. Indeed this assumption provides the whole rhetorical basis for the representational evocation of voice that I am categorizing as idiom: the point of representing a character's idiom is very much to invite inference about that character's subjectivity. Inference of this kind, however, is a much more hazardous and less obviously relevant undertaking when the notional voice is not objectified, as in narrative diegesis. In this case, many of the discursive features commonly embraced by voice are equally, and perhaps better, understood as style: by *style* I mean discourse features understood in their relation to meaning, as conceived within the field of stylistics, rather than as the expression of subjectivity. This substitution makes it easier to recognize that there is no inherent expression of authorial subjecthood—no authentic self-presence—in such discursive features; nor indeed is there inherently a singular authorial subject, either in linguistic media or (more self-evidently) in non-linguistic media. Of course stylistic analysis also relates discourse to ideological import, and this intimates another sense of voice that remains usefully applicable to narrative diegesis, but which relates narrative rhetoric to the constitution of a subject position, rather than to an originary subject as such. I shall return to this distinction later.

For all forms of represented discourse, then, voice as idiom is a particular (idiosyncratic or typical) discursive evocation of character. It is worth insisting upon the correspondence between such rhetorical strategies in different media, in order to grasp the phenomenon at a representational level rather than a specifically linguistic level. The recursive model of represented voice that I have invoked suggests that the place to look for analogies would not be representations of verbal discourse in non-verbal media, but rather those cases where a medium is used to represent an instance of its own use. I have already suggested that the range of represented narrating instances in film might be taken to extend from fairly literal representations of the use of filmic apparatus to representations of the use of the medium's semiotic channels, as mimetic of cognitive narrative processes. On this basis represented narrating instances, which occupy one part of the territory covered by the concept of voice as idiom, would include dream or fantasy sequences, as in the films of *Billy Liar* and *The Secret Life of Walter Mitty*, both of which include filmic representation of their protagonists' day-dreams; but the same principle can be extended to other represented discursive and cognitive acts, including any point-of-view shot that represents the character's own distinct cognitive-perceptual subjectivity. A good example would be the recurrent shot, in *Once upon a Time in the West*, of a blurred figure approaching, which turns out to represent the memory of "Harmonica" (Charles Bronson): it is the perspective of his exhausted younger self (he has been struggling to support the weight of his brother, who has a noose around his neck) as Frank (Henry Fonda) approaches to torment him further by pushing a harmonica into his mouth as he is on the point of collapse.

The most inclusive applications of the term voice in narrative—those that are interchangeable with terms like vision—suggest the equal applicability of linguistic and perceptual metaphors for the concept, which is a helpful support for the proposal that the issue of voice should be placed in the context of representational rhetoric across all narrative media. The analogy with vision also relates directly to another prominent metaphor in narrative theory, which is focalization.[10] But there is a crucial distinction between focalization and the discursive features that fall under idiom. Voice as idiom always constructs a distinct subject (even if generic), by virtue of its objectification—that is, its difference from the narrative diegesis (or a framing narrative mimesis) within which it is represented. Focalization, on the other hand, constructs a subject position only, which may or may not be aligned with a represented character (external focalization is precisely not character centred). When focalization is aligned with a character, its rhetorical means may very well be a representation of idiom. Consider the relation between free indirect discourse (FID) and internal focalization. FID is one of the privileged topics in discussions of narrative voice, and as represented discourse it falls within the scope of voice as idiom. It also necessarily implies internal focalization (however momentary), though the reverse is not true: internal focalization does not always involve FID, or any other representation of idiom. FID is a form of discursive mimesis, whereas focalization is a feature of narrative diegesis (not, I hasten to add, of narrative transmission: it is a product of representational rhetoric, not an information conduit). Where FID and internal focalization

10. Fludernik, discussing the relation between voice and focalization, argues for the theoretical redundancy of the latter (2001: 633–35). I find it helpful to retain it, however, as an aid to discriminating between the different senses of voice, which are often in play at the same time.

coincide, these are two sides of the same coin: the one oriented towards the represented discourse, the other towards the subject position constructed by that representation. The sense in which FID involves some kind of doubling of voice was encapsulated in the title of Roy Pascal's classic study, *The Dual Voice*, as well as in Mikhail Bakhtin's concept of double-voiced discourse, of which it is a very specific instance (I shall return to Bakhtin below). FID is a representation of the idiom—the objectified voice—of another, in neutral or parodic style, with sympathetic or ironic inflection, but in any case with a certain distance inherent in the fact that the representing act itself remains in the fore. The indices of the representational act persist within the representation itself in the form of temporal and perspectival markers (past-tense verbs, third-person pronouns) that correlate with the subject position implied by the narrating instance rather than that implied by the idiomatic voice. That is to say, the narrating voice inhabits FID not as idiom, but as instance (overtly; it also involves interpellation, as we shall see): FID is double-voiced only in the sense that it is a synthetic product of distinct senses of voice.[11]

Whilst certain forms of focalization go hand in hand with representations of voice as idiom, such as FID, this is not the sense in which voice may be understood as applicable to focalization in general. As idiom, voice is an object of representation: it is offered up to the evaluative scrutiny of the narrative's audience, and so held at arm's length. There is a structurally intrinsic detachment, however sympathetic, to the rhetorical function of voice as idiom. Focalization in general, however, does not operate in this way: the perspectival logic of a representation is not manifested as an object, but as an implicit premise of the rhetorical focus of the representational act. That is to say, while voice as idiom serves to characterize a discursive subject as a more or less individuated object of representation, focalization as such functions indirectly, to establish a subject position only; one that may or may not coincide with a specific character, but which in any case is not an object of representation but a tacit rhetorical effect of the discourse's mode of representation of another object. Where a specific character is involved, it is possible to describe represented idiom as an effect of sympathetic or ironic detachment, and focalization as an effect of empathetic subjective alignment (as long as the term empathy can be understood as without evaluative preju-

---

11. The possibility of analogies for FID in other media raises interesting questions: consider the way Hitchcock represents the experience of vertigo in the film of that name, in the famous tower shot combining a zoom out and track in to maintain a constant image size, or frame range, in a view down a (model) stairwell. The device is mimetic of James Stewart's struggle to make sense of his perceptions, but as an overtly filmic technique—a simultaneous track and zoom—it is also part of the representational rhetoric of the diegetic narrative itself.

dice). The more general, abstract concept that applies to the latter effect, however, is interpellation. This is the term I am using to define the third sense in which voice is used in narrative theory and criticism.

Interpellation is the process by which an ideology or discourse "hails" and constitutes individuals as subjects (Althusser 1971: 162). Narration always involves perspectival choices, which necessarily carry with them some set of presuppositions, ranging from the physical (spatio-temporal), through the epistemological, to the ideological. This structure of presupposition may be aligned with a character, as in first-person narration and internal focalization, or it may not; but in every case the act of narrative comprehension requires an imaginative alignment between the reader (or viewer) and the implied subject position of the discourse. Such alignment may, to an extent, be conscious and qualified by reservations of several kinds; but to the extent that it is unconscious, it has the ideological effect of making the implied subject position seem to constitute the authentic selfhood of the narrative recipient.[12]

I have discussed the sense in which voice, as represented idiom, can be understood as a rhetorical means of characterizing the subject of represented discourse. It is a perfectly intelligible and modest figurative leap from there to a usage of voice that refers to the subject position implied by any discourse (represented or diegetic, aligned with a character or not). This is a distinct sense of voice not only because it need not be representationally embodied or owned by a character, or a narrating character, or indeed the author, but also because its scope extends well beyond the category of the discursive, or even the perspectival in any limited perceptual or cognitive sense (the domain of focalization), to become an organizing concept for ideology. Where the concept of voice is invoked in this sense, it seems to do quite various services for critical orientations ranging from Bakhtinian dialogics to identity politics. The figurative instability of the term itself is partly responsible, no doubt: it allows for uncertain fluctuation between a usage in which the ideological subject position is a discursive construct, and a usage in which it is an authentic manifestation of (subaltern) identity.[13]

In *Problems of Dostoevsky's Poetics*, Bakhtin identifies a range of double-voiced phenomena in narrative discourse, the dialogic nature of which is only brought out by a theoretical approach he describes as "metalinguistic"

12. The mechanism of presupposition underlying the interpellation of subjects has been explored by John Frow in relation to genre and Vološinov's concept of the literary enthymeme, or argument with an implied premise (Frow 1986: 77–78).
13. Susan Lanser's *Fictions of Authority* (1992) is a useful example of the politicization of voice from a feminist perspective. Lanser makes a clear distinction between voice in the sense I am calling idiom and a sense that equates with instance/interpellation, though she does not discriminate between the latter two senses.

(181). This is because double-voiced discourse is only perceptible as a feature of concrete, situated language use, from which the discipline of linguistics (including formal stylistics) is necessarily abstracted. Double-voiced discourse emerges, then, when the manifest voice of an utterance can be contextually understood to be in dialogue with some other, implicit voice. Voice in this second sense cannot be assimilated to voice as idiom, since it is not represented; or to voice as instance, since it is not even explicit.[14] Its implicit nature, and the fact that it is not necessarily attributable to a particular subject, or even any specific discursive form, marks this out as a sense of voice that falls within the scope of interpellation. But clearly, since the dialogic interaction that interests Bakhtin is ideological (ideology being the unifying principle of the voice with which the discourse is engaged), the sense of voice that applies on the explicit side of the dialogue also finds its integrity in ideological terms, rather than as a set of formal discourse features, or the represented idiom of a particular subject. So Bakhtin describes Dostoevsky's *Notes from Underground* as double voiced in that the Underground Man's discourse throughout is not only oriented towards its objects, but also in dialogue with the anticipated response of another: "In each of his thoughts about [the world, nature, society] there is a battle of voices, evaluations, points of view. In everything he senses above all *someone else's will* predetermining him" (236). The ideological thrust of his own discourse is precisely to establish the autonomy and integrity of the subject position he claims for himself, yet the attempt itself involves him in an unresolvable dialogic vicious circle: "What he fears most of all is that . . . his self-affirmation is somehow in need of affirmation or recognition by another. And it is in this direction that he anticipates the other's response. . . . He *fears* that the other might think he *fears* that other's opinion. . . . With his refutation, he confirms precisely what he wishes to refute, and he knows it" (229). In other words, the Underground Man's discourse projects a subject position that is nevertheless unoccupiable. In general, Bakhtin's concept of polyphony necessarily dissociates voice from the individual subject; but without some other organizing principle the polyphony would be too diffuse a phenomenon to be conceptually useful—and in fact the notion of monologism, which Bakhtin retains, would be unintelligible. The organizing principle at work in Bakhtin's system is a concept of voice as the relative agglomeration of ideological significance, the

---

14. The need to discriminate between senses of voice is apparent in the conclusion to which Richard Aczel is led by a consideration of this specific Bakhtinian context: "Narrative voice, like any other voice, is a fundamentally *composite* entity, a specific *configuration* of voices" (1998: 483). If every voice is a configuration of voices, the term is being made to work too hard.

integrity of which is not (even in the most monological instance) to be found in the discursive subject as such, but in the projection of virtual subject positions: that is, in the mechanism of interpellation. By distinguishing between voice as instance and as interpellation, I am contrasting a sense of the term in which it represents the narrating agency of a particular individual or collective, with one in which it discursively insinuates an ideological nexus, a subject position with the potential to constitute a particular subject (represented or otherwise). Such a distinction, I think, provides for a politicized sense of voice in which the contextual production of situated political identities is at stake (to be engaged critically, recognized or resisted), without hypostasizing the concept as the authentic expression of such identities.

If my discrimination between the different senses of voice has any merit, it is the result of approaching the issue with two key assumptions in mind. First, an assumption that the senses of voice—instance, idiom and interpellation—need to be conceived in terms of representational rhetoric, and in particular the rhetoric of fictionality; and second, an assumption that the issues covered by the term voice are not exclusively linguistic, but also semiotic, and relevant across the whole range of narrative media. It seems to me that these premises are crucial, not only to expose the inadequacies of the communicative model of narration, but also to take us beyond it. I have insisted upon the metaphoricity of the notion of voice as the precondition for its range of application both within and beyond linguistic media, and the terms I have used to discriminate between senses of voice can only cover that range themselves by virtue of a certain amount of extension and extrapolation. So, I have used the term instance to refer to the sense of voice as an act of narrative representation, which is to say the sense in which the emphasis falls upon communicative agency in narration. I have suggested that the most fundamental distinction to be drawn within this category arises out of the inherent possibility of recursiveness in narration, whereby one narrating instance may represent another. I have shown how this distinction, which corresponds to the Platonic distinction between diegesis and mimesis, cuts across the fourfold typology of narrating instances Genette derives from his oppositions between homodiegetic and heterodiegetic, and intradiegetic and extradiegetic narration, and I have argued further for a rhetorical perspective upon narration that does not confuse representation with transmission. My use of the term idiom serves to group together senses of voice in which the emphasis falls upon the discursive subject as an object of representation—that is, where voice serves purposes of characterization. This definition provides for analogies between literary representations of voice and examples of mimetic recursiveness in other media. It has also allowed me to make a principled distinction between represented voice and focalization (the latter being a form of my third category of voice, interpellation), and to distinguish the different senses of voice that apply in the notably complex case of free indirect discourse. Finally, I have used the term interpellation to refer to those respects in which voice relates to a representational subject position rather than to a represented or actual subject as such. Focalization, I have suggested, is a special, restricted case of voice in this sense, in which the subject position is defined in perceptual and cognitive terms. In the general case, the sense of voice as interpellation embraces more abstract, ideological constructions of a subject position, and I have shown how such a conception of voice can account for its use in the context of Bakhtinian dialogics. If nothing else, this analysis of the metaphor of voice in narrative theory shows that it has already gone a long way beyond words, and indeed that it is perhaps too richly suggestive for its own good. There is little to be gained from attempting to constrain the use of such a metaphor, but it is worth insisting upon the need for more nuanced distinctions; the terms I have suggested here—instance, idiom, and interpellation—offer one way of doing just that.

REFERENCES

Aczel, Richard (1998) "Hearing Voices in Narrative Texts." *New Literary History* 29: 467–500.
Althusser, Louis (1971) *Lenin and Philosophy and Other Essays*. Trans. Ben Brewster. London: New Left Books.
Bakhtin, Mikhail (1984) *Problems of Dostoevsky's Poetics*. Ed. and trans. Caryl Emerson. Manchester: Manchester University Press.
Bal, Mieke (1981) "Notes on Narrative Embedding." *Poetics Today* 2.2: 41–59.
Billy Liar. Dir. John Schlesinger. Vic Films Productions, 1963.
The Blair Witch Project. Dirs. Daniel Myrick and Eduardo Sánchez. Haxan Films, 1999.
Bordwell, David (1985) *Narration in the Fiction Film*. London: Methuen.
Branigan, Edward (1992) *Narrative Comprehension and Film*. London: Routledge.
Citizen Kane. Dir. Orson Welles. RKO Radio Pictures, 1941.
Cohn, Dorrit (1981) "The Encirclement of Narrative: On Franz Stanzel's *Theorie des Erzählens*." *Poetics Today* 2.2: 157–82.
―― (1999) *The Distinction of Fiction*. Bloomington: Indiana University Press.
Fludernik, Monika (1994) "Second-Person Narrative as a Test Case for Narratology: The Limits of Realism." *Style* 28.3: 445–79.
―― (2001) "New Wine in Old Bottles? Voice, Focalization, and New Writing." *New Literary History* 32: 619–38.
The French Lieutenant's Woman. Dir. Karel Reisz. Juniper Films, 1981.
Frow, John (1986) *Marxism and Literary History*. Oxford: Blackwell.

Genette, Gérard (1980) *Narrative Discourse* [1972]. Trans. Jane E. Lewin. Oxford: Basil Blackwell.
—— (1988) *Narrative Discourse Revisited* [1983]. Trans. by Jane E. Lewin. Ithaca, NY: Cornell University Press.
—— (1993) *Fiction and Diction* [1991]. Trans. Catherine Porter. Ithaca, NY: Cornell University Press.
Jahn, Manfred (2001) "Narrative Voice and Agency in Drama: Aspects of a Narratology of Drama." *New Literary History* 32: 659–79.
Lanser, Susan S. (1992) *Fictions of Authority: Women Writers and Narrative* Voice. Ithaca, NY: Cornell University Press.
Once upon a Time in the West. Dir. Sergio Leone. Finanzia San Marco, 1968.
Pascal, Roy (1977) *The Dual Voice: Free Indirect Speech and Its Functioning in the Nineteenth-Century European Novel*. Manchester: Manchester University Press.
Richardson, Brian (2001a) "Voice and Narration in Postmodern Drama." *New Literary History* 32: 681–94.
—— (2001b) "Inhuman Voices." *New Literary History* 32: 699–701.
Ryan, Marie-Laure (1990) "Stacks, Frames and Boundaries, or Narrative as Computer Language." *Poetics Today* 11.4: 873–99.
The Secret Life of Walter Mitty. Dir. Norman Z. McLeod. Samuel Goldwyn Company, 1947.
Stanzel, Franz K. (1984) *A Theory of Narrative* [1979]. Trans. Charlotte Goedsche. Cambridge: Cambridge University Press.
Walsh, Richard (1997) "Who Is the Narrator?" *Poetics Today* 18.4: 495–513.
—— (2007) *The Rhetoric of Fictionality: Narrative Theory and the Idea of Fiction*. Columbus: The Ohio State University Press.

WERNER WOLF

Mise en cadre—
A Neglected Counterpart to Mise en abyme

A Frame-Theoretical and Intermedial Complement to Classical Narratology

POSITIONING THE DISCUSSION OF MISE EN CADRE IN THE FIELD OF (POST-)CLASSICAL NARRATOLOGY

Part of the present "state of the art" of contemporary narratology seems to be a paradox, for rather than presenting a static profile, this "state" of the art is characterized by a highly dynamic situation. Indeed, narratology currently appears to be undergoing a major paradigm shift: most narratologists have recently announced the demise of classical, structuralist narratology and proclaimed the emergence of a "post-classical" era.[1] The manifold alleged or genuinely new developments in this post-classical narratology fall into three categories. There is firstly, as the most radical and also most questionable development, the deconstruction of narratology as a logocentric enterprise, as epitomized by Andrew Gibson (1996). Secondly, there is a large group of "applied narratologists," who are principally interested in new synchronic or diachronic reference fields. They use (and occasionally modify) the tools provided by classical narratology for often highly topical applications to contemporary or past reality and employ narratology for cultural-historical,

---

1. Cf. Herman (1997, 1999), Nünning/Nünning (2002), Fludernik (2003), Kindt/Müller (2003), Nünning (2004).

post-colonial or feminist analyses, to mention a few examples.² And there is, thirdly, a group of "systematic narratologists," who complement classical narratology from a predominantly theoretical point of view by systematically refining and completing its toolbox or by broadening narratology's focus so that it opens up towards other theoretical approaches such as possible-worlds theory, cognitive theory³ and/or towards the non-verbal media, which are increasingly being included in narratological studies.⁴ Not only the first but also both of the latter groups move away from classical structuralist narratology with its all but exclusive focus on intratextual phenomena of literary works as static structures.

In spite of all the current rhetoric of "making it new," one should not forget that all of today's narratology is based on the ground-breaking work of the classical narratologists and that without them there would be nothing to deconstruct, no new outlooks to engage with and no extensions of narratology. In this spirit of acknowledging the achievements of the founders of the discipline such as Gérard Genette, who, among many other notions, introduced a fruitful typology of diegetic levels into the description of narratives (1972: 238 f.), I would in this article like to add something to his findings, a complement to classical narratology that is also meant as a compliment. My contribution thus belongs to the third group of post-classical variants concentrating on systematic supplementation. It is inspired by both structuralist analysis—which for me still has its merits owing to its ideal of methodological and logocentric rigor, its attempt at terminological clarity, and its unparalleled contribution to the understanding of the internal make-up of (literary) texts—and by a number of post-classical approaches, notably frame theory and an intermedial perspective. Owing to this combination of classical and post-classical elements, my approach could also be termed "neo-classical."

My neo-classical complement takes its departure from the well-known concept of *mise en abyme* as investigated by Dällenbach (1989), Hutcheon (1984: 53–6) and others, and consists in highlighting a reciprocal, hitherto neglected phenomenon, which I call *mise en cadre*. To be more precise, I propose to contribute to the study of what, with Jean Ricardou (using "text" in a broad sense) one may call "similitudes textuelles" (1978: 75), that is, simi-

---

2. For a cultural-historical (re-)orientation of narratology see Erll/Roggendorf (2002), Fludernik (2003), and Nünning (2004); for a post-colonial orientation see Birk/Neumann (2002); and for a feminist or gender orientation see Allrath/Gymnich (2002) and Nünning/Nünning (2004).
3. See Surkamp (2002), Zerweck (2002), Herman (2002, 2003).
4. See Cobley (2002), Wolf (2002b, 2004b), Herman (2004), Ryan (2004), and Abbott (2005).

larities that occur within a text or artefact. Thus the following discussion of *mise en cadre* as a complement to *mise en abyme* is also a contribution to the wide field of textual self-referentiality.[5]

POSTCLASSICAL INTERMEDIAL AND FRAME-THEORETICAL APPROACHES AS FRAMES TO *MISE EN CADRE*

Before discussing the concept of *mise en cadre,* I would like to briefly outline the post-classical theoretical frameworks that will be shown to be relevant to this concept.

My first framework is the *theory of intermediality*. I am referring to "intermediality" here in its broad sense, which designates all phenomena that involve more than one conventionally distinct medium of communication. For my present purpose a variant of intermediality is relevant which deals with phenomena that can be observed in more than one medium. In intermediality theory this variant has been called "transmediality."[6] Transmediality is relevant also to many phenomena that have originally been described in literary narratology, notably to the core concept of narratology, namely narrativity.[7] It is moreover important to "descriptivity,"[8] meta-referentiality,[9] to name a few more examples, and it also extends, as we will see, to *mise en cadre*. These are all phenomena that transcend, cross or go beyond the confines of literary texts. The phenomenon of framing equally belongs to these transmedial phenomena, which leads me to the second theoretical framework requisite for the explanation of *mise en cadre,* namely frame theory.

Frame theory, as conceived in linguistics, social psychology and cognitive theory (Bateson 1972, Goffman 1974), is actually the most important theoretical framework for my purposes. It takes its point of departure in the idea, by now generally acknowledged, that all mental activity is ruled by cognitive *frames,* that is, by meta-concepts, which in turn govern individual concepts and thus help us navigate through our experiential and communicative

---

5. I am hereby enlarging on a form of self-referentiality which I first outlined in Wolf (2001: 61–68); cf. also Wolf (2009: ch. 3.2.).
6. For transmediality as one of several basic forms of intermediality (which also includes intermedial transposition, plurimediality and intermedial reference) see Wolf (2002a: 18 f.); Rajewsky (2002: 206) also discusses it in the context of intermediality.
7. See for instance Ryan (2004), and Wolf (2002b).
8. See Wolf/Bernhart (2007).
9. See Hauthal et al. (2007) and Wolf (2009).

universe. Such frames also apply to literature and other media.[10] Literature in itself constitutes a macro-frame, and its production and reception are shaped by further cognitive frames, for example, genres. While the application of some, in particular seemingly natural, frames goes without saying because they operate with implicit "default settings" and without "keyings" (Goffman's term[11]), there are frames which require explicit keying or, as I shall call it, *framing*. The various media, including literature, must be counted among this latter group, since they form specialized modes of communication based on "non-natural" frames that call for special "keyings" or framings. "Framing" in this cognitive sense refers to a concrete coding of abstract cognitive frames as mentally stored schemata, a coding that can occur in mental activities as well as in physical manifestations either within texts and artefacts or in their immediate contexts. In the temporal media, framings in *initial* position are especially important since in this position they are most efficient in contributing to, and controlling, reception processes.[12] In what follows I will be concerned primarily, though not exclusively, with such initial framings.

An important location of cognitive framings in literature are paratexts—another element from Genette's useful classical toolbox (1987). Additional framings can be found in the framing parts of frame narratives (for instance the "General Prologue" of Chaucer's *The Canterbury Tales*) and as we will see, picture frames. In literature as well as in the visual arts such framing parts are commonly called "frames," which could create confusion with the frame-theoretical meaning of frame and framing as introduced above. However, neither the terminological closeness between "frame" as cognitive frame and as physical text segment or picture frame nor the vicinity between cognitive "frame" and "framings" should cause too many difficulties as long as what is meant remains clear. From a cognitive perspective the terminological similarity of "framing" and "frame" in their cognitive as well as common

---

10. For a detailed application of frame theory to literature and other media see Wolf/Bernhart (2006).

11. See Goffman 1974: 40–82. According to Goffman the most important default setting is what he calls the "primary framework" (1974: 21 and passim), which refers to reality; thus it is only when a communicative exchange is *not* seriously meant as "real" that we need "keying" as, for instance, in role playing. Goffman's "keying," which he defines as "[a] systematic transformation [. . .] across materials already meaningful in accordance with a schema of interpretation" (45) is more restricted than my notion of "framing," since "keying," for Goffman, only marks the shift from reality to play, whereas "framing" can mark any cognitive frame that guides mental activities.

12. For more details on frames and (initial) framing in literature and other arts see Wolf/Bernhart (2006), in particular the introduction to that volume (Wolf 2006).

senses may be said to point to a deeper functional relation. It consists in the fact that the frames of frame narratives as well as picture frames are sites on which cognitive framing (the coding of cognitive frames) frequently occurs with particular density, even though such frames-as-text-segments—and this is also true of paratexts and picture frames—can also serve other functions, e.g. create suspense, give summaries of the following story, emphasize the value of the framed work, etc. As regards the following discussion I would like to note that I will primarily deal with framings in the cognitive sense (in particular as physical markers of cognitive frames). More precisely, I will concentrate on two basic forms of how framings can be realized (whether in paratexts, the frames of frame tales, or elsewhere).

The physical codings of cognitive frames can occur either in the explicit mode of telling (that is, by simply naming the relevant cognitive frames) or in the implicit mode of showing (that is, by implying cognitive frames through illustrations). The mode of telling may be illustrated by Chaucer's "General Prologue," namely by the explicit mention of "myrthe" and the wish to "be myrie" as the motivation for the host to ask the pilgrims to tell stories on their way to Canterbury (Chaucer 1957: 773, 782). This triggers the cognitive frame "entertainment" as one of the functions of the embedded tales. The mode of showing, on the other hand, occurs when the text evokes, describes or narrates something in a framing part which—usually proleptically, but in some cases also analeptically—sheds light on the framed part and thus triggers a relevant cognitive frame in the recipient's mind that influences his or her interpretation. In the mode of showing the establishment of similarities between the framing and the framed is a particularly important device, one that is also particularly apt for literature as an art that does not only name concepts but also typically illustrates them. The distinction between telling and showing can even be exemplified in the titles of literary works as important instances of paratexts. There are titles that contain framings in the mode of telling, for instance Defoe's *The Life and Strange Surprising Adventures of Robinson Crusoe, of York, Mariner* (1719), where the generic frame "adventure story" is explicitly mentioned. By contrast, in Oscar Wilde's *The Importance of Being Earnest* (1895) the implicit mode of showing can (retrospectively) be seen at work in the indirect invocation of the generic frame "comedy" through the use of typical devices of comic entertainment: the title establishes a similarity with humorous elements of the play by containing the pun earnest/Ernest and by hinting at the playful non-fulfilment of expectations (seriousness as an "important" theme of a comedy!) that so conspicuously informs Wilde's witty comedy as a whole.

MISE EN CADRE AS A COUNTERPART TO *MISE EN ABYME*: The Concept and Examples from Fiction and Painting[13]

The Concept of Mise en cadre *as Opposed to* Mise en abyme

The implicit mode of showing is particularly relevant to *mise en cadre*, notably when it employs similarities as a form of realizing framings in the cognitive sense. One more—and more complex—example besides the title of Wilde's *The Importance of Being Earnest* shall prepare the ground for the theoretical explanation of the concept in focus here: Joseph Conrad's frametale *Heart of Darkness* (1899), more precisely the relationship between parts of the opening framing section and aspects of the framed text.

As is well known, the embedded story and main part of the text thematically centers on the concept and in particular on the ambivalence of "darkness" not only of colonized "Africa" as a fascinating and disturbingly wild continent, whose "heart" Marlow's expedition attempts to reach in search of the missing Mr. Kurtz, but also of the white colonizers themselves, whose motivations are revealed to have a remarkably dark side. Ultimately, the "heart of darkness" of the novel's title pessimistically refers to the human heart, which is full of gloomy "abominations" underneath a "bright" but deplorably thin varnish of "civilization," consisting of moral and humanist ideals.

This ambivalence, with an emphasis on the dark side of civilization, is already conspicuously present in the landscape description contained in the opening frame (Conrad 1986: 1814–18). This description serves as the coding of major elements of the text's implied worldview and pessimistic view of man and is thus a marker of a complex cognitive frame. The framing scene is set on board a ship anchored in the river Thames. The river, which is made to resemble "an interminable waterway [. . .] leading to the uttermost ends of the earth" (1814–15),[14] foreshadows—and parallels—the great African river on which Marlow sets out on his expedition into the heart of the African darkness. Even more revealing than the similarities in the spatial coordinates is the play of light and gloom which the temporal setting provides, for the framing scene takes place at sunset: "The day was ending in a serenity of

---

13. Parts of this chapter are a revised version of my interpretation of Conrad's *Heart of Darkness* in Wolf (2006: 201–3).

14. Moreover, in Marlow's preface to his tale, the Thames is linked to the ambivalence of the former Roman civilization, whose "[l]ight came out of this river" in the midst of the "darkness" and "wilderness" of early Britain (1817).

still and exquisite brilliance"—yet it is a "brilliance" tarnished in the west by a "gloom, brooding motionless over the biggest, and the greatest, town on earth" (all 1815). This darkness enveloping London, "the monstrous town" (1816) at the center of the British Empire,[15] is repeatedly mentioned and forms one of the most salient features of the framing description. It is a gloom which triggers ideas of decay and death: "[. . .] the sun sank low, and from glowing white changed to a dull red without rays and without heat, as if about to go out suddenly, stricken to death by the touch of that gloom brooding over a crowd of men" (1815). The fact that the crew on board the ship starts a game of dominoes referred to as "bones" (1815) chimes in well with this image of death and decadence. All of these diegetic elements—and there are more in this framing part—are remarkable anticipations of elements in the ensuing hypodiegetic story and show revealing similarities with it. The decadent ambivalence surrounding the Thames resembles the atmosphere surrounding the African river in the embedded tale with its gloomy depictions of the failing aspirations of colonialism and man in general. This ambivalence also anticipates the fate of Kurtz; this "splendid pillar" of Western civilization has apparently had experiences that lead to his famous dying words "The horror! The horror!" (1873), an enigmatic but definitely rather gloomy summing up of his life, which contrasts with its apparent moral splendor.

The entire framing landscape description is a fine specimen of a *mise en cadre*. Like *mise en abyme*, this device rests on two formal criteria: 1) the existence of a hierarchy of at least two different logical or narratological levels; and 2) a similarity or analogy between them (including, as a liminal case, also contrast, for contrast, in order to be discernible as such, always implies a basic common ground between the contrasting phenomena). However, *mise en cadre* differs from *mise en abyme* in the direction in which this similarity is made to operate. While *mise en abyme* is itself a distinct element located on a lower level that sheds light on an upper level through revelatory similarities in a "bottom up" process (Figure 2.1), *mise en cadre* is part of a framing and thus upper-level structure that illuminates a lower, framed text in a "top down" process (Figure 2.2). Narratology has failed to provide a distinct term for this reversal of, and counterpart to, *mise en abyme*. I have therefore proposed elsewhere to baptize it *mise en cadre* (Wolf 1999: 104, Wolf 2001: 63–64), maintaining in the French term the connection with *mise en abyme*. (Already in 1994 Guy Larroux had used the term but in a different sense, namely that of "putting a frame around a tale."[16]) My definition of the

---

15. The British Empire here stands metonymically for all European colonial empires. This includes the Belgian Congo, where the African part of the embedded story is set.

16. Larroux, in his contribution to a colloquium which was held at the Université

term is as follows: As opposed to *mise en abyme,* in which a discrete lower-level element or structure "mirrors" an analogous element or structure on the framing higher level, *mise en cadre* consists of some discrete phenomenon on an upper, framing level that illustrates—frequently, but not necessarily, in an anticipatory way—some analogous phenomenon of the embedded level so that a discernible relationship of similarity is established between the two levels (compare Figures 2.1 and 2.2 below).

In frame-theoretical terms, *mise en cadre* can be said to concern the framing parts of texts or artefacts in which meaning is transmitted by reference to an embedded phenomenon through some kind of similarity with it. The meaning transmitted by *mise en cadre* is often a "framing" in the cognitive sense. Technically, this is frequently an implicit kind of framing, since the eliciting of meaning here typically occurs in the mode of showing, not exclusively in the mode of explicit telling (or thematization)[17]—combinations of both modes being, of course, possible. Functionally, *mise en cadre* can be described as a device that often serves as a framing (coding) of cognitive frames (metaconcepts) and thus contributes to the understanding of the framed (embedded) part of a text or artefact. However, *mise en cadre* can also serve other purposes besides that of marking metaconcepts. Prologues—as in the case of Shakespeare's *Romeo and Juliet*—may, for instance, include miniature narratives summarizing the plot of the ensuing play. In *Romeo and Juliet* the content-related similarity through which the prologue foreshadows the dramatic plot triggers the generic frame "love tragedy," but it also provides information concerning the action and the identification of Verona as the spatial setting.

Interestingly, the aforementioned function of *mise en cadre* to code cognitive frames is also shared by *mise en abyme.* For example, the reflections of Philip Quarles, the novelist within Aldous Huxley's novel *Point Counter Point* (1928), at one memorable moment include extended reflections on a

---

Toulouse le Mirail in 1992 and which was published in 1994 (cf. Larroux 1994: 252), discusses different meanings of *cadre* and employs *mise en cadre* simply for denoting the fact of adding a framing text to another, more important text. He thus does not distinguish *mise en cadre* from "embedding" or *mise en abyme* and actually uses the term "enchâssement" as a synonym of *mise en cadre* (247).

17. One could argue that a mere thematization, as in the mention of a generic frame in a title, can also produce a similarity, namely a similarity of reference (for instance, "Adventures" in the title of *Robinson Crusoe* may be said to refer to the same genre as the novel itself, namely the novel of adventure); for practical purposes and in clarification of a perhaps misleading earlier formulation (in Wolf 2001: 63, where I mentioned "Texttitel" in a discussion of *mise en cadre*) I would like to exclude such liminal cases of simple and exclusively referential "similarity" from the application of the term *mise en cadre* and reserve it for more salient cases in which there is at least some kind of similarity in the mode of showing.

new, experimental kind of novel-writing whose aesthetic principle he explains as "the musicalization of fiction" (Huxley 1978: 302). As this term and the illustration of musicalization given in Quarles's metafictional reflections obviously provide a crucial key to the aesthetics underlying the entire novel (and hence to a cognitive frame of the text), this *mise en abyme* can truly be said to contain a framing in the cognitive sense).

This functional closeness of *mise en abyme* and *mise en cadre* is, of course, no coincidence but stems from the fact that similarities (and contrasts) in works of literature and art are generally among the most common devices of creating or enhancing meaning. It even happens that the coding of cognitive frames occurs in what may be classified as a combination of *mise en abyme* and *mise en cadre*. This is, for instance, the case in the prologue to Longus's classical love romance *Daphnis and Chloe* (2nd to 3rd century A.D.). Here, the narrator or author tells the reader how he once, in a grove dedicated to the nymphs, came across a beautiful picture representing various aspects of love. He then goes on to describe this picture and uses this incident as a motivation for his telling of the story of Daphnis and Chloe in emulation of the painter. This charming episode unfolds a complex web of meaning and similarities. On the one hand, it is an ekphrasis and thus within the prologue a *mise en abyme* of representation. On the other hand, it intermedially anticipates the main theme of the main text, namely love. Owing to its multiple manifestations including parental love, love between animals and humans, heterosexual love, etc., as well as due to its generic value as pointing to the ensuing love romance, the reference to love here clearly provides a cognitive frame in the sense of a metaconcept. As this foreshadowing occurs on the "upper level" of a paratext through a similarity with the main text, this ekphrasis is also a *mise en cadre* with reference to this text.

The reciprocal relationships between *mise en cadre* and *mise en abyme* discussed above can be illustrated as follows in Figures 2.1 and 2.2. The arrows in the figures indicate the direction in which the "mirroring" implied in both devices works in order to create or enhance meaning (this includes the reference of framings in the cognitive sense): *mise en abyme* "mirrors" or points to the "upper level," thereby clarifying or shedding light on it bottom-up, while *mise en cadre* does so with reference to the "lower level" and thus works top-down:

Figures 2.1 and 2.2 actually illustrate particular cases of *mise en abyme* and *mise en cadre* which are especially suited to enhancing the meaning of a text or artefact by means of similarities. The particularity does not so much relate to the mention of diegetic and hypodiegetic levels, which points to narrative, perhaps even literary texts: the reference to this medium (fiction) is

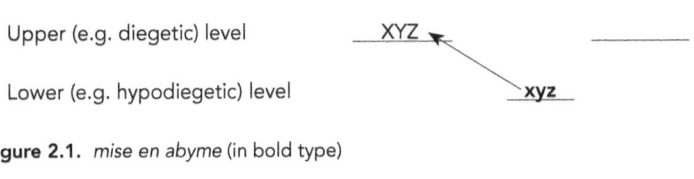

Figure 2.1. *mise en abyme* (in bold type)

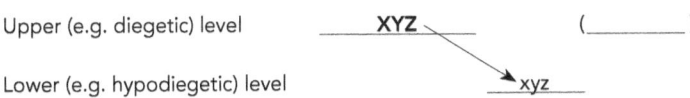

Figure 2.2. *mise en cadre* (in bold type)

only incidental, and our example could in principle be taken from other, even non-narrative texts, artefacts or media as well. The same openness applies to the exemplification of levels through *diegetic* levels: other kinds of levels would serve the same purpose, e.g. the difference between paratext and main text in literature, or between frame and canvas in painting. Rather, the particularity in focus here refers to a special quantitative relationship between "center'" and "periphery" or, in other words, between *the dominant and other, non-dominant parts of a text or artefact:* in Figure 2.1 the "dominant" is clearly the upper level, in Figure 2.2 the lower one. Even if ultimately the relationship between "dominant" (in the sense of carrying the most important text or constituent of the artefact) and other parts is not really a binary opposition but a scale allowing for many degrees in between two poles, one can immediately see that there are quite different possibilities of shaping this relationship. As for representational *mises en abyme* in the form of dramatic plays within plays, Richard Hornby (1986: 33–35) aptly differentiates between an "'inset' type" as opposed to a "'framed' type." In the former case the inner play is secondary and the framing play most important and longest (as in Shakespeare's *Hamlet*), while in the latter case it is the embedded play that forms the center or "dominant" as opposed to a short framing part (an instance of this latter case would thus be Shakespeare's *The Taming of the Shrew*). It should be noted that both of these types, including the basic relationships between dominant and other parts, are transgenerically as well as transmedially applicable (e.g., in film), and this is not only the case in *mises en abyme* but also in *mises en cadre*. As for the coding of cognitive frames as an important function of both *mises en abyme* and *mises en cadre,* it can in principle also occur in dominant *mises en abyme* (in Hornby's terminology in the "framed type") as well as in dominant *mises en cadre*, yet this is not typically so. The reason for this is that framings are functionally subservient to the framed and therefore also tend to be quantitatively non-dominant. Therefore, Figures 2.1 and 2.2 represent the typical cases of cognitively functionalized *mises en abyme* and *mises en cadre,* namely a *mise en abyme* that is non-dominant with reference to the upper level, and a *mise en cadre* that is non-dominant with reference to the lower level.

Mise en reflet *as an Additional Counterpart to* Mise en abyme

For the sake of completing the picture of the variants of creating meaning in discrete textual or artistic units that are related to other parts of the same text or artefact through similarities, one may mention that such similarities can basically also operate on the same level. In fact, as opposed to *mise en abyme* and *mise en cadre,* which both presuppose a difference of levels across which the similarity operates, there is, of course, the possibility of juxtaposing, for instance, similar stories or text elements on the same hypodiegetic, diegetic or extra-diegetic level. As in the case of *mise en cadre,* literary theory has not provided a term for this phenomenon—in particular when referring to complex similarities (and not only to mere semantic isotopies or other recurrences of individual elements, as described by Jakobson [1960] in the context of his theory of the "poetic function"). I have therefore called this phenomenon *mise en série* or *mise en reflet* (Wolf 2001: 66), maintaining in the French wording again a link with *mise en abyme. Mise en série* refers to cases where there are more than two instances of similar entities on the same level; for only two instances of similar entities on the same level, the term used was *mise en reflet.* As in the case of *mise en abyme* and *mise en cadre,* the elements of such same-level parallels can be of variable quantity, but there is here, too, a tendency to find cognitive framings predominantly in non-dominant, smaller or shorter elements (in the temporal media in preceding parts) which code cognitive frames that are relevant to a dominant (subsequent) element—and this for the same reason as mentioned above. Therefore, *mise en reflet* (with one non-dominant element carrying framings that shed light on a dominant one) is typical here, as illustrated in Figure 2.3.

An example of this phenomenon would be the "thought-reading episode" in E. A. Poe's inaugural detective fiction "The Murders in the Rue Morgue" (1841). After an initial essay-like framing regarding "the analytical power" (1908: 381) as the main prerequisite of a good detective (a framing located on the extradiegetic level), the text illustrates master-detective Dupin's analytical abilities by a surprising instance of his seeming thought-reading when he analyses the mindset of his friend, the story's Watson-like narrator, and

one and the same level

Figure 2.3. *mise en reflet* (in bold type)

provides an *ex post facto* rational explanation. As opposed to *mise en abyme* and *mise en cadre*, this episode is located on the same (intra-)diegetic level as the crime story which follows. The murder mystery of this tale clearly forms the center of the text, but the structure and the constituents of its telling—initial mystery, the subsequent process of detection carried out by Dupin with his "analytical power," and the surprising final solution—are illustrated and foreshadowed in the "thought-reading episode" in remarkable detail. Over and above this structural similarity, this episode also furnishes important keys to the understanding of the main story, in particular of the frame "rational solution of mysteries through observation and analysis," and thus constitutes a graphic illustration of a *mise en reflet* with a framing function.

HOW TO BECOME AWARE OF INITIAL *MISES EN CADRE*, AND THE COMBINATION OF INITIAL AND TERMINAL FORMS OF *MISE EN CADRE*

Mise en cadre has been defined as a "discrete phenomenon on an upper, framing level" which shows a "discernible relationship of similarity" with reference to the lower level. This definition raises two problems. The first refers to the "discernibility" of the similarity required for *mise en cadre*. As a solution one may point out that there are different degrees of similarity, which result in different degrees of saliency of *mises en cadre*—from liminal to clear cases.[18] The second problem is that of how one can know in literary texts, in particular at a first reading, what discrete textual element forms a *mise en cadre*. This is indeed a pertinent problem, not least with reference to the aforementioned frequent function of *mise en cadre* as an *implicit* means of marking cognitive frames in the mode of showing (as opposed to the explicit marking in the mode of telling). Moreover, although *mises en cadre* by definition occur in upper level or framing parts of texts or artefacts, they need not be co-extensive with such framings.

In the temporal media, *mises en cadre*—their occurrence as well as their extension—are particularly difficult to identify in the process of reception if they foreshadow something that has not yet been read or perceived. In this

---

18. Cf. above, note 17.

context it is helpful when such a *mise en cadre,* as is so frequently the case with other implicit devices, is supported by explicit devices. We can indeed note such explicit clarifying elements in the framing part of *Heart of Darkness.* Shortly before Marlow starts with his tale, the narrator expressly warns the reader that in Marlow's storytelling "the meaning [. . .] was not inside like a kernel but outside, enveloping the tale which brought it out only as a glow brings out a haze [. . .]" (1817). This metatextual warning not only points to the extra attention that the reader should invest in the quest for a hidden meaning of the embedded tale, but, through the repeated use of the terms "haze" and "glow," points back to the description of the increasingly obscure landscape, in which these terms also occur[19] and which, as a part of the framing, literally "envelop[s]" Marlow's "tale." This explicit emphasis on "obscurity" foregrounds the framing description and marks it as relevant for the ensuing story, thus signalling a *mise en cadre*. In addition, the general emphasis on the landscape description in Conrad's framing is such that an experienced reader, who knows that descriptions are rarely merely "innocent" visualizations of a setting, arguably already expects some further relevance. This very expectation also provides a sort of "keying" for the reading of Marlow's story, a keying that later on becomes confirmed when the similarities on the embedded level become apparent and can be related back to the framing in a process of spatialized reading, where, to borrow from Joseph Frank's seminal essay, "attention is fixed on the interplay of relationships [. . .] independently of the progress of the narrative" (Frank 1945: 44). Of course, the confirmation of this expectation of later relevance can only be gained after having read the embedded tale, and thus, in a temporal medium such as the novel, initial *mises en cadre* are usually revealed as such only when one has the benefit of hindsight.

This is, however, not to say that all *mises en cadre* occur exclusively in initial positions. Rather, they can also be observed in internal and terminal positions as well as employing a combination of these possibilities. An example of the combination of initial with terminal *mises en cadre* is Mary Shelley's Gothic frame-tale *Frankenstein* (1818). The opening frame, letters of Captain Walton to his sister Margaret in England, already displays revealing similarities with the ensuing story by Frankenstein in the mode of a traditional initial *mise en cadre*. Walton is about to transgress a boundary, though a relatively harmless geographical one, since he is engaged in a quest for a "passage near the pole" (Shelley 1968: 270). Walton's enterprise foreshadows

---

19. See "A haze rested on the low shores [. . .]" (1814), and "the sun sank low, and from glowing white changed to a dull red [. . .]" (1815).

Frankenstein's fateful ethical and religious transgression of the limits imposed on man, rivalling God as a creator of animate beings. Moreover, Walton, like Frankenstein, acts contrary to his father's wish,[20] purports to act for the benefit of humankind[21] while in reality being propelled by an overheated Romantic "imagination," "enthusiasm," and scientific "curiosity."[22] Many of these correspondences can even be traced to verbatim parallels on the level of discourse, to phrases and keywords in Frankenstein's hypodiegetic tale that are anticipated by similar expressions in Walton's diegetic story,[23] while others remain on the story level, for instance the fatal consequences which both men risk, owing to their "ardent curiosity" (270). While Frankenstein's quest for artificial life produces a monster that actually kills several people, Captain Walton is prepared to sacrifice human lives for his mission.[24] Again, this initial *mise en cadre* may be said to be difficult to identify at first reading, but—as in *Heart of Darkness*—in this case, too, the text contributes to the discernibility of the correspondence between Walton and Frankenstein by explicitly making Frankenstein thematize the parallel shortly before starting with his narrative: "Unhappy man! Do you share my madness? Have you drunk also of the intoxicating draught?" (284).

At any rate, the *mise-en-cadre* correspondences between an initial frame and the embedded story which trigger the frame "guilty scientific curiosity" become clear retrospectively when reading Frankenstein's story, and this will arguably sensitize the reader for possible further correspondences between this story and the terminal frame (which reverts to Walton's diary-like letters). In fact, when reaching the framing part that concludes the novel the reader

---

20. Compare, in reference to Walton: "[. . .] my father's dying injunction had forbidden my uncle to allow me to embark in a seafaring life" (270), and Frankenstein, whose father equally tried to keep him from what he nevertheless ventured into: "In my education my father had taken the greatest precautions that my mind should be impressed with no supernatural horrors. [. . .] I knew well therefore what would be my father's feelings, but I could not tear my thoughts from my employment [. . .]" (311, 315).

21. Walton dreams of "the inestimable benefit which [he] shall confer on all mankind to the last generation, by discovering a passage near the pole to those countries, to reach which at present so many months are requisite; or by ascertaining the secret of the magnet, which, if at all possible, can only be effected by an undertaking such as mine" (270). Frankenstein claims that: "Life and death appeared to me ideal bounds, which I should first break through, and pour a torrent of light into our dark world" (314).

22. Thoughts of the pole kindle Walton's "imagination," "curiosity," and "enthusiasm" (269 f.). This foreshadows Frankenstein's "enthusiasm" (297), "curiosity" (295) and "imagination" (313) with reference to the "physical secrets of the world" (296).

23. See the preceding note.

24. He says: "[. . .] gladly I would sacrifice my fortune, my existence, my every hope, to the furtherance of my enterprize. One man's life or death were but a small price to pay [. . .]" (283).

is again confronted with correspondences. This time they are centered on the motif of failure and its evaluation. Walton must acknowledge that his quest for the north passage has failed and that he must return. This mirrors Frankenstein's previous double failure, as narrated in his hypodiegetic story: his failure as a God-like creator (he has created a monster instead of a being that is beneficial to humankind); and his failure as an avenger, for he dies before he is able to kill his murderous creature (which ultimately commits suicide). In combination with the cognitive frame "guilty scientific curiosity" marked by the initial *mise en cadre* this could be interpreted as the coding of the cognitive frame "punishment" or "poetic justice," and both together point to a worldview in which providential justice seems to play an important role.

However, this terminal *mise-en-cadre* correspondence between Walton's and Frankenstein's failures, which rounds off the impact of the initial *mises en cadre,* is implicated, through the parallel reactions to these failures, in a remarkable relativization of such a providential (moral or religious) reading, and this not only of Frankenstein's tale but of the entire novel. Frankenstein, in the initial frame, explicitly thematizes the similarity between Walton and himself, and he moreover prefaces his story by giving it a clear morally didactic function. Frankenstein sees his own experience as a warning for Walton, who shares his curiosity:

> I do not know that the relation of my disasters will be useful to you; yet, when I reflect that you are pursuing the same course, exposing yourself to the same dangers which have rendered me what I am, I imagine that you may deduce an apt moral from my tale; one that may direct you if you succeed in your undertaking and console you in case of failure. (285 f.)

However, when we read Walton's letters at the end, he does not appear to have learnt anything from Frankenstein's biography. He is aware that the lives of his crew "are endangered" through him, but his "courage and hopes do not desert" him (486). He even says, "I had rather die than return shamefully, my purpose unfulfilled" (488). When he is nevertheless finally forced to abandon his quest, he does not do so out of moral considerations, but merely yields to the force of circumstances in bitter disappointment: "I have consented to return if we are not destroyed. Thus are my hopes blasted by cowardice and indecision; I come back ignorant and disappointed [. . .]" (488–89). His frustration is most clearly discernible in the way in which he answers the dying Frankenstein's question, "'Do you, then, really return?,'" Walton responds with a revealing sigh: "'Alas! Yes [. . .]'" (489). All of this renders the alleged moral effect of the embedded story highly questionable.

The failure of Frankenstein's didactic intention with reference to Walton thus retrospectively sheds light on the hypodiegetic story itself, undermining its moral effect. Frankenstein himself, shortly before his death, acts in a curiously ambivalent way as recounted in the concluding frame. On the one hand, he continues to emphasize the moral function of his life's story by a final admonition: "Farewell Walton! Seek happiness in tranquillity and avoid ambition [. . .]" (491). On the other hand, his own moral sensibility turns out to be curiously blunt when he says, "I have been occupied in examining my past conduct; nor do I find it blameable" (490). He concludes by giving utterance to a frustration similar to Walton's when he thinks about his "apparently innocent" ambition "of distinguishing [him]self in science and discoveries": "I have myself been blasted in these hopes, yet another may succeed" (491). This final *mise en cadre,* not of a moral concern but of a re-affirmation of the very scientific curiosity which we witnessed at work in his hypodiegetic autobiography, again undermines the moral message of the embedded story. The monster's terminal appearance in the concluding frame only partly re-establishes the text's moral message, since it centers on his own guilt and remorse as a "fallen angel" (494); Frankenstein's sin, his Prometheus-like usurpation of God's creative power ungraced with concomitant love and responsibility, is not mentioned. Thus it appears that the *mise en cadre* of the motif of failure is combined with a deeply disturbing ambivalence in the effect which *Frankenstein* as a whole arguably has on the reader. The powerful impact of this Gothic novel does not so much stem from its character as a moral tale but derives from something else, above all from its capacity to "awaken thrilling horror," as announced in the "Author's Introduction to the Standard Edition" (262). Frankenstein's didactic failure to morally convince the fictitious recipient of his tale, Captain Walton, can thus be regarded as a *mise en abyme* of the dubious moral function of the entire novel *Frankenstein* for the real recipient/reader. For the novel, while succeeding as a horror story, may also very well fail to appeal to its readers if read only with an eye to the "moral tendencies" and the "exhibition of the amiableness of domestic affection, and the excellence of universal virtue," which P. B. Shelley claimed for the text in his "Preface" (268).

THE TRANSMEDIAL RELEVANCE OF *MISE EN CADRE,* AND AN EXAMPLE FROM PAINTING

As said before, *mise en cadre* in a terminal position, such as in the concluding frame of *Frankenstein,* is less frequent in literature than its initial, foreshadowing variant and therefore often gives rise, in literature, to the aforementioned problems regarding the difficulty of recognizing the structural and thematic similarities at play. In contrast to literature—a temporal medium—spatial media tend to facilitate the deciphering of *mises en cadre* since here the limitations of a first reading do not apply and similarities between framing and framed can be accessed more or less at first glance.

As an example let us turn to Caspar David Friedrich's *Tetschen Altar* (Illustration 2.1). As is well known in art history, this altar piece was revolutionary (and controversial) in that it introduced the representation of landscape into the genre of religious painting to the extent that the picture could be mistaken for a "mere" landscape painting[25]—that is, if one disregards the gilt frame. This frame, which was produced by the sculptor Kühn (cf. Kemp 1995: 13) following the directions of the painter himself, contains clear clues—"framings" in the cognitive sense—which sufficiently clarify the religious content and thus the affiliation with religious painting, provided one is prepared to disregard narrow generic boundaries and admit possibilities of cross-fertilizations between genres. What renders these clues especially interesting in our context is the fact that some of them operate on the basis of a *mise en cadre*, that is, through a significant similarity between framing and framed. Thus, the rays emanating from the triangular symbol of God's eye in the lower part of the frame unmistakably echo the sun's rays in the painting which appear behind a curiously triangular rock and touch the cross erected on top of it. By this framing sign of God's eye the frame announces and stabilizes the religious meaning of the framed landscape and indeed codes the canvas a "religious painting" (as opposed to a "mere" landscape painting). This coding occurs in a logical (albeit not topological) "top-down-process" (from frame to framed) and is based on the device of "showing" through meaningful similarities. It is therefore as much a *mise en cadre* as in the literary examples discussed above and in fact the clearest case of *mise en cadre* occurring in the *Tetschen Altar*.

The other religious symbols on the frame (the puttos and the eucharistic signs of bread and wine) serve the same function of providing framing signals for the correct decoding of the framed picture. Their similarity with reference to the picture is, however, more indirect. It primarily operates on the level of belonging to the same paradigm of religious symbols as the framed represented as a part of the framed landscape, which amounts to a merely referen-

---

25. For a detailed art-historical discussion of the *Tetschen Altar* with special reference to its frame see Kemp (1995: 13–15).

tial similarity that is analogous to the mode of "telling" in verbal texts. Yet the shape of the ears of corn and the vine in addition mirrors the clouds in the picture and thus adds a note of formal similarity in the mode of showing. Owing to the fulfilment of the condition of a "top-down" similarity of discrete higher level elements mirroring lower level ones, these religious symbols of the frame can thus also be classified as instances of a *mise en cadre,* albeit less obvious ones. As opposed to this, the caption "Tetschen Altar," which accompanies the book illustration of the painting under discussion (Mendgen 1995: 14), while equally coding the religious cognitive frame, should not be regarded as a *mise en cadre,* as it does not operate on the basis of similarity in the mode of showing but exclusively through a simple reference in the mode of (intermedial) telling.[26]

As we have seen, *mise en cadre,* like *mise en abyme,* in spite of having originally been theorized in narratology, is actually a transmedial phenomenon that can be observed to occur beyond narrative and even beyond verbal artefacts (the same applies to *mise en reflet/série*). It may, for instance, not only be found in picture frames but also in paratextual sections of films that already show relevant elements of the film proper or in opera overtures anticipating important themes of the ensuing opera.[27] *Mise en cadre* arguably has this wider relevance as a transmedial phenomenon that occurs across many media, since, besides coding cognitive frames, it also contributes to one of the most essential features of human artefacts, namely the production of meaningful and beautiful similarities and recurrences. Adding this concept to the toolbox of scholarly description of media and artefacts of various kinds is thus not a trivial matter: it allows us to see what the concept of *mise en abyme* did not highlight, namely that in artefacts similarities can work not only "bottom-up" but also "top-down." Becoming aware of this fact and being able to identify it by a specific term can form a substantial contribution to our understanding of narratives and other artefacts. It can also provide a description of how meaning is produced and how recipients are guided by self-referential structures of artefacts of various media, narrative and otherwise.

---

26. For the classificatory problem involved here, see above, note 17.

27. For further examples see in Wolf/Bernhart (2006): e.g. on film Roy Sommer's contribution ("Initial Framings in Film," 383–406), including examples of framing metareferences foreshadowing highly metareferential films (401–3 on *Adaptation* and *The Truman Show*), and on opera Michael Walter's essay "Framing and Deframing the Opera: The Overture" (429–48).

Illustration 2.4. Caspar David Friedrich: *Tetschen Altar* (1807–8)

MISE EN CADRE—
WHY YET ANOTHER NARRATOLOGICAL NEOLOGISM? OR
Why Post-Classical Narratology Should Continue the Project of Classical Narratology

The "scientism" and terminological rage of classical narratology in particular has been the butt of much criticism over the past few decades.[28] One must therefore also expect such antagonism in the present context: is it really necessary to introduce yet another neologism (*mise en cadre*) into narratology, and a French one to boot? The answer ought to be emphatically yes! For, in comparison to the many hundreds if not thousands of neologisms and technical terms used in other disciplines (e.g. in medicine; even in rhetoric there is a remarkable amount of terminology), the fuss about a few dozen narratological terms appears exaggerated and ultimately negligible. Actually, the real issue should not be the number of neologisms nor their euphonic or cacophonic quality, but their heuristic value. Whether *mise en cadre* turns out to be a useful concept is for the reader to judge. At any rate, it designates a relatively frequent phenomenon, particularly regarding framing parts in literature and other media, for which so far no precise term has been coined. "Foreshadowing" is at once too narrow, since it is inapplicable to terminal *mises an cadre,* and too imprecise, since it denotes only a function without the device through which it is achieved. Moreover, *mise en cadre* (like *mise en reflet/série*) forms an obvious counterpart to a well-known structural device, namely *mise en abyme,* whose heuristic value is generally accepted. Generally speaking, there should be a consensus in the humanities similar to the natural sciences that the endeavor to classify and name phenomena is an indispensable prerequisite for any study meriting the name of scholarship. Moreover, it is a well-known cognitive fact that the existence of a term triggers recognition: having a concept at one's disposal often helps one to become aware of the corresponding phenomenon. Thus narratology should decidedly *not* abandon its search for general features and its classical "rage" to describe, classify and name them, if necessary by means of yet another neologism.

Of course, this enterprise rests on the premise that narratology—and theory in general for that matter—are rational, logocentric projects. This includes, for instance, the acknowledgment of narrative levels in narrative texts on the lines of Rimmon-Kenan's differentiation between diegetic levels (1983: 94 f.). Detractors of logocentrism such as Gibson may sneer at this,

---

28. For a particularly pungent attack on "[t]he language of literary criticism and theory" as "the ugliest private language in the world" see Currie (1998: 33) in a chapter aptly entitled "Terminologisation."

but without a really valid reason. Gibson, for instance, claims that in some texts levels are blurred, but this constitutes no argument at all against a hierarchical text model. Rather, it is only against the background of such a model that transgressive devices such as metalepsis (yet another term provided by classical narratology, see Genette 1972: 243–51) can adequately be described with reference to narratives in the first place since most metalepses form a (really or seemingly) illogical transgression of boundaries between extra- and intradiegetic or intra- and hypodiegetic levels. As for the majority of cases in which such transgressions do not occur, a distinction of narrative levels on the theoretical plane nevertheless makes sense, all the more so as the frequency of frame narratives in literature requires an appropriate descriptive terminology.

To conclude: where classical narratology has left lacunae, it is perfectly legitimate to continue its project of systematically describing and naming general features in literary texts. *Mise en cadre* provides a good example of a useful extension of narratological terminology, all the more so as this text-based, "structural" phenomenon can in fact be linked with post-classical issues. As the above examples from fiction and painting show, *mise en cadre* can be inscribed both into an intermedial context and into a frame-theoretical one.[29] It is in the latter framework that I originally coined the term (Wolf 1999: 104). In addition, the example from Conrad shows that *mise en cadre* could also be used for a reader-response (or, transmedially speaking, recipient-response) approach as well as for post-colonial or culturalist interpretations. Yet this relevance of the concept under discussion to currently debated specific contexts is not actually its most important point. For the core of narratology—as of any theory—ought to be the potentially *general*;[30] though I hasten to add that the generalities involved in, or related to, narratives go beyond what was in focus in classical narratology, and include, for instance, cognitive processes elicited by narratives. It is indeed the general nature of a theoretical concept that permits its application to, or modification for, a plurality of contexts, and this certainly applies to *mise en cadre*, whether occurring in narrative or non-narrative contexts.

As can be seen in the case of *mise en cadre* (or *mise en reflet/série* for that matter), the study of "textual" generalities is not yet exhausted nor com-

---

29. It may indeed be the lack of a cognitive and a frame-theoretical awareness of classical narratology that made it neglect *mise en cadre* as opposed to *mise en abyme*, for this latter phenomenon can be described from an exclusively text-centered perspective.

30. I here agree with Gorman's definition of narratology as "the study of narrative as a set of potential features of any work" rather than "studies of individual works" (2004: 395).

pleted.[31] I therefore would like to plead for the continuation of the narratological endeavor, not in the narrow frame of structuralist, exclusively text-centered classical narratology but in a neo-classical narratology which includes textual features but also opens up towards non-structuralist approaches, other media, and the various contexts in which texts are embedded—as long as the focus on the general is maintained. In fact, this focus on the general is what legitimates narratology as the theory of narrative artefacts in the first place. Therefore I doubt if it really makes sense to speak of narratologies in the plural as has become fashionable (Herman 1999), let alone of a "postcolonial" or a "feminist narratology."[32] At best, these so-called "narratologies" are specific approaches to, and extensions of, classical narratology or deal with special kinds of artefacts that are characterized by certain contents and/or thematic concerns. Be that as it may, in view of phenomena such as *mise en cadre*, it should be acknowledged that even after half a century of systematic investigation of narratives something new or useful can be found from the perspective of a general narratology. Nor should this perspective be abandoned altogether in a (by now perhaps outmoded) postmodernist, centrifugal spirit. For this perspective has revealed a rich trove of analytical tools in the past, tools which, as the above example from painting shows, can even be applied beyond the confines of literary narratives.[33] There is every reason to be confident that such a generalist, neo-classical approach may continue to prove useful in the future, too.

31. Thus, to name but a few examples, the entire field of self-reference and metareference in the media, narrative and otherwise, has only recently come into focus, and the same is true of what actually constitutes "narrativity" across media. As a consequence, there is as yet much to be done in these areas.
32. See Lanser (1986), Birk/Neumann (2002), and Allrath/Gymnich (2002).
33. For some possibilities but also the problems of exchanging terminology across disciplinary and medial boundaries see Wolf (2007).

REFERENCES

Abbott, H. Porter (2005) "The Future of All Narrative Futures." *A Companion to Narrative Theory*. Eds. James Phelan and Peter J. Rabinowitz. Blackwell Companions to Literature and Culture 33. Oxford: Blackwell. 529–41.

Allrath, Gaby, and Marion Gymnich (2002) "Feministische Narratologie." *Neue Ansätze in der Erzähltheorie*. Eds. Ansgar Nünning and Vera Nünning. WVT Handbücher zum literaturwissenschaftlichen Studium. Trier: WVT. 35–72.

Bateson, Gregory (1972) "A Theory of Play and Fantasy" [1955]. *Steps to an Ecology of Mind*. Ed. Gregory Bateson. New York: Ballantine. 177–93.

Birk, Hanne, and Birgit Neumann (2002) "*Go-between*: Postkoloniale Erzähltheorie." *Neue Ansätze in der Erzähltheorie*. Eds. Ansgar Nünning and Vera Nünning. WVT Handbücher zum literaturwissenschaftlichen Studium. Trier: WVT. 115–52.

Chaucer, Geoffrey (1957) *The Canterbury Tales* [1380]. *The Works of Geoffrey Chaucer*. Ed. F. N. Robinson. 2nd ed. London: Oxford University Press. 17–265.

Cobley, Paul (2002) *Narrative*. The New Critical Idiom. London: Routledge.

Conrad, Joseph (1986) *Heart of Darkness* [1899]. *The Norton Anthology of English Literature*. Vol. 2. Ed. M. H. Abrams. New York: Norton. 1814–80.

Currie, Mark (1998) *Postmodern Narrative Theory*. Transitions. New York: St. Martin's Press.

Dällenbach, Lucien (1977) *Le Récit spéculaire: Essai sur la mise en abyme*. Collection Poétique. Paris: Seuil. English version: (1989) *The Mirror in the Text*. Transl. J. Whiteley and E. Hughes. Oxford: Polity Press.

Erll, Astrid, and Simone Roggendorf (2002) "Kulturgeschichtliche Narratologie: Die Historisierung und Kontextualisierung kultureller Narrative." *Neue Ansätze in der Erzähltheorie*. Eds. Ansgar Nünning and Vera Nünning. WVT Handbücher zum literaturwissenschaftlichen Studium. Trier: WVT. 73–113.

Fludernik, Monika (2003) "The Diachronization of Narratology." *Narrative* 11.3: 331–48.

Frank, Joseph (1962) "Spatial Form in the Modern Novel." *Critiques and Essays on Modern Fiction 1920–1951*. Ed. John W. Aldridge. New York: Ronald Press. 43–66.

Genette, Gérard (1972) *Figures III*. Collection 'Tel Quel.' Paris: Seuil.

—— (1987) *Seuils*. Collection "Poétique." Paris: Seuil.

Gibson, Andrew (1996) *Towards a Postmodern Theory of Narrative*. Postmodern Theory. Edinburgh: Edinburgh University Press.

Goffman, Erving (1974) *Frame Analysis: An Essay on the Organization of Experience*. Cambridge, MA: Harvard University Press.

Gorman, David (2004) Rev. of *What Is Narratology? Questions and Answers Regarding the Status of a Theory*. Eds. Tom Kindt and Hans-Harald Müller. *Style* 38.3: 392–96.

Hauthal, Janine, Julijana Nadj, Ansgar Nünning, and Henning Peters, Eds. (2007) *Metaisierung in der Literatur und anderen Medien: Theoretische Grundlagen, historische Perspektiven, Metagattungen, Funktionen*. Spectrum Literaturwissenschaft. Berlin: de Gruyter.

Herman, David (1997) "Scripts, Sequences, and Stories: Elements of a Postclassical Narratology." *PMLA* 112: 1046–59.

———, Ed. (1999) *Narratologies: New Perspectives on Narrative Analyses*. Columbus: The Ohio State University Press.
——— (2002) *Story Logic: Problems and Possibilities of Narrative*. Lincoln: University of Nebraska Press.
———, Ed. (2003) *Narrative Theory and the Cognitive Sciences*. CSLI Lecture Notes 158. Stanford: Center of the Study of Language and Information. 163–93.
——— (2004) "Toward a Transmedial Narratology." *Narrative across Media: The Languages of Storytelling*. Ed. Marie-Laure Ryan. Lincoln: University of Nebraska Press. 47–75.
Hornby, Richard (1986) *Drama, Metadrama, and Perception*. London/Toronto: Associated University Press.
Hutcheon, Linda (1984) *Narcissistic Narrative: The Metafictional Paradox* [1980]. London/New York: Methuen.
Huxley, Aldous (1978) *Point Counter Point* [1928]. London: Granada.
Jakobson, Roman (1960) "Closing Statement: Linguistics and Poetics." *Style in Language*. Ed. Thomas A. Sebeok. Cambridge, MA: Technology Press of MIT. 350–77.
Kemp, Wolfgang (1995) "Heimatrecht für Bilder: Funktionen und Formen des Rahmens im 19. Jahrhundert." *In Perfect Harmony: Bild und Rahmen 1850—1920*. Ed. Eva Mendgen. Amsterdam/Vienna: Waanders. 13–25.
Kindt, Tom, and Hans-Harald Müller, Eds. (2003) *What Is Narratology? Questions and Answers Regarding the Status of a Theory*. Narratologia, 1. Berlin/New York: de Gruyter.
Lanser, Susan Sniader (1986) "Toward a Feminist Narratology." *Style* 20.1: 341–63.
Larroux, Guy (1994) "Mise en cadre et clausularité." *Poétique* 25: 247–53.
Mendgen, Eva, Ed. (1995) *In Perfect Harmony: Picture and Frame 1850–1920*. Amsterdam/Vienna: Waanders.
Nünning, Ansgar (2004) "Where Historiographic Metafiction and Narratology Meet: Towards an Applied Cultural Narratology." *Style* 38.3: 352–75.
Nünning, Ansgar, and Vera Nünning (2002) Eds. *Neue Ansätze in der Erzähltheorie*. WVT Handbücher zum literaturwissenschaftlichen Studium. Trier: WVT.
———, Eds. (2004) *Erzähltextanalyse und Gender Studies*. Stuttgart: Metzler.
Poe, Edgar Allan (1908) "The Murders in the Rue Morgue" [1841]. *Tales of Mystery and Imagination*. Ed. Padraic Colum. London: Dent. 378–410.
Rajewsky, Irina O. (2002) *Intermedialität*. UTB 2261. Tübingen: Francke.
Ricardou, Jean (1978) *Le Nouveau roman*. Ecrivains de toujours. Paris: Seuil.
Rimmon-Kenan, Shlomith (1983) *Narrative Fiction: Contemporary Poetics*. New Accents. London/New York: Methuen.
Ryan, Marie-Laure, Ed. (2004) *Narrative across Media: The Languages of Storytelling*. Lincoln: University of Nebraska Press.
Shelley, Mary (1968) *Frankenstein* [1818]. *Three Gothic Novels*. Ed. Peter Fairclough. Harmondsworth: Penguin. 256–497.
Surkamp, Carola (2002) "Narratologie und *possible-worlds theory*: Narrative Texte als alternative Welten." *Neue Ansätze in der Erzähltheorie*. Eds. Ansgar Nünning and Vera Nünning. WVT Handbücher zum literaturwissenschaftlichen Studium. Trier: WVT. 153–83.

Wolf, Werner (1999) "Framing Fiction: Reflections on a Narratological Concept and an Example: Bradbury, *Mensonge*." *Grenzüberschreitungen: Narratologie im Kontext/Transcending Boundaries: Narratology in Context*. Eds. Walter Grünzweig and Andreas Solbach. Tübingen: Narr. 97–124.

—— (2001) "Formen literarischer Selbstreferenz in der Erzählkunst: Versuch einer Typologie und ein Exkurs zur '*mise en cadre*' und '*mise en reflet/série*.'" *Erzählen und Erzähltheorie im zwanzigsten Jahrhundert. Festschrift für Wilhelm Füger*. Ed. Jörg Helbig. Heidelberg: Winter. 49–84.

—— (2002a) "Intermediality Revisited: Reflections on Word and Music Relations in the Context of a General Typology of Intermediality." *Word and Music Studies: Essays in Honor of Steven Paul Scher and on Cultural Identity and the Musical Stage*. Eds. Suzanne M. Lodato, Suzanne Aspden, and Walter Bernhart. Word and Music Studies 4. Amsterdam: Rodopi. 13–34.

—— (2002b) "Das Problem der Narrativität in Literatur, bildender Kunst und Musik: ein Beitrag zu einer intermedialen Erzähltheorie." *Erzähltheorie transgenerisch, intermedial, interdisziplinär*. Eds. Ansgar Nünning and Vera Nünning. WVT-Handbücher zum literaturwissenschaftlichen Studium 5. Trier: WVT. 23–104.

—— (2004) "'Cross the Border—Close that Gap': Towards an Intermedial Narratology." *European Journal of English Studies* 8.1: 81–103.

—— (2006) "Framing Borders in Frame Stories." *Framing Borders in Literature and Other Media*. Eds. Werner Wolf and Walter Bernhart. Studies in Intermediality 1. Amsterdam: Rodopi. 181–208.

—— (2007) "Möglichkeiten und Grenzen der Übertragung literaturwissenschaftlicher Terminologie auf Gegenstände der Kunstwissenschaft: Überlegungen zu einem Weg interdisziplinärer Verständigung am Beispiel von 'Erzählsituationen' und 'Metafiktion.'" *Festschrift für Götz Pochat um 65. Geburtstag*. Ed. Johann Konrad Eberlein. Grazer Edition 2. Vienna: Lit. 355–90.

—— (2009) "Metareference across Media: The Concept, its Transmedial Potentials and Problems, Main Forms and Functions." *Metareference across Media: Theory and Case Studies—Dedicated to Walter Bernhart on the Occasion of his Retirement*. Ed. Werner Wolf in collaboration with Katharina Bantleon and Jeff Thoss. Studies in Intermediality 4. Amsterdam: Rodopi. 1–85.

Wolf, Werner, and Walter Bernhart, Eds. (2006) *Framing Borders in Literature and Other Media*. Studies in Intermediality 1. Amsterdam: Rodopi.

——, Eds. (2007) *Description in Literature and Other Media*. Studies in Intermediality 2. Amsterdam: Rodopi.

Zerweck, Bruno (2002) "Der *cognitive turn* in der Erzähltheorie: Kognitive und 'Natürliche' Narratologie." *Neue Ansätze in der Erzähltheorie*. Eds. Ansgar Nünning and Vera Nünning. WVT Handbücher zum literaturwissenschaftlichen Studium. Trier: WVT. 219–42.

3

ALAN PALMER

Large Intermental Units in *Middlemarch*

Intermental thought is joint, group, shared or collective thought, as opposed to intramental, or individual or private thought. It is also known as *socially distributed*, *situated*, or *extended cognition*, and also as *intersubjectivity*. Intermental thought is a crucially important component of fictional narrative because much of the mental functioning that occurs in novels is done by large organizations, small groups, work colleagues, friends, families, couples and other intermental units. It could plausibly be argued that a large amount of the subject matter of novels is the formation, development and breakdown of these intermental systems.[1] However, this aspect of narrative has been neglected by traditional theoretical approaches such as focalization, characterization, story analysis and the representation of speech and thought. Intermental thought in the novel has been invisible to traditional narrative approaches and the many examples of intermental thought that follow would not even count as examples of thought and consciousness within these approaches. Nevertheless, this type of thought becomes clearly evident within a cognitive approach to literature that is informed by findings in cognitive, social and discursive psychology and the philosophy of mind. This philosophical and psychological background to the concept of intermental thought is contained in chapter five of my book *Fictional Minds* (2004) and so I will not repeat it here.

---

1. For an excellent analysis of the small intermental unit of a marriage in a Virginia Woolf short story, see Semino (2006).

I have explored the issue of intermental functioning in George Eliot's *Middlemarch* in two previous essays. In "The Lydgate Storyworld" (2005a) I discussed some small intermental units in the novel: chiefly the marriage of Lydgate and Rosamond and the friendship between Lydgate and Farebrother. In "Intermental Thought in the Novel: The Middlemarch Mind" (2005b), I argued that one of the most important characters in the novel is the town of Middlemarch itself. I called the intermental functioning of the inhabitants of the town "the Middlemarch mind." I went much further than simply suggesting that the town of Middlemarch provides a social context within which individual characters operate, maintaining instead that the town literally and not just metaphorically has a mind of its own. To illustrate, I discussed the construction of the Middlemarch mind in the opening few pages of the novel and attempted to show that the initial descriptions by the heterodiegetic narrator of the three individual minds of Dorothea, Celia and Mr. Brooke were focalized through it.

This essay is my third and final one on the subject of intermental thought in *Middlemarch*. Its purpose is to build on the work done previously and take the analysis a stage further. I wish now to try to convey the subtlety of the fine shades of intermental thought in the novel and the complexity of the relationships between intermental and intramental thought in the novel. First, I discuss the various ways in which, over the course of the whole text, readers are able to identify a number of distinct, separate Middlemarch minds within the single intermental unit that is constructed at the beginning of the novel. After saying a little about the techniques used for the constructions of these various minds, I suggest that an analysis of the class structure of the town reveals the existence of separate and well-defined upper class, middle class and working class minds. I then refer to the complexity and fluidity of the myriad other intermental units that occur at various points in the text and introduce a tentative typology for the various forms of intermental focalization that are present in the novel. The essay then turns to the roles played by individuals: not only those inside the large intermental units who act as spokespeople or mouthpieces for their views, but also those who, like Lydgate, Dorothea and Ladislaw, find themselves outside these units and become the object of their intermental judgments. These various intramental/intermental relationships have a substantial impact on the plot of the novel.

A close study of *Middlemarch* reveals that George Eliot was fascinated by the intermental process: its complexity, its causes and effects, its relationship with individuals and so on. Thought in general and intermental thought in particular are discussed frequently and explicitly. Group minds are capable of great sophistication and of a wide range of cognitive functioning and they cannot be understood in purely social terms. A very wide range of cognitive terms are used to describe intermental activity in the novel: knowing, thinking, considering, believing, noticing, conjecturing, implying, suspecting, tolerating, hating, opposing, liking, wanting, and so on. These and the many other examples that are to be found in the rest of this essay are verbs of thought and of consciousness. The whole novel is saturated with clear evidence of a variety of this intermental thought. The selection of this evidence that is presented in this essay comprises only a very small proportion of the total; ruthless pruning was required in order to present my argument in a manageable form.

In the longer, indented quotes that follow, I will put all references to large intermental units in italics. I do this for ease of reference, but also to emphasize in visual form the sheer number of these phrases in the text. I sometimes refer to *the* Middlemarch mind when it is clear from the context that I am talking about the large intermental unit of the whole town; I will also refer to *a* Middlemarch mind when it is clear that a subgroup of the whole town mind is being discussed. This essay is about large intermental units and I will not therefore be considering small units such as marriages, friendships and families. It is no exaggeration to say that a short book could be written about all of the intermental units in *Middlemarch*, both large and small.

Fictional minds form part of the storyworld or diegetic universe of the novel. Put another way, they occur within the story, as opposed to the discourse, level. As I explained in chapter three of *Fictional Minds*, in studying the mental functioning of characters that takes place in the storyworlds of novels, I go beyond the information provided directly to the reader within the categories of direct thought, free indirect thought, and thought report (or *psychonarration*) that are the basis of the study of thought representation. I go beyond them because I also take into account the information that is made available to the reader by, for example, presentations of characters' speech and behavior.

THE CONSTRUCTION OF INTERMENTAL MINDS

In my earlier essay on the Middlemarch mind (2005b), I identified four linguistic techniques that are used in its construction. In order of degree of directness, they are: explicit reference to an actual group, reference to a hypothetical group in order to make a particular rhetorical point, use of the passive voice, and presupposition. The following passage neatly illustrates all of these:

(1) Doctor Sprague [a] *was more than suspected* of having no religion, but somehow [b] *Middlemarch* tolerated this deficiency in him ... it was perhaps this negation in the doctor which made [c] *his neighbours* call him hard-headed and dry-witted. ... At all events, it is certain that if any medical man had come to Middlemarch with [d] *the reputation* of having very definite religious views ... [e] *there would have been a general presumption* against his medical skill. (125; emphasis added)

The passage marked (a) is the passive voice: it is the Middlemarch mind that is doing the suspecting. The letters (b) and (c) indicate explicit references, and (d) presupposition: a Middlemarch mind is presupposed because it is that that would create Sprague's reputation. Although (e) is also an example of presupposition (a group would do the presuming), it is there to make a specific rhetorical point about intermental views on medicine and religion.

I will say a little more here about the first category: explicit references to the names of a variety of intermental groups in the town. The most obvious names relate to the town itself. There are a number of variations: "the Middlemarchers" (106) and (114), "good Middlemarch society" (108), "Middlemarch company" (463) and so on. Another group of terms refers to "the town" (112), "the respectable townsfolk" (105), etc. References to Middlemarch can also be more specific when related to a particular context. For example, during a discussion of the political situation, the text refers to "buyers of the Middlemarch newspapers" (246). During consideration of Bulstrode's possible hypocrisy in example (18) below, there is an ironical reference to "the publicans and sinners in Middlemarch" (83). Finally, a description of Rosamond's popularity refers to "all Middlemarch admirers" (114).

The Middlemarch narrator, as I mentioned earlier, is fond of explicitly acknowledging the cognitive element in the book, particularly as it applies to intermental cognition. Some of the many examples include "civic mind" (65), "public mind" (99) and (246), "the unreformed provincial mind" (424) and "many crass minds in Middlemarch" (106). There are other sightings in the examples used below. At other times, very general terms are used such as: "that part of the world" (151), "midland-bred souls" (71), "mortals generally" (105), "the company" at a party (107), "vulgar people" (114), "all people young and old" (16), "public feeling required" (16), it was "sure to strike others" (17) and so on. Some of the general and vague descriptions of the workings of the Middlemarch mind involve oblique references to speech: "gossip" (344), "the air seemed to be filled with gossip" (344), "the conversation seemed to imply" (124), "general conversation in Middlemarch" (181) and "It's openly said" (72). Sometimes the reporting of the speech is focalized through an individual: Mr. Featherstone "had it from most undeniable authority, and not one, but many" (73), Lydgate "heard it discussed" (106) and (an example of what David Herman [1994] calls *hypothetical focalization*) "If Will Ladislaw could have overheard some of the talk at Freshitt that morning . . . " (433). Later, it is made clear what he would have heard being said:

> (2) "Young Ladislaw the grandson of a thieving Jew pawnbroker" was a phrase which had entered emphatically into the dialogues about the Bulstrode business at *Lowick, Tipton* and *Freshitt*. (533; emphasis added)

The three locations mentioned in example (2) deserve further attention. We can only follow what happens in a storyworld if we follow the mental functioning of the people in that storyworld. However, it is also essential to have a certain amount of knowledge, however rudimentary, of the geographical or material aspects of storyworlds. In the case of *Middlemarch*, we have to have a rough idea in our heads of the fact that Middlemarch is a town surrounded by a number of large country houses with accompanying parishes or villages. These include Tipton (home of Mr. Brooke, and also Dorothea and Celia before they marry), Freshitt (the home of Sir James Chettam, and Celia after she marries), and Lowick (the home of Casaubon, and also of Dorothea after she marries him). However, as this list shows, knowledge of the geographical storyworld is closely linked with knowledge of the mental and social storyworld. Tipton, Freshitt and Lowick are important only because they are the homes of these particular members of the gentry or upper classes who are leading characters in the story. This is demonstrated by the fact that references to the upper classes are couched in geographical terms, as in example (2), as well as in more obviously social terms. In other words, these place names function as metonymies for the upper classes or the gentry. Similarly, references to the town of Middlemarch itself sometimes act in the same way for the middle classes (as the Tankard pub does for the working classes).

As this discussion shows, the three social classes are amongst the most prominent of the subgroups of the Middlemarch mind. The upper classes consist primarily of the Brookes, the Chettams, the Cadwalladers and the other members of the local landed gentry. The middle classes comprise the professional classes and, in particular, the various medical men. The working classes are much less well represented and are confined mainly to Mrs. Dollop's pub, the Tankard. Sometimes the text refers to the upper classes as the "Middlemarch gentry" (186), the "county" (4) or "the county people who looked down on the Middlemarchers" (114). At other times, as in example (2), there are more specific references to the place names: "all Tipton and its neighbourhood" (151), "no persons then living—certainly none in the neighbourhood of Tipton" (17), "the unfriendly mediums of Tipton and Freshitt" (24), "all the world around Tipton" (32) and "opinion in the neighbourhood of Freshitt and Tipton" (58). Very occasionally, it is made clear that these place names describe the middle or working classes who live in them, as in "both the farmers and labourers in the parishes of Freshitt and Tipton" (34).

There are several passages that illustrate the class structure behind the intermental functioning in the town. Here is one example:

> (3) The heads of this discussion at "*Dollop's*" had been the common theme among *all classes in the town*, had been carried to *Lowick Parsonage* on one side and to *Tipton Grange* on the other, had come fully to the ears of *the Vincy family*, and had been discussed with sad reference to "poor Harriet" by *all Mrs Bulstrode's friends*, before Lydgate knew distinctly why *people* were looking strangely at him, and before Bulstrode himself suspected the betrayal of his secrets. (500; emphasis added)

This single sentence contains references to the whole social spectrum. "All classes" can be subdivided into upper (Lowick Parsonage and Tipton Grange), middle (the Vincy family and Mrs. Bulstrode's friends) and lower (Dollop's pub).

At several points in the discourse the views of the Middlemarch mind are arrived at through what Bronwen Thomas calls "multiparty talk" (2002) (that is, conversations between more than two people). A surprisingly large number of conversations, at least twenty I would say, feature three or more people. Scenes of this sort in which Middlemarch minds are clearly at work include the following:

- A The dinner party at which Lydgate is introduced to Middlemarch society (60–63)
- B The public meeting at which the vote on the chaplaincy takes place (126–29)
- C Sir James Chettam, the Cadwalladers and Mr Brooke talk about politics (261–67)
- D Hackbutt, Toller and Hawley discuss Lydgate (308–9)

E   The Chettams, the Cadwalladers, Dorothea and Celia have a discussion about widowhood (378–79)
F   The Bulstrode scandal breaks and comes to a climax at the public meeting (494–505)
G   The Chettams, the Cadwalladers and Mr. Brooke exchange views on Dorothea's second marriage (560–65)

There are two sorts of multiparty talk here. C, E and G are conversations between members of the gentry that establish a set of characteristically upper-class views on Dorothea's marriages and on politics. By contrast, B, D and F are the town or middle class views on Lydgate and Bulstrode (together with the working class view in F). A is, as the text explicitly states, an uneasy mixture of the upper and middle classes. In most cases, but particularly in F, there is a mixture of direct speech in the form of dialogue and multiparty talk, and intermental thought report. The hypothetical book on intermental thought in *Middlemarch* that I referred to earlier would allow space for a detailed analysis of the endlessly fascinating ways in which the intricately shifting dynamics of the various group minds are traced in these passages. Unfortunately, there is not enough space in this paper for such an analysis.

In addition to these big set pieces there are many short passages, often only a paragraph in length, in which intermental views are presented. These paragraphs act as a kind of low-level, continuous intermental commentary on events in between the big set pieces. Several of these paragraphs are used for illustrative purposes during the rest of this essay. In addition, there are several dialogues that make it clear that intermental norms have been internalized to such an extent that they have a subtle and indirect, though still profound and pervasive, influence on intramental thought processes. This point is particularly true of concerns about reputation or honor. To take just one example, there is an important discussion between Sir James Chettam and Mr. Brooke on the codicil to Casaubon's will in which Mr. Brooke says:

(4) "As to *gossip,* you know, sending [Ladislaw] away won't hinder *gossip*. *People* say what they like to say, not what they have chapter and verse for [. . . .] In fact, if it were possible to pack him off . . . *it would look* all the worse for Dorothea." (336–37; emphasis added)

Every word spoken by Mr. Brooke is informed by concern for intermental approval. All their thoughts are dominated by these four, dreaded words: what will people think?

SUBGROUPS AND THE DISCURSIVE RHYTHM

Although the most common of the intermental minds at work in the town are divided along class lines, such a distinction comes nowhere near reflecting the complexity of intermental thought in the novel. A large number of other ephemeral, localized, contextually specific groups can be identified. In a number of the examples given in this essay, there is a bewilderingly complex variety of perspectives, usually comprising the whole Middlemarch mind together with some of its subgroups. Sometimes the subgroups appear to be in agreement and therefore form *the* Middlemarch mind. They may be separate from each other but have an overlap in membership; they may be distinct from and even opposed to each other; sometimes sub-subgroups of a particular subgroup are featured. With the exception of the social classes, it is rare for subgroups to be referred to more than once in different parts of the novel. In the discussions that follow, it will be apparent that many of these groups are mentioned in a particular context in order to provide a very specific perspective on a particular issue and then vanish. I was originally tempted to try to create a kind of taxonomy or map of intermental thought in the novel by listing all the groups mentioned and analyzing their relations with each other. However, it took only a quick look at the large amount of evidence of intermental thought in *Middlemarch* to see that such a task would be impossible. The complexity would simply be overwhelming. In any event, little would be achieved because of the contextual nature of many of the references to subgroups.

The narrator can sometimes be self-knowingly ironic about the imprecision that is required when discussing these intermental units:

> (5) At Middlemarch in those times a large sale was *regarded* as a kind of festival. . . . The second day, when the best furniture was to be sold, "*everybody*" was there. . . . "*Everybody*" that day did not include Mr Bulstrode. (415; emphasis added)

The reader is alerted to the fact that locutions such as "everybody" and "all Middlemarch" must not be taken literally. It is difficult to be precise about the membership of large intermental units. Generalizations are required even thought they may not be strictly accurate. To pursue this line of thought, the narrator sometimes uses a particular example of intermental thought, as in the discussion on prejudice in (6), to muse on the nature of intermentality generally and the imprecision of descriptions of it in particular:

(6) *Prejudices* about rank and status were easy enough to defy in the form of a tyrannical letter from Mr Casaubon; but *prejudices*, like odorous bodies, have a double existence both solid and subtle. (300; emphasis added)

The narrator repeatedly points out that intermental units have a double existence which is both solid and subtle. On the one hand, the Middlemarch minds are collections of very different individuals, all with slightly different perspectives on the social issues affecting the town: they are subtle. On the other hand, and at the same time, these large units come together with a collective force, particularly as it appears to an individual, which is far greater than the sum of their parts: they become solid.

It is obviously too simplistic to suggest that intermental units are so fixed and clearly bounded that individuals are either inside or outside of them. The situation is more complex than that. Some people occupy ill-defined positions with regard to any intermental consensus. The vicar, Farebrother, is one who is on the fringes of the consensus. He regrets the common view on the Bulstrode/Lydgate affair because he likes Lydgate and, although he dislikes Bulstrode, he does not like to see him hounded. His case is made explicit because he is a major character and his views of the matter add to the complexity of the whole situation. However, the reader will know that other characters will have their own, individual views even if the precise nature of these views is not articulated. It is an important part of the capacity of readers to comprehend fictional narrative that they appreciate that, when intermental thinking takes place, significant intramental variations will always occur within it.

One example of this complex combination of intramental and intermental functioning takes place at a dinner party at the Vincey's household. The various members of the middle classes that are present discuss the chaplaincy. Individual views are expressed and they are often in disagreement with each other. People are thinking intramentally. Then: "Lydgate's remark, however, did not meet the sense of the company" (107). What happens here is that the individuals who were previously expressing conflicting views coalesce and close ranks in the presence of an outsider, as families tend to do. The presence of a "company" with a common view is explicitly acknowledged. The party is no longer a random collection of intramental perspectives; it becomes an intermental unit.

The attention paid in the text of the novel to the bewildering variety of the intricately interlocking subgroups results in the presence of a characteristic discursive rhythm. This highly distinctive rhythm is sometimes there in single sentences, sometimes in a group of two or three sentences, sometimes in a whole paragraph. Once it has been noticed, it is difficult to understand how it could have been overlooked. The tone of this rhythm is often ironic and even playful. The narrator regularly seems to backtrack on earlier statements and qualify generalizations. The language seems to meditate on the difficulty of pinning down precisely how these fluid and protean minds are initially and temporarily constituted, then dissolve, reform and dissolve again and so on. Example (1) gives a flavor of this rhythm. Other examples include (18), (19) and (20). Note the prose rhythms contained in the following two passages, and the careful balancing of different intermental perspectives, all trained on a single intramental mind:

> (7) However, Lydgate was installed as medical attendant on the Vincys, and the event was a subject of *general conversation in Middlemarch*. *Some* said, that the Vincys had behaved scandalously. . . . *Others* were of the opinion that Mr Lydgate's passing by was providential. . . . *Many people* believed that Lydgate's coming to the town at all was really due to Bulstrode; and Mrs Taft . . . had got it into her head that Mr Lydgate was a natural son of Mr Bulstrode's. . . . (181–82; emphasis added)

> (8) *Patients who had chronic diseases* . . . had been at once inclined to try him; also, *many who did not like paying their doctor's bills,* thought agreeably of opening an account with a new doctor . . . and *all persons thus inclined to employ Lydgate* held it likely that he was clever. *Some* considered that he might do more than others "where there was liver." . . . But these were *people of minor importance. Good Middlemarch families* were of course not going to change their doctor without reason shown. (305–6; emphasis added)

In both (7) and (8), a view is attributed to a large group and then modified or expanded by subgroups in what might be called a "many people thought . . . some said . . . others considered . . . " rhythm. Example (7) is particularly illustrative because it starts with the whole Middlemarch mind, "general conversation in Middlemarch," and then refers to three subgroups: some, others, and many people. The relationship between these three groups is unclear. Are they mutually exclusive or is there an overlap in membership? We cannot be sure. Example (8) concerns an implicit subgroup, patients, instead of the whole Middlemarch mind, but is otherwise similar in shape. Again, it would be very difficult indeed to establish the precise relationship between the various sub-subgroups of patients: those willing to change to Lydgate for very different reasons and those who are not. Some readers of this essay may be familiar with the mathematical tool of Venn diagrams, in which circles are used to express the relationships between classes of objects. Some of the examples in this essay could, I think, be expressed very usefully in this diagrammatic form, but in other cases insufficient evidence is available for their use.

The illustrated rhythm is characteristic of descriptions of intermental thinking because it is an acknowledgment of the messiness or complexity of this kind of mental functioning. It is invariably inaccurate and uninteresting to claim that everybody in an intermental unit thinks in exactly the same way for exactly the same reasons. Within the Middlemarch minds, the strength of view on the Bulstrode/Lydgate case will vary. Some people will be convinced of their guilt; others will be less so; some will care very much; others will not; some will be pleased at the general view because they dislike Bulstrode and/or Lydgate or because a loss of their status will benefit them; others will regret it because they like one or both of them or have moral objections. The narrator is invariably scrupulous in reflecting these fine shades of opinion. The delicate balance between intramental and intermental thought is always maintained.

INTERMENTAL FOCALIZATION

The points made in the previous section about the narrator reflecting fine shades of intermental opinion can be restated in terms of the concept of focalization. In what follows, I wish to propose the following three binary distinctions within the umbrella term *focalization* that, I think, go some way to reflecting the complexity of the passages quoted in this essay:

- intramental and intermental;
- single and multiple; and
- homogeneous and heterogeneous

The difference between *intramental* and *intermental* focalization refers to the distinction between mental activity by one (intramental) and by more than one (intermental) consciousness. *Single focalization* occurs when there is one focalizer. The term *multiple focalization* refers to the presence of two or more focalizers of the same object. These multiple focalizers may be intramental individuals or intermental groups or a combination of the two. However, a further distinction is required. In the case of *homogeneous focalization*, the two focalizers have the same perspective, views, beliefs and so on relating to the object. By contrast, *heterogeneous focalization* reflects the fact that the focalizers' views differ, and their perspectives conflict one with another.

If focalization is single, then it can be either intramental (one individual) or intermental (one single group), but it will be homogeneous and not heterogeneous unless an individual or group has conflicting views on an issue. One example of single focalization is (1), where all of the italicized phrases look superficially as though they are references to different groups, but in fact are simply different means of naming the Middlemarch mind. Other examples are (5) and (14). However, two points should be made. First, the majority of the examples quoted in this essay show multiple points of view. Most display a balance of distinct and distinctive collective views and fine shades of subtly differing judgments. Second, a succession of single focalizations will become multiple in a Bakhtinian effect on the reader when aggregated over the course of a novel.

If focalization is multiple, then it can involve different individuals, or different groups, or a combination of both; and, completely independently, it can be homogeneous or heterogeneous. Obviously, a fairly large number of possible combinations can be derived from these variables. I have not conducted an exhaustive analysis of the *Middlemarch* text to find out, but my guess is that most combinations are contained in this novel. Of the various examples of multiple intermental focalizations used in this essay, some are homogeneous and some are heterogeneous. Multiple intermental heterogeneous focalization is featured in examples (7), (8), (11), (13) and (18). In all these cases, the various intermental units mentioned have different views on the object of their cognitive functioning. To be strictly accurate, examples (7) and (11) have an intramental element as well and so are, in fact, examples of multiple intermental and intramental heterogeneous focalization. Multiple intermental *homogeneous* focalization is present in examples (2), (3), (10), (12), (16), (19) and (22). Again, examples (12) and (22) also have an intramental element.[2]

INDIVIDUALS INSIDE INTERMENTAL UNITS

This section and the following one focus on the relationships between groups and individuals. This one will say a little about how the leaders or spokespeople of each of the three classes are used to present the results of the class-based mental functioning. The next section will consider those individuals

---

2. For more on multiperspectivism, see Nünning (2000).

who are outside the social groups in the sense that they are the objects of their intermental cognitive activity.

Both Mrs. Cadwallader and Sir James Chettam act as powerful mouthpieces for the upper class mind. Here is a very dramatic illustration of this function:

> (9) But Sir James was a power in a way unguessed by himself. Entering at that moment [as Ladislaw is saying goodbye to Dorothea], he was an incorporation of the strongest reasons through which Will's pride became a repellent force, keeping him asunder from Dorothea. (377)

Chettam embodies or represents—or, to use the word chosen in the passage, "incorporates"—the upper class Middlemarch mind. It is stressed that he, thinking of himself as an individual, is not aware of this power and this may make his role even more powerful. His mouthpiece role is also clearly evident in example (22). Mrs. Cadwallader has a similar role. Two whole pages are devoted to an explanation of it (39–40): "She was the diplomatist of Tipton and Freshitt, and for anything to happen in spite of her was an offensive irregularity" (40). When something does happen in spite of her (the reference is to Dorothea's engagement to Casaubon instead of Chettam), "It followed that Mrs Cadwallader must decide on another match for Sir James" (40). This is intramental thought and action in the sense that it relates to a single individual, but her power to take this action results from her ability to represent the intermental consensus. Her intentionality is much more clearly foregrounded than with the Sir James quote. "It followed" implies that it followed for Mrs. Cadwallader in her capacity as a mouthpiece for the Middlemarch mind and, in addition, to her as an individual agent. Example (9) is different in that Sir James does not actually do, say or even think anything. He simply has a representative role in Ladislaw's uneasy consciousness. At that moment, for Ladislaw, Sir James is less an individual and more the incorporation of the town's collective view.

The middle-class mind has several mouthpieces: they include at various times Sprague, Minchin, Toller, Chicheley, and Standish. It is made explicit that they regard "themselves as Middlemarch institutions" (126). The following quote gives a useful insight into the dynamics or mechanics of the middle-class Middlemarch mind:

> (10) What *they* [Sprague and Minchin] disliked was [Lydgate's] arrogance, which *nobody* felt to be altogether deniable. *They* implied that he was insolent, pretentious, and given to that reckless innovation for the sake of noise

and show which was the essence of the charlatan. The word charlatan once thrown on the air *could not be let drop*. (313; emphasis added)

Here we have a balance between a small intermental unit (the pair formed by Sprague and Minchin) and the much larger middle class mind. The wider group acquiesces in the views of the pair. The final sentence makes use of the passive voice and presupposition to give a very accurate indication of how views spread. People seize on an idea or a word and hang onto it. It is in this way that the use of the term charlatan becomes attached to Lydgate. However, in keeping the intramental/intermental balance referred to above, it is important to look out for individual characteristics. Fred's illness "had given to Mr Wrench's enmity towards Lydgate more definite personal ground" (312). Despite the fact that Mr. Wrench is a mouthpiece for a large intermental unit, his thinking here has conscious intramental shading.

Mrs. Dollop is the acknowledged leader of working class opinion. This is a group that is based in the Tankard pub. (The middle class pub is the Green Dragon.) As the passages describing the working classes are amongst the weakest in the book and, to be honest, make for quite painful reading, I will only briefly describe this topic here. Here are two passages that illustrate the workings of the working class mind and the leadership role of Mrs. Dollop:

> (11) This was *the tone of thought chiefly sanctioned by Mrs Dollop*, the spirited landlady of the Tankard in Slaughter Lane, who had often to resist the shallow pragmatism of *customers* disposed to think that their reports from the outer world were of equal force with what had "come up" in her mind. (498; emphasis added)

> (12) If that was not reason, Mrs Dollop wishes to know what was; but there was *a prevalent feeling* in her audience that her opinion was a bulwark, and that if it were overthrown there would be no limits to the cutting-up of bodies, as had well been seen in Burke and Hare with their pitch-plaisters—such a hanging business as that *was not wanted in Middlemarch*. (305; emphasis added)

The use of a representative voice and a supporting chorus is a notable characteristic of both passages. Regarding (11), the term *sanctioned* is revealing of Mrs. Dollop's power. The group-defining force of the phrase "outer world" is also worth noting. This "outer mind" stands in clear contrast to Middlemarch conceived as a homogeneous unit of familiarity and home-like interiority. Finally, I would like to draw the reader's attention to the occurrence towards the end of (12) of intermental free indirect discourse. It is clear from some of the phrases in this sentence ("Mrs Dollop wishes to know what was"; "as had well been seen in Burke and Hare with their pitch-plaisters"; and "such a hanging business as that was not wanted in Middlemarch") that the narrator is making use of the distinctive speech and thought patterns that are characteristic of Mrs. Dollop and her customers. I have also found examples of this phenomenon in Evelyn Waugh's *Vile Bodies* (Palmer 2004, 208–9). It seems to me that this type of free indirect thought merits further attention.

Having examined the role of the mouthpieces of the three class-based intermental units, I will now consider the ways in which the text presents the judgments of units such as these on individuals who are outside of them.

INDIVIDUALS OUTSIDE INTERMENTAL UNITS

There are a number of different ways to describe the cognitive relationships that exist in the novel between intermental units and the individuals who are outside them. I will refer here briefly to four. The first two (focalization, and what I call *cognitive narratives*) are narratological terms; the other two (theory of mind and attribution theory) are cognitive theories.

Focalization

As I explained above, individuals are frequently focalized through an intermental mind. For example, both Dorothea's and also Lydgate's character and behavior are, at various times, focalized through a variety of Middlemarch minds. The relentlessly judgmental quality of intermental thought in the novel remains fairly constant in relation to both of them. However, intermental units can also be focalized through intramental cognitive functioning. For example, within Lydgate's free indirect discourse, there are references to "Middlemarch gossip" (240) and to "the circles of Middlemarchers" (299). Dorothea is critical of the "society around her" (23). Sometimes the two directions are at work simultaneously. In a very good example of a reciprocal intermental/intramental relationship, Lydgate comments that "I have made up my mind to take Middlemarch as it comes, and shall be much obliged if the town will take me in the same way" (112). It is clear that Lydgate talks here of Middlemarch in the way that the narrator does in the final sentence of

(19), as a sentient being that is capable of mental thought. In (13), the presentation of power relations in the town is focalized through Lydgate:

> (13) The question whether Mr Tyke should be appointed as salaried chaplain to the hospital was an exciting topic to *the Middlemarchers*; and Lydgate *heard it discussed* in a way that threw much light on the power exercised in the town by Mr Bulstrode. The banker was evidently a *ruler*, but there was *an opposition party*, and even among *his supporters*, there were *some* who allowed it to be seen that their support was a compromise. . . . (106; emphasis added)

Lydgate is aware that, on this question, the whole intermental mind ("Middlemarchers") is subdivided into support for Bulstrode and opposition to him (and perhaps those who have no strong opinion?). The support is then further subdivided into strong and weak or "compromise" support.

Cognitive narratives

This term designates a character's whole perceptual, cognitive, ethical and ideological viewpoint on the storyworld of the novel. It is intended to be an inclusive term that conveys the fact that each character's mental functioning is a narrative that is embedded within the whole narrative of the novel. In "The Lydgate Storyworld" (note the title), I argued that Lydgate's mind in action is the Middlemarch storyworld as seen from his viewpoint. Double cognitive narratives are versions of characters' minds that exist in the minds of other characters. So, one way to describe this cognitive relationship is to say that Middlemarch minds regularly form double cognitive narratives of individuals. Equally, double cognitive narratives can be reversed. As Lydgate's wish that the town take him as it finds him shows, some individuals form their own double cognitive narratives for the Middlemarch mind.

Theory of mind

This is the term used by philosophers and psychologists to describe our awareness of the existence of other minds, our knowledge of how to interpret other people's thought processes, our mind-reading abilities in the real world. This mind reading involves readers in trying to follow characters' attempts to read other characters' minds.[3] Theory of mind is usually considered to work in the novel on the intramental level. For example, in *Persuasion*, when Wentworth is snubbed by Anne's father and sister, Anne knows that he feels contempt and anger; Wentworth knows that Anne knows what he feels; Anne knows that Wentworth knows that she knows, and so on. There are other points in the novel at which Anne and Wentworth use their theory of mind on each other. However, it is part of the purpose of this essay to show that groups can also use their theory of mind and, in addition, be the subject of individuals' theory of mind.

For example, when Lydgate takes Bulstrode out of the public meeting in which he, Bulstrode, has been humiliated:

> (14) It seemed to him [Lydgate] as if he were putting his sign-manual to that *association* of himself with Bulstrode, of which he now saw the full meaning as it must have presented itself to *other minds*. [And then, within Lydgate's free indirect discourse:] The *inferences* were closely linked enough: the *town* knew of the loan, believed it to be a bribe, and believed that he took it as a bribe. (504; emphasis added)

In theory of mind terms, the passage can be decoded as follows:

A   Lydgate believes
B   that the Middlemarch mind believes
C   that Bulstrode believed
D   that Lydgate was bribable
E   and that Bulstrode intended to bribe him
F   and that Lydgate knew of Bulstrode's intention
G   and that Lydgate did accept Bulstrode's bribe

Note that this cognitive chain involves intermental (item B) as well as intramental reasoning.

Attribution theory

An alternative approach is to use the language of attribution theory and say that a wide range of different attributions are made by intermental minds

---

3. For more on theory of mind, see Palmer (2005b) and Zunshine (2006).

regarding the supposed workings of intramental minds.[4] Throughout the novel, Middlemarch minds are focused on the construction of their views on individuals in order to judge them and to place them. "Most of those who saw Fred . . . thought that young Vincey was pleasure-seeking as usual" (163). So Fred is constructed as a pleasure seeker. In example (1), Sprague is defined as "hard-headed and dry-witted." Attributions by large intermental units also have a profound effect on smaller units such as marriages: "In Middlemarch a wife could not long remain ignorant that the town held a bad opinion of her husband" (511).

All this inter- and intramental complexity is a vital element in the development of the various plots in the novel. The two most important examples are the Lydgate and Bulstrode crisis and the Dorothea and Ladislaw relationship. Example (9) shows very clearly that intermental units play a very powerful teleological role in the plot of the novel. The point is made explicit there in the reference to the upper class mind keeping Dorothea and Ladislaw apart, mainly through their, and especially his, uneasy awareness of its workings. For example:

> (15) Will was in a defiant mood, his consciousness being deeply stung with the thought that the *people* who looked at him probably knew a fact tantamount to an accusation against him as a fellow with low designs which were to be frustrated by a disposal of property. (417; emphasis added)

This is an example of what Bakhtin calls the *word with a sideways glance*: the nervous and uneasy anticipation of the view of another. It was also apparent in example (4). The end result for Dorothea and Ladislaw is that they are kept apart for some time:

> (16) His position [in Middlemarch] was threatening to divide him from her with those *barriers of habitual sentiment* which are more fatal to the persistence of mutual interest than all the distance between Rome and Britain. (300; emphasis added)

The focus of intermental units on intramental thinking raises important questions regarding the construction of identity:

> (17) There was *a general impression,* however, that Lydgate was not altogether a common country doctor, and in Middlemarch at that time such an

---

4. For more on attribution theory, see Palmer (2007).

impression was significant of great things being expected from him. (96–97; emphasis added)

Lydgate is considered to be a gentleman doctor. That is the intramental identity that is constructed by the intermental consensus. It is clear that George Eliot was very interested in how these socially situated identities are constructed. For example, the narrator emphasizes in the following quote that intermental minds tend to pay a good deal of attention to the past lives of individuals. While a cognitive narrative is being constructed for these individuals, their origins are carefully examined for any clues relating to their identities. Here, Bulstrode's lack of known social origins is held to be deeply suspicious:

> (18) Hence Mr Bulstrode's close attention was not agreeable to *the publicans and sinners in Middlemarch;* it was attributed by *some* to his being a Pharisee, and by *others* to his being Evangelical. *Less superficial reasoners among them* wished to know who his father and grandfather were, observing that five-and-twenty years ago nobody had ever heard of a Bulstrode in Middlemarch. (83; emphasis added)

Obviously, talk of a single, stable, assured social identity is misleading. All of these groups (loud men; those persons who thought themselves worth hearing; others; the publicans and sinners in Middlemarch; some; others; less superficial reasoners among them) have their own conflicting, colliding, contradictory perspectives on poor Bulstrode.

This interest in the past is even more explicit in the next example, which is very revealing about the ways in which intermental constructions of intramental cognitive narratives require individuals' pasts to be filled out:

> (19) *No one in Middlemarch* was likely to have such a notion of Lydgate's past as has here been faintly shadowed, and indeed *the respectable townsfolk* there were not more given than *mortals generally* to any eager attempt at exactness in the representation to themselves of what did not come under their own senses. *Not only young virgins of that town,* but *grey-bearded men also,* were often in haste to conjecture how a new acquaintance might be wrought into their purposes, contented with very vague knowledge as to the way in which life has been shaping him for that instrumentality. *Middlemarch,* in fact, counted on swallowing Lydgate and assimilating him very comfortably. (105; emphasis added)

The passage starts by saying, reasonably enough, that the Middlemarch mind is not going to know what had actually happened to Lydgate before he arrives in the town. But it then goes on to say that the hypothetical construction of his cognitive narrative (in the absence of real evidence) will owe more to the Middlemarch mind's own needs ("wrought into their purposes") than any disinterested pursuit of the truth of his history. The final sentence emphasizes the point. It will make use of Lydgate as it wishes. The need is to create a "Middlemarch Lydgate" who can be comfortably "swallowed" and easily assimilated. This "Lydgate" need only have a tenuous relationship with the "real" Lydgate (whatever and whoever that is).

In example (19) above, and also in examples (20) and (22), there is a strong emphasis on the almost mythic power of especially intermental but also intramental minds to modify reality to their own requirements. This is especially true, as can be seen above, of the construction of Lydgate's cognitive narrative. The intricate and messy detail of a life as actually lived by a particular individual is smoothed and flattened out into a simple story, a narrative that is molded according to the intermental desire for a simple moral to the tale. In (20) the narrator again uses the opportunity of some complex intermental views of an individual, this time Bulstrode, for some general musings on how intermental minds construct intramental embedded narratives:

> (20) But *this vague conviction* of interminable guilt, which was enough to keep up much head-shaking and biting innuendo even among *substantial professional seniors,* had *for the general mind* all the superior power of mystery over fact. *Everybody* liked better to conjecture how the thing was, than simply to know it; for *conjecture* soon became more confident than knowledge, and had a more liberal allowance for the incompatible. Even the more definite *scandal* concerning Bulstrode's earlier life was, *for some minds,* melted into the mass of mystery, as so much lively metal to be poured out in dialogue, and to take such fantastic shapes as heaven pleased. (498; emphasis added)

This is a general assessment by the narrator of a certain type of intermental thought. Although it is related to the workings of the Middlemarch mind, it appears to have a wider application. The narrator seems to be suggesting that this is how intermental systems generally work. It is heavily ironic and rather jaundiced. It makes the obvious point that the cognitive investigations of the Middlemarch mind are not aimed at a pure disinterested pursuit of the objective truth. Rather, in this case, the driving force is the enjoyment of mystery, as opposed to the discovery of fact. This is because fact might result in an uninteresting narrative being constructed for the two individuals, Bulstrode and Lydgate. Also, the resulting narrative might not suit the purposes or interests of those people who are hostile to the two. Even the "more definite" facts are warped to fit into a more satisfying narrative. There is then a reference to "some minds" going further "even" than the majority in modifying the known facts to construct a satisfying narrative. A cognitive narrative that fits the needs of the group is created.

In fact, in a typically explicit passage, the narrator muses on the question of identity and warns the reader against the distortions in the construction of intramental identity inherent in the myth-making process:

> (21) For surely *all* must admit that a man may be puffed and belauded, envied, ridiculed, counted upon as a tool and fallen in love with, or at least selected as a future husband, and yet remain virtually unknown—*known* merely as a cluster of signs for *his neighbours'* false suppositions. (96; emphasis added)

The myth-making process continues even after death. The following passage occurs at the very end of the book:

> (22) *Sir James* never ceased to regard Dorothea's second marriage as a mistake; and indeed this remained *the tradition concerning it in Middlemarch,* where she was spoken of to a younger generation as a fine girl who married a sickly clergyman, old enough to be her father, and in little more than a year after his death gave up her estate to marry his cousin—young enough to have been his son, with no property, and not well-born. *Those who had not seen anything of Dorothea* usually observed that she could not have been "a nice woman," else she would not have married either the one or the other. (577; emphasis added)

Dorothea is focalized though the Middlemarch mind for ever. Her life exists now only as a double cognitive narrative that is constructed by the Middlemarch mind. In its reductive simplicity and naivety, this narrative is completely different from the warm, sympathetic, complex one that is presented by the narrator over the course of the novel. It is a very long way indeed from the woman described in the final paragraph, the one whose "finely-touched spirit had still its fine issues," "who lived faithfully a hidden life" and who rests in an unvisited tomb (578).

CONCLUSION

I have tried in this essay to describe the various ways in which the narrator of *Middlemarch* organizes the mosaic of intermentality that makes up the text of the novel. I hope to have shown that the various intermental units are so integral to the plot of the novel that it would be difficult for a reader to follow the plot without an understanding of them. Now that the existence of this fundamentally important aspect of the novel has been established, the resulting lines of inquiry could go in a number of different directions. One would be to consider in more detail the different purposes that are served by the depictions of these units, in particular the creation of various ironic effects. Another would be to find out how the representations of intermental units in this novel both differ from, and are similar to, the representations in texts written by other novelists of the same period, as well as those from different periods.

REFERENCES

Eliot, George (1977) *Middlemarch* [1872]. Ed. Bert G. Hornback. New York: Norton.
Herman, David (1994) "Hypothetical Focalization." *Narrative* 2.3: 230–53.
Nünning, Ansgar (2000) "On the Perspective Structure of Narrative Texts: Steps Towards a Constructivist Narratology." *New Perspectives on Narrative Perspective*. Eds. Willi van Peer and Seymour Chatman. Albany: State University of New York Press. 219–31.
Palmer, Alan (2004) *Fictional Minds*. Lincoln: University of Nebraska Press.
——— (2005a) "The Lydgate Storyworld." *Narratology Beyond Literary Criticism*. Ed. Jan Christoph Meister. Berlin: de Gruyter. 151–72.
——— (2005b) "Intermental Thought in the Novel: The Middlemarch Mind." *Style* 39.4: 427–39.
——— (2007) "Attribution Theory." *Contemporary Stylistics*. Eds. Marina Lambrou and Peter Stockwell. London: Continuum. 81–92.
Semino, Elena (2006) "Blending and Characters' Mental Functioning in Virginia Woolf's 'Lappin and Lapinova.'" *Language and Literature* 15.1: 55–72.
Thomas, Bronwen (2002) "Multiparty Talk in the Novel: The Distribution of Tea and Talk in a Scene from Evelyn Waugh's *Black Mischief*." *Poetics Today* 23.4: 657–84.
Zunshine, Lisa (2006) *Why We Read Fiction: Theory of Mind and the Novel*. Columbus: The Ohio State University Press.

MONIKA FLUDERNIK

Mediacy, Mediation, and Focalization

The Squaring of Terminological Circles

The issue to be discussed in this essay concerns narratological terminology, but involves different conceptualizations of theoretical design as well. The essay will be concerned with the relationship between Stanzel's fundamental defining feature of narrative, its *mediacy*, on the one hand, and the discussions of narrative *mediation* or *transmission* (Chatman) on the other. While Stanzel's *mediacy* focuses on the mediateness of narrative, on the fact that the story (*histoire*) is mediated through the narrative report (*Erzählerbericht*) of a narrator figure, Chatman's *transmission* and what has recently come to be called *mediation* concern the process of (re)medialization of one *histoire* or one version of a story into different, especially multi-medial, discourses (e.g., film, ballet, drama, etc.). The contrasting of mediacy and mediation, as I will explain below, thematizes *different definitions of narrativity* and partially incompatible notions of *discourse*. Both models do, however, rely on a distinction between a deep-structural *histoire* (story) and a surface-structural discourse conceived in a variety of ways.

A second term of continuing prominence in narratological debates is that of focalization. In classical models such as Mieke Bal's, focalization is positioned as a process applying between the story and discourse levels of narrative (see Chatman 1986: 22; Bal 1985: 50[1]). Especially in Bal, focalization does not entirely synchronize with mediation, though some media presum-

---

1. Bal divides her levels into fabula (≈ Chatman's story), plot ("restructured fabula") and text (i.e. the words on the page). In her model, focalization mediates between the levels of fabula and plot.

ably involve the application of necessary or standard types of focalization. While focalization and mediation can therefore be argued to have some overlap, focalization and mediacy seem to stand in a relationship of complementary distribution both practically and theoretically. *Practically,* focalization (*qua* point of view) in Stanzel's model seems unrelated to mediacy since it does not have any direct impact on the mediating discourse of the narrator; story is not transformed into text by means of adding a point of view. Paradoxically, since the mediating narrator does not "see," this opens up a "who sees" (the reflector mode protagonist) versus "who speaks" (the narrator) dichotomy within Stanzel's theory. *Theoretically,* focalization and mediacy clash in their role as representatives of Genette's versus Stanzel's models. As the reader will remember, focalization is a term invented by Genette, whereas Stanzel's three narrative situations combine different types of storytelling or narration with different types of focalization ("perspective"), and he also distinguishes between *perspective* and *mode,* both of which have affinities with standard conceptions of point of view or focalization. Looking at the interrelations between focalization and mediacy in Stanzel's model and contrasting mediacy and mediation may help to bring out some underlying parallels between a number of processes that are said to operate between the story and discourse levels of narratives. Such an inquiry also poses the question of to what extent a reconstruction of story from the discourse can be parallelized with the medial transformation of stories, plots or already existing discourses (Babes in the Wood as material, as story/plot, as a fairy tale transposed into film, cartoon, novel, etc.).

REVISITING STORY AND DISCOURSE—
NO MEDIA/CY/TION WITHOUT DICHOTOMIZATION

Practically all models of narrative theory repose on the story/discourse dichotomy, and they usually approach this binary opposition as a before/after sequence: first there is the story and then one transforms it into a discourse by means of narration by a narrator or through a specific medium like film or theatrical performance or ballet. The origins of the dichotomy lie in Russian formalism and its distinction between *fabula* and *syuzhet* (Shklovsky 1965: 57; Eichenbaum 1965: 121–22; Erlich 1965: 240–1), complemented (and muddied) by the story/plot opposition according to E. M. Forster (1990: 42; 86–87). Forster, as one remembers, contrasts *story* as a sequence of actions with *plot* (sequence of actions plus motivation): on the one hand, *The king died. Then the queen died;* on the other, *The king died. Then the queen died of grief.* By contrast, the Russian formalist distinction focuses on the rhetorical *rearrangement* of story elements in the discourse, illustrated with panache by Shklovsky on the example text of *Tristram Shandy* (Shklovsky 1965). In the later development of narratology, Forster's distinction has been relegated to the deep structure of narrative: plot and story are now often treated as *one level* that is anterior to the narrative discourse. In fact, the journey from the events themselves (*Geschehen,* cp. Schmid 2005: 241–72) to story or plot (*Geschichte*), and then on to discourse has been represented in a number of different ways as Korte (1985) and Fludernik (1993: 61–62) already outlined.[2] In Seymour Chatman's *Story and Discourse* (1978/1986), *narrative transmission* in verbal and visual narrative includes focalization (1986: 158–61). The move from the story level (focusing on existants and actions) to the discourse level (words, images) includes not only a possible rearrangement in the order of plot events (Genette's anachrony in the category of tense), but also the introduction of focalization and voice ("who sees" and "who speaks"), the latter inflected in a medium-specific manner (see Chatman's cinematic narrator—1990: 124–38). However, the assumed inclusion of focalization in narrative transmission will have to be modified in a close reading of *Story and Discourse* and in consideration of Chatman's newer distinctions (1990: 139–60) between *filter* and *slant* (see below in the section Mediation and Focalization).

All of these models depart from the assumption that the story is a given and the discourse transforms it into the text as we have it before our eyes. Such a viewpoint is generative and production-oriented, assuming that the author creates a narrator, who then transforms the story (what happened) into the text/discourse we read. As has been pointed out, from the reader's perspective the situation is entirely different since the reader *reconstructs* the story from the discourse, a process that may be quite laborious in some Modernist novels like James Joyce's *Ulysses* (1922), William Faulkner's *Absalom, Absalom!* (1936), or even in newer fiction like Timothy Findley's *Famous Last Words* (1981) or Rudy Wiebe's *The Temptations of Big Bear* (1995). All of these narratives require heroic efforts on the part of their readers to work out what happened in what order. What I would like to suggest, though, is that the readerly perspective is not exclusively a reception-oriented view of the story/discourse dichotomy, but that it also applies to the generative perspective. The story is *always* a construction and an idealized chronological outline. On the other hand, it also needs to be noted that nonfictional narra-

---

2. See also the very useful summary in Wenzel (2004: 16–17), who even distinguishes between two layers of discourse.

tives and re-medializations clearly rely on a prior story (though not necessarily referent) which they transform into discourse.

As regards authors' compositional practices, it is now widely established that these do not start with a story or plot and then literally choose between, say, an omniscient or first-person narrator, between a chronological or analeptic presentation of events, or between types of focalization. On the contrary, pronouncements by various authors on how they came to write their stories often allow us to glimpse a character trait, a key scene, a moral problem, and so on as the germ of the later narrative, and it is from that significant detail that decisions about presentation are developed. Specifically, many plot details are not known to authors when they start to write, as Dickens's outlines for his later novels demonstrate to perfection. Taking plot as the basic ground on which discourse builds is therefore not very convincing from a generative perspective. The situation is, however, very different if there already exists a prior textual source for the narrative, for instance another novel, a fairy tale, a history book, or if the core of the story is a historical sequence of events which has already been canonized. Under these circumstances, transformations do indeed take place on a prior event sequence. Angela Carter's rewritings of, respectively, "Beauty and the Beast" and "Bluebeard's Chamber" in her "The Courtship of Mr. Lyon" and "The Bloody Chamber" in *The Bloody Chamber* (1979) obviously rely on their model reader's familiarity with these fairy tales; only then can he/she optimally appreciate Carter's feminist anti-patriarchal revisions of these sources. One should, however, note that such revisions also change the plot by reintroducing different settings and characters (the piano tuner in "The Bloody Chamber") and therefore actually create a new plot (and a new discourse). Since the revision of the plot has ideological importance, it cannot be set aside as irrelevant to the creative process.[3]

Historical writing is even more complicated. On the one hand, there is no historical plot to start with, as Paul Veyne notes in his classic analysis (1971: 13–20); on the other hand, once historians have created the "history of the Peloponnesian War" or the "history of the rise of the gentry," certain key events have been selected as prominent causes and results in a sequence whose teleological argument provides a storyline. This configuration (Ricoeur 1984–88) is then taken over by other historians, who add to the data, revise in accordance with new sources, and summarize "the story" in their own

3. For a superb discussion of such adaptations, as she calls them, see Hutcheon (2006). Hutcheon in particular discusses modifications of theme, character and plot as common foci of the adaptive process (7–8), thus indicating that adaptations often tend to rewrite the story level.

words. Historiography thus originally creates a new story, but often rewrites it once it has been outlined; indeed, only when a completely new interpretation becomes necessary in the light of recently retrieved evidence (e.g. the discovery and decipherment of the Linear B tablets) is a new story created. At the same time, owing to its factual pretensions, historiography always claims to tell a story that is prior to its narration since history is "out there" and supposedly independent of the individual historian's text. (Hence the controversial status of Hayden White among historians; he *seems to say* that there are no events outside the historians' inventions of stories, though in actual fact he merely queries our representations of those occurrences in story form.)

The story/discourse dichotomy, and especially the priority of the story, has recently been attacked by Richard Walsh (2001, reprinted in Walsh 2007), who also refers to a debate between Barbara Herrnstein Smith (1980) and Seymour Chatman (1981) in *Critical Inquiry*. Smith's article is a sarcastic review of Chatman's 1978 classic, *Story and Discourse*, basically from her perspective of a speech act paradigm of speech and writing, which is Smith's preferred mode of approaching literature in her *On the Margins of Discourse* (1978). Smith's major point of attack is the "Platonic," as she terms it (1980: 213), nature of story in Chatman; in her view, story, like Plato's ideas, does not exist in the real world. The only thing that exists is *versions* of stories (specifically discourses of Cinderella), including summaries, which are also discourses. Smith proposes that the reason that most people agree on a similar summary of a text is because they share a cultural background, have similar expectations of what a summary should look like, and deploy the same culturally transmitted genre conventions. Chatman's reply to Smith focuses on the linguistic model and parallelizes story and discourse with the phonological phoneme/phone dichotomy: "The phonemes are as real as their actualizations on people's lips; they are not some fuzzy Platonic idea but a reality, a construct by linguists from actual utterances and attributable to the configuration of articulational and semantic features" (1981: 804–5). Chatman's more basic model is, however, Chomsky's transformational grammar, since the entire point of reconstructing the underlying story for Chatman is to determine in what way the discourse differs from it (by way of anachronies, focalization, etc.).

It makes perfect sense to contrast the messy text that one has in hand with an idealized chronological story, which the reader needs to piece together in order to understand the narrative. One can also sympathize with narratological tendencies to logically put the story first (though not in terms of actual production). The point of Smith's criticism that Chatman responds to only vaguely and insufficiently is the one about the impossibility of finding a core version of Cinderella in its many manifestations from China to Peru. Chatman never really addresses this question. Smith, on the one hand, clearly confuses the chronology of a hypostatized story which belongs to any one discourse *with the mythic kernel* that supposedly lies beneath all Cinderella retellings in three hundred and more versions of that fairy tale. Most of the difficulties that Smith outlines actually touch on the existants (the prince is not a prince but the captain of a ship; Cinderella is the oldest sister) or the setting (cp. Hutcheon 2006: 7–8). The transformation of a chronological into an anachronistic discourse, on the other hand, presupposes the positing of the *same plot* for both versions. Or, in other words, story/discourse transformations only make sense for *one* specific story version of Cinderella that is transformed into one specific verbal narrative or film or ballet. Different discourse versions of Cinderella in different media, on the other hand, all have their individual stories. Narrative transmission does not in fact coincide with remedialization (the rewriting of a myth), i.e. the presumed Ur-Cinderella responsible for the three hundred or more Cinderella tales on this globe. Where Smith is quite correct, therefore, is in showing that a *remedialization* cannot take the original text (and its story) as a starting point for the *same kind* of transformation that occurs between story and discourse in *one medium*. A rewriting of fairy tales and myths such as Angela Carter's "The Erl-King," "Puss in Boots" or "Penetrating to the Heart of the Forest" produces a different discourse (and a different story).

In his brilliant "Fabula and Fictionality in Narrative Theory" (2001; 2007: 52–68), Walsh inverts the classic story before discourse dichotomy by not only emphasizing discourse's priority over story but by additionally arguing that "sujet (discourse) is what we come to understand as a given (fictional) narrative, and fabula (story) is how we come to understand it" (2007: 68). Rather than focusing on how we deform story to yield a rearranged discourse, Walsh sees the construction of fabula as a means of explicating the rhetoric of fiction: "Fabula is not so much an event chain underlying the sujet as it is a by-product of the interpretative process by which we throw into relief and assimilate the sujet's rhetorical control of narrative information" (67); rather, fabula is "an interpretative exercise in establishing representational coherence" in order to achieve "rhetorical perceptibility" (ibid.). The construction of fabula is needed for the interpretation of narrative (65). Walsh here seems to first cast out story (fabula) as the rock on which narratology reposes, but then ends up entrenching the distinction, yet does so from a functionalist rather than temporal (chronology-related) or generic perspective.

To return to our problem of mediacy, mediation, and focalization. One needs to point out that in classic narratological models, all three concepts rely on the opposition between the two levels of story and discourse and that the notions of mediation and focalization presuppose the priority of the deep structural level. (I am using Chatman's classic formulation here.) Particularly in the case of mediation, this poses the question of whether a remediation of one story into another in a different medium (from novel to film, from fairy tale to Walt Disney production) actually is a remediation, or whether film or cartoon versions do not in reality have different plots which relate to the plots of the source narratives in a framework of family resemblances. Does the process of selection, restructuring, and media-related refocalization create a new story through a new discourse, or is it still the same story?

We will keep these conundra in mind. For the moment we have established that the dichotomy between story and discourse is basic to all recent theorizing about mediacy, mediation, and focalization. We also saw that traditional narratology in practice (though not always in theory[4]) saw the story level as prior to the discourse level and conceived of the discourse as a transformation of the story through the medium of narration (which then included medial and focalizational aspects). We additionally noted that a reception-oriented perspective would tend to emphasize the construction of story from the discourse. A mediational focus, on the other hand, requires a stable plot on which mediation can build and therefore seems to argue for the priority of story. However, as I have suggested, remedialization and narrative transmission are perhaps two entirely different animals and should not be treated as equivalent.

MEDIACY VERSUS MEDIATION

When Stanzel introduced the notion of mediacy in 1955, he defined it in the following manner:

> Die vorliegende Untersuchung nimmt ihren Ausgang von dem zentralen Merkmal der Mittelbarkeit der Darstellung im Roman. Mittelbarkeit charakterisiert auch die Darstellungsweise im Epos. [. . .] Im Roman bezeichnet

---

4. The *de facto* priority of discourse is noted by Genette when he sees the story as the signified of the discourse. For criticism of the story/discourse relation see also Fludernik (1993: 61–63; 1994; 1996: 333–37). Wolf Schmid even has a diagram that visualizes the priority of discourse over story by arrows pointing from narration to discourse, from discourse to plot, and from plot to events (2005: 270).

die Mittelbarkeit der Darstellung jenen Sachverhalt, der von den oben angeführten Theoretikern des Romans in der Anwesenheit eines persönlichen Erzählers gesehen wird. [...] [D]ie Auffassung, daß echte Darstellung im Roman nur durch die Vermittlung eines persönlichen Erzählers möglich wäre, ist in ihrem normativen Anspruch ebenso unhaltbar wie jene besonders von Spiegelhagen vertretene Ansicht, daß der Erzähler völlig unsichtbar zu bleiben habe. [...] In der Regel ist die Erzählung in einem Roman jeweils auf eine ganz bestimmte Art des Vermittlungsvorganges abgestimmt, die dann im ganzen Roman durchgehalten wird. Sie soll hier Erzählsituation genannt werden. Die Mittelbarkeit des Romans erhält in der Erzählsituation ihren konkreten Ausdruck: ein Autor erzählt, was er über eine Sache in Erfahrung gebracht hat, ein anderer tritt als Herausgeber einer Handschrift auf, jemand schreibt Briefe oder erzählt seine eigenen Erlebnisse, um nur einige geläufige Einkleidungen der Erzählsituation zu nennen. Solche Einkleidungen haben alle zum Ziel, im Leser die Illusion zu stärken, daß das Erzählte ein Teil seiner eigenen Wirklichkeitserfahrung sei. (1969: 4–5)

The present investigation takes as its point of departure one central feature of the novel—its mediacy of presentation. Mediacy or indirectness also characterizes the technique of presentation in the epic. [...] For these theoreticians [Petsch, Hamburger, Friedemann] the novel's mediacy of presentation consists in the presence of a personal narrator. [...] The view that authentic presentation in the novel is only possible through the mediation of a personal narrator is as untenable a normative criterion as the view, held notably by Friedrich Spielhagen, that the narrator ought to remain fully invisible. [...] As a rule, the narration in a given novel maintains a single fixed type of mediative process throughout the work. This mediative process will be called the narrative situation. The mediacy of the novel finds its concrete expression in the narrative situation: one author narrates the facts he has learned about a given subject; another appears as the editor of a manuscript; yet another writes letters or narrates his own experiences. These are only a few common guises of the narrative situation. Such guises all have the aim of strengthening the reader's illusion that the narrated material is a part of his own experience of reality. (1971: 6–7)

In the first sentence of this passage Stanzel notes that mediation of the story by the narrator has generally been taken for granted and was thematized by Robert Petsch (1934), Käte Hamburger (1993), and Käte Friedemann (1965). His contribution to these antecedents is to show that Spielhagen's ideal of objective, seemingly narrator-less type of narration (1883: 220) is also mediated, and that mediation therefore manifests itself through a number of different narrative situations.

In his 1979/1984 *Theory of Narrative,* the concept of mediacy is elaborated differently, in relation to the opposition of narrative (epic) with drama, a contrast that Stanzel borrows from Pfister (1977/1991):

> The three *narrative situations* distinguished below must be understood first and foremost as rough descriptions of basic possibilities of rendering the mediacy of narration. It is characteristic of the *first-person narrative situation* that the mediacy of narration belongs totally to the fictional realm of the characters of the novel: the mediator, that is, the first-person narrator, is a character of this world just as the other characters are. [. . .] It is characteristic of the *authorial narrative situation* that the narrator is outside the world of the characters. [. . .] Here the process of transmission originates from an external perspective, as will be explained in the chapter on "perspective." Finally, in the *figural narrative situation,* the mediating narrator is replaced by a reflector: a character in the novel who thinks, feels and perceives, but does not speak to the reader like a narrator. [. . .] (Stanzel 1984: 4–5)

Stanzel then goes on to equate his concept of mediacy with Seymour Chatman's *narrative transmission* (5). He proceeds to align foregrounded mediacy with the literariness of a narrative, citing Shklovsky's *Tristram Shandy* essay as an analysis of foregrounded mediacy (6). Later in the introduction Stanzel reduces narrative transmission (mediacy) to the narratorial function. The narrator is either openly active in the telling of the tale or hides behind it:

> All those narrative elements and the system of their coordination which serve to transmit the story to the reader belong to the surface structure. The main representative of this transmission process is the narrator, who can either perform before the eyes of the reader and portray his own narrative act, or can withdraw so far behind the characters of the narrative that the reader is no longer aware of his presence. (16–17)

The main grounding of Stanzel's mediacy thus lies in the verbal mediation of story by means of a narrator's act of narration. Narrative is to be distinguished from drama by its mediacy. Whereas the story of drama is enacted on stage and therefore presented without mediation, im-mediately, narratives represent the events through the medium of verbal narration by a narrator figure. Stanzel's model therefore relies on a definition of narrative that excludes drama from it—a traditional German axiom that goes back to Goethe's genre distinction between epic, poetry, and drama as the basic triad of available generic forms. Narrativity, in the sense of what constitutes a narrative,[5] in Stanzel therefore includes a story versus discourse distinction and entails a mandatory narrational level figured in a narratorial persona (who/which may, however, be laid back, covert or even seemingly nonexistent, as in reflector-mode narrative, i.e. in narratives of global internal focalization). Such a definition does not cover nonverbal narratives or drama; its presuppositions, especially that of the distinction between narrative, lyric, and dramatic modes, clearly proclaim that such an extension is not desired.

Although the exclusiveness of Stanzel's definition of mediacy, and implicitly of narrativity, seems restrictive today, one does well to remember that the necessary existence of a narrator, and the privileging of the verbal act of narration, can also be found in Gérard Genette, who has been drastically outspoken regarding his rejection of Banfield's no-narrator theory:

> Narrative without a narrator, the utterance without an uttering, seem to me pure illusion [...]. I can therefore set against its devotees only this regretful confession: "Your narrative without a narrator may perhaps exist, but for the forty-seven years during which I have been reading narratives, I have never met one." *Regretful* is, moreover, a term of pure politeness, for if I were to meet such a narrative, I would flee as quickly as my legs could carry me: when I open a book, whether it is a narrative or not, I do so to have the author *speak to me*. And since I am not yet either deaf or dumb, sometimes I even happen to answer him. (Genette 1988: 101–2)

Parallelizing the reading process with narration, Genette humorously presents the activity of reading as a conversation with a person, the real author or narrator (in the case of a fictional narrative). Genette's model goes beyond Stanzel's in its focus on the level of narration, separating as it does the narrator as extradiegetic communicative instance on the one hand, and the product of his/her act of narration, the narrative discourse, on the other. It is precisely this split in the mediacy-constituting narrational transmission between sender and textual message that opened up the way for Seymour Chatman to include first film and later other media under the banner of narrative transmission. Chatman's model allows for the existence of different "texts"—purely verbal, filmic, dramatic. It therefore implies the hypostatizing of a narrating instance

---

5. In opposition to different definitions of narrativity as constructedness in Hayden White (1981) and in opposition to narrativehood in Gerald Prince (1982, 2008).

in film, drama, and even in other visual media (see Chatman's cinematic narrator, 1990: 124–38).

Although both Stanzel and Genette anchor a narrator telling the story in their theoretical models, for Stanzel the narrator splits into two types—on the one hand an explicit teller in most first-person narratives and in authorial narratives with a foregrounded narrator figure; and on the other a disguised narrator in reflector-mode narratives, where the narrator is in abeyance, covert, seemingly absent, and the story seems to be "told," i.e. conveyed, by a reflector figure (often called "narrator" by Booth, e.g. 1983: 274) or Jamesian "center of consciousness" (James 1934: xvii–xviii; 322–25). By contrast, Genette takes the narrator as fundamental, but combines voice, mode, and tense as inflections of the relationships between story, discourse, and narration. Although every narrative has a narrator, there is actually no real *mediation* going on since the narrator produces a discourse (the discourse being the signified of the narration as signifier), and the discourse in turn is the signifier of the story, its signified. This means that in Genette the one necessary thing is a narrator, and the story emerges indirectly as the signified of the narrational acts' signified—it is at second remove from the story. Rather than subscribing to a story–discourse model, then, Genette's typology actually consists of a double dyad or triad: A. narration-B. *récit* [B1 discourse-B2 story]. In fact, this dichotomy, in which one term of the binary opposition splits into a further dichotomy, is a recurring structure in Genette's model. His model of focalization also works in the same way: focalization versus no focalization (*focalization zéro*), with focalization divided into internal versus external. One cannot speak of mediacy or mediation proper in Genette, but only of signification.

Stanzel, on the other hand, entirely focuses on mediation *qua* mediacy, but he exclusively means mediation through the narratorial discourse. The *point* of Stanzel's model, however, is not so much to thematize mediation—this he really takes for granted as the constitutive feature of narrative (epic) in contrast to drama in so far as both genres tell a story—but to propose *two types* of mediacy, namely explicit and implicit or overt and covert, and to demonstrate how the pretense of immediacy in figural narrative can be achieved. Since the reflector character does not narrate and all narrative is mediate, how is mediacy achieved in this type of fiction which seems to provide im-mediate access to the experience of the characters, to the story? If immediacy were actually possible, this would militate against the axiomatic distinction between drama and narrative, but such dramatic immediacy is possible only rarely in dialogue novels; in figural narrative, instead, mediacy is camouflaged by the narrator's sly disappearance behind the scenes, allowing the reflector character's psyche to move to the foreground, supplying a deictic center of orientation and evaluation. Stanzel therefore sees mediacy as a kind of mediation, but not in terms of different media (verbal telling versus visual, performative narrative), but of different types of verbal narrative—by means of either overt telling (first-person or authorial narrative) or "reflecting" through the center of consciousness within a narrative discourse that, as to its source, remains disguised, occulted, camouflaged. From the perspective of later Balian, Chatmanesque or Wolfian models, Stanzel's theory is therefore not a theory of medi*ation* but of mediacy—in so far the translation of *Mittelbarkeit,* literally "mediability," is correct. It is a theory of the foregrounding or backgrounding of mediacy by the narratorial discourse, which is the one and only medium of narrative.

Stanzel, as the quotations cited above show, alternates between a dual and a triple manifestation of mediacy. On the one hand, the three narrative situations (first-person, authorial, and figural) are said to instantiate mediacy; on the other hand, the modal difference between telling and showing (reflecting) is constitutive of mediacy. This inconsistency could be related to the existence of two levels of mediacy. At some points, as in our first quotation (1969: 4–5), Stanzel seems to focus on the generic forms of mediacy, including the diary, the editor's report and other frames in the various manifestations of mediacy; at other times the emphasis is on the (missing) narrator persona and veiled act of narration or on the foregrounding/backgrounding of narratorial mediation. From that latter perspective, the triad of narrative situations begins to slide into a dichotomy, since both first-person and authorial narratives have a clear narrator persona, with the exception (in Stanzel's model) of the autonomous interior monologue. Cohn's suggestion to reduce the three axes in Stanzel's *Theory of Narrative* therefore articulates the unease triggered by the slide between a clear triadic and an equally obvious dual set-up within the model (Cohn 1981).

My own model in *Towards a 'Natural' Narratology* extends Stanzel's theoretical edifice by revising two of his presuppositions. First, it became clear to me that reflector-mode narrative substitutes consciousness for narration; the medium of figural narrative is therefore less a covert narrator hiding behind the mind of a protagonist than a different mode of cognitive conceptualizing of characters' experience—*telling* versus *experiencing*. This then led to my addition of two further such frames—based on conversational narrative formats posited as prototypical and therefore of cognitive salience: *viewing* and *reflecting* (ideating) (see Fludernik 1996: 43–52). In my model there are thus four different ways in which forms of consciousness mediate narrative experience within frames. Later in the book I also integrated readers' immersive projections into that model when discussing Banfield's empty center and Stanzel's reflectorization technique (his *Personalisierung*) in contrast with what I called forms of figuralization (using Stanzel's English term for his *personale Erzählsituation*, i.e. the *figural* narrative situation).[6]

Because viewing and experiencing are not based on discourse or language, this model additionally opened the way to a broader understanding of narrative and narrativity, which no longer remained limited to verbal narrative. Note, however, that the mediation of experientiality through cognitive frames, i.e. mediacy, is not at all equivalent or even comparable to media-related mediation per se—different cognitive frames may come into play in different media. The model therefore welcomes considerations of medi*ation*, but without dropping the notion of medi*acy* as a separate category. For these reasons, it is important to continue to distinguish between the concepts of mediacy and mediation.

MEDIATION AND FOCALIZATION

Whereas, as we have seen, Genette's focalization can be added to any possible narrative, Stanzel's internal perspective is central to figural narrative texts, combining with the reflector mode: *grosso modo* one can say that mediacy comes either in teller or in reflector mode, and if in the latter, one has internal focalization à la Genette. (It is not important for our argument here that Genette's internal focalization, Stanzel's internal perspective, Stanzel's figural narrative and his reflector mode do not all refer to precisely the same thing and have some very jagged edges.[7]) Since Stanzel excludes all nonverbal narratives

---

6. See Fludernik (1996: 178–221).

7. Stanzel's perspective "involves the control of the process of apperception which the reader performs in order to obtain a concrete perceptual image of the fictional reality" (1984: 111); thus "[i]nternal perspective prevails when the point of view from which the narrated world is perceived or represented is located in the main character or in the centre of events" (ibid.). Reflector-mode narrative, which also covers first-person texts, is marked by "a close correspondence between internal perspective and the mode dominated by a reflector character" (141), while the figural narrative situation contains a dominance of internal perspective with a prevailing reflector mode. But first-person reflector-mode narratives in Stanzel belong to the first-person narrative situation. As for Genette's focalization, it is defined through a restriction of point of view *within* the narrative world (Genette 1972/1980: 185–6). This internal focalization seems to correspond almost precisely with Stanzel's internal perspective, except that their opposites, external focalization and external perspective, differ radically. Internal focalization in Genette contrasts with external focalization—an external view of the fictional world which disallows insight into characters' minds; whereas Stanzel's external perspective characterizes the narrator's all-encompassing vision on the fictional world including "his" omniscient ability to look into the protagonists' minds. Thus, Fielding's depiction of his

from consideration, the question of how to treat focalization in film does not pose itself within his theory. Nor is there a question of *where* to locate focalization. Since Stanzel only has one type of "focalization," namely reflector mode narrative,[8] which is one of two ways in which mediacy manifests itself, focalization therefore clearly "occurs" between the story level and the discourse level. Hence, it comes to rank with those transformations usually positioned in this space: the rearrangement of chronology (Genette's category *order*) and the selection and compression process (Günther Müller's *Erzählzeit* versus *erzählte Zeit* [1948]).[9]

Once one starts to consider narrative as existing in several media, however, a long list of theoretical imponderables emerges; these have given rise to a number of diverse solutions. The possible relations between focalization and mediation clearly depend on which of these solutions one has espoused.

Let us start with Chatman since he is the prime exponent of the story and discourse definition of narrative, and the inventor, or at least popularizer, of the cinematic narrator concept. For Chatman, "point of view" (1986: 151–61) comes in three forms: perceptual point of view, conceptual point of view and interest point of view (1978: 152). Perceptual point of view refers to what a character sees; conceptual point of view refers to cognition and attitude; and interest point of view to the "passive state" (152) of being concerned, of practical interest, or life-orientation. Already in *Story and Discourse,* Chatman relates point of view to the story level: "point of view is the physical place or ideological situation or practical life-orientation to which *narrative events* stand in relation" (153; my emphasis). He clearly opposes point of view and voice: "Perception, conception, and interest points of view are quite independent of the manner in which they are expressed. [. . .] Thus point of view is *in* the story (which is the character's), but voice is always outside, in the discourse" (154; Chatman's emphasis). Rather than seeing point of view constitutively as part of a transformation process, Chatman actually locates character's point of view in the story, and allows the narrator a separate point of view which is separate from the action of telling, though still part of the transformation from story into discourse, I suppose.

In Chatman's *Coming to Terms* (1990), the narrator is no longer allowed any point of view, but may have a *slant,* whereas characters' point of view

---

characters' consciousness would be *global zero focalization* (plus extradiegetic heterodiegetic narrative), possibly with minimal pockets of internal focalization, in Genette, but *external perspective* (and hence authorial narrative situation) in Stanzel.

8. In heterodiegetic narrative internal perspective coincides with the reflector mode; in homodiegetic narrative, internal perspective is just part of the dynamics of the first-person narrative situation.

9. In Genette, time of narration versus narrated time is subsumed under *duration.*

becomes a *filter* through which they perceive the narrative world (1990: 139–60). Chatman's revised model foregrounds ideology,[10] and it allows perceptual point of view only on the level of the characters: "I propose *slant* to name the narrator's attitudes and other mental nuances appropriate to the report function of discourse, and *filter* to name the much wider range of mental activity experienced by characters in the story world—perceptions, cognitions, attitudes, emotions, memories, fantasies, and the like" (1990: 143; Chatman's emphasis). Note that in *Coming to Terms* the point of view on the narratorial level is now subsumed under the "function of discourse" and not a stance superimposed on the narrational act. Focalization, perceptual and cognitive or ideological, therefore only relates to characters—there is no *external* focalization as in Genette (Chatman 1990: 145)! It has nothing to do with the point from which events are perceived but in fact seems to be equivalent to Stanzel's reflector-mode: characters' point of view is a filter through which the characters "experience" themselves and the world around them. Filter, in fact, "captur[es]" the "mediating function of a character's consciousness" (144). It therefore emerges that the model which was most crucially responsible for entrenching the story/discourse dichotomy actually does *not* integrate focalization into it. In Chatman (1990) focalization does not arise from transformations between story and discourse, despite the explicit statement in *Story and Discourse* that it does: "Narrative transmission concerns the relation of time of story to the recounting of time of story [. . .]: narrative voice, point of view, and the like" (1986: 22).

Let us now turn to Genette. In Genette, decisions about focalization for a whole text (what one could call macrofocalization, to distinguish it from Mieke Bal's microfocalization in individual sentences), like the choice of homo- versus heterodiegesis, most probably take their origin in the author. (Genette rejects the construct of the implied author—Genette [1988: 136–45]—which/who would be held responsible for it by theorists like Rimmon-Kenan [1983] or Nünning [1989], who replaces the implied author by what he calls level 3 of communication, N3). If focalization is rooted in authorial decisions, it has no business with the mediational process (i.e. the transmission of story into discourse) because it would be located already at the level of the plot. Note that this conclusion crucially depends on definitional choices. Thus, the discourse is here taken to be the product of the narratorial process of narration, the words on the page. As soon as one moves into a different medium such as cartoon or film, the existence of a narrator and the descrip-

---

10. Interest, renamed "interest-focus" (148–9), is now linked to the audience's attention, wishing a character "good luck" (148).

tion of the "text" as the utterance by that narrator become less convincing propositions.

Once the concept of mediation is extended to media contexts, the theoretical problems multiply exponentially. One of these problems is to what extent focalization happens in the mediational process (see above) or is superimposed *by the medium*. This is an important question in film. One can, for instance, argue that, since film is a predominantly visual medium, in which the camera serves as a focalizer, film narrative is inherently focalizing so that there exists no zero focalization in accordance with Genette's model (1980: 189–94; 1988: 121). Other theorists have argued that *all* films have external focalization since the default shot is one in which the scene is presented in an overview or bird's-eye view which does not correspond to human vision. Subjective (internal focalization) shots are rare and require some manipulation: close-up shots, shot-reverse shot, eye-level shots that unnaturally cut off objects one would usually see as part of the picture, e.g. a shot taken from the perspective of a seated person looking at people passing by that cuts off people's heads, or low-angle shots for individuals who seem overpowered by what is bearing down on them, such as children's low-angle perspectives on the adult world.[11] For film, Mieke Bal's focalization terminology is even more useful than Genette's since her distinction between focalizer and focalized allows one to contrast those shots in which the camera serves as focalizer and those in which a character focalizes events (Bal 1985). The latter are subjective shots. The waters become muddied, however, when the camera presents us with a face distorted by fear. This is clearly meant to be a subjective shot (in Bal's terms of an invisible focalized, i.e. a character's emotions), yet in the filmic medium this shot has to be visible, and it may be both the camera's presentation of a character's mind frame and the rendering of another character's impressions of the fearful person. The camera's pan from the scene as a whole to a character's internal focalization corresponds to a shift from authorial narration to free indirect discourse or interior monologue; the already subjective vision of a character focusing on the emotions depicted or reflected in another character's face corresponds to narrated perception (the observer's impression of his/her interlocutor), and this impression may be objective in the sense that the visual medium would tend to show us the face of the fearful person as he/she really looked, but it might also be subjective (unreliable) in portraying the deranged or biased vision of the observer character (I do not have an example for this; but then I am no film specialist). The zoom on the

---

11. See Chatman (1978: 158–61). Compare also his section on slant and filter in film (1990: 155–8).

character's fear-distended face would clearly mark a departure from neutral or objective camera shots, and it could be compared to an authorial or figural handling of the lens. Yet a close-up only becomes necessary in the framework of (authorial) wide-angle shots, since these do not allow the viewer to notice the expression on a character's face (too small on the screen).

It is still relatively easy to determine whether or to what extent one can find equivalents of Genette's three types of focalization or of Bal's in films or cartoons; when it comes to plays, the problems proliferate, as we will see below. Moreover, once one starts to include other types of focalization models, the theoretical issues multiply even further. For instance, when using Manfred Jahn's distinction between strict, ambient, and weak focalization (Jahn 1999), all films would presumably lie somewhere between strict and ambient, and some perspective camera-eye high-angle shots might even be regarded as weak focalization.[12] The problem with this is that it entirely casts out subjectivity, which was of course the leading motive behind the introduction of *focalization* as a term designed to improve on the concepts of *point of view* and *perspective*. Another question is: to what extent can linguistic or ideological perspective, or affect, be rendered in film, and how does one describe the combination of visual, aural, and verbal elements that might result in similar effects? (I am here thinking of suggestive music hinting at a protagonist's anxiety, or at impending danger; or of voice-over for interior monologue, usually combined with a close-up of the protagonist's face.)

Drama poses problems of a different nature. In Stanzel's paradigm (where there is no category of focalization), one simply has an immediate presentation of the story, with the admittedly unrealistic convention of the soliloquy or the aside. The audience apparently watches what is happening from their external perspective. (This description clearly leaves out questions of selection as well as the presence of metadramatic and narrative elements in drama.) If one tries to apply Genettean terminology to plays, drama would seem to have external focalization throughout (even more extensively than film), and again there is no good explanation for soliloquy (it could not easily be categorized as internal focalization). Drama therefore on the whole resembles early fiction in which the conventions allow characters to soliloquize, i.e. utter their thoughts out loud (rather than the narrative depicting their interiority in free

12. Jahn defines these terms as follows: F1 refers to the "burning point of an eye's lens" (87), F2 to the object of focalization. In *strict focalization*, "F2 is perceived from (or by) F1 under conditions of precise and restricted spatio-temporal coordinates" (97). *Ambient focalization*, on the other hand, depicts F2 "summarily, more from one side, possibly from all sides" and "allow[s] a mobile, summary, or communal point of view" (97). *Weak focalization* is weak because it dispenses with F1, and thus with "all spatio-temporal ties"; there is "only a focused object to F2" (97).

indirect discourse or psycho-narration or interior monologue). Characters cannot focalize in drama, so, within Mieke Bal's model, one has a consistent "narrator-focalizer" who focuses on the visible. I am not sure how she would deal with the soliloquies, though. Experiments in twentieth-century drama have tried to get around these genre conventions by means of a variety of techniques. Dreams and memories, in particular, are depicted on stage and externalize a subjective perspective of certain characters. Clues such as verbal repetition or a change of lighting, or simple inconsistency serve to alert the audience to a segment of memory or fantasy. (See, for instance, Tom Stoppard's *Travesties,* Sebastian Barry's *The Steward of Christendom,* and Christina Reid's *The Belle of the Belfast City*.[13]) However, these tactics are mostly used to present the contrast of a character's mind rather than their focalized perception.

The relationship between mediation and focalization is therefore fraught with complications. The most crucial of these are the variety of models of focalization and the dissensus among narratologists regarding where exactly focalization "happens" (connected with the disagreement between different narratological models). Thus, if focalization is conceived of as vision of something (as in Bal), it can become part of the plot (a character focalizing another character); on the other hand, focalization conceived of as mind-reading (zero focalization) vs. internal focalization à la Genette locates the source of this technique with the author or narrator. Since the figure of a narrator does not necessarily exist in other media (again a point of dissensus), imponderables mushroom.

One of the ways out of this dilemma is to concentrate on the discourse in one particular medium, and to discuss what strategies are employed to create spatial perspective and to transmit insights into characters' minds, or from within characters' minds on their surroundings. Such a pragmatic approach will list the function of close-ups, zooms, shot-reverse shots and so on in film to indicate interiority and subjective vision. It will also discuss dolly-shots and pans to track spatial orientations of a neutral or subjective kind. (For instance, a film in which we see a character enter a house and then get a shot of the lobby and a pan up the staircase obviously represents the character's viewpoint on entering.) In drama, such an analysis will tend to focus on gestures and soliloquy as indicators of characters' interiority, and it will note that there exists no psycho-narration (looking into characters' minds from a

---

13. All three plays are memory plays. *Travesties* (1974) focuses on Henry Carr's memories of World War I in Zürich; *The Steward of Christendom* (1995) has its protagonist Thomas Dunne re-experiencing crucial moments of his life; and in *The Belle of the Belfast City* (1987), scenes from Dolly's past help to explain attitudes and moods in the present.

quasi-extradiegetic viewpoint) in drama. (Clearly, postmodernist experiments such as David Edgar's *Entertaining Strangers* [1985], where the play sports a narrator who psychonarrates characters' minds in tandem with them [cp. Fludernik 2008: 370–71], need to be taken as exceptions to this rule.) Drama is also singularly lacking in spatial focalizing since it traditionally presents one setting from one particular perspective. Yet, again, recent experiments in dramaturgy and staging have discovered ways and means to get around these restrictions. Thus, looking into more than one space at the same time (e.g. the kitchen and Biff's bedroom in Arthur Miller's *Death of a Salesman* [1949]; or several rooms in Tennessee Williams's *Vieux Carré* [1978]) can allow the audience an "omniscient" (spatially omnipresent) viewpoint; filmic montage on a screen, on the other hand, may suggest a character's subjective view of a narrowing tunnel through which he is climbing. Nevertheless, in contrast to experiments in temporality, plot disjunction or the dissolution of the boundary between the fictional world and fantasy, such spatial manipulations are not particularly prominent in the theater.

THE NO-NARRATOR AND NO-MEDIATION THESIS

In his book *The Rhetoric of Fictionality* (2007) Richard Walsh has reiterated the controversial no-narrator thesis which had already been popularized by Ann Banfield (1982) and has recently been revived by Sylvie Patron (2005, 2009). Walsh also proposes a no-mediation thesis, although he does not call it that; that is, he rejects the idea that there is one story which is then mediated into different manifestations in novels, films, ballets, and so on. This thesis takes us right back to Barbara Herrnstein Smith (1980) and her remarks on the multiplicity of different versions of Cinderella.

I do not want to engage with the no-narrator thesis here; Walsh is applying Occam's razor even more aggressively than Genette did to rid himself of the implied author. Unlike radical no-narrator proponents, I myself have always held that there is a narrator persona when one has clear linguistic signs of a speaker's (writer's) "I" and "his"/"her" subjective deictic center (cp. Fludernik 1996: 169); authorial narrative of the *Tom Jones*ian kind with an intrusive narrator persona for me clearly has a narrator. Walsh's phrasings are perhaps too hedged to indicate clearly whether or not he regards the narrator in *Tom Jones* as legitimate *qua* narrator. (I rather think he does, despite impressions to the contrary.[14]) Like myself, Walsh clearly "repudiate[s] the

---

14. See, for instance, his remark that there may be a "local effect" narrator, who then does

narrator as a distinct narrative agent intrinsic to the structure of fiction [. . .]" (84), though perhaps for different reasons. Walsh intends to critique the notion that fictionality in fiction resides in the figure of an invented fictional speaker, the narrator, whereas I reject the obligatory narrator proposition because I need to see linguistic evidence for a speaker in the text and do not want to hypostasize the existence of a narrator for texts in which there are no such evidential markers.

Walsh's no-mediation thesis proposes that, since in his model fabula is not prior to sujet, stories in different media do not transform a common plot (story) in different ways, but that each establishes their own fabula. He goes on to argue that sujets (discourses) in different media are medium-dependent (this in agreement with most narratologists) and that (in disagreement with the narratological community) plot (fabula) is likewise medium-dependent: "The idea of representation is not intelligible without a medium" (104–5). Walsh links this theoretical insight to the fact that stories abound both as objects of analysis and as tools of sense-making:

> That is to say that, both across and within media, narrative representations are intelligible in terms of other narrative representations. Narrative sense-making always rides piggyback upon prior acts of narrative sense-making, and at the bottom of this pile is not the solid ground of truth, but only the pragmatic efficacy of particular stories for particular purposes in particular contexts. (106)

The first example that Walsh adduces for his thesis is Neil Gaiman's *Sandman* cartoon, in which the reader needs to figure out that the two characters sleeping together in the central area of the cartoon page are dreaming the sequence of images on the bottom and top of the page: "The event is a product of narrative processing, an instance of cognitive chunking in which the mind negotiates with temporal phenomena" (111). Walsh's second example comes from early film. He demonstrates convincingly that early film sequences are quite non-dramatic or plotless. His focus, however, is a film called *The Countryman and the Cinematograph* from R. W. Paul (1901), in which the naïve country person encounters a movie screen showing a train rushing towards the viewer. Since the country yokel cannot distinguish between the "space of representation" and the "space of exhibition" (125), he runs away—to the audience's amusement. In this film, the frame, as Walsh claims, corresponds to the "*concept* of the frame": "[. . .] the frame is not a representational

---

not have to be presumed to exist for the rest of the text (2007: 81).

feature of the narrative transmission, but a rhetorical feature of imaginative orientation" (126). I take it that what Walsh means to say is that what happens in that movie can only be explained in a media-related way—and hence the "plot" is actually a function of the medium.

Personally, I do not find either of these examples convincing as support for Walsh's thesis. Both rely on the conventions of the media in question, and both take the reader's perspective to be central to the question of plot. One will of course agree that in some media it may be difficult to grasp what is the plot of the narrative and that certain conventions help one to do so (clearly, the convention of the flashback requires a learning process, too); it is also true that one will need to understand at some point that a represented object is not the real thing—"This is not a pipe" (René Magritte; see Foucault 1968/1986). But such conventions of representation apply to all types of media (including non-narrative ones) and not to specific media in specific ways.

Be that as it may, in the context of an essay on mediacy, mediation, and focalization, Walsh's insights can stimulate some interesting conclusions regarding the conundra that we have been puzzling over. For one, the notion of mediacy does indeed appear to be equivalent to mediation if one sees it as a synonym for representation. The fictional world is represented, and it is most obviously represented in different medial forms: verbal (the novel or short story), performative (verbal or nonverbal, musical or non-musical—theater, ballet, opera), visual and non-performative (pictures, cartoon, film). It is now generally accepted that mediation through a storyteller occurs not only in novels but also in plays or cartoons (see Richardson 1988, 2001; Fludernik 2008; Nünning/Sommer 2008 and Schüwer 2009). Such mediation through a represented narrator persona (who is a character) is in fact a frame, and this frame may be introduced in a medium different from that of the inset—a character in film may be shown to read or verbally tell a story, a novel may describe what story a picture tells to the viewer (cp. Ryan's category 5 of her areas of remedialization—Ryan 2004: 33). This would suggest that *narration as mediacy* and *narration as mediation* overlap: one either has a definite character as a narrational agent (in language or performance or pictures or operatic music or a combination of these); or mediacy is not personalized. Non-personalized mediacy can be conceived of as mediation through a medium. Representation would then appear as either person-related and subjective (there is a teller) or as impersonal and objective (medium-related).[15]

    15. On a transmedial perspective that looks at narrative aspects common to several media, though in medium-specific manifestation, see also Rajewsky (2002, 2007) and Mahne (2007).

On the other hand, if one returns to *Towards a 'Natural' Narratology* and cognitive frames that serve as agents of mediacy, one can also regard *mediacy as medium-independent*. Besides *telling*—a frame that calls up a narrative agent and hence the figure of the narrator—*Towards a 'Natural' Narratology* also had the frames of *viewing, experiencing, reflecting,* and *action*. Each of these frames can be activated in various media, though not each one in each medium. Whereas mediacy in Stanzel or narrative transmission in Chatman is therefore constituted by mediation through a narrator (overt or covert, personalized or dissimulated), in *Towards a 'Natural' Narratology* mediacy can, but need not, rely on the presence of a narratorial agent whether explicit or implicit. *Viewing* is clearly the most basic frame for all the visual arts, but subjective camera shots and symbolic techniques can also invoke the *experiencing* frame, and some rare close-ups with voice-over not only instantiate *telling* but may even call up the *reflecting* frame. The fundamental *viewing* frame operates for the audience's experience of witnessing the fictional world on screen; however, it may also begin to overlap with the *experiencing* frame, since immersion into the filmic world occurs not only for characters' consciousness but also for the audience's spatial feeling of being inside the fictional world. *Action* of course plays a crucial role as a subsidiary element or subset to *viewing,* as it does in drama, painting, and cartoon.

No-narrator theories make perfect sense for painting and ballet; though even there one will be able to introduce the figure of a teller. The point is that a teller is an optional element in all media where the main protagonist does not function as the narrator. The *no mediation* thesis makes sense only to the extent that one treats the medium as primary so that there is no medial choice on the basis of a plot, resulting in a film, text, picture, etc. One must here be especially wary of introducing arguments from remedialization into the analysis. Remedialization can, however, point to characteristic advantages of one medium over another. It is certainly the case that, in the interest of a maximally effective narrative, the discourse in any medium is extremely selective in what it renders and how. This starts with length—a filming of a novel will always have to be shorter and therefore highly selective. The veracity of a film will focus not on reproducing the extensive dialogue from the novel in toto but on providing the "feel" of the novel, evoking the characters, the atmosphere, the mood of the text. It will introduce, say, sequences of landscape description and cloud formations in cheery or dark weather to call up the gaiety or bleakness of the characters' lives, and it may also do so simply to add a visual aesthetic quality to the film which may or may not correspond to the style of the narrative in the written version. The point of a remedialization is not necessarily a one-to-one correspondence between a plot element and a rendering of it in the original novel and the later film, but an independent play with the material of the novel, whether that material belongs to the plot or to the discourse. A good film will make use of the specific potential of the filmic medium for a particular scene or a particular effect which is part of the artistic design of the film. As a result, the plot of a filmed version of a novel will inevitably turn out to differ in part from the plot of the novel itself, though for the film to be a reasonably reliable remedialization, these plot differences need to be kept within bounds; after all, the film most often wants to be recognizable as a film version of the novel.

What this suggests theoretically is that, for any narrative token in and by itself, no mediation need be assumed; there is no separate layer of additional effects or processes added on to a prior plot that would convert a story into a medialized version of discourse. Mediacy—how the medium presents the fictional world—may be conceived of as medium-independent, though it will of course be medium-inflected in its specific manifestations. When it comes to remedialization, however, there is a prior model that orients the new version of the story, but very rarely is the remedialized version a faithful translation of the original. Like all good translation, a filming of a novel or a dramatization of a short story or a novelistic rewriting of a TV show need to concern themselves with an individual perspective and design, taking from the original only what allows them to fulfill their vision. Hence, the no-mediation theory of narrative makes as much sense as does the no-narrator theory.

CONCLUSION

In this paper I have tried to find connections between the concepts of mediacy, mediation, and focalization in the classic narratological paradigms. What the comparison has underlined is, to begin with, the dependence of all of these terms on the story/discourse dichotomy. Both Stanzel's concept of mediacy and the process of mediation in the sense of transforming deep-structural plot into a medium-related surface structure rely on the idea that im-mediate representation of story is impossible. In Stanzel's case, this is the logical consequence of his contrasting of drama and narrative; im-mediate representation supposedly exists in drama. The assumption that all narrative undergoes a transformation into medial manifestation clearly rules out im-mediacy from an axiomatic perspective. Yet again from Walsh's representational perspective, all narrative is a representation of plot or of a fictional world and hence by definition medialized. Im-mediate telling does not exist.

A second important point that emerged from the discussion is the crucial question of narratorial transmission in relation to mediacy and mediation. Stanzel's mediacy and Genette's conception of discourse as the product of a narrational act both place the (verbal) narrator and the process of telling the story at the heart of their conception of narrative transmission (to use Chatman's phrase). However, Stanzel allows for the illusion of im-mediacy and can be argued to imply the existence of a variety of mediational options (by means of telling, by means of reflecting; or by means of the three narrative situations; by means of generic molds such as the editor, the diarist, etc.). By contrast, Genette's emphasis on the narrator (overt or covert—to use Chatman's terminology) locates what in Stanzel's model would be the illusion of im-mediacy in focalizational choices in conjunction with the category of voice (internal focalization roughly corresponding to reflector-mode narrative; zero focalization to the authorial narrative situation; and the alternation of external and internal focalization typical of first-person narrative). In Genette, therefore, focalization is clearly distinct from mediacy or mediation. In privileging the act of narration, Genette's narrative transmission remains a non-medialized mediacy.

The problem of narratorial presence or absence plays an even more crucial role in discussions of mediation. Film has been the prime example of a medial narrative for narratologists. Chatman's cinematic narrator and the French term *auteur* in film studies have tended to dominate this discussion. However, as we have seen, the hypostasizing of an obligatory narratorial agent in film, drama, ballet or cartoons lacks any kind of logical or textual evidence, except perhaps in some kinds of plays, where the stage directions echo novelistic conventions of narratorial commentary (as they do in the work of George Bernard Shaw, for instance—see Fludernik 2008). A narrator figure can, as I have shown, be introduced into narratives in almost any medium; but such instances of voice-over, stage managers or cartoon-drawers depicted in the margins between cartoons are rare and tend to emphasize the fact that in these media most often there are no such teller figures. This would suggest that narratorial transmission is a specific kind of mediacy, and—as I suggested—that the medialized renderings of a fictional world can be analyzed as deploying a variety of cognitive frames in combination, though with one cognitive frame dominant over the others, depending on which medium one is dealing with.

In this essay I have also proposed that one distinguish between mediation and remedialization, since the two are often thrown together (as in the exchange between Herrnstein Smith and Chatman). The controversial questions all relate to mediation *qua* narrative transmission. Chatman's answers to Herrnstein Smith rely on the linguistic, in fact, Chomskyan, model and analogize the deep structure of transformational grammar with the story of narratives. However, this analogy is wrong. Chomsky's deep structure is grounded cognitively as a prototype of syntax; the transformations that result in the surface structure of sentences explain departures from the ground figuration. By contrast, where narrative is concerned, the transformational rules are not the point of the exercise at all; what narratologists are keen to examine is, for instance, what the chronology of a story is when the discourse turns out to be full of flashbacks and ellipses. No "rules" apply between the two levels—it is not the case that a particular chronology always gets rearranged in a specific manner; nor does it make sense to hypothesize the existence of a transformational rule to explain a flashback as A → B → C transformed into A → C → B since that very reversal of the reconstructed plot elements B and C is what the concept "flashback" already denotes. Compare the passive transformation, in which the syntactic reshuffling results in a semantic effect (active → passive). The theoretical existence of a deep structure and of transformational rules makes sense from a methodological perspective where syntax is concerned, but it does not clarify issues in the same way for narrative or narratology. As in Genette's category of *voice*, the deep and surface structure model in narrative uses a *metaphor* in order to talk about patent versus latent structure, for instance in relation to chronology or order.

One can take these arguments a step further by exploding the notion of focalization as a process that occurs between the deep and surface structure. As I demonstrated in the section on Mediation and Focalization above, even Chatman himself vacillated on the issue and seems to have ended by adopting a theory that locates point of view independently on the narratorial and plot levels. While it makes sense to reconstruct a chronology in interpreting texts that deliberately disguise that order of events, one cannot convincingly argue that the plot inherently has no focalization. At best it could have zero or external focalization, which might then be shifted into internal focalization in some passages. The problem is that if one defines focalization as access to interiority, then the deep structure of the story would simply be the bare plot sequence without any stylistic elements and human details (*The king died and then the queen died*). By adding "of grief" we already add not just the cause of the queen's dying but the experiential parameters of the story, and then the discourse can only be said to elaborate (rather than add) aspects like focalization, description, dialogue, etc. If, on the other hand, focalization is defined as "who sees," the plot must be a neutral version in which nobody sees and the discourse would add who is doing some seeing. This is of course how focalization and Stanzel's mediacy have traditionally been understood. Yet the point of this seeing is not whether (factually) a character was there to see and note an occurrence; the point is whether the narrative "sees through the mind" of a character or whether there is evaluative slant (Chatman) on the story world. The decision taken in narrative mimesis is therefore that *from which perspective* the telling or representation is to be modulated, which takes us right back to the question of mediacy, i.e. whether we are to be presented the fictional world through the voice of a narrator or character (in Walsh's view, a narrator would be a character) or through the consciousness or filter of one (or several) characters (in succession). In this case, focalization and mediacy would collapse into one another, as they do in Stanzel.

One final point on this issue. All of these discussions assume that one can indeed establish a chronology and a realistic, consistent fictional world "out there." Although readers will expect to find such a world, experimental texts may deliberately foil their attempts to establish it. Nevertheless, technically innovative texts frequently do include, for instance, passages of internal focalization. Yet, since in these texts there is no determinable deep structure on which to apply focalizational transformations, the existence of such focalized passages must then be laid at the door of the author (reader, note, this is tongue-in-cheek!), and an analysis in terms of mediation and transmission desisted from. We will take the foregoing argument as yet another piece of support of the Walshian no-mediation thesis.

What we have been struggling with is the incompatibility of axiomatic narratological assumptions. The problems discussed in this paper are perhaps quite arcane; to raise them may—metaphorically speaking—reflect nothing but narratologists' inevitable critical urge to read metaphors literally, which puts them in danger of drowning in the theoretical waves that they have provoked.

REFERENCES

Bal, Mieke (1985) *Narratology: Introduction to the Field of Narrative.* Trans. Christine von Boheemen. Toronto: University of Toronto Press.
Banfield, Ann (1982) *Unspeakable Sentences. Narration and Representation in the Language of Fiction.* Boston: Routledge & Kegan Paul.
Barry, Sebastian (1997) *The Steward of Christendom* [1995]. London: Methuen.
Booth, Wayne C. (1983) *The Rhetoric of Fiction* [1961]. Chicago/London: Chicago University Press.
Carter, Angela (1973) *The Bloody Chamber and Other Stories.* London: Gallancz.
Chatman, Seymour (1981) "Critical Response. V. Reply to Barbara Herrnstein Smith." *Critical Inquiry* 7.4: 802–9.
―――― (1986) *Story and Discourse: Narrative Structure in Fiction and Film* [1978]. Ithaca, NY: Cornell University Press.
―――― (1990) *Coming to Terms: The Rhetoric of Narrative in Fiction and Film.* Ithaca, NY: Cornell University Press.
Cohn, Dorrit (1981) "The Encirclement of Narrative: On Franz Stanzel's *Theorie des Erzählens.*" *Poetics Today* 2.2: 157–82.
Eichenbaum, Boris (1965) "The Theory of the Formal Method" [1927]. *Russian Formalist Criticism. Four Essays.* Trans. and intro. Lee T. Lemon and Marion J. Reis. Lincoln: University of Nebraska Press. 99–139.
Erlich, Victor (1965) *Russian Formalism: History—Doctrine.* 2nd rev. ed. The Hague: Mouton.
Fludernik, Monika (1993) *The Fictions of Language and the Languages of Fiction: The Linguistic Representation of Speech and Consciousness.* London/New York: Routledge.
―――― (1994) "Second-Person Narrative As a Test Case for Narratology: The Limits of Realism." *Style* 28.3: 445–79.
―――― (1996) *Towards a 'Natural' Narratology.* London/New York: Routledge.
―――― (2008) "Narrative and Drama." *Theorizing Narrativity.* Narratologia, 12. Ed. John Pier and José Ángel García Landa. Berlin: de Gruyter. 355–83.
Foucault, Michel (1986) *Ceci n'est pas une pipe* [1968]. Ill. René Magritte. Montpellier: Fata Morgana.
Friedemann, Käte (1965) *Die Rolle des Erzählers in der Epik* [1910]. Darmstadt: Wissenschaftliche Buchgesellschaft.
Forster, E. M. (1990) *Aspects of the Novel* [1927]. London: Edward Arnold.
Genette, Gérard (1980) *Narrative Discourse: An Essay in Method [Discours du récit,* 1972]. Trans. Jane E. Lewin. Ithaca, NY: Cornell University Press.
―――― (1988) *Narrative Discourse Revisited [Nouveau discours du récit,* 1983]. Trans. Jane E. Lewin. Ithaca, NY: Cornell University Press.
Hamburger, Käte (1993) *The Logic of Literature* [1957]. Trans. M. J. Rose. 2nd rev. ed. Bloomington: Indiana University Press.
Hutcheon, Linda (2006) *A Theory of Adaptation.* New York: Routledge.
Jahn, Manfred (1999) "More Aspects of Focalization: Refinements and Applications." *Recent Trends in Narratological Research. Papers From the Narratology Round Table, ESSE 4, September 1997, Debrecen, Hungary. GRAAT,* 21. Ed. John Pier. Tours: University of Tours. 85–110.

James, Henry (1934) *The Art of the Novel: Critical Prefaces.* Intro. Richard P. Blackmur. New York/London: Scribner's.

Korte, Barbara (1985) "Tiefen- und Oberflächenstrukturen in der Narrativik." *Literatur in Wissenschaft und Unterricht* 18: 331-52.

Mahne, Nicole (2007) *Transmediale Erzähltheorie. Eine Einführung.* Göttingen: Vandenhoeck & Ruprecht.

Müller, Günther (1948) "Erzählzeit und erzählte Zeit." *Festschrift für P. Kluckhohn und H. Schneider. Gewidmet zu ihrem 60. Geburtstag.* Ed. by his students from Tübingen. Tübingen: Mohr. 195-212.

Nünning, Ansgar (1989) *Grundzüge eines kommunikationstheoretischen Modells der erzählerischen Vermittlung. Die Funktionen der Erzählinstanz in den Romanen George Eliots.* Horizonte, 2. Trier: Wissenschaftlicher Verlag Trier.

Nünning, Ansgar, and Roy Sommer (2008) "Diegetic and Mimetic Narrativity: Some Further Steps Towards a Transgeneric Narratology of Drama." *Theorizing Narrativity.* Narratologia, 12. Ed. John Pier and José Ángel Garcia Landa. Berlin/New York: de Gruyter. 331-53.

Patron, Sylvie (2005) "Le narrateur et l'interprétation des termes déictiques dans le récit de fiction." *De l'énoncé à l'énonciation et vice-versa. Regards multidisciplinaires sur la deixis. From Utterance to Uttering and Vice-Versa. Multidisciplinary Views on Deixis.* Eds. Daniele Monticelli, Renate Pajusalu, and Anu Treikelder. Tartu: Tartu University Press. 187-202.

—— (2009) *Le narrateur. Introduction à la théorie narrative.* Paris: Armand Colin.

Petsch, Robert (1934) *Wesen und Formen der Erzählkunst.* Halle/Saale : Niemeyer.

Pfister, Manfred (1991) *The Theory and Analysis of Drama* [*Das Drama,* 1977]. Trans. John Halliday. Cambridge: Cambridge University Press.

Prince, Gerald (1982) *Narratology: The Form and Functioning of Narrative.* Berlin: Mouton.

—— (2008) "Narrativity, Narrativehood, Narrativeness." *Theorizing Narrativity.* Narratologia, 12. Ed. John Pier and José Ángel García Landa. Berlin: de Gruyter. 19-28.

Rajewsky, Irina O. (2002) *Intermedialität.* Tübingen: Francke.

—— (2007) "Von Erzählen, die (nichts) vermitteln: Überlegungen zu grundlegenden Annahmen der Dramentheorie im Kontext einer Transmedialen Narratologie." *Zeitschrift für französishe Sprache und Literatur* 117: 25-68.

Reid, Christina (1987) "The Belle of the Belfast City." *Plays 1.* London: Methuen. 177-250

Richardson, Brian (1988) "Point of View in Drama: Diegetic Monologue, Unreliable Narrators, and the Author's Voice on Stage." *Comparative Drama* 22.3: 193-214.

—— (2001) "Construing Conrad's *The Secret Sharer:* Suppressed Narratives, Subaltern Reception, and the Act of Interpretation." *Studies in the Novel* 33.3: 306-21.

Ricoeur, Paul (1984-88) *Time and Narrative.* Vols. I-III. Chicago: University of Chicago Press.

Rimmon-Kenan, Shlomith (1983) *Narrative Fiction. Contemporary Poetics.* New Accents. London: Methuen.

Ryan, Marie-Laure (2004) Ed. *Narrative Across Media: The Language of Storytelling.* Lincoln: University of Nebraska Press.

Schmid, Wolf (2005) *Elemente der Narratologie.* Narratologia, 8. Berlin: de Gruyter.

Schüwer, Martin (2009) *Wie Comics erzählen. Grundriss einer intermedialen Erzähltheorie der grafischen Literatur.* Trier: WVT.
Shklovsky, Victor (1965) "Sterne's *Tristram Shandy*: Stylistic Commentary" [1921]. *Russian Formalist Criticism. Four Essays.* Trans. & Intro. Lee T. Lemon and Marion J. Reis. Lincoln: University of Nebraska Press. 25–57.
Smith, Barbara Herrnstein (1980) "Afterthoughts on Narrative. III. Narrative Versions, Narrative Theories." *Critical Inquiry* 7.1: 213–36.
—— (1983) *On the Margins of Discourse. The Relation of Literature to Language* [1978]. Chicago: The University of Chicago Press.
Spielhagen, Friedrich (1883) *Beiträge zur Theorie und Technik des Romans.* Leipzig: Staackmann.
Stanzel, Franz Karl (1969) *Die typischen Erzählsituationen im Roman. Dargestellt an Tom Jones, Moby-Dick, The Ambassadors, Ulysses u.a.* [1955]. Wien: Braumüller.
—— (1984) *A Theory of Narrative* [*Theorie des Erzählens*, 1979]. Trans. Charlotte Goedsche. Cambridge: Cambridge University Press.
—— (1971) *Narrative Situations in the Novel. Tom Jones, Moby-Dick, The Ambassadors, Ulysses.* Trans. James Pusack. Bloomington: Indiana University Press.
Stoppard, Tom (1975) *Travesties* [1974]. London: Faber & Faber.
Veyne, Paul (1971) *Comment on écrit l'histoire: essai d'épistémologie.* Paris: Seuil.
Walsh, Richard (2001) "Fabula and Fictionality in Narrative Theory." *Style* 35.4: 592–606.
—— (2007) *The Rhetoric of Fictionality. Narrative Theory and the Idea of Fiction.* Columbus: The Ohio State University Press.
Wenzel, Peter (2004) *Einführung in die Erzähltextanalyse. Kategorien, Modelle, Probleme.* Trier: Wissenschaftlicher Verlag Trier.
White, Hayden (1981) "The Value of Narrativity in the Representation of Reality." *On Narrative.* Ed. W.J.T. Mitchell. Chicago: Chicago University Press. 1–23.

II

Transdisciplinarities

5

DAVID HERMAN

Directions in Cognitive Narratology

Triangulating Stories, Media, and the Mind

TOOLS FOR TRIANGULATION

Writing in 1991, on the brink of what Alan Richardson and Francis Steen (2002) subsequently termed "the cognitive revolution" in literary research, Mark Turner presciently argued in his book *Reading Minds* that English studies needs to set itself new goals in the age of cognitive science. Specifically, Turner suggested that "[o]ur profession touches home base when it contributes to the systematic inquiry into [. . .] linguistic and literary acts as acts of the human mind" (18). To quote Turner more fully:

> I propose that what the profession lacks is a concept of language and literature as acts of the everyday human mind. If we had such a concept, our grounding activity would be the study of language and of literature as expressions of our conceptual apparatus. We would focus on how the embodied human mind uses its ordinary conceptual capacities to perform those acts of language and literature. (6)

In this groundbreaking, agenda-setting contribution to the field, Turner draws on ideas from cognitive linguistics to triangulate literary scholarship with the study of language and of mind. Working against the grain of what he characterizes as default assumptions in the humanities in general and literary studies in particular, Turner suggests that practitioners should shift from producing ever more sophisticated readings of individual works, to developing an account of the basic and general principles underlying the process of reading itself. Cognitive linguistics, Turner argues, affords invaluable tools when it comes to this reprioritizing of reading over readings. At issue is a reassessment that places systematicity over nuance; common, everyday cognitive abilities over ostensibly unique or special capacities bound up with literary expression; and unconscious sense-making operations over what falls within the (narrow) domain of conscious awareness. Thus Turner draws on the work of theorists like George Lakoff and Mark Johnson (1980) to describe poetic scenes and figures as a skillful exploitation of generic, cognitively based linguistic abilities, rather than as a special, separate form of verbal creativity limited to literary writing. Likewise, Talmy's (2000) account of force dynamics (409–70)—his theory of how the semantic structures of natural language encode a folk physics of force, movement, friction, etc.—helps Turner build a cognitive-linguistic framework for understanding the rhetoric of argument. Ways of understanding arguments, Turner suggests, are grounded in embodied human experience; for example, arguments are defined in terms of positions and counter-positions that must be resisted and overcome, in parallel with how a swimmer must fight against the current or a runner is buffeted by countervailing winds.

This essay revisits the project of triangulation envisioned in—and programmatically articulated by—Turner's study more than fifteen years ago. In one respect, the scope of my discussion will be more restricted than Turner's, since I am examining not literature in general but rather literary narrative in particular, as exemplified in William Blake's short narrative poem "A Poison Tree." My discussion, however, focuses on Blake's text as a specific realization of what might be called the narrative system. At issue is narrative viewed as a representational system that operates across various communicative media (Herman 2004, 2009, and 2010; Ryan 2004; Wolf 2003), including print texts, film, face-to-face discourse, graphic novels, and so on, and that enables people to use those media in particular ways to structure, express, and comprehend their experiences.[1] Thus the focus of the research program

---

1. In other studies (Herman 2009, 2010), I propose a general framework for analyzing multimodal storytelling, or forms of narrative practice that exploit more than one semiotic channel to represent situations, objects, and events in narrated worlds or *storyworlds* (see below for a fuller characterization of this term). These other studies suggest the relevance of the distinction that theorists like Kress and van Leeuwen (2001) draw between *modes* and *media*. For such researchers, modes are semiotic channels (better, environments) that can be viewed as a resource for designing representations within a particular type of discourse, which is in turn embedded in a specific kind of communicative interaction. By contrast, media can be viewed as means for disseminating or (re)producing what has been designed in a given mode. In this essay, though I will refer to narrative/storytelling media in my discussion of Blake's combination of verbal and visual designs in "A Poison Tree," this poem and Blake's oeuvre more generally

from which the present essay derives is in another respect broader than the one outlined by Turner. My overall research goal—a goal that indicates the scope of *cognitive narratology,* broadly conceived—is to triangulate not just literary narratives, theories of language, and research on the mind, but more capaciously, to inquire into (1) the structure and dynamics of storytelling practices; (2) the multiple semiotic systems in which those practices take shape, including but not limited to verbal language; and (3) mind-relevant dimensions of the practices themselves—as they play out in a given medium for storytelling.

In the account sketched here, cognitive narratology can be viewed as a subdomain of the broader enterprise of cognitive semiotics (cf. Brandt 2004; Fastrez 2003); cognitive linguistics also belongs to this broader domain.[2] Cognitive semiotics studies how the use and interpretation of sign-systems of all sorts are grounded in the structure, capacities, and dispositions of embodied minds. Cognitive narratology studies the design principles for narratively organized sign-systems in particular. Drawing on tools from a variety of fields, including (cognitive) linguistics, ethnography, the philosophy of mind, and social and cognitive psychology, cognitive narratology explores the interfaces among narrative structure, semiotic media, and humans' cognitive dispositions and abilities. Hence my aim here is to suggest a range of strategies for triangulating narrative, media, and minds—strategies not necessarily anchored in the traditions for studying verbal language that factor most prominently in Turner's pioneering book.

In the pages that follow, I use as a case study Blake's "A Poison Tree," first published in 1794 as part of *Songs of Innocence and Experience,* to discuss several research foci that fall within the scope of cognitive narratology. These foci correspond to areas of intersection among the three key concerns of this essay, namely, storytelling practices, communicative media, and the mind:

- Research on the cognitive processes that support inferences about the structure and inhabitants of a narrated world, or *storyworld;* relatedly, the study of what constitutes (across media) distinctively narrative ways of worldmaking (Gerrig 1993; Goodman 1978; Herman 2009: 105–36).

- Studies of how narratives can stage discourse practices in storyworlds—

---

exemplify multimodal narration in the sense just indicated.
2. Hence, in contrast with Turner's (1991, 1996) general approach, in the approach developed here cognitive linguistics constitutes not the sole basis for triangulating narrative, media, and mind, but only one toolkit (or group of toolkits) among others.

where discourse is defined as the rule-based manipulation of symbols (verbal, visual, or other) in multiparty contexts of talk. At issue is how stories reflexively model cognitive, interactional, and other dimensions of acts of narration along with other forms of communicative practice. Under this heading I subsume questions about how narratives like Blake's present folk theories of discourse, how they mobilize emotion discourse in particular, and how their representation of acts of discourse positions characters and readers in various ways.

- Research on the nexus of narrative and consciousness. One pertinent question in this connection is how stories represent the felt, conscious awareness of narrators as well as characters—what philosophers of mind might refer to as the "what-it's-like" dimension of conscious experiences (Nagel 1974). A second key question is the extent to which narrative might afford scaffolding for conscious experience itself (Herman 2009: 137–60).

My next section provides further context for analyzing "A Poison Tree" as a case study, situating my approach in some of the commentary that has grown up around Blake's work. Indeed, I have chosen Blake's poem as a test case in part because Blake's own poetic practices resonate with the later frameworks for inquiry explored here; texts like "A Poison Tree" suggest that Blake himself was deeply concerned with developing new ways of understanding the relationships among modes of narration, storytelling media, and the human mind. Then, in the remainder of my essay, I turn to the research foci just listed, putting them into dialogue with the poem to extend the project of triangulation already anticipated in Blake's work. I conclude with some reflections on what my analysis suggests about future directions—and outstanding challenges—for narrative inquiry today.

THE CASE STUDY
William Blake's "A Poison Tree"

As Phillips (2000) notes, Blake invented in 1788 a method of creating and reproducing word-image combinations that he called "Illuminated Printing," and that subsequent commentators have termed "relief etching": "It was composed of writing and drawing on a copper plate using an acid-resistant varnish, etching the unprotected surfaces away leaving both text and design standing in relief, and then inking and printing the relief surfaces on

a printmaker's rolling press" (15; see Essick 1985 and Viscomi 2003 for further details about Blake's techniques). This method, which Blake may have adopted in part because it entailed about one-fourth of the cost of engraving (Mitchell 1978: 42), was used to create the version of "A Poison Tree" whose image is reproduced above.[3] I also provide a verbal transcription of Blake's text.

3. From Copy C of *Songs of Innocence and Experience*. Lessing J. Rosenwald Collection, Library of Congress. Copyright (c) 2009 the William Blake Archive. Used with permission.

I was angry with my friend;
I told my wrath, my wrath did end.
I was angry with my foe;
I told it not, my wrath did grow.

And I waterd it in fears, 5
Night & morning with my tears:
And I sunned it with smiles,
And with soft deceitful wiles.

And it grew both day and night,
Till it bore an apple bright. 10
And my foe beheld it shine,
And he knew that it was mine,

And into my garden stole,
When the night had veild the pole;
In the morning glad I see: 15
My foe outstretchd beneath the tree.

It is important to stress that the version of the poem reproduced here is just one realization of Blake's original design. As Gleckner and Greenberg (1989) observe, "Blake printed and individually hand colored *Songs of Innocence* and *Songs of Innocence and Experience* from 1789 to 1818. Twenty-one copies of *Innocence* and twenty-eight of the combined work are known to exist. No two are alike, Blake having altered his coloring more often than not, his arrangement, and even certain aspects of the plates' iconography from copy to copy" (xii; cf. Essick 1985: 883; Viscomi 2003).[4]

    4. For example, in the existing copies of the first issue of *Songs of Experience*, two different color schemes are used for "A Poison Tree" (Phillips 2000: 104), and in "the twenty-eight extant copies of the combined volume, Blake offers nineteen different arrangements of the poems" (Gleckner and Greenberg 1989: xiv; xv). Though I will not comment further on the production methods used to create "A Poison Tree," nor on the design considerations affecting its placement among the other poems in *Songs of Innocence and Experience*, Blake's manifest concern with these issues warrants equal care when it comes to examining the interplay between the verbal and visual elements of his work. As Mitchell puts it, "The free interpenetration of pictorial and typographic form so characteristic of Blake's books is technically impossible in a medium which separates the work of the printer from that of the engraver [. . .] In one sense, then, there is almost something perverse about discussing the 'relations' between the constituent parts of an art form which is so obviously unified in both conception and execution" (1978: 15).

What interpretive traditions have grown up around this poem in particular and around Blake's multimodal poetic practices more generally? And how can those traditions be used to underscore the relevance of "A Poison Tree" for the project of triangulating narrative, media, and mind? For his part, Gallagher (1977) considers whether "A Poison Tree" should be read as a parabolic poem, in which the specific scenario presented in the poem (the vehicle) is subordinated to the general theme or moral principle it is designed to instantiate (the tenor). As Gallagher puts it, "in a narrative whose tenor ([the idea] that deliberate repression of anger is far more destructive than its spontaneous expression) is a deceptively obvious cliché, it is all too easy to dismiss the poetic vehicle (a poison tree) as merely a convenient parable construed allegorically for the sake of articulating the moral which can be drawn from it" (237). For Gallagher, however, interpreting Blake's text as merely a parable amounts to underreading the poem, and more specifically failing to come to terms with "the astonishing allegation that *anger can become literally incarnate as a physical object* (a poison tree can be made to materialize out of thin air)" (237).[5] Gallagher instead construes the poem as a dark parody of the account of the fall stemming from the Book of Genesis, with a self-deifying narrator playing the role of an angry, punitive God in a sinister version of the creation myth (247–48).

Furthermore, Gallagher draws attention to the final couplet of Blake's poem (lines 15–16), with its shift to the present tense via the verb *see* ("In the morning glad I see: / My foe outstretchd beneath the tree"). Although, as I discuss below, *see* could be glossed as an instance of the historical present tense, designed to underscore the special significance of the narrator's past act of looking vis-à-vis the other events recounted in the poem, for Gallagher the poet's shift of tenses accentuates the ongoing impact of events on the narrator's mind:

> Although the shift can be interpreted as necessitated by the demands of rhyme, Blake would hardly compromise sense merely for the sake of sound. The meaning of the poem's concluding couplet is clear: a single past act (the murder of the narrator's foe) brings about an effect which has decisive

---

5. Here Gallagher (cf. Welch 1995: 243–44) distinguishes Blake's poison tree from the more properly allegorical representation of another tree in *Songs of Experience*, namely, the Tree of Mystery in "The Human Abstract" ("The Gods of the earth and sea/ Sought thro' Nature to find this Tree;/ But their search was all in vain:/ There grows one in the Human Brain" [lines 21–24].) In contrast to this figurative usage, "Blake's poison tree is no metaphor: it is rather the physical instrument by which the narrator allegedly effects his enemy's death" (242).

reverberations in the eternal present: in the morning—any morning, every morning—I see my foe *now* dead beneath the tree. This is precisely true of original sin, for in Adam's mortal transgression all men have already died. (Gallagher 1977: 248)

This interpretation emphasizes the continuing legacy of the narrator's world-disrupting (or world-corrupting) actions—in this case, his act of choosing not to tell someone (who thereby became his foe) about his wrathful feelings toward that person or his reasons for having such feelings.[6] The interpretation also highlights the world-configuring power of the narrator's remembering/perceiving mind. Visually re-mediating the narrator's verbal report of his own act of seeing,[7] the design of the text foregrounds this moment to suggest that the most destructive of the narrator's acts are acts of mind—including the act of gladly seeing the death of someone whom the narrator has himself (through yet another act of mind) transformed into a foe.

The poem thus supports Mitchell's (1978) claim that in Blake's images, "[p]ictorial space does not exist as a uniform, visually perceived container of forms, but rather as a kind of extension of the consciousness of the human figures it contains" (38; cf. Connolly 2002: 26). Reacting against Newton's conception of space as a pre-existing container in which material bodies are impinged upon by physical forces (Ault 1986: 163–69; Hagstrum 1991: 76–77; Peterfreund 1998: 54), Blake instead emphasizes the active, form-giving operations of embodied minds as they configure spaces into scenes organized around particular, situated perspectives. Or, as Mitchell puts it, "[t]he essential unity of Blake's composite art [. . .] lies in the convergence of each form [verbal as

---

6. Although Blake's phrasing might be read as suggesting that the two persons mentioned in the first stanza of the poem were already the narrator's friend and his foe before he ever discussed or refrained from discussing with them his wrathful feelings, and that these prior relationships are thus simply a premise of the narrative, I would resist this interpretation. Instead, I construe the poem as developing a genealogy of the very concept of "foe," by tracing the destructive consequences of not engaging in open discourse with others when conflicts first arise. In accordance with this interpretation, I read the first stanza as an instance of the trope of hysteron proteron, in which later events are mentioned before earlier ones, and which in this case is motivated by the poem's sparse verbal style and the constraint imposed by its use of end rhymes. On this reading, the narrator mentions the effects of his own past conduct—namely, someone's being categorized, or constituted, as a friend or a foe—before he mentions the conduct that caused these effects—namely, engaging or not engaging in open talk with others when a conflict arises.

7. Mitchell (1978), however, argues that "in contrast to the general practice of eighteenth-century illustrators," Blake's method "is to provide not a plausible visualization of a scene described in the text but rather a symbolic recreation of ideas embodied in that scene" (18). The relationship of the image track to the verbal track in Blake is thus one of transformation rather than translation (19).

well as visual] upon the goal of affirming the centrality of the human form (as consciousness or imagination in the poetry, as body in the paintings) in the structure of reality" (1978: 38). In the case of "A Poison Tree" consciousness and body converge in precisely this way, with the verbal and visual information tracks jointly foregrounding the destructiveness for self and other of a specific way of seeing. The poem's visual design bears out Mitchell's diagnosis of Blake's pictorial style, which involves not the projection of "inner," mental realities onto an "outer," material world, in proto-expressivist fashion, but rather an emphasis on "the continuity and interplay between body and space, as a symbol of the dialectic between consciousness and its objects" (59). Note, for example, how the lower branches of the poison tree, i.e., the branches constituting the lower border of the verbal text, echo the curve of the supine figure's ribcage and also have the same span as the dead foe's outstretched arms. Here the observing consciousness, from whose vantage-point on the represented world the image can be assumed to emanate, construes the spatial layout of that world as conditioned by the human form's situation within it— even as that observing mind's representation is shaped by its own, situated perspective, including its position in time and space vis-à-vis the scene portrayed.

As these last remarks suggest, beyond figuring a dialectic between consciousness and its objects, mind and world, Blake's text suggests that storytelling practices mediate between these two poles—and do so by projecting, through various semiotic channels (and combinations of channels), worlds inhabited by embodied minds. In what follows, I put Blake's own narrative practice into dialogue with recent research that suggests strategies for triangulating—modeling the relations among—stories, media, and the mind. This research can shed new light on Blake's work; but more than this, considering how the research bears on "A Poison Tree" can help chart new directions for cognitive narratology as a theory-building enterprise.

NARRATIVE WAYS OF WORLDMAKING

Tools for triangulation have been developed by theorists who describe language use as a process of building mental models of the discourse entities evoked by verbal cues, including those deployed by literary authors (see, e.g., Clark 1996; Zwaan 1996). Recently, scholars of story have built on this and related work to characterize the mental models used to parse texts, discourses, and other kinds of representations that are narratively organized (see, e.g., Doležel 1998; Emmott 1997; Gerrig 1993; Herman 2002, 2009; Pavel 1986; Ryan 1991; Werth 1999).

Classical, structuralist narratologists failed to come to terms with the referential or world-creating properties of narrative, partly because of the exclusion of the referent in favor of signifier and signified in the Saussurean language theory that informed the structuralists' approach. Yet mapping words onto worlds is arguably a fundamental—perhaps *the* fundamental—requirement for narrative sense making. The question is how readers of print texts, interlocutors in face-to-face discourse, viewers of films, and interpreters of other kinds of narratives use textual cues to build up representations of the worlds evoked by stories, or storyworlds.[8] Approaches such as deictic shift theory (Duchan, Bruder, and Hewitt 1995), text world theory (Werth 1999), and contextual frame theory (Emmott 1997) suggest how configuring narrative worlds entails mapping discourse cues onto the WHAT, WHERE, and WHEN dimensions of mentally projected narrative worlds. In the present section I draw on this work to explore the range of cognitive processes that support inferences about the modal status, inhabitants, and spatiotemporal profile of storyworlds like Blake's.

The storyworld of "A Poison Tree" features a relatively limited constellation of persons, non-human entities, and states of affairs: the narrator, a friend, and a foe; a real or imagined conflict of some kind; an iteratively narrated passage of time which follows the conflict and during which the narrator experiences a range of emotions (notably, fear and sadness), and strategically adopts a variety of behaviors and dispositions (smiles but also wiles); a garden, tree, and apple intertextually linked to their counterparts in the story of the fall; and a final glimpse by the narrator of the foe lying outstretched and presumably dead beneath the tree. This stripped-down ontology—together with the way Blake has populated it with situations, objects, and events imported from a religious master narrative about the irruption of sin in paradise and the resulting loss of innocence—contributes to the poem's parable-like quality. As already noted, Gallagher (1977) disputes any narrow interpretation of "A Poison Tree" as a parable, in which poetic vehicle is wholly subordinated to thematic tenor. More broadly, however, interpretation of the poem activates inferencing strategies that Turner (1996) associates with fundamental mechanisms of human intelligence and subsumes under the heading of *parabolic projection,* or the projection of a source story onto a

---

8. Hence, as discussed in Herman (2002: 9–22), the notion *storyworld* is consonant with a range of other concepts proposed by cognitive psychologists, discourse analysts, psycholinguists, philosophers of language, and others concerned with how people make sense of texts or discourses. Like *storyworld*, these other notions—including *deictic center, mental model, situation model, discourse model, contextual frame,* and *possible world*—are designed to explain how interpreters rely on inferences triggered by textual cues to build up representations of the overall situation or world evoked but not necessarily explicitly described in the discourse.

target story—as when the story of someone's death from a protracted illness is framed as a narrative of struggle with a murderous agent. In this account, making sense of one story in terms of another (e.g., reading "A Poison Tree" vis-à-vis accounts of the fall) is a basic and general principle of mind that supports all forms of narrative worldmaking, rather than a processing strategy limited to a particular literary genre.

In any case, a focus on narrative ways of worldmaking underscores the need to consider how the WHAT dimension of a given storyworld interacts with the dimensions of WHERE and WHEN. Along these lines, deictic shift theory seeks to illuminate the cognitive reorientation required to take up imaginary residence in a narrative world like Blake's. This theory holds that a "location within the world of the narrative serves as the center from which [sentences with deictic expressions such as *here* and *now*] are interpreted" (Segal 1995: 15), and that to access this location readers must shift "from the environmental situation in which the text is encountered, to a locus within a mental model representing the world of the discourse" (15). The theory also suggests that over longer, more sustained experiences of narrative worlds, interpreters may need to make successive adjustments in their position relative to the situations and events being recounted—as prompted by the blueprint for world building included in the narrative's verbal texture. To make sense of Blake's poem, readers have to track these shifts in orienting vantage-points in order to update their emergent models of the unfolding storyworld as a whole. For example, in the poem's verbal track there is a shift from the speaker's perspective on events, which dominates the account, to the foe's vantage-point beginning with line 11, and then a shift back to the speaker's in the final two lines. (Line 14 is a different case: it is not clear whose cognitive vantage-point orients the report about the state of this storyworld "when the night had veild the pole.") Temporally speaking, Blake's use of the past tense in lines 1–14 prompts the inference that the younger, experiencing I encountered the foe, nourished the poison tree, and so forth at some time earlier than the present moment of narration by the older, narrating I.

Yet here Blake's management of verb tenses complicates the world-building process. Having initially used the past tense to situate the narrated events in a time-frame earlier than the present moment of speaking, in line 15 the narrating I switches to the present tense. Not only does this tense shift reinforce that the glimpse of the dead foe is an especially salient event;[9] what is more, use of the present tense also creates a context in which aspects of the

---

9. For perspectives on the role of tense shifts in narrative, see Johnstone (1987); Schiffrin (1981); and Wolfson (1982).

current moment of telling can be elided with past occurrences. The morphology of English verbs does not distinguish between the simple present and the historical present; rather, discourse context must be used to determine which functional interpretation of the tense marking is preferable. Blake's narrative exploits this feature of the language—i.e., the way English present-tense verbs can both signify the here and now and presentify what is past—to construct the foe's death less as a localized incident than as complex event-structure distributed across time(s) (cf. Herman 2007: 320–21). In other words, the narrator's shift to the present tense promotes polychrony (Herman 2002: 211–61), or the situation of events at multiple points in time, with the figurative, historical-present reading of *"see"* locating the narrator's perceptual act in the past and the literal interpretation of *"see"* anchoring that act in the current moment of narration—and potentially in all moments that have led up to and will extend beyond the present. True, the first part of line 15, with its mention of a particular morning, would seem to favor the historical-present reading of the tense shift. But the strategic placement of *"see"* in the poem's final couplet, and the possibility of interpreting *"the morning"* as a generic reference to any morning (Gallagher 1977), licenses an alternative reading of the narrator's perceptual act as co-occurrent with the act of narration.

Blake's representation of this same pregnant moment in the visual design contributes to the temporal unmooring of the foe's demise. The represented scene visually presides over or dominates the entire time-span covered by the poem's sixteen lines; the branches of the poison tree not only stretch over the full extent of the foe's supine body but also encompass the whole of the text. And again, the placement of the image after the conclusion of the poem suggests that the effects of this death, rather than being encapsulated within the current speech event as a past moment recounted by the narrator, flows forward, ongoingly, into the future.[10] In short, in concert with its tense patterning, the visual design of the poem inhibits knowledge about the position of events along the timeline stretching from past to present to future—from the experiencing I to the narrating I and beyond. Attempts to parse the temporal logic of the text generate an unresolvable question: exactly where along the narrative timeline can the narrator's perception of—or affective response to—the death of the foe be situated?

Emmott's (1997) contextual frame theory provides other tools for characterizing how Blake's text sets into play narrative ways of worldmaking,

---

10. Here it is worth re-emphasizing how the verbal component of the text is intertwined with the branches of the tree that bore the poison apple as fruit. Thus, taken as a verbal-visual complex, the poem metaleptically suggests that the language used to recount these events is itself the fruit of the destructive discord rooted in the storyworld.

and in doing so invites exploration of the interfaces of narrative, media, and mind. Emmott's model is premised on the assumption that readers of narratives like "A Poison Tree" use semiotic cues to bind characters into and out of particular contexts (that is, mentally modeled environments for being and doing), and that these contexts will be distributed spatially as well as temporally over the course of a narrative. Once characters and other elements have been integrated into contextual frames, readers of print texts can use those frames to disambiguate pronouns that refer to different discourse entities at various points in the narration. Thus, the friend is bound out of what Emmott would call the primed contextual frame after line 2, whereas the foe is bound into the frame with an initial mention in line 3, and line 4 binds in the speaker's wrath as well. The pronoun "*it*" in lines 5, 7, and 9 refers back to this entity, or rather psychological state, whereas the binding in of the apple in line 10 allows readers to parse the same pronoun ("*it*") differently when it occurs in lines 11 and 12. From this perspective, more generally, narrative worldmaking can be analyzed as a process of mentally configuring contexts, as well as scanning for specific textual cues that prompt readers to engage in the binding, priming, recalling, switching, and other processing operations that involve such contexts.

But how does the poem's inclusion of a visual track impinge on the construction of contextual frames? In a way that complements the effects of Blake's strategic shift to the present tense for a verb of perception in line 15, the poem's multimodal design raises questions about the scope and application of contextual frames even as it triggers their use. The tense shift prompts readers to situate the act of seeing in multiple frames, each with a different "timestamp." In this manner, the poem promotes what might be termed cognitive flexibility, suggesting how some modes of worldmaking require oscillating between multiple frames to trace through the consequences of particularly salient events—to understand how those events have shaped the whole history of a world. Conversely, the image of the dead foe primes, in the visual channel, only one of the several contextual frames activated over the course the verbal text's unfolding. In this manner, the poem promotes what can be called cognitive economy, inducing readers to select one frame as the point of reference for interpreting a sequence of events that spans multiple places and times. Here the terminal event in the sequence provides, in the visual track, the primary frame of reference. The poem would have cued a very different way of worldmaking if the initial event in the sequence—viz., the narrator's failure to engage openly and directly with the person who thereby became his foe—had been represented visually. Equally important is how these contrasting and complementary methods of framing are set into play at one and the same time, thanks to the interaction between the text's verbal and visual channels.

Finally, in evoking a storyworld, the degree to which a narrative foregrounds a more or less marked (and thus noteworthy or tellable) disruption of the canonical or expected order of events is one of the factors that accounts for how readily the text or discourse can be interpreted as a narrative in the first place. Once a world has been evoked and interpreters have relocated to it, orienting themselves to its canonical order or "givens," the procedures specific to narrative worldmaking require that the world be one in which those givens are called into question, jeopardized by events that are more or less radically noncanonical, more or less antithetic to the normal order of things (Bruner 1990; Herman 2009: 133–36). Thus, in the storyworld associated with "A Poison Tree," the dissipation of anger through discourse is not tellably transgressive; hence the encounter with the friend receives only a bare report in lines 1–2. By contrast, the failure to address the cause of a dispute, and its resultant flowering into full-blown, destructive hatred, is reportably at odds with the world-order encapsulated in the first two lines. Hence 87.5 percent of the verbal portion of the text (lines 3–16) is devoted to an account of the narrator's experiences with the person who became his foe. For its part, the entirety of the poem's visual design is given over to representing (the effects of) world-disrupting events, not the canonical order against which those events stand out—in the manner of a foreground against a background.

Yet the different degrees of disruptiveness that the same sort of event might have in various contexts suggests the impossibility of attempting to fix in advance what makes something tellable, what constitutes a narratable disruption in the order of a world. Literary narratives can be viewed as a resource for exploring such threshold conditions for narrativity, and for generating counterfactual contexts in which situations and events become tellable in ways they might not otherwise. To put the same point in other terms, texts like Blake's suggest how narrative is both a product of and a resource for the (re)modeling of worlds.

STAGING DISCOURSE PRACTICES IN STORYWORLDS

In other studies, I have explored literary authors' representations of discourse practices—their figuring of "scenes of talk" (Herman 2006) in which characters engage in communicative acts, including acts of storytelling. In this section, shifting to a different set of tools for triangulating stories, media, and the mind, I examine Blake's multimodal staging of discourse practices in "A

Poison Tree." Literary narratives like Blake's bear importantly on folk theories of discourse in general; they also reflect—and help shape—understandings of discourse about emotions in particular. Further, the poem reflexively models, through its visual as well as verbal design, how the production and understanding of discourse requires interlocutors to position themselves with respect to one another as well as discourse referents.

"A Poison Tree" and Folk Theories of Discourse

In contrast with the texts used in my previous work, such as the final interchange between Mr. and Mrs. Ramsay before the "Time Passes" section of Virginia Woolf's *To the Lighthouse* (Herman 2006), or the complex, sometimes disingenuous interaction between the male character and Jig in Hemingway's "Hills Like White Elephants" (Herman 2010b), Blake's poem evokes in its first stanza a quite minimal scene of talk—or rather of talk withheld, which is what allows the speaker's wrath to grow and thereby nourish the bright poison apple. But even so, the poem sketches a folk theory of discourse as a means to understanding, and for that matter as a remedy against the discord and strife that define a fallen world. Specifically, in a way that anticipates Nietzsche's 1887 diagnosis of the causes and consequences of *ressentiment* (Nietzsche 1968) Blake's text interlinks the emotion of anger, the absence of talk, and the having of enemies; more precisely it characterizes the having of an enemy in terms of the inability to dissipate anger through open discourse. The poem's reflexive representation of discourse thus suggests the potentially destructive consequences, for self as well as other, of not using talk to assemble jointly a world-picture that encompasses multiple perspectives on events. At issue is the process whereby I come to imagine the world from another's vantage-point, and reciprocally cue the other to imagine the world from my own situation. The storyline involving the narrator and his enemy traces through what happens when there is no attempt to exchange and negotiate accounts of situations and events around which conflicting interpretations have grown up.

The poem also raises broader questions about ways in which folk theories of discourse can be encapsulated in literary narratives like Blake's. How does a given text reflexively model the processes by which discourses are produced and interpreted, as when a narrative uses an embedded storytelling scenario to comment on the nature and possibilities of narrative in general (Prince 1992)? How does the text situate acts of discourse production in the storyworld relative to other forms of activity, e.g., nonverbal behaviors, acts of perception not accompanied by talk, and so on? And in narratives exploiting more than one semiotic channel, how is the information about scenes of talk distributed between the various channels or tracks—and with what effect? In "A Poison Tree," for example, the visual channel represents the *effects* of the withheld talk, but information about the act of withholding is found only in the verbal text. What would have been the consequence for readers' engagement with the text—or, to revert to the terms of the previous section, for the world-building process—if this relationship had been inverted in the poem's overall design?

Emotion Discourse and Emotionology

Recent accounts of emotion talk throw further light on Blake's staging in words and images of discourse practices—and of the cognitive processes that both support and are supported by such practices. For his part, Stearns (1995) contends that there is a basic tension between naturalist and constructionist approaches. Naturalists (cf. Ekman 1982) argue for the existence of innate, biologically grounded emotions that are more or less uniform across cultures and subcultures. By contrast, constructionists argue that emotions are culturally specific—that "context and function determine emotional life and that these vary" (Stearns 1995: 41). Griffiths (1997: 137–69) accuses constructionists of engaging in straw-person argumentation with a version of naturalism that no practicing researcher would actually endorse. Putting that objection aside, however, work by Adolphs (2005) suggests how the naturalist and constructionist positions can be reconciled if emotions are viewed as (1) shaped by evolutionary processes and implemented in the brain, but also (2) situated in a complex network of stimuli, behavior, and other cognitive states. Because of (2), the shared stock of emotional responses is mediated by culturally specific learning processes. In turn, to explore the contribution of cultural contexts to humans' emotional life, analysts can study "[e]motion discourse [as] an integral feature of talk about events, mental states, mind and body, personal dispositions, and social relations" (Edwards 1997: 170). This approach gave rise to the concept of "emotionology," which was proposed by Stearns and Stearns (1985) as a way of referring to the collective emotional standards of a culture as opposed to the experience of emotion itself (cf. Harré and Gillett 1994: 144–61; Edwards 1997: 170–201). The term functions in parallel with recent usages of "*ontology*" to designate a model of the entities, together with their properties and relations that exist within a particular domain. Emotionologies are systems of emotion terms and concepts deployed by participants in discourse to ascribe emotions to themselves as well as their cohorts.

On the one hand, the visual design of "A Poison Tree" both draws on and contributes to a broader cultural system for understanding emotions. The relatively large size of the image of the dead foe and the encirclement of the text by the branches of the poison tree suggest a dominant emotionological motif: namely, the ease with which anger grows to all-consuming and thus poisonous proportions. Further, the branches extending upward along the right margin of the poem, before curling over the top of the text and then back down the left margin, are stick-like, bare of leaves, perhaps even dead. Not only does anger or wrath, when left unexpressed (and thus unaddressed), come to overshadow the worlds in which we act and interact; what is more, its only fruits are a bleak, unhospitable environment, with no possibility for renewal or regeneration.

On the other hand, the verbal design of Blake's poem also features a richly emotionological profile. Of its 101 words, a substantial percentage is drawn from the lexicon of emotion: *"angry," "wrath," "fears," "tears," "glad."* The poem thereby mirrors the way, in everyday discourse more generally, people draw on emotion terms to make sense of their own and one another's minds *as* minds. What is more, the poem recounts actions that are, in the cultural, generic, and situational contexts in which Blake's discourse is embedded, pragmatically rather than lexically linked with the emotions it figures. It suggests a complex network of cognitive and behavioral connections among unresolved (or unexpressed) anger or resentment, fear, sadness or depression, and schadenfreude, or the taking of satisfaction in another's suffering. This same underlying network of concepts—in other words, the emotionology in which the poem is embedded and to which it contributes in turn—allows readers to reconstitute unstated causal links among emotional states, such as the way unexpressed anger can foster a sociointeractional environment that breeds other life-destroying emotions. Thus, when the narrator reports that "my foe beheld it [the apple] shine, / And he knew that it was mine" (line 11–12), the use of the possessive pronoun in a position of emphasis at the end of line 12, together with the "mine"/"shine" rhyme, suggests that envy may have been one of the foe's motivating impulses for stealing into the narrator's garden at night—presumably, to obtain the "apple bright" (line 10). By contrast, when the narrator openly expresses his anger at the person who thereby becomes his friend in lines 1–2, the possibility for envy is dissipated along with the narrator's own ill will.

In short, literary narratives such as Blake's do not just recruit from emotionologies but also contribute to their formation and reconfiguration.

Arguably, Blake's poem seeks to make an emotionological intervention, by using words and images to underscore the importance of uncoupling the emotion of anger from the secretive, deceitful pursuit of recompense for anger-causing grievances and to suggest that anger or wrath, if brought out into the open and addressed explicitly, need not eventuate in life-negating practices.

Positioning

Theories of positioning afford another strategy for investigating the reflexive modeling of discourse practices (and their after-effects) in multimodal narratives like Blake's. In Harré and van Langenhove's account (1999: 1–31), speech acts are used to assign positions to social actors. Positions, in this account, are places along scales or continua that correspond to polarities of character such as "strong versus weak," "flashy versus understated," etc. Over time, self- and other-positioning speech productions help build overarching storylines in light of which people make sense of their own and others' doings. Reciprocally, those overarching narratives provide the means for linking position-assignments with utterances, as when a snide or affirming remark about someone does its work thanks to the way it shores up (or undercuts) a larger story about that person.

In "A Poison Tree," positioning is a relevant parameter for analysis on at least two levels: the level of the characters, and the level of the reader's engagement with the text, given the narrative techniques used in the poem.[11] At the first level, the text suggests how the positioning of self and other as foes translates into a particular strategy for relating to someone viewed as an enemy. Thus, the narrator's use of the designation of "*foe*" arises not during his interaction with that other person but at a distance, during his subsequent taking stock of the encounter—the narrational act corresponding to the poem itself being one method for taking stock *ex post facto*. By contrast, although the poem does not mandate this interpretation,[12] one possible reading of the opening lines is that the narrator's positioning of self and other as friends translates into an "*I-you*" mode of encounter, with the narrator directly informing his friend about his wrathful feelings. And conversely, the continuing possibility of encounters of that kind is ensured by open acts of

---

11. See, e.g., Bamberg (1997) and Herman (2009: 55–63) for a fuller discussion of levels of positioning.

12. As Peter Rabinowitz pointed out in his helpful comments on an earlier draft of this essay, "the poem never says that [the narrator] told his wrath to his friend; he might have told it to someone else and have been relieved of the burden [in that way]."

telling. The poem thereby suggests how positioning practices both afford and result from certain protocols regulating communicative encounters, which in turn derive from ways of conceptualizing social space. Positioning someone as an enemy at once requires and entails eliminating any genuine mutuality of encounter—as well as any world-model that includes such mutuality as a possible development.

At a second level, Blake's words and images position readers vis-à-vis (the narrator's account of) events in the storyworld. Here again both the shift to the present-tense verb "*see*" in line 15, and the image capturing the contents of the perceptual act corresponding to this verb, play a key role. Up until line 15, actions and events are focalized through the older, narrating I; the narrator thus positions himself and readers at a remove from these past occurrences. But on the historical-present interpretation of "*see*," the shift to the present tense can be viewed as a shift to internal focalization: the text registers how things looked to the narrator at the moment he first saw the dead foe outstretched beneath the tree. The poem's positioning logic likewise changes, bringing both teller and reader into a less mediated relation to the event of the foe's death, whose impact *at that past moment* is strikingly reinforced by the image. Meanwhile, the eternal-present reading of "*see*" positions readers in yet another way, and leads to a different construal of word-image relations in the text. In this second reading the impact of the foe's death lives on into the present, and is directly encountered by the narrating I rather than filtered retrospectively through the remembered perceptions of the experiencing I. In comparison with the historical-present interpretation of "*see*," further, the event of the foe's death is presented in an even less mediated fashion; the image now suggests that the ongoing perception of the dead foe dominates and predetermines the narrator's act of telling, even before it begins.

Blake thus combines verbal and visual designs to prompt reflection on narrative itself as a method of positioning self and other with respect to reported events—events whose varying degrees of accessibility to memory, cognition, and emotion can be signaled (or created) via shifts in storytelling style.

NARRATIVE AND CONSCIOUSNESS

I come now to the third and final strategy for triangulating research on narrative, media, and mind to be discussed in this essay: namely, the strategy of examining the nexus of narrative and consciousness. In one manifestation, this triangulation strategy focuses on how stories represent the felt, conscious awareness of narrators as well as characters; in another manifestation, the focus is on the extent to which narrative might afford scaffolding for conscious experience itself.

On both the historical-present and the eternal-present readings of "*see*" in line 15, a key feature of the poem is the way it accentuates both verbally and visually the impact of the sight of the outstretched dead foe on the narrator's consciousness. Blake's emphasis on lived quality of this perceptual act supports a hypothesis about the nature of narrative itself: namely, that a distinguishing feature of narrative worldmaking is the way it highlights the pressure of events on real or imagined consciousnesses affected by storyworlds-in-flux (cf. Fludernik 1996). To put the same point otherwise, narrative is centrally concerned with *qualia,* a term used by philosophers of mind to refer to the sense of "what it is like" for someone or something to have a particular experience (Levin 1999; Levine 1983; Nagel 1974). Cutting across differences of genre, communicative context, and storytelling media is a common focus on the what-it's-like dimension of consciousness; stories more or less explicitly foreground how one or more human or human-like minds is affected by what is going on in narrated worlds (Herman 2009: 137–60). But if it is part of the nature of narrative to focus on the impact of events on experiencing minds, the converse question also suggests itself: does narrative afford scaffolding for consciousness experience? Are there grounds for making the strong claim that narrative not only represents what it is like for experiencing minds to live through events in storyworlds, but furthermore constitutes a basis for having—for knowing—a mind at all, whether it is one's own or another's?

Relating qualia to the notion of the intrinsically first-person nature of conscious awareness, Searle (1997) for his part argues that consciousness cannot be observed, since consciousness itself resides in the structure of observing. As Searle puts it, there is "no way for us to picture subjectivity as part of our worldview because, so to speak, the subjectivity in question is the picturing" (98). Consciousness, in this account, is equivalent to the qualia associated with observing or experiencing the world from a particular, irreducibly subjective or first-person vantage point. But the isomorphism between the structure of narrative and the structure of consciousness may indicate a way beyond the paradox identified by Searle. Narratives, thanks to the way they are anchored in a particular vantage point on the storyworlds that they evoke, and thanks to their essentially durative or temporally extended profile, do not merely convey semantic content but furthermore encode in their very structure a way of experiencing the world. Thus, even granting Searle's point that we cannot *picture* our own or another's subjectivity because it is built into the process of picturing the world, it can still be argued that engaging with a narrative enables interpreters to *experience* the subjectivity that it manifests (cf. Zahavi 2007). On this reading, Blake's tense shift in line 15 does not just provide information about but moreover enacts the temporally unlocatable impact of the foe's death on the narrator, or rather its multiple locations along the (the narrator's experience of the) timeline connecting past and present. What is more, multimodal narratives like Blake's afford especially rich possibilities for representing what it is like to experience events in storyworlds. For example, aspects of the narrator's subjective experience, or the what-it's-like dimension of his encounter with the dead foe, are encapsulated in the perspective structure of the image: the onlooker is situated near the head of the body (hence the comparatively small size of the legs and feet), and appears to be looking at the body not from a full standing position, but almost as if he is crouching down—or perhaps has been brought to his knees by the sight of the outstretched foe. To put the same point another way, it would be inconsistent with the perspective structure of the image to suggest that the narrator-observer experienced the sight of the dead foe from high above, say in the uppermost branches of the poison tree, or from a situation closer to the feet than the head of the body. And the narrator's conscious experiences are re-experienced by readers who use the perspective structure of the image as scaffolding for knowing what it was like (or, given the fictivity of this scenario, what it would be like) to encounter this body in this specific way in this particular storyworld.

In sum, unlike other modes of representation such as deductive arguments, stress equations, or the periodic table of the elements, narrative is uniquely suited to capturing what the world is like from the situated perspective of an experiencing mind. More than just representing minds, stories emulate through their temporal and perspectival configuration the what-it's-like dimension of conscious awareness itself. And if narrative in general provides a discourse environment optimally suited for the world-picturing process, another broad project of triangulation would involve studying how specific modes and media of storytelling can be used to emulate the structure of conscious experience.[13]

---

13. Although it cuts against the grain of aspects of Hamburger's (1993 [1957]) account, and in particular her claim that the worlds created through first-person versus third-person narration have a different ontological status, from another perspective the line of argument being sketched here can be viewed as an extension of Hamburger's model. Not only fictional narrative but narrative more generally, the argument suggests, can be used to evoke or emulate the experiencing consciousness of another (cf. Fludernik 2007: 265–66). Meanwhile, for a wide-ranging discussion of types of empathy facilitated by such narrative emulations of consciousness (among other techniques used in novels), see Keen (2007).

POSTSCRIPT
New Challenges for Postclassical Narratology

In this essay, I have used Blake's multimodal text to argue that cognitive narratology can be productively characterized as a triangulation project, that is, a framework for inquiry that explores the interfaces among narrative, media, and the mind. In making this argument, I have implicitly suggested the advantages of weaving together two strands of postclassical narratology that have for the most part been pursued separately up to now, namely, *transmedial narratology* (Herman 2004; Ryan 2004; Wolf 2003) and *cognitive narratology*.

Unlike classical, structuralist narratology, transmedial narratology disputes the notion that the fabula or story level of a narrative remains wholly invariant across shifts of medium. However, it also assumes that stories do have "gists" that can be remediated more or less fully and recognizably—depending in part on the semiotic properties of the source and target media.[14] Transmedial narratology is thus premised on the assumption that, although narrative practices in different media share common features insofar as they are all instances of the narrative text type, stories are nonetheless inflected by the constraints and affordances associated with a given medium. Meanwhile, theorists developing cognitive approaches to narrative have worked to enrich the original base of structuralist concepts with ideas about human intelligence either ignored by or inaccessible to earlier story analysts, thereby building new foundations for the study of cognitive processes vis-à-vis various dimensions of narrative structure. And here the cognitive and transmedial approaches overlap. As already suggested, the target of cognitive-narratological research is the nexus of narrative and mind not just in print texts but also

14. For example, cinematic adapations of print texts reveal the story-configuring, and not just story-transmitting, properties of the media at issue. Thus, if voice-over narration is used to remediate in a film extended passages of free indirect discourse or thought report in the print-text source, the particular voice chosen to deliver the narration can affect film viewers' assessments of the situations and events being represented. In John Huston's 1987 film adaptation of James Joyce's "The Dead," the use in the final scene of a voice-over by Donal McCann, the actor who plays Gabriel Conroy, cues the inference that the images of a snowy Ireland are subworlds glimpsed by Gabriel's mind's eye. By contrast, in the opening sequence of Todd Field's 2006 film *Little Children*, an adaptation of the novel by Tom Perrotta, the third-person narration is recast in the form of a voice-over delivered by Will Lyman, whose deep, authoritative voice American viewers will associate with the news magazine *Frontline*, produced by the Public Broadcasting Service. In this case the particular voice chosen provides a kind of hyper-authentication of the events being shown on screen—and creates an incongruity that Fields exploits to comic effect. Examples of this sort suggest how narrative remediation can impinge on judgments about the modality status of events being recounted and hence on the configuration of storyworlds.

in face-to-face interaction, cinema, radio news broadcasts, computer-mediated virtual environments, and other storytelling media. In turn, "mind-relevance" can be studied vis-à-vis the multiple factors associated with the design and interpretation of narratives across media, including the story-producing activities of writers, the processes by means of which interpreters make sense of storyworlds evoked by multimodal as well as monomodal narrative artifacts, and the cognitive states and dispositions of characters in those variously configured storyworlds. In addition, the mind-narrative nexus can be studied along two other dimensions, insofar as stories function not only as a target of interpretation but also as a means for making sense of experience in their own right. The integrative framework outlined here thus underscores the pertinence of new questions for postclassical narratology: what sense-making possibilities do multimodal storytelling practices afford that are not afforded by monomodal or single-channel narrative practices, and vice versa? Do multimodal narratives that exploit different semiotic channels (e.g., words and images vs. utterances and gestures) draw on, and support, different ways of navigating the world (cf. Herman 2010a)? And what investigative probes might be developed to explore these sorts of issues?

To extrapolate: if postclassical narratology in a first phase involves incorporating ideas that fall outside the domain of structuralist theory, in order to reassess the possibilities as well as the limitations of classical models, new challenges emerge in a second phase. What is now required is to bring into closer dialogue the full variety of postclassical approaches—feminist, transmedial, cognitive, corpus-narratological, and other. By juxtaposing the descriptions of narrative phenomena (narration, perspective, character, etc.) made possible by these approaches, testing for overlap among the descriptions, and then exploring the degree to which the descriptions' non-overlapping aspects might complement one another, theorists can begin to engage in a more coordinated effort to accomplish what remains the overarching goal of narrative inquiry: coming to a better understanding of what stories are and how they work.[15]

---

15. A different version of portions of this essay will be published as "Stories, Media, and the Mind: Narrative Worldmaking through Word and Image," in a special issue of the Chinese journal *Foreign Literature Studies*. Coedited by Shang Biwu and James Phelan, the issue is devoted to "Postclassical Narratology: Western Approaches." I am grateful to Jan Alber, Shang Biwu, Monika Fludernik, Jim Phelan, Peter Rabinowitz, Les Tannenbaum, Jim Zeigler, and Lars Franssen for their invaluable comments on earlier drafts of the analysis presented here. I am also grateful for the Arts and Humanities Seed Grant from Ohio State University and the fellowship from the American Council of Learned Societies that have supported this research.

REFERENCES

Adolphs, Ralph (2005) "Could a Robot Have Emotions? Theoretical Perspective from Social Cognitive Neuroscience." *Who Needs Emotions: The Brain Meets the Robot.* Eds. Michael Arbib and Jean-Marc Fellous. Oxford: Oxford University Press. 9–28.

Ault, Donald (1986) "Incommensurability and Interconnection in Blake's Anti-Newtonian Text [1977]." *Essential Articles for the Study of William Blake, 1970–1984.* Ed. Nelson Hilton. Hamden, CT: Archon Books. 141–73.

Bamberg, Michael (1997) "Positioning Between Structure and Performance." *The Journal of Narrative and Life History* 7.1–4: 335–42.

Blake, William (1794) "A Poison Tree." From Copy C of *Songs of Innocence and Experience.* Lessing J. Rosenwald Collection, Library of Congress. http://www.blakearchive.org/blake/indexworks.htm

Brandt, Per Aage (2004) *Spaces, Domains, and Meaning: Essays in Cognitive Semiotics.* Bern: Peter Lang.

Bruner, Jerome (1990) *Acts of Meaning.* Cambridge, MA: Harvard University Press.

Clark, Herbert H. (1996) *Using Language.* Cambridge: Cambridge University Press.

Connolly, Tristanne J. (2002) *William Blake and the Body.* Basingstoke: Palgrave Macmillan.

Doležel, Lubomír (1998) *Heterocosmica: Fiction and Possible Worlds.* Baltimore: Johns Hopkins University Press.

Duchan, Judith F., Gail A. Bruder, and Lynne E. Hewitt (1995) Eds. *Deixis in Narrative: A Cognitive Science Perspective.* Hillsdale, NJ: Lawrence Erlbaum.

Edwards, Derek (1997) *Discourse and Cognition.* London: Sage.

Ekman, Paul (1982) *Emotion in the Human Face* [1972]. Cambridge: Cambridge University Press.

Emmott, Catherine (1997) *Narrative Comprehension: A Discourse Perspective.* Oxford: Oxford University Press.

Essick, Robert N. (1985) "William Blake, William Hamilton, and the Materials of Graphic Meaning." *English Literary History* 52.4: 833–72.

Fastrez, Pierre (2003) Ed. *Sémiotique Cognitive—Cognitive Semiotics.* Special issue of *Recherches en communication/Research in Communication* 19.

Fludernik, Monika (1996) *Towards a 'Natural' Narratology.* London: Routledge.

——— (2007) "Identity/Alterity." *The Cambridge Companion to Narrative.* Ed. David Herman. Cambridge: Cambridge University Press. 260–73.

Gallagher, Philip J. (1977) "The Word Made Flesh: Blake's 'A Poison Tree' and the Book of Genesis." *Studies in Romanticism* 16: 237–49.

Gerrig, Richard J. (1993) *Experiencing Narrative Worlds: On the Psychological Activities of Reading.* New Haven: Yale University Press.

Gleckner, Robert F., and Mark L. Greenberg (1989) "Introduction: Teaching Blake's Songs." *Approaches to Teaching Blake's Songs of Innocence and of Experience.* Eds. Robert F. Gleckner and Mark L. Greenberg. New York: Modern Language Association. x–xvi.

Goodman, Nelson (1978) *Ways of Worldmaking.* Indianapolis: Hackett.

Griffiths, Paul E. (1997) *What Emotions Really Are: The Problem of Psychological Categories.* Chicago: University of Chicago Press.

Hagstrum, Jean H. (1991) "William Blake Rejects the Enlightenment." *Critical Essays on William Blake* [1963]. Ed. Hazard Adams. Boston: G.K. Hall & Co. 67–79.

Hamburger, Käte (1993) *The Logic of Literature* [1957]. 2nd, revised edition. Trans. Marilyn J. Rose. Bloomington: Indiana University Press.

Harré, Rom, and Grant Gillett (1994) *The Discursive Mind*. London: Sage.

Harré, Rom, and Luk Langenhove (1999) Eds. *Positioning Theory: Moral Contexts of Intentional Action*. Oxford: Blackwell.

Herman, David (2002) *Story Logic: Problems and Possibilities of Narrative*. Lincoln: University of Nebraska Press.

—— (2004) "Toward a Transmedial Narratology." *Narrative across Media: The Languages of Storytelling*. Ed. Marie-Laure Ryan. Lincoln: University of Nebraska Press. 47–75.

—— (2006) "Dialogue in a Discourse Context: Scenes of Talk in Fictional Narrative." *Narrative Inquiry* 16.1: 79–88.

—— (2007) "Storytelling and the Sciences of Mind: Cognitive Narratology, Discursive Psychology, and Narratives in Face-to-Face Interaction." *Narrative* 15.3: 306–34.

—— (2009) *Basic Elements of Narrative*. Oxford: Wiley-Blackwell.

—— (2010a) "Word-Image/Utterance-Gesture: Case Studies in Multimodal Storytelling." *New Perspectives on Narrative and Multimodality*. Ed. Ruth Page. London: Routledge. 78–98.

—— (2010b) "Narrative Theory after the Second Cognitive Revolution." *Introduction to Cognitive Cultural Studies*. Ed. Lisa Zunshine. Baltimore: Johns Hopkins University Press. 115–75.

Johnstone, Barbara (1987) "'He says . . . so I said': Verb Tense Alteration and Narrative Depictions of Authority in American English." *Linguistics* 25: 33–52.

Keen, Suzanne (2007) *Empathy and the Novel*. Oxford: Oxford University Press.

Kress, Gunther, and Theo van Leeuwen (2001) *Multimodal Discourse: The Modes and Media of Contemporary Communication*. London: Arnold.

Lakoff, George, and Mark Johnson (1980) *Metaphors We Live By*. Chicago: University of Chicago Press.

Levin, Janet (1999) "Qualia." *The MIT Encyclopedia of the Cognitive Sciences*. Eds. Robert A. Wilson and Frank C. Keil. Cambridge, MA: MIT Press. 693–94.

Levine, Joseph (1983) "Materialism and Qualia: The Explanatory Gap." *Pacific Philosophical Quarterly* 64.4: 354–61.

Mitchell, W. J. T. (1978) *Blake's Composite Art: A Study of the Illuminated Poetry*. Princeton: Princeton University Press.

Nagel, Thomas (1974) "What Is It Like to Be a Bat?" *The Philosophical Review* 83.4: 435–50.

Nietzsche, Friedrich (1968) *On the Genealogy of Morals: Basic Writings of Nietzsche* [1887]. Trans. and ed. Walter Kaufmann. New York: The Modern Library. 437–599.

Pavel, Thomas G. (1986) *Fictional Worlds*. Cambridge, MA: Harvard University Press.

Peterfreund, Stuart (1998) *William Blake in a Newtonian World*. Norman: University of Oklahoma Press.

Phillips, Michael (2000) *William Blake: The Creation of the Songs (from Manuscript to Illuminated Printing)*. Princeton: Princeton University Press.

Prince, Gerald (1992) *Narrative as Theme: Studies in French Fiction.* Lincoln: University of Nebraska Press.

Richardson, Alan, and Francis F. Steen (2002) *Literature and the Cognitive Revolution,* Special issue of *Poetics Today* 23.

Ryan, Marie-Laure (1991) *Possible Worlds, Artificial Intelligence, and Narrative Theory.* Bloomington: Indiana University Press.

——— (2004) Ed. *Narrative Across Media: The Languages of Storytelling.* Lincoln: University of Nebraska Press.

Schiffrin, Deborah (1981) "Tense Variation in Narrative." *Language* 57: 45–62.

Searle, John R. (1997) *The Mystery of Consciousness.* New York: The New York Review of Books.

Segal, Erwin M. (1995) "Narrative Comprehension and the Role of Deictic Shift Theory." *Deixis in Narrative: A Cognitive Science Perspective.* Eds. Judith F. Duchan, Gail A. Bruder, and Lynne E. Hewitt. Hillsdale, NJ: Lawrence Erlbaum. 3–17.

Stearns, Peter (1995) "Emotion." *Discursive Psychology in Practice.* Eds. Rom Harré and Peter Stearns. Thousand Oaks, CA: Sage. 37–54.

Stearns, Peter, and Carol Stearns (1985) "Emotionology: Clarifying the History of Emotions and Emotional Standards." *American Historical Review* 90: 13–36.

Talmy, Leonard (2000) *Toward a Cognitive Semantics.* Vol. 1. Cambridge, MA: MIT Press.

Turner, Mark (1991) *Reading Minds: The Study of English in the Age of Cognitive Science.* Princeton: Princeton University Press.

——— (1996) *The Literary Mind.* Oxford: Oxford University Press.

Viscomi, Joseph (2003) "Illuminated Printing." *The Cambridge Companion to William Blake.* Ed. Morris Eaves. Cambridge: Cambridge University Press. 37–62.

Welch, Dennis M. (1995) "Blake's Songs of Experience: The Word Lost and Found." *English Studies* 3: 238–52.

Werth, Paul (1999) *Text Worlds: Representing Conceptual Space in Discourse.* Ed. Michael Short. London: Longman.

Wolf, Werner (2003) "Narrative and Narrativity: A Narratological Reconceptualization and Its Applicability to the Visual Arts." *Word & Image* 19: 180–97.

Wolfson, Nessa (1982) *The Conversational Historical Present in American English Narrative.* Dordrecht: Foris.

Zahavi, Dan (2007) "Expression and Empathy." *Folk Psychology Re-Assessed.* Eds. Matthew Ratcliffe and Daniel D. Hutto. Dordrecht: Springer. 25–40.

Zwaan, Rolf (1996) "Toward a Model of Literary Comprehension." *Models for Understanding Text.* Eds. Bruce K. Britton and Arthur C. Graesser. Malwah, NJ: Lawrence Erlbaum. 241–55.

6

JAN ALBER

Hypothetical Intentionalism

Cinematic Narration Reconsidered

Cinematic narration figures prominently in the work of several narratologists. Basically, three schools of thought exist. The first, represented by David Bordwell, argues that film has narration but no narrator (1985: 61). According to Bordwell, cinematic narration is created by the *viewer*, who uses cognitive schemata to transform the film's visual images and sounds into a series of perceptible configurations, which he or she then interprets as a story.[1] In contrast to Bordwell's approach, the second school, represented by Seymour Chatman, argues that films are narrated by a *cinematic narrator*. Chatman defines this narrator in terms of "the organizational and sending agency" (1990: 127) behind the film. In his view, films "are always presented—mostly and often exclusively shown, but sometimes partially told—by a narrator or narrators." The overall agent that does the showing is "the 'cinematic narrator'" (133–34).[2] The third school, represented by theoreticians such

---

1. See also Bordwell (1989), Fleishman (1992: 13; 19), Bordwell and Thompson (2003: 86–87), and Grodal (2005: 169).
2. Other terms for the same concept are "image-maker" (Kozloff 1988: 44), "grand Imagier" (Gaudreault 1999: 107; 2000: 56), "narrateur filmique" (Burgoyne 1991: 272), "external narrator" (Stam et al. 1992: 103), "perceptual enabler" (Levinson 1996a: 252), "film narrator" (Lothe 2000: 30), and "implied narrator" (Laass 2008: 22). Diehl argues that he is "a firm defender of the conceptual claim that any narrative of necessity requires a narrator" and puts the matter as follows: "Regardless of the medium in which a narrative is presented, I claim that we are prescribed to imagine a fictional narrator for a narrative work N if and only if we are prescribed to imagine *de re* of the text of N that it occurs within the world of the fiction generated by N" (2009: 23, 15).

as George Wilson (1986: 135), Michaela Bach (1999: 245–46), and Berys Gaut (2004: 248) argues that it is *the implied filmmaker* who mediates the film as a whole, guides us through it, and directs our attention to important issues. Similarly, Katherine Thomson-Jones argues that "the narrator guide is sometimes just the filmmaker as manifest in the film" (2007: 82), while Manfred Jahn de-anthropomorphizes the source of the discourse and speaks of a "filmic composition device (FCD)," which he defines as "the theoretical agency behind a film's organization and arrangement." According to Jahn, the FCD "need not be associated with any concrete person or character, particularly neither the director nor a filmic narrator" (Jahn 2003: F4.1.2–F4.1.3).

Up until now, the discussion has been dominated by analyses that focus on the conceptual foundations of film narration, rather than on how concepts of cinematic narration might be developed in ways that are productive for the business of interpreting films. For instance, some theoreticians try to verify their claims concerning the cinematic narrator on the basis of the so-called A Priori Argument ("narration without narrator does not exist because the former is conceptually dependent on the other")[3] or the so-called Argument for Means of Access ("only the fictional persona of the narrator can give us access to the fictional world of a narrative"),[4] while others—such as Currie (1995: 266), Gaut (2004: 235–37), and Thomson-Jones (2007: 82–89)—attempt to refute these arguments on logical grounds.[5] Although these attempts to develop a "philosophy of the movies" (Gaut 2004: 230) constitute a valuable and important contribution to the understanding of movies, my focus is elsewhere. The most pressing question for me is whether the concept of a cinematic narrator helps us come up with better readings or interpretations of movies.

To address this practical, interpretive issue, I begin by exploring the way viewers rely on folk psychology[6] to make sense of films. In doing so, I will try to both synthesize and transcend the three approaches mentioned above. Second, I want to reconsider analytical tools such as the implied filmmaker and

3. Chatman argues that both "a communication with no communicator" and "a creation with no creator" (1990: 127) are impossible, and hence, cinematic narratives need to have a narrator.

4. For Levinson, "the presenter in a film [. . .] gives perceptual access to the story's sights and sounds; the presenter in a film is thus, in part, a sort of *perceptual enabler*. Such perceptual enabling is what we must implicitly posit to explain how it is we are, even imaginarily, perceiving what we are perceiving of the story [. . .]"(1996: 252).

5. Also, theoreticians exist who try to refute the prior refutations of others. See, for example, Diehl (2009: 16, 19).

6. The term "folk psychology" denotes "our standard, everyday, unthinking, 'commonsense' assumptions about how our minds and the minds of others work" (Palmer 2004: 244).

the cinematic narrator from the perspective of their usefulness for actual film analysis and cinematic criticism. Third, I develop a new model of cinematic narration and I show that this model may serve as a frame of reading that helps us to make strange and incomprehensible experimental films such as David Lynch's *Lost Highway* (1997) more readable.

HYPOTHETICAL INTENTIONALISM AND THE READING OF FILMS

In our everyday interaction, we try to understand others by attributing mental states and dispositions to them. Alan Palmer argues that "consciousness allows us to adapt intelligently to our environment" (2004: 89). Similarly, Lisa Zunshine points out that we continuously engage in processes of mindreading and try "to explain people's behavior in terms of their thoughts, beliefs, and desires" (2006: 6). If we did not speculate about or try to interpret the intentions of our fellow human beings, most, if not all, types of interaction (such as human communication) would become impossible.

Numerous critics have argued that the way in which we try to make sense of other people is similar to the way in which we attempt to make sense of fictional narratives (Palmer 2004, Zunshine 2006, and Herman 2007). I would like to propose that when viewing a film, most viewers try to find out what the film means or "is trying to say."[7] Indeed, Daniel O. Nathan argues that "interpretation is in general and essentially a matter of asking 'why,' of seeking an explanation of whatever it is that we have before us" (1992: 196).

Films are directed by individuals such as Alfred Hitchcock, Stanley Kubrick, Fritz Lang, or David Lynch, and they are typically very influential with regard to the end product that we as viewers get to see. However, it is of course ultimately impossible to determine the filmmaker's intentions. To begin with, in film analysis it does not even make sense to speak of a single author or filmmaker. While writing a novel is typically something done by an individual, a film is usually so expensive and technically so complicated that it can only be realized through a complex production process in which many professionals work together: the author of the script, the producer, the director, the editor, actors and actresses, photographers, sound directors, etc. (Lothe 2000: 31).[8] For these reasons, it is impossible for us to know whether

---

7. This is obviously not true of films that were designed for "pure" entertainment such as action movies or porn films.
8. At the same time, it is worth noting that the producer and the director typically exercise more power over the final product than all the others.

our interpretations reveal the intentions of this multitude of professionals who produced the film. Arguably, however, it would be equally impossible if there were only one professional such as the director.[9]

Some critics speak of an "implied author" (Booth 2002) or an "implied filmmaker" (Gaut 2004: 248) rather than the real filmmaker. However, I would also like to avoid these terms because they suggest that certain critics are able to transcend the mere forming of hypotheses about a narrative's purpose or "point," and that they are somehow right about the intentions that a narrative evokes. For example, according to Wayne C. Booth, the implied author is the real author's "second self," and as such satisfies "the reader's need to know where, in the world of values, he stands, that is, to know where the author *wants* him to stand" (1983: 73). Booth believes that analyses along the lines of the concept of the implied author enable us "to come as close as possible to sitting in the author's chair and making this text, becoming able to remake it, employing the author's 'reason-of-art'" (1982: 21).

Since we can never be sure that we have formed correct hypotheses about the implied author or filmmaker's intentions, I want to follow instead David Herman's slightly more modest proposal to move beyond the "compartmentalized intentionality" of the implied author or filmmaker—that is, beyond an approach that is grounded in a view of intentions as inner, mental objects (cf. Hutto 2000)—and toward "an approach of narrative understanding that more fully and more openly grounds stories in intentional systems, that acknowledges the extent to which the process of interpretation hinges on making defeasible (= possibly wrong) inferences about communicative intentions" (2008: 244). This proposal closely correlates with the idea that intentions are not located in one particular and/or fixed area (such as the real or implied filmmaker). Rather, they are distributed across the inventers and interpreters of narratives, narrative designs, and the communicative context in which narratives are produced and interpreted (Herman 2006).

More specifically, I propose to look at the way in which we make sense of films from the perspective of hypothetical intentionalism, a cognitive approach in which "a narrative's meaning is established by *hypothesizing intentions authors might have had,* given the context of creation, rather than relying on, or trying to seek out, the author's subjective intentions" (Gibbs 2005: 248; my italics; see also Kindt and Müller 2006: 170–76). More to the point, I use what Daniel C. Dennett calls "the intentional stance" (1996: 27) and Alan Palmer's "*continuing-consciousness frame*" (2004: 175) to shed

---

9. On the intentional fallacy in literary studies, see Wimsatt and Beardsley (2001) and Barthes (2002).

new light on cinematic narration. My basic assumption is that we all attribute intentions and motivations to films in order to find out what they might mean. Dennett defines the intentional stance as "the strategy of interpreting the behavior of an entity (person, animal, artifact, whatever) by treating it *as if* it were a rational agent who governed its 'choice' of 'action' by a 'consideration' of its 'beliefs' and 'desires'" (1996: 27). Similarly, according to Alan Palmer, "the working hypothesis that visibly coherent behavior is caused by a directing consciousness in the actual world is used by extension in the application of the continuing-consciousness frame to the storyworld" (2004: 178).

When we view a film, we treat it as "a rational agent who governed its 'choice' of 'action' by a 'consideration' of its 'beliefs' and 'desires'" (Dennett 1996: 27). We do not merely engage in processes of mind-reading to understand the minds of the characters; rather, we also apply the continuing-consciousness frame to the film as a whole and construct some kind of mind or consciousness behind the film. In a second step, we then form hypotheses about this mind's intentions or what one might call the film's potential "point." However, since we can never be sure that we have interpreted a film correctly, it does not make sense to ascribe our hypotheses about the intentions and motivations behind the film to the real or implied filmmaker.

Jerrold Levinson, one of the major supporters of hypothetical intentionalism, in reconsidering Booth's concept of the implied author, argues that "instead of speaking of beliefs and attitudes that would be *reasonably attributed* to the actual author on the basis of the work contextually grasped, we can speak of the beliefs or attitudes that *just straightforwardly belong* to the implied author—he or she is being a construction tailor-made to bear them" (Levinson 1996b: 229). While Booth thinks that the concept of the implied author ultimately enables us to "employ [. . .] the author's 'reason-of-art'" (1982: 21), Levinson redefines the implied author as a more or less fictional construct created in the reader's mind on the basis of signals or cues in the narrative text. Since, as Tom Kindt and Hans-Harald Müller point out, the term "implied author" has been used so differently in the past, one might want to dispense with the implied author: "it would hardly be sensible to continue using the old name to refer to the new, refined concept" (2006: 176).[10]

Hence, with regard to the medium film, I propose to ascribe our hypotheses about the intentions underlying a movie to what I would like to call the "hypothetical filmmaker," a term which denotes *the single entity to which*

---

10. To put this slightly differently, the term "implied author" has by now acquired so much baggage that it makes sense to use new terminology.

the viewer ascribes conscious or unconscious motivations that actuated the professionals who were responsible for the making of the film in question.[11] In this model, the intentions and motivations that played a role in the production of a film are distributed across the film's inventors, the film's interpreters, and the film's narrative designs (which viewers use as the basis of their hypotheses).

THE CINEMATIC NARRATOR RECONSIDERED

Let us for a second assume that films are narrated by a cinematic narrator in Chatman's sense (1990: 127). Would it, then, somehow be possible to discern the presence of this narrator or to get a sense of how the film narrator mediates a film as a whole? At first glance, one might feel that in film, no deictic or expressive markers exist that would warrant the existence of a film narrator. In particular, in films that follow the classical paradigm of transparency (such as Fritz Lang's *You Only Live Once* [1937]) and avoid intertitles, non-diegetic inserts, non-diegetic music,[12] and so forth, nothing really suggests the presence of a cinematic narrator; indeed, we have a sense of the immediacy of presentation: the film seems to merely show a fictional world without any narratorial inflection or commentary. Hence, one may feel that it is unnecessary to introduce a narrator for film and that what we are observing in theorists needing such a persona is an illicit transfer of real-world frames of storytelling onto the (much more complex) communicational process of cinematic narration. In films using non-diegetic music or sound effects, intertitles, captions, non-diegetic inserts, voice-over- or character-narrators, however, some sort of mediacy does indeed make itself felt. This is also true of such filmic peculiarities as slow-motion sequences or speed-ups, garish colors, surprising cuts, and wipes.

If we posit the existence of a cinematic narrator, it is clear that this "overall agent that does the showing" (Chatman 1990: 134) has to be both extradiegetic and heterodiegetic. Furthermore, the film narrator is typically covert and only occasionally slightly more overt, though never as overt as the first-person or authorial narrator of a novel. Hence, David A. Black (2001: 301) argues that the cinematic narrator differs from the prototypical narrators

---

11. Similarly, Nathan argues that "given the weaknesses of ordinary intentionalism, appeal to a hypothetical author is the only adequate response" (1992: 200) to the demands of literary interpretation.

12. Non-diegetic inserts and sound effects are not part of the fictional world and cannot be seen or heard by the characters in the film.

of novels or short stories. Indeed, the film narrator is typically covert like the narrative medium in reflector-mode narratives (such as Virginia Woolf's novel *Mrs. Dalloway* [1925]) or third-person narratives of external focalization (such as Ernest Hemingway's short story "The Killers" [1927]).

According to Seymour Chatman, it is of utmost importance to discriminate between "the *inventor*" of a film (what he calls the implied filmmaker) on the one hand, and its *"presenter"* (what he calls the cinematic narrator) on the other (1990: 133). However, from the perspective of actual film criticism, this distinction does not really matter because the functions of these two entities or constructs clearly converge. Interestingly, the functions that critics ascribe to the cinematic narrator are virtually identical with the functions that others attribute to what they call the implied filmmaker: both are rather neutral or covert shower or arranger functions.[13]

Since everything for which the cinematic narrator is said to be responsible (the mediating, presenting, showing, arranging, or organizing of the film) can in fact be attributed to what I call the hypothetical filmmaker, we can do away with the concept of the film narrator.[14] From the perspective of hypothetical intentionalism, the only really important thing is that we formulate hypotheses about the intentions and motivations that played a role in the production of the film. I would therefore like to redefine cinematic narration as the interaction between the film's inventers, its viewers, and the film's narrative designs. As I see it, cinematic narration correlates with the idea that the viewer uses Dennett's intentional stance and Palmer's continuing-consciousness frame to speculate about the film's intentions. And I want to argue that he or she formulates these hypotheses on the basis of the narrative designs used in the film.

---

13. For instance, Seymour Chatman uses the term "cinematic narrator" to denote "the organizational and sending agency" (1990: 127) behind the film; Jerrold Levinson speaks of a *"perceptual enabler"* who "gives perceptual access to the story's sights and sounds" (1996a: 252); Jakob Lothe defines the "film narrator" as "the superordinate 'instance' that presents all the means of communication that film has at its disposal" (2000: 30); and Kozloff speaks of an "image-maker" who is responsible for "all the selecting, organizing, shading, and even passive recording processes that go into the creation of a narrative sequence of images and sounds" (1988: 44). Similarly, Booth defines the "implied author" of films as "a creative voice uniting all the choices" (2002: 125); Manfred Jahn (2003: F4.1) speaks of a "filmic composition device (FCD)" which denotes "the theoretical agency behind a film's organization and arrangement"; and Gaut simply argues that "the implied filmmaker" mediates the film as a whole (2004: 248).

14. Similarly, Richard Walsh suggests eradicating extra- and heterodiegetic narrators in narrative fiction: "Extradiegetic heterodiegetic narrators (that is, 'impersonal' and 'authorial' narrators), who cannot be represented without thereby being rendered homodiegetic or intradiegetic, are in no way distinguishable from authors." He therefore concludes that "the narrator is always either a character who narrates, or the author" (2007: 84; 78).

THE HYPOTHETICAL FILMMAKER AS THE FILM'S HIGHEST AUTHORITY

The concept of the hypothetical filmmaker (seen as the "agent" projected by the viewer) offers us an organizational hierarchy that helps us describe the functioning of film narratives. From the perspective of hypothetical intentionalism, it makes sense to attribute the totality of a film's stimuli (including non-diegetic music or sound, garish colors, non-diegetic inserts, surprising cuts, as well as paratextual elements, i.e. intertitles, captions, and the film's opening and final credits) to some kind of agency and to then ponder their potential "point." Some viewers will (not without reason) maintain that such choices ultimately issue from the director of the film. However, since we can never be entirely sure of the director's true intentions (and since his or her intentions are not the only ones that play a role), I suggest attributing these choices and the motivations behind them to the hypothetical filmmaker or, in a different manner of speaking, simply to the film as a whole. From my perspective, the only important thing here is that we speculate about the potential purpose of the movie, scene, or shot under discussion; it does not matter whether we attribute these choices to the filmmaker or to the film as a whole. Let me present a couple of examples that illustrate how viewers typically impute intentions to cinematic stimuli.

For instance, by continuously juxtaposing Alex's (Malcolm McDowell) violent outbursts with (non-diegetic) Beethoven music, the film *A Clockwork Orange* (1971) proposes a connection between violence and art. Indeed, Sobchack argues that in the film, "art and violence spring from the same source; they are both expressions of the individual, egotistic, vital, and non-institutionalized man" (1981: 98). Furthermore, the garish red screen during the opening credits may be a visual hint at the extreme emotions (related to sex and violence) that are at work in *A Clockwork Orange*. Similarly, the film *Fury* (1936) presents us with a surprising cut from gossiping housewives to a (non-diegetic) shot of clucking hens, and thus urges us to look for similarities between these two entities. More specifically, we are invited to (metaphorically) see the women as hens (Bordwell and Thompson 2003: 336). Likewise, the film *2001: A Space Odyssey* (1968) suddenly cuts from a bone employed by a primitive ape-man and then thrown up in the air to a spacecraft of the future. This juxtaposition may suggest that the same primitive motives and instincts that drove the ape-man to construct a weapon out of a bone also drive us to manufacture space-age hardware (Whittock 1990: 51–52).[15]

---

15. Both cuts urge us to see one entity as a different one and thus involve cinematic meta-

For their part, the films *Metropolis* (1926) and *The Bourne Identity* (2002) use intertitles or captions to inform the audience about the story's temporal and spatial whereabouts. In this context, it is worth noting that the choices concerning the color and the typographical presentation of the letters do not only convey narrative information but additionally set a particular tone.[16] For example, *The Bourne Identity*, a film about a non-conformist CIA agent called Jason Bourne (Matt Damon), who suffers from amnesia after the CIA has tried to kill him, presents us with white captions that look as if they could have come from a report written on a computer. The film thus suggests objectivity and aloofness—a tone that highlights the cool and merciless way in which the CIA tries to eradicate Bourne, and simultaneously contrasts sharply with the strong emotional attachment we develop for the major protagonist as he desperately tries to find out who he is.

Furthermore, films may occasionally supply voice-over narrators who comment on what we see on the screen or character-narrators who tell stories to other characters. For instance, the film *A Clockwork Orange* confronts us with a homodiegetic voice-over narrator (Alex) who comments on the action on the screen, while the movie *The Cabinet of Dr. Caligari* (1920) uses a character-narrator (Francis) who tells another inmate how he ended up in the lunatic asylum. Since the images continue on the screen regardless of whether such verbal narrators speak (and also regardless of whether non-diegetic sounds, captions, or intertitles are present), the theoretical construct of the hypothetical filmmaker has to be seen as the film's highest authority: all information is a consequence of its mediation, choice, organization, and arrangement. In other words, voice-over narrators, character-narrators, non-diegetic sounds, and intertitles are all components of the hypothetical filmmaker's options; they are some of the various devices that can be used in film.

Films sometimes also present us with unreliable character-narrators, and the concept of the hypothetical filmmaker helps us explain and conceptualize cinematic unreliability. In cases of unreliable narration in film, it is always the case that the film as a whole (or, in a different manner of speaking, the hypothetical filmmaker) draws our attention to and simultaneously counteracts a character-narrator's norms, values, tastes, judgments, or moral sense (Prince 1987: 101), and sometimes even the character-narrator's "actual and overt misinterpretation or distortion of story facts" (Chatman 1990: 225, n. 21).

---

phor. For more on film metaphors, see Whittock (1990) and Alber (forthcoming). Generally speaking, I would attribute cinematic metaphors to choices made by the hypothetical filmmaker.

16. Also, *Metropolis* is a silent film and therefore required intertitles above and beyond "intent."

Thus, it makes sense to discriminate between cinematic forms of normative unreliability on the one hand, and cinematic forms of factual unreliability on the other (see also Laass 2008: 30–32). In both cases, we are invited to see that the character-narrator's norms differ significantly from the norms of the film, and our hypotheses about intentions and motivations obviously play a crucial role.

A well-known example of cinematic unreliability is Hitchcock's *Stage Fright* (1950). In this film, Jonathan Cooper (Richard Todd) tells Eve Gill (Jane Wyman) that he and Charlotte Inwood (Marlene Dietrich) are secret lovers and that he is wanted by the police for killing Charlotte's husband. Jonathan (or "Johnny") also tells Eve that Charlotte committed the crime. According to his story, he only helped her to get rid of her blood-stained dress but was seen leaving the scene. The camera enacts Jonathan's story, which Eve and we as viewers assume to be true. "Only retrospectively, after Johnny admits to Eve his criminal tendency and a previous murder, do we realize that the camera has conspired with Johnny to deceive us, that Johnny's flashback was a lie" (Chatman 1990: 131).

Another example of cinematic unreliability can be found in the film *The Usual Suspects* (1995), in which Roger "Verbal" Kint (Kevin Spacey), apparently a disabled low-profile criminal, tries to get immunity for his involvement in a drug deal by testifying to US Customs Special Agent Dave Kujan (Chazz Palminteri). As in *Stage Fright,* the camera enacts Kint's story, which Kujan and we as viewers assume to be true. However, as we learn at the end of the film, Kint only made up this story in order to mislead Kujan about his true identity. That is to say, the images we saw only conformed to Kint's fabricated story but not to what actually happened.[17] Toward the end of the film, Kint receives his immunity and leaves the investigation room, while Kujan realizes that important details and names from Kint's story are actually words appearing on objects in the room, and that Kint is actually Keyser Söze, the criminal mastermind Kujan had been looking for.

I agree with Volker Ferenz's argument that all unreliable narration in film emerges from an unreliable character-narrator (like Jonathan Cooper in *Stage Fright* or Kint in *The Usual Suspects*).

---

17. One might argue that in such cases, a film narrator translates the narration visually to the audience and that this cinematic narrator is unreliable. However, I would argue that since what we see is identical with what we hear, most viewers attribute both the spoken words and the resulting images to the character-narrator. From my perspective, there is no need for the concept of the film narrator in these cases either. The character-narrator is unreliable and this is clearly what we are supposed to realize.

In film, only in the case of [. . .] the character-narrator who "takes over," and thus appears to be the driving seat of, the narration, [. . .] do we deal with narrators whom we treat like "real persons" and "new acquaintances" and whom we can hold "responsible" for being unreliable about the facts of the fictional world. Only then do we have a clearly identifiable fictional scapegoat with sufficient "authority" over the narrative as a whole whom we can blame for textual contradictions and referential difficulties. (Ferenz 2005: 135)[18]

At first glance, one might feel that a film like *A Beautiful Mind* (2001) also presents us with a form of unreliable narration because it uses a lying camera as well (Helbig 2005, Lahde 2006, Laass 2008: 28). However, upon closer inspection we realize that in this case, the camera presents us with the deranged perception of John Forbes Nash (Russell Crowe), a mathematical genius, who begins to endure delusional and paranoid episodes, and Nash does not relate his life through a narrative; rather, he is a focalizer who simply misperceives the world. For example, at one point in the film, Nash begins to work for a secret Defense Department facility in the Pentagon, and it takes us quite some time to realize that he has never done so and that we have shared Nash's deranged perception all along. Toward the end of the film, we learn that the people from the Defense Department (such as William Parcher [Ed Harris]) do not exist outside Nash's mind (even though we see him interacting and dealing with them). According to Ferenz, focalizers like Nash cannot be unreliable: they "cannot be held accountable for distorting the fictional world simply because they do not narrate it" (2005: 140). Nash cannot misrepresent the world of *A Beautiful Mind* because he does not even try to narrate or represent it; rather, he inhabits it.[19]

18. Greta Olson argues along the same lines, when she claims that "the less personalized the narrative voice is, [. . .] the more inappropriate it is to infer unreliability" (2003: 106, n14). To put this slightly differently, the more personalized the narrative voice is, the more appropriate it is to infer unreliability.
19. Similarly, it would also be odd to speak of the unreliability of Septimus Warren-Smith in Virginia Woolf's novel *Mrs. Dalloway* (1925). Septimus is a reflector-character who suffers from schizophrenia following World War I. For instance, he frequently sees Evans, his commanding officer during the war, who is dead: "There was his hand; there the dead. White things were assembling behind the railings opposite. But he dared not look. Evans was behind the railings!" (2000: 21). Since Septimus misperceives the world but does not try to convince us of his deranged worldview, it does not really make sense to speak of unreliability here. Eva Laass mentions a number of films such as *The Sixth Sense* (1999), *Memento* (2000), *Donnie Darko* (2001), *A Beautiful Mind* (2001), and *Mulholland Drive* (2001), which, in her view, "encourage the attribution of unreliable narration [. . .] in spite of their non-personalised narrative mediation" (2008: 28). She sees these cases as forms of unreliable narration because for her, they are presented by the cinematic narrator (whom she rechristens as "the implied narrator"

Inferences about intention also come into play in connection with other forms of focalization. Generally speaking, films can use images that are internally focalized (such as point-of-view shots or memory sequences) or images that are externally focalized. In the latter case (which is far more common in film), the perspective "corresponds to that place where a hypothetical observer of the scene, present at the scene, would have to stand in order to give us the space as pictured" (Branigan 1984: 6). Numerous recent films confront us with images that seem to be externally focalized but then turn out to represent a character's worldview or misperception. For instance, Christine Edzard's two-part film adaptation of Charles Dickens's novel *Little Dorrit* (1855–57) (*Nobody's Fault* and *Little Dorrit's Story* [1987]) presents us with sequences in which the images of Amy Dorrit (Sarah Pickering) and Arthur Clennam (Derek Jacobi) are shaped by their respective worldviews. *Nobody's Fault* confronts us with the worldview of Arthur, while *Little Dorrit's Story* focuses on Amy's worldview. For instance, the room at the Marshalsea debtors' prison in *Little Dorrit's Story* is bigger and brighter than the room we see in *Nobody's Fault*. According to March, "the walls of the set have been bodily moved out by several feet; the set has been repainted, redressed in slightly brighter colors; potted plants blossom [. . .]; Dorrit's bare chair grows a cover, and his dressing gown sprouts tendrils of embroidery" (1993: 255). These two perspectives on the prison and William Dorrit (Alec Guiness) reflect Arthur's and Amy's perception. While Arthur has a pessimistic worldview and feels oppressed in the room, Amy has become accustomed to the prison and has a more optimistic worldview. The "point" of this technique is presumably to suggest that both Amy and Arthur live in their own worlds, and that it is difficult (or impossible) for one to understand the other (Alber 2007: 48). Since no narrator misleads us in this case, and since the filmic images here clearly relate to focalization, i.e. a character's worldview, rather than narration, I think that such scenarios cannot be described as cinematic forms of unreliable narration. I would like to argue that they are better understood as forms of internal focalization.[20]

To summarize: it makes sense to attribute a film's various stimuli to an agent like the hypothetical filmmaker because their presence follows a

---

[ibid.: 22]). Since I have done away with this concept, I would suggest categorizing all of these cases as forms of internal focalization: in each case the images we see are dominated by the distorted worldview of one of the characters, and they are *focalizers* who do not represent (or even try to represent) what we see.

20. Most of the alleged examples of cinematic unreliability discussed by Jörg Helbig also involve internal focalization, i.e., reflector-characters (or focalizers) that *perceive* but do not *narrate* (2005: 134–36; 140). The only exception is *Fight Club* (1999), where we can attribute unreliability to Jack (Edward Norton), the film's voice-over narrator (ibid.: 136–39).

particular purpose. In other words, they are interpretive clues and we are invited to ponder their implications. The concept of the hypothetical filmmaker allows us to speculate about the "point" of the film's various stimuli and its overall design without suggesting that we can definitely know the real or implied filmmaker's intentions. It is also worth noting that we assume that the hypothetical filmmaker follows the Gricean Cooperative Principle. That is to say, we approach the filmic data on the assumption of encountering a well-informed composition guided by the Gricean maxims of quality, quantity, relevance, and manner (1989: 22–40). Indeed, Marie-Louise Pratt has shown that no matter how odd the textual structure of a narrative is, we will always try to read it as a purposeful and meaningful communicative act by utilizing the Gricean Cooperative Principle (Pratt 1977: 170–71). And, as I will show in what follows, we can use this (very basic) assumption to make filmic oddities more readable.

THE HYPOTHETICAL FILMMAKER
AS A FRAME OF READING: The Strange Case of *Lost Highway*

In this section, I show that the concept of the hypothetical filmmaker may serve as a frame of interpretation that helps us to make strange and incomprehensible experimental films such as David Lynch's *Lost Highway* (1997) more readable. *Lost Highway* is a particularly strange and disconcerting film because it is full of unnatural, i.e., physically and logically impossible, scenarios or events (Alber 2009a: 80, 2009b). In this film, some of the characters are inexplicably transformed into other characters. Also, characters exist who can be at two different locations at the same time.[21] In the words of Murray Smith, "appearance and reality are dislocated; motivations are obscure, cognitive dissonance disturbs the very foundations of narrative coherence; temporal and causal sequences become paradoxical" (2003: 159). As I show in what follows, the application of Alan Palmer's continuing-consciousness frame to the characters but also to the film as a whole helps us to (at least partly) explain this odd narrative.

Lost Highway opens with a sequence in which we see Fred Madison (Bill Pullman) in his house. Somebody rings the bell and, through the intercom, delivers the (apparently meaningless) message that "Dick Laurent is dead." The film then introduces us to the tense atmosphere in the marriage

---

21. Inexplicable transformations of characters are physically impossible, while violations of the principle of non-contradiction are logically impossible (see also Doležel 1998: 165).

between Fred, who works as a saxophone player, and his wife, Renée (Patricia Arquette). Among other things, she does not want to go to his concert at the Luna Lounge. After the concert, he tries to call her but she does not answer the phone (either because she does not want to or because she is not there). In another scene, they have sex but he is obviously unable to satisfy her. Fred's and Renée's body language and their conversations (which are full of long and awkward pauses) also give us a clear sense of their alienation. "Renée's desire is a source of unbearable agony for Fred, precisely because he has no idea what she wants, let alone how to give it to her" (McGowan 2000: 54). The film underlines this feeling of discomfort by using a minimalist décor, low-key illumination,[22] and non-diegetic lugubrious string sounds. At one point, we witness a flashback in which Fred remembers that Renée left another concert by Fred together with a character called Andy (Michael Massee). When Fred then asks her how she got to know Andy, she remains extremely vague and tells him that Andy has offered her an unspecified "job." Fred suspects Renée of having an affair, and he becomes so jealous that he eventually kills her.

In his prison cell, Fred is mysteriously transformed into the car mechanic Pete Dayton (Balthazar Getty) who has an affair with Alice Wakefield. Interestingly, Alice is played by Patricia Arquette, the actress who also plays Renée. One way of explaining Fred's transformation and the existence of Pete's parallel universe would be to argue that Fred re-experiences the tragedy of his marriage with Renée from a different perspective, and in his fantasy assumes the identity of Pete, who is in many senses diametrically opposed to him: Fred is a melancholy and lonely musician who does not seem to have any friends. Pete, on the other hand, is a promiscuous car mechanic (and also a small-time criminal) who has numerous buddies. Also, Pete goes out with Sheila (Natasha Gregson Wagner) and at the same time, he begins an affair with Alice who seems to be the fantasy version of Renée since both are played by the same actress, Patricia Arquette. In the second part of the film, Fred tries to achieve something he did not achieve in the first part, namely to gain power and control over (or solve the mystery of) Renée (who is "reincarnated" as Alice).

The hypothetical filmmaker presents us with various clues that corroborate my hypothesis that the second part of the film enacts Fred's fantasies. First of all, before the transformation, we see an opening curtain which conveys the idea that we are about to witness something staged, theatrical, or

---

22. "Low-key" illumination primarily correlates with a lack of lighting and is frequently used in horror films to create suspense (see Bordwell/Thompson 2003: 196).

invented. Second, it is worth noting that the curtain opens to a shot of an exploding hut in the desert that runs backward: we see the exploding hut turning into a complete one. By using this backward-running shot, the film seems to tell us that we will learn how the hut came to explode, i.e., how the marriage between Fred and Renée came to be so unworkable that Fred finally killed his wife. Third, although the film contrasts the worlds of Fred and Pete through the use of lighting, colors, depth,[23] and music,[24] it remains very clear to us that the two worlds are related; the film establishes a connection between these worlds by having Patricia Arquette play both Renée and Alice, and by having Pete and Alice often speak the same dialogs as Fred and Renée. Fourth, when Fred realizes that, even in his role as Pete, he cannot understand, "have," or control Renée/Alice, the fantasy world begins to crumble and we return to the primary level of the film, i.e. Fred's world.[25] We can make sense of the film by applying Alan Palmer's continuing-consciousness frame to the characters Fred/Pete and Renée/Alice (Pete and Alice are fantasy versions of Fred and Renée created in Fred's mind), and we can also assume a continuing consciousness (the frame of the hypothetical filmmaker) that tries to communicate a meaningful message behind the film as a whole.

At this point, one may wonder about the differences between the concept of the implied filmmaker and the concept of the hypothetical filmmaker. I think the advantage of my concept is an ethical or moral one, namely a higher degree of honesty, modesty, and cautiousness. In contrast to Booth, I do not know for sure whether my reading correlates with the place "where the author *wants* [me] to stand" (1983: 73) and I do not know whether I have approximated the position of the authorial audience. I would like to suggest my reading as a hypothesis or speculation, and (as in everyday interaction) I want to allow for the possibility that I might be wrong. Nevertheless, I wish

23. "The first part (reality deprived of fantasy) is 'depthless,' dark, almost surreal, strangely abstract, colorless, lacking substantial density, and as enigmatic as a Magritte painting, with the actors acting almost as in a Beckett or Ionesco play, moving around as alienated automata. Paradoxically, it is in the second part, the staged fantasy, that we get a much stronger and fuller 'sense of reality,' of depth of sounds and smells, of people moving around in a 'real world'" (Žižek 2000: 21).

24. According to Smith, "the first half is dominated by a mixture of 'dark ambient' or 'illbient' atmospheres, and 'industrial' music—recalling the soundtracks of *Eraserhead* and *The Elephant Man*. The second half shifts the emphasis to, on the one hand, a kind of lite jazz (best exemplified by Antonio Carlos Jobim's bossa nova composition 'Insensatez'), and on the other hand those gaudy cousins, 'black' metal, 'death' metal, and shock rock (in the form of tracks by Rammstein and Marilyn Manson)" (2003: 160).

25. Since a seemingly supernatural event (Fred's transformation into Pete) gets explained as a dream or fantasy, *Lost Highway* bears certain structural similarities to what Todorov calls "the uncanny" (1973: 41).

to stress that the process of interpretation closely correlates with speculations about intentions.

I would now like to speculate about the potential purpose or "point" of the parallel universe that *Lost Highway* projects. First of all, it is worth noting that in Fred's fantasy world, Fred's alter ego Pete has an affair with Alice. Alice, some kind of *femme fatale,* is the girlfriend of Mr. Eddy (Robert Loggia), a pornographer, and she also plays roles in his porn films. At one point, Alice tells Pete that Andy offered her a "job," which consisted of taking her clothes off in front of Mr. Eddy while one of his gangsters put a gun to her head. Pete asks her why she did not decline and speculates that she actually "liked it." Since we witnessed exactly the same dialog between Fred and Renée earlier on, the film here informs us that in its primary world, it was actually Fred's wife Renée who accepted Andy's job offer. Indeed, toward the end of the film, when we return to Fred's world, we learn that Renée had an affair with the pornographer Dick Laurent, the equivalent of Mr. Eddy in Fred's world (also played by Robert Loggia), and starred in his porn films. More specifically, we see Renée having sex with Dick Laurent in a room at the so-called Lost Highway hotel. Once Renée has left the hotel, Fred overpowers Dick Laurent, throws him into the boot of his car, and then shoots him in the desert. This scene is followed by a sequence in which Fred rings the bell of his own house to speak the sentence "Dick Laurent is dead" into the intercom. That is to say, at the beginning of the film, Fred must have (at least unconsciously) known that "Dick Laurent is dead" because he had already killed him. I think that one can explain this logically impossibly scenario (in which Fred tells himself through the intercom that "Dick Laurent is dead") as the visualization of an unconscious process. In other words, the images tell us that Fred knows that he killed Dick Laurent but represses this knowledge so that he is no longer consciously aware of it.

As Fred begins to realize that, even in his role as Pete, he cannot "have" or control Renée/Alice,[26] the fantasy world gradually dissolves. All the characters disappear or are retransformed. At first, Pete's girlfriend Sheila disappears, and she is followed by Pete's parents. Later on, when Pete and Alice have sexual intercourse in the desert, he tells her, "I want you, I want you," to which she coldly responds, "You'll never have me." It is notably at this

---

26. As I have shown in Alber (forthcoming), Pete's obsession with Alice borders on self-destruction. At one point, she tells him that she will not be able to see him. Pete is full of despair, and the film cuts from a close-up of Pete's face to a shot of moths inside a ceiling light, where they die in their attempt to fly into a light bulb. This juxtaposition involves cinematic metaphor and allows us to see Alice as the light and Pete as a moth in so far as he destroys himself in his desperate attempts to reach or possess her.

point that Pete turns into Fred again. Fred's second attempt to gain control over Renée did not work either, and as a consequence Pete is retransformed into Fred. Alice, on the other hand, walks into the hut and disappears like all the other characters. *Lost Highway* thus seems to argue that Fred should learn to let go and to accept things as they are because he will not be able to control Renée anyway. One potential message of the film might be that our desperate attempts to control others by understanding every aspect of them will not work out, and that we should thus refrain from trying to do so.

There are two final aspects of this film that I would like to discuss in the context of my attempt to develop an interpretation of the film using the idea of hypothetical intentionalism, namely the identity of the spooky and devil-like "Mystery Man" (Robert Blake) and the videotapes that Fred and Renée find on the stairs to their house. Both seem to be closely related to the problems that exist between Fred and Renée. To begin with, it is worth noting that the pasty-faced Mystery Man enters the world of the film through Renée, or, more specifically, through Fred's vision of Renée. We first see this old man when Fred wakes up during the night, looks at his wife but instead of her face sees the face of the Mystery Man.[27]

Later on, Fred talks to the Mystery Man at Andy's party. The Mystery Man tells Fred that he is in Fred's house, and offers to call him there. Strangely enough, the Mystery Man, who stands before Fred, answers the phone in Fred's house. When Fred asks him how this is possible, the old man replies, "You invited me. It is not my custom to go where I am not wanted." The Mystery Man thus seems to embody Fred's desire to be at two places at the same time to be able to gain absolute control over Renée (for instance, when he phones her after the concert and she does not answer the phone). In what follows, the movie (or the hypothetical filmmaker) establishes a close link between Fred and the Mystery Man. For example, both can be at two different locations at the same time: the Mystery Man can simultaneously stand before Fred at Andy's party and answer the phone in Fred's house. Similarly, at the end of the film, we see Fred telling himself through the intercom that "Dick Laurent is dead." Also, the Mystery Man notably helps Fred to kill Dick Laurent. One way of explaining the existence of the Mystery Man would thus be to argue that he exists in Fred's mind and constitutes some kind of materialization or embodiment of Fred's desire to understand and control the split within Renée, i.e., her hidden desires and drives. In other

---

27. This superimposition involves cinematic metaphor and invites us to see Renée as the Mystery Man with the consequence that the beautiful woman becomes threatening, scary, and ugly. And, indeed, Renée is in a sense quite threatening for Fred: he cannot have a "normal" relationship with her because of her mysterious desires (Alber, forthcoming).

words, we can explain the Mystery Man by attributing his existence to Fred's unconsciousness. Anne Jerslev, on the other hand, reads the Mystery Man as "a personified, perverse visual principle" (2004: 161). This reading also makes sense if one extends this principle to all the men in the film. Interestingly, both Fred/Pete and Mr. Eddy/Dick Laurent follow the desire to master the riddle of femininity through voyeuristic surveillance but ultimately fail.

In the first part of the film, Fred and Renée find three different videotapes on the steps to their house. The first one depicts the exterior of their house; the second one presents a strange shot in which somebody walks into their bedroom and films them as they sleep; the third one shows Fred next to the mutilated corpse of his wife. These videotapes are disconcerting because we never learn where they come from. The most obvious answer is the Mystery Man, who, however, only exists in Fred's mind. I would therefore like to argue that, like the Mystery Man, the videotapes are actually materializations of the problems that exist between Fred and Renée. And it is worth noting that their problems have got to do with both videotapes and the idea of surveillance. Renée plays roles in Dick Laurent's porn films, and this is arguably a severe problem for Fred.[28] Fred, on the other hand, would like to observe every move that his wife makes in order to gain complete control over her.

In other words, the film *Lost Highway* depicts psychological processes and problems as existing in the outside world where they can be filmed. Many shots in this film seem to convey the idea that internal processes can have very drastic consequences in the outside world, and that we should pay attention to them. Also, by confronting us with entities such as the Mystery Man and the videotapes, both of which cut across the distinction between "internal" and "external," the hypothetical filmmaker illustrates that it can be difficult to clearly separate illusion and reality. And this is particularly true of extreme emotional states like jealousy. One might argue that the film is ultimately about Fred's feelings of jealousy and his desperate attempts to come to terms with them (through a fantasy of omniscience). The Mystery Man and the videotapes highlight that in extreme emotional states like jealousy, reality and illusion often become indistinguishable. As a matter of fact, the film puts us into a position that is similar to that of a jealous person: we frequently do not know what to believe or which images to trust. And this is another effect that I would like to attribute to the hypothetical filmmaker. The ultimate message of the film might be that like Fred, we should not follow the human urge to create significance; we should rather learn to let go.

---

28. Colin Odell and Michelle Le Blanc also argue that the connection between these tapes and Pete's world is "via video" (2007: 99).

But it is worth noting that if we had not tried to impute intentions, we would not have arrived at this conclusion.

CONCLUSION

In this paper, I have looked at the process of cinematic narration from the perspective of hypothetical intentionalism. More specifically, I have redefined the process of cinematic narration as a complex process that involves the film's inventers, the viewer, and the narrative designs used in the film. I argue that viewers try to make sense of films by applying Dennett's intentional stance or Palmer's continuing-consciousness frame to characters but also to films as a whole. This redefinition of cinematic narration has the following advantages. First, it does justice to the folk-psychological reasoning viewers typically use to make sense of films. Second, we can avoid the odd suggestion that we can determine the real or implied filmmaker's intentions and motivations; in contrast to the implied author or filmmaker (Booth 1982: 21; Phelan 2005: 45), the hypothetical filmmaker is an emergent product of the interaction between narrative designs and processes of production and interpretation. Third, the concept of the hypothetical filmmaker can be used to replace the cinematic narrator, and it offers us a hierarchy that makes it possible for us to describe the complex functioning of cinematic narrative (including the phenomenon of cinematic unreliability). Fourth, the hypothetical filmmaker helps us to make experimental films such as David Lynch's *Lost Highway* more readable. This particular film might argue that it makes no sense to try to control others, and that we should learn to let go. I would like to hypothesize that these ideas played a role in the production of the film, and attribute them to what I call the hypothetical filmmaker.[29]

---

29. I wish to thank Johannes Fehrle, Monika Fludernik, Per Krogh Hansen, David Herman, Tilmann Köppe, Jim Phelan, Peter Rabinowitz, and the anonymous reader of the manuscript for their extremely helpful comments on an earlier version of this essay.

REFERENCES

2001: A Space Odyssee. Dir. Stanley Kubrick. Metro-Goldwyn-Mayer, 1968.

Alber, Jan (2007) *Narrating the Prison: Role and Representation in Charles Dickens' Novels, Twentieth-Century Fiction, and Film.* Youngstown, NY: Cambria Press.

────── (2009a) "Impossible Storyworlds—and What to Do with Them." *Storyworlds: A Journal of Narrative Studies* 1.1: 79–96.

────── (2009b) "Unnatural Narratives." *The Literary Encyclopedia.* 28 October 2009. *www.litencyc.com*

────── (forthcoming) "Cinematic Carcerality: Prison Metaphors in Film." *The Journal of Popular Culture.*

Bach, Michaela (1999) "Dead Men—Dead Narrators: Überlegungen zu Erzählern und Subjektivität im Film." *Grenzüberschreitungen: Narratologie im Kontext. Transcending Boundaries: Narratology in Context.* Eds. Walter Grünzweig and Andreas Solbach. Tübingen: Narr. 231–46.

Barthes, Roland (2002) "The Death of the Author [1968]." *The Book History Reader.* Eds. David Finkelstein and Alistair McCleery. London: Routledge. 221–24.

Baudry, Jean-Louis (1980) "Ideological Effects of the Basic Cinematographic Apparatus [1974–75]." *Film Theory and Criticism. Introductory Readings.* Eds. Leo Braudy and Marshall Cohen. Oxford: Oxford University Press. 345–55.

A Beautiful Mind. Dir. Ron Howard. Universal, 2001.

Black, David A. (2001) "Narrative." *Critical Dictionary of Film and Television Theory.* Ed. Roberta E. Pearson and Philip Simpson. London and New York: Routledge. 300–303.

Booth, Wayne C. (1982) "Between Two Generations: The Heritage of the Chicago School." *Profession* 82: 19–26.

────── (1983) *The Rhetoric of Fiction* [1961]. Chicago: University of Chicago Press.

────── (2002) "Is There an 'Implied' Author in Every Film?" *College Literature* 29.2: 124–31.

Bordwell, David (1985) *Narration in the Fiction Film.* London: Routledge.

────── (1989) *Making Meaning: Inference and Rhetoric in the Interpretation of Cinema.* Cambridge, MA: Harvard University Press.

Bordwell, David, and Kristin Thompson (2003) *Film Art: An Introduction.* 7th ed. New York: McGraw Hill.

The Bourne Identity. Dir. Doug Liman. Universal Pictures, 2002.

Branigan, Edward (1984) *Point of View in the Cinema: A Theory of Narration and Subjectivity in Classical Film.* Berlin and New York: Mouton.

Burgoyne, Robert (1990) "The Cinematic Narrator: The Logic and Pragmatics of Impersonal Narration." *Journal of Film and Video* 42.1: 3–16.

────── (1991) "Le narrateur au cinéma: Logique et pragmatique de la narration impersonelle [1990]." *Poétique* 22. 87: 271–88.

The Cabinet of Dr. Caligari. Dir. Robert Wiene. Decla-Bioscop AG, 1920.

Chatman, Seymour (1990) *Coming to Terms: The Rhetoric of Narrative in Fiction and Film.* Ithaca, NY and London: Cornell University Press.

────── (1999) "New Directions in Voice-Narrated Cinema." *Narratologies: New Perspectives on Narrative Analysis.* Ed. David Herman. Columbus: The Ohio State University Press. 315–39.

A Clockwork Orange. Dir. Stanley Kubrick. Warner Bros., 1971.
Currie, Gregory (1995) *Image and Mind: Film, Philosophy, and Cognitive Science*. Cambridge: Cambridge University Press.
Dennett, Daniel C. (1996) *Kinds of Minds: Towards an Understanding of Consciousness*. London: Weidenfels and Nichols.
Diehl, Nicholas (2009) "Imagining *De Re* and the Symmetry Thesis of Narration." *The Journal of Aesthetics and Art Criticism* 67.1: 15–24.
Doležel, Lubomír (1998) *Heterocosmica: Fiction and Possible Worlds*. Baltimore and London: The Johns Hopkins University Press.
Ferenz, Volker (2005) "Fight Clubs, American Psychos and Mementos: The Scope of Unreliable Narration in Film." *New Review of Film and Television Studies* 3.2: 133–59.
Fight Club. Dir. David Fincher. Twentieth-Century-Fox, 1999.
Fleishman, Avrom (1992) *Narrated Films: Storytelling Situations in Cinema History*. Baltimore and London: The Johns Hopkins University Press.
Fury. Dir. Fritz Lang. Metro-Goldwyn-Mayer, 1936.
Gaudreault, André (1999) *Du littéraire au filmique: Système du récit*. Paris: Armand Colin.
——— (2000) *Le récit cinématographique. Cinéma et récit II* [1990]. 2nd ed. Paris: Nathan.
Gaut, Berys (2004) "The Philosophy of the Movies: Cinematic Narration." *The Blackwell Guide to Aesthetics*. Ed. Peter Kivy. Malden, MA: Blackwell. 230–53.
Gibbs, Raymond W. (2005) "Intentionality." *Routledge Encyclopedia of Narrative Theory*. Eds. David Herman, Manfred Jahn, and Marie-Laure Ryan. London: Routledge. 247–49.
Grice, H. P. (1989) "Logic and Conversation [1975]." *Studies in the Way of Words*. Cambridge, MA: Harvard University Press. 22–40.
Grodal, Torben (2005) "Film Narrative." *The Routledge Encyclopedia of Narrative Theory*. Eds. David Herman, Manfred Jahn, and Marie-Laure Ryan. London: Routledge. 168–72.
Helbig, Jörg (2005) "'Follow the White Rabbit': Signale erzählerischer Unzuverlässigkeit im zeitgenössischen Spielfilm." *Was stimmt denn jetzt? Unzuverlässiges Erzählen in Literatur und Film*. Eds. Fabienne Liptay and Yvonne Wolf. Munich: Edition Text + Kritik. 131–46.
Herman, David (2006) "Genette Meets Vygotsky: Narrative Embedding and Distributed Intelligence." *Language and Literature* 15.4: 357–80.
——— (2007) "Cognition, Emotion, and Consciousness." *The Cambridge Companion to Narrative*. Ed. David Herman. Cambridge: Cambridge University Press. 245–59.
——— (2008) "Narrative Theory and the Intentional Stance." *Partial Answers* 6.2: 233–60.
Hutto, Daniel D. (2000) *Beyond Physicalism*. Amsterdam: John Benjamins.
Jahn, Manfred (2003) "A Guide to Narratological Film Analysis." 28 October 2009. www.uni-koeln.de/~ame02/pppf.htm
Jerslev, Anne (2004) "Beyond Boundaries: David Lynch's *Lost Highway*." *The Cinema of David Lynch—American Dreams, Nightmare Visions*. Eds. Erica Sheen and Annette Davison. London and New York: Wallflower Press. 151–64.
Kindt, Tom, and Hans-Harald Müller (2006) *The Implied Author: Concept and Controversy*. Berlin: de Gruyter.

Kozloff, Sarah (1988) *Invisible Storytellers: Voice-Over Narration in American Fiction Film.* Berkeley: University of California Press.

Laass, Eva (2008) *Broken Taboos, Subjective Truths: Forms and Functions of Unreliable Narration in Contemporary American Cinema. A Contribution to Film Narratology.* Trier: WVT.

Lahde, Maurice (2006) "Den Wahn erlebbar machen: Zur Inszenierung von Halluzinationen in Ron Howards *A Beautiful Mind* und David Cronenbergs *Spider*." *"Camera doesn't lie": Spielarten erzählerischer Unzuverlässigkeit im Film.* Ed. Jörg Helbig. Trier: WVT: 43–72.

Levinson, Jerrold (1996a) "Film Music and Narrative Agency." *Post-Theory: Reconstructing Film Studies.* Eds. David Bordwell and Noël Carroll. Madison: University of Wisconsin Press. 248–82.

⸺ (1996b) "Messages in Art." *The Pleasures of Aesthetics: Philosophical Essays.* Ed. Jerrold Levinson. Ithaca and London: Cornell University Press. 224–41.

Lost Highway. Dir. David Lynch. Asymmetrical Productions/Ciby 2000, 1997.

Lothe, Jakob (2000) *Narrative in Fiction and Film: An Introduction.* Oxford: Oxford University Press.

McGowan (2000) "Finding Ourselves on a *Lost Highway*: David Lynch's Lesson in Fantasy." *Cinema Journal* 39.2: 51–73.

March, Joss (1993) "Inimitable Double Vision: Dickens, *Little Dorritt*, Photography, Film." *Dickens Studies Annual* 22: 239–82.

Metropolis. Dir. Fritz Lang. Ufa, 1926.

Nathan, Daniel O. (1992) "Irony, Metaphor, and the Problem of Intention." *Intention and Interpretation.* Ed. Gary Iseminger. Philadelphia: Temple University Press. 183–202.

Odell, Colin, and Michelle Le Blanc (2007) *David Lynch.* Harpenden: Kamera Books.

Olson, Greta (2003) "Reconsidering Unreliability: Fallible and Untrustworthy Narrators." *Narrative* 11.1: 93–109.

Palmer, Alan (2004) *Fictional Minds.* Lincoln: University of Nebraska Press.

Phelan, James (2005) *Living to Tell about It: A Rhetoric and Ethics of Character Narration.* Ithaca, NY: Cornell University Press.

Pratt, Mary Louise (1977) *Toward a Speech Act Theory of Literary Discourse.* Bloomington and London: Indiana University Press.

Prince, Gerald (1987) *A Dictionary of Narratology.* Lincoln: University of Nebraska Press.

Smith, Murray (2003) "A Reasonable Guide to Horrible Noise (Part 2): Listening to *Lost Highway.*" *Film Style and Story: A Tribute to Torben Grodal.* Eds. Lennard Højberg and Peter Schepelern. Copenhagen: Museum Tusculanum Press. 153–70.

Sobchack, Vivian C. (1981) "Décor as Theme: *A Clockwork Orange.*" *Literature/Film Quarterly* 9.2: 92–102.

Stage Fright. Dir. Alfred Hitchcock. Warner Bros., 1950.

Stam, Robert, Robert Burgoyne, and Sandy Flitterman-Lewis (1992) *New Vocabularies in Film Semiotics: Structuralism, Post-Structuralism, and Beyond.* London and New York: Routledge.

Thomson-Jones, Katherine (2007) "The Literary Origins of the Cinematic Narrator." *The British Journal of Aesthetics* 47.1: 76–94.

Todorov, Tzvetan (1973) *The Fantastic: A Structural Approach to a Literary Genre.*

Trans. Richard Howard. Cleveland and London: The Press of Case Western Reserve University.
The Usual Suspects. Dir. Bryan Singer. Polygram Filmed Entertainment, 1995.
Walsh, Richard (2007) *The Rhetoric of Fictionality: Narrative Theory and the Idea of Fiction*. Columbus: The Ohio State University Press.
Whittock, Trevor (1990) *Metaphor and Film*. Cambridge: Cambridge University Press.
Wilson, Eric G. (2007) *The Strange World of David Lynch*. New York and London: Continuum.
Wilson, George (1986) *Narration in Light: Studies in Cinematic Point of View*. Baltimore and London: The Johns Hopkins University Press.
Wimsatt, William K., and Monroe C. Beardsley (2001) "The Intentional Fallacy [1946]." *Norton Anthology of Theory and Criticism*. Eds. Vincent B. Leitch et al. New York: Norton. 1374–87.
Woolf, Virginia (2000) *Mrs. Dalloway* [1925]. Oxford: Oxford University Press.
You Only Live Once. Dir. Fritz Lang. Walter Wanger Productions, 1937.
Žižek, Slavoj (2000) *The Art of the Ridiculous Sublime: On David Lynch's Lost Highway*. Seattle, WA: Walter Chapin Simpson Center for the Humanities.
Zunshine, Lisa (2006) *Why We Read Fiction: Theory of Mind and the Novel*. Columbus: The Ohio State University Press.

7

SUSAN S. LANSER

Sapphic Dialogics

Historical Narratology and the Sexuality of Form

Literary critics have long acknowledged that form is (a kind of) content and, as such, socially meaningful. Even scholars whose focus is hermeneutic rather than poetic cannot wholly escape attending to the formal elements that shape—and arguably *are*—the text. It would seem, then, that narratologists and interpreters of narrative would acknowledge considerable common ground. Yet the relationship between narratology and studies of the novel—to take one example—still remains something of a standoff, and nowhere more vividly than on the turf of history. As Monika Fludernik observes, narratologists have demonstrated "comparatively little interest on a theoretical level in the history of narrative forms and functions" (2003: 331). Conversely, scholars invested in the history of the novel tend to evince little more than passing interest in the novel's changing formal practices. As Marjorie Levinson observes, the "historical turn" in literary studies, with its emphasis on texts as "documents" rather than "monuments" (to borrow René Wellek's famous terms), has been accompanied by a rather widely acknowledged "eclipse" of form (Levinson 2007: 559, 566). Thus it would seem that, as Brian McHale willfully overstates it, "historicism represses narratology, just as [. . .] narratology represses history" (2005: 65). It is safe to speculate that typically, though of course not universally, the more historicized a narrative project, the less likely it is to be narratological, and that the more narratological a project, the less likely it is to be historical.

And yet some of the most important contributions to narrative studies are rich amalgams of poetics and history. I think of Erich Auerbach's inimitable *Mimesis,* which offers a history of techniques by which narrative has changed under the pressure of imitative representation. Or Ian Watt's groundbreaking *Rise of the Novel,* which provides a brilliant delineation of "formal realism" as "the sum of literary techniques [. . .] whereby the novel embodies [a] circumstantial view of life" by providing "such details of the story as the individuality of the actors concerned, [and] the particulars of the times and places of their actions" (Watt 1957: 31–32). Or the concept of homology between the formal structures of literary texts and the economic conditions of society that we owe to such theorists as Georg Lukács and Lucien Goldmann. And I think of course of Bakhtin, whose explorations of the "dialogic imagination" are at once historicized and formalized, and of Fredric Jameson, whose *Political Unconscious: Narrative as a Socially Symbolic Act* (1981) arguably relies almost as much on Greimas as on Marx.

Ansgar Nünning would seem to be right, then, in predicting that "the more narratological literary and cultural history becomes and the more historically and culturally oriented narratology becomes, the better for both" (2000: 345). One recent model of just such a serious narratological inquiry that is also a serious literary history is Hilary Dannenberg's *Coincidence and Counterfactuality: Plotting Time and Space in Narrative Fiction* (2008). My essay offers a more modest contribution to that aim by studying narrative form as sexual content in the context of lesbian—or what I prefer to call sapphic—literary history.[1] I am of course far from the first to marry the study of lesbian representation with the study of narrative form: Marilyn Farwell's *Heterosexual Plots & Lesbian Narratives* (1996) asks what counts as "lesbian narrative" and explores lesbian subjectivity as it is constituted in a range of modern and postmodern incursions against a heterosexual masterplot; Judith Roof's *Come As You Are: Sexuality & Narrative* (1996) investigates the reciprocal relationship of narrative and sexuality in twentieth-century Western discourse to ask what textual locations homosexualities can occupy; and a fruitful "Sexuality and Narrative" issue of *Modern Fiction Studies* (1995) likewise explored this imbrication. But these several works discuss twentieth-century texts almost exclusively and, like most studies of sapphic representations in the novel (Lisa Moore's *Dangerous Intimacies* [1997] and George Haggerty's *Unnatural Affections* [1999] for eighteenth-century English texts, and Sharon Marcus's *Between Women* [2007] for Victorian narra-

---

1. Terms such as "lesbian" and "sapphic" are equally problematic for exploring a historical sweep. I prefer "sapphic" in part for its emergence in the eighteenth century, the period that will constitute the central focus of this essay, and in part simply for its *Verfremdungseffekt*: it reminds us that sexuality, like narrative, is historically contingent.

tives), focus primarily on plot and character. My own much briefer work on "Queering Narratology" (1996) does attempt to sharpen awareness of the significant place gender and sexuality might occupy in narration itself, but like these other studies, it remains essentially a project of synchrony.[2]

My purpose here, in contrast, is both diachronic and formalist: to sketch the ways in which a particular cultural *topos*—in this case, female same-sex desire—may be linked with historically variable narrative practices. By looking at the changing ways in which the sapphic operates narratively, I hope to suggest that we have something to learn about the history of sexuality from studying narrative form; conversely, by looking at the ways in which narrative—and in particular narration—operates sapphically, I hope to suggest that we have something to learn about narrative *tout court* from its sapphic inscriptions. And in tracing the rudiments of an arc from the sixteenth to the nineteenth century of one such structure, I will suggest that the intersections of narrative history with the history of sexuality make the case for both a more consciously historicized narratology and a more consciously narratological history of sexuality.[3]

More specifically, I will explore a form of narrative intersubjectivity that I call the "sapphic dialogic," in which erotic content is filtered through a (usually intradiegetic) female pairing of narrator and narratee. Attending to narration rather than only to narrated events allows me to argue that female same-sex desire underwrites both early pornography and, in more muted and unexpected ways, the courtship novel of the eighteenth century. Such a claim might well seem counterintuitive, for as many scholars have persuasively argued, the "rise" of the novel is swept up in the constitution of sexual difference and the consolidation of a heterosexual subject. And if, as Nancy Armstrong has famously argued, the "modern individual is first and foremost a woman" (1987: 4), certainly that woman—Pamela, Elizabeth Bennet, Jane Eyre—is defined by her place in a social order that is heterosexual as well as class-stratified. But reading narrative form as sexual content brings a more complex textual story—both in and of the novel—to light. Put differently, I am suggesting that what Michael McKeon has called the "secret history of domesticity" carries the deeper secret of domesticity's dependence on the structural deployment of female same-sex desire.

---

2. A somewhat lengthier version of this essay appears in Lanser (1998).
3. Lisa Moore's *Dangerous Intimacies: Toward a Sapphic History of the British Novel* (1997) nods to the potential for the sapphic to inflect the "rise" of the novel but does not take up this challenge more than in passing and not through an analysis of narrative form.

PORNOGRAPHY AND SAPPHIC FORM

Mikhail Bakhtin has famously argued that "the speaking person and his [sic] discourse" (1981: 332) constitute the novel's primary distinctiveness, and it is a commonplace that homodiegetic voice "rose" with the novel itself. It is also a commonplace that female voice characterizes many an eighteenth-century novel. But the prehistory of the novel's homodiegetic practices turns out to be quite differently gendered. If we can trace the genesis of a work like *Robinson Crusoe* to such seventeenth-century genres as the spiritual autobiography and the traveler's tale, it is worth noting that these forms relied almost exclusively on male voices.[4] One of the few places where early modern literature does deploy female homodiegesis is in the formal dialogue, a genre that experienced a dramatic resurgence in early modernity. While the preponderance of Renaissance dialogues remained true to the Platonic tradition of male interlocutors, female voices were put to two primary purposes, both of which entail transgressions of "woman's place": protofeminist discourses about the status of women and erotic conversations about sexuality. Both practices can trace their roots to Lucian's *Dialogues of the Courtesans* of the second century C.E., to my knowledge the only classical instance that relies almost exclusively on the voices of women. Indeed, it is fair to say that the genres both of the *querelle des femmes* and of early modern pornography were born in female voice. Christine de Pisan's *Cité des dames* (1405), which launched the *querelle*, relies entirely on the voices of "Christine" and her allegorical but explicitly female guides to the utopian women's "city" to make its case for women's contributions to history. Later instances of the *querelle* are more prone to relying on male voices, although Moderata Fonte's *Il merito delle donne* (1600) breaks new ground by creating conversations among seven women friends who undertake a scathing critique of patriarchy, marriage, and men's treatment of women.

It is in the more clearly narrative of these two genres, however, that we find the most direct antecedent of female voice in the novel. In the final dialogue of Pietro Aretino's *Ragionamenti* (1534), arguably Europe's first post-classical pornographic fiction and one structured entirely as a series of conversations between women, a midwife/procuress describes to a wetnurse an illicit encounter that she has arranged between a married lady and her lover. But in an act of dialogic imagination, the midwife adds a sapphic narrative layer to this heterosexual story by telling another woman what the

---

4. As Felicity Nussbaum argues in *The Autobiographical Subject*, women also produced spiritual autobiographies, but these were available only privately. Among others, Nussbaum mentions works by Elizabeth Bury, Mary Mollineux, Alice Thornton, and Elizabeth West.

sight of a third woman—the adulterous wife who is undressing for her male lover—does to her. Re-presenting the view from her hiding place, and in effect occupying a focalizing position that aligns her with the man as he examines his paramour "carefully, in every nook and cranny," the midwife rhapsodizes:

> I saw her strip herself stark naked [. . .] for he examined her carefully [. . .]. My God, her neck! And her breasts, Nurse, those two tits would have corrupted virgins and made martyrs unfrock themselves. I lost my wits when I saw that lovely body with its navel like a jewel at its center, and I lost myself in the beauty of that particular thing, thanks to which men do so many crazy deeds [. . .]. The front parts of her body drove me wild, but the wonder and marvel which really drove me wild were due to her shoulders, her loins, and her other charms. I swear to you [. . .] that as I looked at her, I put my hand on my you-know-what and rubbed it just the way a man does when he hasn't place to put it. (Aretino 2005: 341–42)[5]

In this moment, a heterosexual story produces, in effect, a second and quite sapphic narrative. And this stimulation of one woman's desire when watching another is multiplied yet again when the midwife's interlocutor, the nurse, is herself stimulated by listening to the midwife: "I feel, as you tell me all this, that sweet delight which you feel when dreaming that your lover is doing it to you and then awake just as you come" (Aretino 2005: 342). The arousal of women by women that happens on the level of narration thus depends on a heterosexual story, while the heterosexual story depends on the sapphic structure of its narration. The effect is dialogic not only in the formal but in the Bakhtinian sense: the heterosexual story becomes heteroglossic; it is capable of being turned into a homoerotic text, and the renowned "male gaze" is rendered simultaneously female.

It is fair to say that formally speaking, early modern pornography was born in this woman-to-woman narrative structure, and that what I call "sapphic dialogic" thus warrants recognition both in the history of sexuality and the history of narrative. I do not, of course, mean that actual lesbians by

5. For reference to this scene I am indebted to Denise A. Walen (2000). Aretino's Italian original reads as follows: "la vidi spogliare ignuda [. . .] perchè egli la contemplò in ogni parte [. . .]. Un collo Iddio! Un petto balia! E due poccie da far corrompere i vergini, et da sfratare i martiri; io mi smarrii nel vedere il corpo con la sua gioia per elico in mezzo, e mi perdei ne la vaghezza di quella cosa, bontà de la quale si fanno tante pazie, tante nimicizie, tante spese, e tante parole; ma le coscie, le gambe, i piedi, le mani, e le braccia lodino per me chi sa lodarle. E non solo le parti dinanzi; lo stupore che mi cavò fuor del sentimento, uscì da le spalle, da le reni, e da l'altre sue galanterie. Io ti giuro per lo mio mobile, e lo do a sacco, al fuoco, e ai ladri, e ai birri, se non mi posi nel vederlo la mano a la cotale, menandomela non altrimenti che si menino i cotali da chi non ha dove intignergli" (Aretino 1979: 275).

whatever name had anything to do with the construction of Aretino's dialogues, which are doubtless written for the titillation of men and which also use transgressive women to expose a range of social and intellectual hypocrisies. But it is not insignificant that pornography takes this turn, for I will argue that the dialogic structuring of a heterosexual story through female same-sex narration becomes a significant practice not only overtly in seventeenth-century erotica, but covertly in eighteenth-century courtship narratives. Aretino's sapphic structure is thus a foundational practice in the history of European narrative as it edges toward the genre recognizable as the novel. We can readily see the more overtly erotic and the more conventionally chaste (and historically sequential) versions of this dynamic in two of the most popular erotic fictions of the 1680s, and again, if more chastely, in such novels by women writers as Eliza Haywood's *The Masqueraders; or, Fatal Curiosity* (1724), Marie-Jeanne Riccoboni's *Lettres de Milady Juliette Catesby à Milady Henriette Campley, son amie* (1759), Frances Sheridan's *Memoirs of Miss Sidney Bidulph* (1761), and Eliza Fenwick's *Secresy, or The Ruin on the Rock* (1796), and perhaps most tortuously in the two most famous novels of the eighteenth century, Samuel Richardson's *Clarissa* (1747–48) and Jean-Jacques Rousseau's *Julie, ou la nouvelle Héloïse* (1762). That we can also mark a relative endpoint to this practice of sapphic narration is equally significant.

While the stories that Aretino's midwife tells the nurse are not dependent on—but only back-inflected by—their sapphic narration, two erotic fictions of the 1680s, Nicolas Chorier's *L'Académie des dames ou la Philosophie dans le boudoir du Grand Siècle* (c. 1680) and Jean Barrin's *Vénus dans le cloître, ou, La religieuse en chemise: entretiens curieux* (1683), and several other texts to a lesser degree take sapphic narration beyond the imbrication of two temporalities to a "here-and-now" dynamic in which sapphic dialogue not only revises but constitutes the plot.[6] That these texts are invested in the formal realism and especially the "chronotope" that characterizes modern fiction aligns what are otherwise loosely-plotted erotic encounters with the novel that will "rise" in their wake. *L'Académie des dames* consists of seven dialogues between the newly betrothed Octavie and her more experienced,

---

6. Texts with erotic content that use female-female narration during the same period include the anonymous *L'école des filles, ou la philosophie des dames*, printed multiple times from 1655 on and set forth in an English version as *The School of Venus* (1680); Ferrante Pallavicino's *La Retorica delle Puttane* (1642 and 1671); the anonymous English contribution based upon Pallavicino, *The Whores Rhetorick: Calculated to the Meridian of London; and conformed to the Rules of Art* (1683); and, in a somewhat different vein, Bernard Mandeville's *The Virgin Unmask'd: or, Female Dialogues Betwixt an Elderly Maiden Lady and her Niece* (1724).

married cousin Tullie, who has come to teach her the sexual ways of the world. *Vénus dans le cloître* uses a similar structure to enact five dialogues between the innocent Soeur Agnes and the sexually experienced Soeur Angélique. Both works circulated widely throughout Europe in their original languages and in translation; both discuss, describe and enact sex acts in the context of philosophically wide-ranging conversations; both texts deploy narrative strategies that keep same-sex intimacy in motion throughout the text, even when heterosexual acts are being recounted or enacted; and both also resist closure by promising further sapphic encounters or by insisting that they live on in memory.

These narratives take sapphic structure beyond Aretino's retrospective and voyeuristic form; here the interlocutors are also the actors, and the textual events become inseparable from their narration. The narrator-characters effectively perform sex acts through speech acts: they *discuss* sex, *report* sex, and *enact* sex, mostly between one another and sometimes with men in one another's presence, in a discourse that joins narration and action in a single chronotope. This is no external view such as the one through the peephole that allows Aretino's midwife to participate in a man's seduction of a woman; here both narrators and readers are located in effect *within* the sexual events. The merging of *Erzählzeit* (narrating time) and *erzählte Zeit* (narrated time), marked both by the "ahs" and "ohs" of sexual pleasure and by ellipses that signal ecstasy beyond language, sustains a sense that the represented acts are proceeding at something like the pace in which they would actually occur, creating a stimulating synchrony that makes sex available to readers *as an experience* and makes time "in effect, palpable and visible" (Bakhtin 1981: 250) in a way that the novel will come to depend on. Even heterosexual encounters are filtered through sapphic narration, effectively "queering" these fictions' ostensibly phallocentric plots. In effect, all sex becomes sapphic sex, and heteroerotic pleasure—for both characters and readers—is dependent on the sapphic word and gaze. Without denying that these fictions are man-made fantasies produced primarily for men's pleasure, they nonetheless constitute a *formal* innovation in the gendering—and sexing—of narrative voice.

SAPPHIC DOMESTICITY
The Eroticism of Confidence

Libertine fictions continue to proliferate, of course, in the eighteenth century. Diderot's *La Religieuse* (circulated in manuscript in 1760 but not published until 1796) is easily read as an *implicit* revision of *Vénus dans le cloître* (though with a single female narrator addressing a male narratee) and Sade's *Philosophie dans le boudoir* (1795) as an *explicit revision of *L'Académie des dames* (though with male as well as female dialogic voices). It is especially worth noting that England's best-known indigenous libertine novel, John Cleland's *Fanny Hill or Memoirs of a Woman of Pleasure* (1749), is structured as a sexual confidence between women: each volume begins with a salutation to an anonymous "Madam" whose "desires" Fanny considers "as indispensable orders" to provide the "stark naked truth" (39) even though she wishes her narratee would be "cloyed and tired" with the "repetition of near the same images, the same figures, the same expressions" in recounting the "*joys, ardours, transports, ecstasies*" in a narrative of which "the *practice of pleasure* [. . .] professedly composes the whole basis" (129). Clearly, this "practice of pleasure" constitutes on the level of narration the very relationship between narrator and narratee.

In terms of manifest content, these libertine fictions are rather distant from the domestic novels that dominate the eighteenth century. Yet Bakhtin reminds us that the novel is in a sense pornographic at its core: it is essentially the practice of prurience, "of snooping about, of overhearing 'how others live'" (1981: 123). If, as the novel gets domesticated, it foregoes its most overtly pornographic "snooping," then it seems to me all the more significant that the structure of narration underlying so many libertine writings also sustains a major strand of the domestic novel. For I will argue that the convention of sapphic interlocutors set in motion by libertine fiction finds a muted counterpart in one of the most common narrative devices of the courtship novel: the device of confidantes whose letters, journals, or conversations place two women in a *structurally* erotic relationship in which same-sex secrets become the narrative vehicle for cross-sex desires. The sexual history of narrative form thus argues for a line of continuity between the libertine dialogues and the more decorous novels of desire that appear to affirm and even to celebrate a firmly heterosexual trajectory. In this way, the sapphic is not simply propelled by the novel but propels it, holding an originary place in the new narrative order from which the novel springs.

We find a cautionary version of this structure in Eliza Haywood's *The Masqueraders or, Fatal Curiosity* (1724). In a fiction that I would situate midway between the libertine and the domestic, the rake Dorimenus seduces a willing widow named Dalinda to the apparent bliss of both. Yet for Dalinda, sex requires the supplement of its *telling*:

> Whatever Company she happen'd to be in, she always found some pretence to make [Dorimenus] the Theme of her Discourse, and even among those

who were the greatest Strangers to him, would invent some way to introduce his Name—But all this fell short of the Satisfaction she wanted:—Her Soul, full of his Charms, wild 'twixt Desire and Transport, could not contain the vast Excess.—She long'd to impart the mighty Bliss. (13)

Here Haywood in effect sets up the primacy of narration over story as a *sexual* practice. When Dalinda "pour[s] out the overwhelming Transport" (7) to her friend Philecta, her own narration of her sexual encounters is not merely mentioned but transcribed, and it occupies far more textual space than the heterodiegetic narrator's initial account of those acts. Moreover, the narration is explicitly represented as an erotic experience: while Dalinda "related to [Philecta] the particulars of her Happiness," she

[. . .] felt in the delicious Representation, a Pleasure, perhaps, not much inferiour to that which the Reality afforded [. . .]. She no sooner parted from [Dorimenus's] Embraces, than she flew to her fair Friend, gave her the whole History of what had pass'd between them—repeated every tender Word he spoke—not the least fond Endearment was forgot—describ'd his Looks—his melting Pressures—his Ardours!—his Impatiences!—his Extasies!—his Languishments!—and endeavour'd to make her sensible how different he was from other Lovers!—how much beyond his Sex!—with what a God-like Sublimity of Passion he ador'd her!—and what was more prodigious than the rest, assur'd her, that each Enjoyment but encreased Desire. (14)

Here we have a sapphic supplement that turns the heterosexual event, structurally speaking, into sex "between women," so that the narrative becomes the story of the pleasure both of (hetero)sexual act and (homo)sexual discourse. But if Dalinda needs narration to supplement story, the supposedly dependable but, it turns out, envious confidante needs story to supplement narration: she uses what Dalinda has told her in order to lure Dorimenus to herself, her "fatal curiosity" thereby turning narration back into plot. Philecta's ruin is likewise doubly an effect of story and narration; after she becomes pregnant, it is less the pregnancy than Dalinda's exposure of Philecta's betrayal that ultimately destroys Philecta: "The Affair shall be no Secret—I will, at least, have the satisfaction of Revenge" (40). The tragic outcome of this particular structure of narration takes us far from the collusive eroticism of the libertine fictions I have discussed above; indeed, one could argue that Haywood's representation serves as a cautionary tale locating female interlocutors as rivals for men rather than erotic partners. That the sapphic structure is enclosed within a heterodiegetic narrative both fosters and symbolizes the unreliability of female confidence.

More domesticated and subtler deployments of same-sex narrative confidence structure two midcentury novels by women: Marie-Jeanne Riccoboni's *Lettres de Milady Juliette Catesby à Milady Henriette Campley, son amie* (1759) and Francis Sheridan's *Memoirs of Miss Sidney Bidulph* (1761). Riccoboni's epistolary novel is effectively a one-way correspondence from Juliette to her confidante Henriette, narrating Juliette's flight from Lord Ossery, to whom she had been secretly engaged but who had abandoned her to marry another. Ossery's wife has died, and he is now pursuing Juliette in an effort to explain himself; it turns out that he did not love his wife but married her as the honorable response to a peccadillo. After Juliette yields to her own desire and marries him, it is Ossery who writes the news to Henriette, appropriating Juliette's pen and effectively silencing her to tell Henriette that there is no longer a "Lady Catesby," but "if in place of this friend so dear to your heart you'll accept a new one, then Lady Ossery is ready to receive your warm congratulations" (172–73; translation mine). Ossery is emphatic: Juliette is now "mine, forever mine. No more Lady Catesby; she's my wife, my friend, my mistress" (173). But Juliette recovers her pen from Ossery to suggest that she is not simply "forever his": the novel's last avowal of love is for the confidante: "We await you impatiently here: no parties, no balls, without my dear Henriette; I would say no pleasures, if the person who is following my pen with his eyes were not already a little jealous of my tender *amitié*" (39).[7] In the final narration, in contradistinction to the apparent plot, it is the husband who gets abandoned and the female friendship that gets the last word. *Juliette Catesby* thus participates in the extensive revisionist project which I have discussed elsewhere (Lanser 1998–99), that gives to friendship between women the primacy that classical and early modern writers from Aristotle to Montaigne accorded friendship between men.

The same-sex intimacy sustained by narration more vividly overtakes the cross-sex intimacy that dominates the plot of Frances Sheridan's *Memoirs of Miss Sidney Bidulph*. Constructed as journal written for Cecilia, for whose "embrace" Sidney "longs" and to whom, in conventional fashion, "she revealed all the secrets of her heart," *Sidney Bidulph* is built upon blatant trade-offs in the object of desire. Just as Cecilia leaves to *go* abroad, Sidney's brother returns *from* abroad with Faulkland, the man with whom Sidney will fall in love. One might argue that the unacknowledged task of this novel,

---

7. In a fuller analysis of this novel in *Fictions of Authority* (1992: Ch. 2), I discuss the ways in which Ossery's own narration undermines itself even before Juliette regains the pen.

like the task that Freud assigns to female development and the task that the story of Iphis and Ianthe assigns to the gods, is to turn a woman's intimacy with another woman into a socially mandated union with a man. If so, however, *Sidney Bidulph* demonstrates not the ease but the difficulties of such a transformation, for Faulkland will become Sidney's husband only after a first marriage that turns tumultuous and ends tragically and a series of tribulations that thwart her happiness with Faulklaud both before and after their (legally questionable) union. The novel's maidenly title, *Memoirs of Miss Sidney Bidulph,* provides a telling counterpoint to Sidney's marriages.

It is thus also significant that *Sidney Bidulph* retains its sapphic narrative structure to the end. In a reversal of the opening drama, Cecilia returns *from* the continent just after Faulkland again leaves *for* it. Although newly married at last to the man she has loved for so many years, Sidney still writes to Cecilia that she "shall not be sorry if I am detained from Mr. Faulkland till I have the happiness of first embracing you, as our separation may be afterwards of a long continuance" (455). As it turns out, the separation of long—indeed permanent—continuance will be from Faulkland, as it is Cecilia who narrates Faulkland's death, having "immediately on [her] arrival in London [. . .] fl[own] to the dear friend of [her] heart" and "found the dear Sidney alone, in her bed-chamber [. . .] prepared to receive me" (459). It is as if Faulkland's death enables a new kind of marriage effected through the novel's structure and affirmed by the fact that after this bedroom scene Cecilia takes over as narrator and completes Sidney's text. In yet another exchange of narration and story, then, heterosexual marriage is replaced by a same-sex narrative union on the level of form.

If it is possible to read the narrative structure of *Juliette Catesby* or *Sidney Bidulph* as attenuated and sanitized sapphic dialogue, then arguably the novel of domesticated heterosexuality has its *narrational* roots in the intimacy of sexual knowledge shared between women. These examples render marriage far from the simple "tomb of friendship" (24) that the fictional Eliza Wharton of Hannah Foster's *The Coquette* proclaims it—or that the historical Elizabeth Carter avowed when she lamented that "people when they marry are dead and buried to all former attachments" (I, 56–57). Indeed, in *Sidney Bidulph,* it is heterosexuality itself that ends up "dead and buried." Such is also the case with Eliza Fenwick's *Secresy* (1796), which uses the structure of confidence to create a more openly erotic intimacy between Caroline, the text's primary *narrator,* and Sibella, its primary *character,* within a convoluted plot of multiple desires: Sibella's for the libertine Clement, the sensitive Arthur Murden's for Sibella, Caroline's for Murden. Through it all, the relationship between Caroline and Sibella is manifestly eroticized through Caroline's overtly physical rhapsodies over Sibella and reciprocated in Sibella's emotional dependence on Caroline, in whose arms Sibella finally dies after bearing a stillborn child conceived with Clement.[8] Narratively speaking, the sapphic is arguably the ultimate open secret in *Secresy*; the intimacy between Caroline and Sibella coexists uneasily enough with the triangulated plot for Caroline to report that others have noticed it. Fittingly, the novel's last words conjoin the intimacy of narration with the intimacy of story, as Caroline grieves both Sibella and Murden: "I loved them both as I never loved man nor woman beside" (359).

As novels like *The Masqueraders* and *Secresy* make clear, however, the distinction between (sapphic) narration and (heterosexual) story with which I have been working here does not entirely hold up. That is, the "events" that constitute the narration—i.e., the interactions between narrators and narratees that are in theory separable from the events of the story—are, in most of these instances, implicated in the turns of the plot. In a few cases—for example, *Memoirs of a Woman of Pleasure* and *Juliette Catesby*—the intimacy between women enacted through narration is little more than an overlay upon—rather than an altering factor in—a manifestly heterosexual story. But narration has a stronger connection to the plot of *Sidney Bidulph* and *Secresy,* and *The Masqueraders,* like *L'Académie des dames* and *Vénus dans le cloître* before it, is entirely dependent on the workings of same-sex confidence. These variations suggest that the relationship between the dynamic of narration and the dynamic of plot in any given text is itself a variable worth further narratological scrutiny.

SAPPHIC RESURRECTION AND THE TRAGIC TURN

The trajectory in which sapphic narration ends up complicating a heterosexual plot also characterizes, in ways too often overlooked, what are arguably the eighteenth-century's two most important and popular domestic fictions, Samuel Richardson's *Clarissa* (1747–48) and Jean-Jacques Rousseau's *Julie, ou la Nouvelle Héloïse* (1762). Each of these epistolary novels structured through multiple intradiegetic voices features a female confidante (Anna Howe for Clarissa, Claire for Julie) who is herself resistant to marriage and professes an excess of love for the heroine. At the end of both novels, the confidante attempts to reclaim the heroine's dead body for herself in a bed-

---

8. I discuss this novel in passing, along with *Clarissa* and *La Nouvelle Héloïse,* in "Befriending the Body" (1998).

room scene with profound if differing implications for the novel's inability to sustain a marriage plot. That the erotic relationships between Anna and Clarissa and between Julie and Claire are under-attended by critics seems to me symptomatic of the ways in which scholars both of sexuality and of the novel have given short shrift to narrative form as textual content.

Anna Howe's pledges of love for Clarissa are threaded throughout Richardson's long text: "I love thee as never woman loved another," Anna professes repeatedly. But Clarissa does not run off to, or off with, Anna nor does Anna come to Clarissa's rescue (and the novel's structure of letter-writing requires, of course, that the confidantes remain apart). In this way, *Clarissa* effectively renders the implications of Anna's love insignificant on the level of story while requiring that love as a central feature of narration. Thus separated from Clarissa for 1400 pages, Anna Howe turns up to make good on her loverly pledges only when Clarissa is a corpse. With heaving bosom, in what she herself calls a "wild frenzy," Anna repeatedly kisses Clarissa's lips, attempting "by her warm breath" to bring Clarissa back to life (1402–3). When Anna twice asks "is this all [. . .] of my Clarissa's story!" (1402), she suggests that this *is not* all, that the female intimacy that has structured the narration cannot be killed off by the closure that Clarissa's death implies.

Julie's cousin Claire is likewise set up early on as an intimate, in a desire that triangulates the relationships of Claire, Julie, and Julie's lover Saint-Preux and that culminates in Claire's excess of grief when Julie contracts a fatal illness after rushing into cold waters to save her child. Rousseau makes the eroticism of the death scene even more explicit than does Richardson when Claire shares the dying Julie's bed after exiling both the husband and the chambermaids. In a language that could be describing sex as readily as dying, unexplained "comings and goings" precede the "moans" that draw Julie's husband, Monsieur de Wolmar, to the chamber, where he sees "the two friends motionless, locked in each other's embrace; the one in a faint, and the other expiring." Claire has to be dragged away and locked up to stop her from continuing to "thr[ow] herself upon [Julie's] body, warm it with hers, endeavor to revive it, press it, cl[ing] to it in a sort of rage, call it loudly by a thousand passionate names" (602) and from literally going mad with grief.

Both Anna and Claire attempt in the narration of their devastating loss to create a kind of sapphic after-plot: in the novel's last letter, Claire insists that Julie lives on, that "her coffin does not contain all of her . . . it awaits the rest of its prey . . . it will not wait for long" (612; ellipses in original). And Anna Howe imagines that she and Clarissa may "meet and rejoice together where no villainous *Lovelaces,* no hard-harted *relations,* will ever shock our innocence, or ruffle our felicity" (1403). Thus two of the eighteenth-century's most widely read and now canonical novels embed a sapphic structure in which narration writes beyond the plot's ostensible closure to turn death into a kind of same-sex marriage.

With the exception of *Memoirs of a Woman of Pleasure* and *Juliette Catesby*, in neither of which the confidante plays a substantive role in the narrated events, all of the novels I have described as bearing a sapphic narrative structure end tragically. In this respect they differ both from the libertine fictions of the seventeenth century, in which sapphic and heterosexual elements coexist quite cheerfully, and from a number of homoerotically-inflected eighteenth-century novels with comic plots. Richardson's *Pamela* and *Sir Charles Grandison*, Edgeworth's *Belinda*, and Diderot's *La Religieuse*, for example, all feature characters marked implicitly or explicitly as sapphic, and all of these novels require the *forcible* exclusion of the sapphic character through exile or alteration: *Pamela*'s leering Mrs. Jewkes turns innocuous; *Grandison*'s mannish lover of women, Miss Barnevelt, is dropped from the narrative; *Belinda*'s duelling feminist Mrs. Freke is symbolically castrated after she is caught in a "man-trap"; and the advances of the lesbian mother superior in *La Religieuse* become the last straw—implicitly worse than the cruel physical and psychological punishments of Suzanne's previous abbess—that impels Suzanne's narratee finally to intervene in order to get her out of the convent. None of these novels displays the sapphic structure of *narration* that I have discussed here; conversely, none of the eighteenth-century novels with sapphic narration, arguably excepting the *Memoirs of a Woman of Pleasure*, features any character who is overtly marked, let alone mocked, as lesbian.[9] The more covertly homoerotic courtship fictions that I have been discussing here seem less able to put their sapphic strains to rest. To be sure, the comic irony of Juliette Catesby's final demurral has less operative force than the tragic irony of Anna Howe's final reunion with Clarissa, and the difference between these endings may be related not only to major distinctions between comic and tragic fiction but to very different degrees of narrative agency: Henriette is but a silent receiver; Anna a major textual voice. Yet the divergent resolutions of *Juliette Catesby* and *Clarissa* both locate the eighteenth-century domestic novel within an erotic nexus that is far from straightforward, and the fact that scholars so often pass over the sapphic potential of these endings

9. The character Phoebe in Cleland's novel is marked by a queer pleasure in sexual encounters with women (as is the young Fanny herself before having heterosexual intercourse), but Fanny goes to some length to reassure her narratee that Phoebe "really" prefers male partners even as she undermines that claim: "Not that she hated men or did not even prefer them to her own sex; but when she met with such occasions as this was, a satiety of enjoyments in the common road, perhaps to a secret bias, inclined her to make the most of pleasure wherever she could find it, without distinction of sexes" (1985: 49–50).

may remind us of the shared investment in heteronormativity that characterizes our own century and that we may be too stringently reading back into the eighteenth century. For the story of the heterosexual subject, which the eighteenth-century novel has seemed bent on consolidating, is also the story of the incompleteness or sometimes even the failure of that consolidation, an incompleteness arguably produced not only by blatant moves against queer subjects such as Miss Barnevelt but also by structures in which the narration of erotic pleasure and erotic danger is filtered through the intimacy between a female narrator and her female narratee.

HETERODIEGESIS AND HETEROSEXUAL PLOTTING

In linking the erotically muted courtship novel with the blatantly sapphic dialogues of early pornography, I am not claiming any direct lineage, though the possibility of influence cannot be wholly ruled out. Rather, I am suggesting that the sapphic gets put in motion as an early modern problem that is intimately tied both to the project of the novel and to the broader cultural challenge of regulating the regimes of gender and sexuality to which the novel is indentured. That Clarissa, Julie, and Sibella must be killed off, Dalinda and Philecta done in and Sidney Bidulph widowed, sometimes in ways that give female confidantes an entry point into the plot, suggests that as the eighteenth-century continues, the discursive project of regulating sexual subjectivity through the novel might be growing not simpler but more complex.

No wonder, then, that the nineteenth-century novel expunges the dialogic structure of female confidence, as if heterosexual subjectivity requires a walling off of same-sex narration even more complete than of same-sex event. It may be no accident, for example, that the heterodiegetic narrator's strongest affirmations of sisterly intimacy in Jane Austen's *Sense and Sensibility* and *Pride and Prejudice* occur at the end of these novels, after the sisters are safely married off. More pointedly, it is worth remembering that Elinor Dashwood says almost nothing to Marianne of her feelings for Edward and that even the ebullient Marianne speaks only what and when she must about her relationship with Willoughby. Elizabeth Bennet likewise holds back so much of her belated desire for Darcy that her ostensible confidante Jane is as surprised as Mr. and Mrs. Bennet when Elizabeth agrees to marry him. What in light of the novel's history amounts to a wary withholding of female intimacy on the level of narration becomes all but completed in a novel like *Jane Eyre*, in which the confidante is an anonymous and voiceless reader and Jane's beloved friend Helen Burns has been killed off (perhaps so that Jane herself may live, since as Jane puts it, "I was no Helen Burns" [59]). While I would agree with Lisa Sternlieb that in *Jane Eyre* "the reader is repeatedly pitted against Rochester for Jane's affections" and that "she woos her reader as Rochester has wooed her" (475), these qualities make the genderlessness of Jane's "dear reader" all the more significant.[10] It is only a step from Jane's anonymous narratee to the "you" that is "merely dead paper" to which the narrator of Charlotte Perkins Gilman's "The Yellow Wall-Paper" (1892) addresses her words, or for that matter to the narrative form of Helen Fielding's *Bridget Jones' Diary* (1996), whose narrator does not explicitly address even a paper narratee even though some kind of narratee is, of course, implied.

These examples suggest that the arc of what I am calling the sapphic dialogic reaches its most explicit form in the seventeenth century, becomes sexually muted in the eighteenth, and all but disappears by the nineteenth century. I am not arguing, of course, that the sapphic itself disappears with it. Sharon Marcus is right to say that the Victorian novel does not negate bonds between women, though I would not quite agree that "almost every Victorian novel that ends in marriage has first supplied its heroine with an intimate female friend" (76). I read the coexistence of female friendship with the marriage plot as a sign of the consolidation of heterosexuality, all the more as it is the shared desire for a specific man that sometimes most unites the women (*Middlemarch,* as Marcus shows us, is a case in point). I suggest, however, that because these female intimacies are rendered in extradiegetic and often also heterodiegetic narration, they are better able to remain instrumental rather than to offer resistance to the heterosexual marriage plot. By contrast, in both the libertine fictions and domestic novels I have been discussing, at least one of the female interlocutors is assigned or enacts a protofeminist critique of men and/or marriage. Anna, Claire, Juliette, Philecta, and Caroline all make clear their resistance to some domestic or patriarchal *status quo.*

It is also worth recognizing that this textual pattern of same-sex dialogics, while produced by male as well as female writers, is gendered female: the male-male homoerotic dialogue or structure of intersubjective confidence does not take root in the novel in the same way. One could argue, of course, that the dialogue form enacted between two or more male interlocutors lies firmly at the heart of the "Western tradition," given its primacy as Plato's great structuring technique and its subsequent use in myriad dialogues across literary history. And, as Robert Sturges points out, male-male dialogue structures several important discourses on male friendship, from Cicero's to that

---

10. I discuss the narrative strategies of *Jane Eyre* more fully in *Fictions of Authority* (1992: 176–93).

of the twelfth-century cleric Aelred to the seventeenth-century pederastic dialogue of Rocco's *L'Alcibiade fanciullo a scola* (1651), in which, says Sturges, the dialogue mode once again becomes "a form of seduction" as it was in Plato's *Lysis* (138). The dialogic mode continues without much erotic content in Diderot's philosophical fictions (*Le Rêve d'Alembert*, *Le Neveu de Rameau*), but it is otherwise a rare phenomenon among novels of the eighteenth century. It is uncommon even in men's works for a male narrator to address a male narratee to recount erotic desires or deeds, though one might consider the (ultimately competitive) ways in which Clarissa functions as a love object in the correspondence between Lovelace and Belford, and one must also, of course, recognize those rarer novels from Aphra Behn's *Love Letters Between a Nobleman and His Sister* (1688) to Pierre Choderlos de Laclos's *Les Liaisons dangereuses* (1784) in which sexual secrets are the stuff of male-female confidence.

On the whole, then, it is not through intradiegetic narration that the novel engages male-male desire, with the slight exception of Goethe's *Die Leiden des jungen Werthers* (1774), at least until Mary Shelley's *Frankenstein* (1817), in which men (the creature, Victor) talk to men (Victor, Walton) and in which the first-level narrator Walton, while writing to his (silent) sister, speaks passionately of his desire for intimacy with a man. Those eighteenth-century narratives in which men recount erotic experience are more likely to be directed to extradiegetic narratees who stand in for the public reader. Such a difference in gendered narrative patterns is plausible given the fact that men are culturally more authorized to speak to a "public" both in general and about the erotic in particular.

This by no means signifies an absence of male homoeroticism in the eighteenth-century novel; such a claim would be patently false, as numerous scholars have shown.[11] Rather, I am claiming a more limited and less frequently erotic presence of male-male narrative interlocutors during the period in which the novel "rose." In short, it is safe to say that the male-male dialogic has a quite different trajectory from the sapphic structure that I have been discussing. This difference reminds us not only that the eighteenth-century novel genders both the structures of desire and the mechanisms of its narration, but that, as I have argued elsewhere and often, narration itself has gendered properties.[12]

In arguing for sapphic form as an underpinning of the eighteenth-century novel's domestic agenda, I also hope to have shown that narrative form can

---

11. See, for example, MacFarlane and Haggerty.
12. I make this argument in several essays, most recently in "Sexing the Narrative" (1995) and "Queering Narratology" (1996).

function as novelistic content and that the novel's history of sexuality thus needs to encompass a history of form. Nor should narration be considered the only element—though I believe it remains a central and underexplored one—in which form arguably embeds what manifest content seems to be overlooking or even contradicting. The ways in which several of the novels I have been discussing write "beyond the ending," to take a phrase from Rachel Blau DuPlessis, suggests, for example, that the formal qualities of plot embodied in narrative order and narrative time might also be fruitful locations for a history of the novel and its sexualities. Years after Helen's death, Jane Eyre has the word *Resurgam*—"I shall rise again"—engraved on her friend's tomb. This textual detail gives the story of Jane and Helen a kind of afterlife metaphorically related to that accorded female intimacy through its reappearance after the resolution of the marriage plots in several of the novels I have been discussing. In this spirit, we might speculate that what narrative content "killeth" may likewise find a *Resurgam* in narrative form. It is my hope that such prospects will challenge historicism no longer to repress but rather to welcome narratology, and narratology likewise to welcome history. Both fields have little to lose and much to gain from such a new dialogic relationship.

REFERENCES

Aretino, Pietro (2005) *Dialogues* [*Ragionamenti*] [1534]. Trans. Raymond Rosenthal. Toronto: University of Toronto Press.
Aretino, Pietro (1979) *Ragionamenti* [1534]. Rome: Savelli.
Armstrong, Nancy (1987) *Desire and Domestic Fiction: Toward a Political History of the Novel*. Oxford: Oxford University Press.
Auerbach, Erich (1953) *Mimesis: The Representation of Reality in Western Literature* [1946]. Trans. Willard Trask. Princeton, NJ: Princeton University Press.
Bakhtin, M. M. (1981) *The Dialogic Imagination: Four Essays*. Trans. Caryl Emerson and Michael Holquist. Austin: University of Texas Press.
Barrin, Jean (1683) *Vénus dans le cloître*. Paris, n.p.
Brontë, Charlotte (2008) *Jane Eyre* [1848]. Oxford and New York: Oxford World Classics.
Carter, Elizabeth (1809) *A Series of Letters between Mrs. Elizabeth Carter and Miss Catherine Talbot, From the Year 1741 to 1770*. Ed. Montagu Pennington. 3 vols. London: Rivington.
Chatterjee, Ranita (2004) "Sapphic Subjectivity and Gothic Desires in Eliza Fenwick's *Secresy* (1795)." *Gothic Studies* 6.1: 45–56.
Chorier, Nicolas (1680) *L'Académie des dames*. Paris, n.p.
Cleland, John (1985) *Fanny Hill or Memoirs of a Woman of Pleasure* [1749]. Harmondsworth, England: Penguin.

Dannenberg, Hilary (2008) *Coincidence and Counterfactuality: Plotting Time and Space in Narrative Fiction*. Lincoln: University of Nebraska Press.
DuPlessis, Rachel Blau (1985) *Writing Beyond the Ending: Narrative Strategies of Twentieth-Century Women Writers*. Bloomington: Indiana University Press.
Farwell, Marilyn (1996) *Heterosexual Plots & Lesbian Narratives*. New York: New York University Press.
Fenwick, Eliza (1994) *Secresy; or, The Ruin on the Rock* [1796]. Peterborough, ON: Broadview Press.
Fludernik, Monika (2003) "The Diachronization of Narratology." *Narrative* 11.3: 331–48.
Foster, Hannah Webster (1986) *The Coquette* [1797]. New York: Oxford University Press.
Haggerty, George (1999) *Men in Love: Masculinity and Sexuality in the Eighteenth Century*. New York: Columbia University Press.
Haywood, Eliza (1724) *The Masqueraders or, Fatal Curiosity*. London: Printed for J. Roberts.
Jameson, Fredric (1981) *The Political Unconscious: Narrative as a Socially Symbolic Act*. Ithaca: Cornell University Press.
Lanser, Susan S. (1998–99) "Befriending the Body: Female Intimacies as Class Acts." *Eighteenth-Century Studies* 32.3: 179–98.
——— (1992) *Fictions of Authority: Women Writers and Narrative Voice*. Ithaca: Cornell University Press.
——— (1995) "Sexing the Narrative: Propriety, Desire, and the Engendering of Narratology." *Narrative* 3.1: 85–94.
——— (1996) "Queering Narratology." *Ambiguous Discourse: Feminist Narratology and British Women Writers*. Ed. Kathy Mezei. Chapel Hill: University of North Carolina Press. 250–61.
——— (1998) "Sexing Narratology: Toward a Gendered Poetics of Narrative Voice." *Grenzüberschreitungen: Narratologie im Kontext/Transcending Boundaries: Narratology in Context*. Ed. Walter Grünzweig and Andreas Solbach. Tübingen: Narr. 167–83.
——— (2007) "The Political Economy of Same-Sex Desire." *Structures and Subjectivities: Attending to Early Modern Women V*. Ed. Joan E. Hartman and Adele Seeff. Newark: University of Delaware Press. 157–75.
Levinson, Marjorie (2007) "What is New Formalism?" *PMLA* 122.2: 558–69.
Marcus, Sharon (2007) *Between Women: Friendship, Desire, and Marriage in Victorian England*. Princeton, NJ: Princeton University Press.
McFarlane, Cameron (1997) *The Sodomite in Fiction and Satire, 1660–1750*. New York: Columbia University Press.
McHale, Brian (2005) "Ghosts and Monsters: On the (Im)Possibility of Narrating the History of Narrative Theory." *A Companion to Narrative Theory*. Ed. James Phelan and Peter J. Rabinowitz. Oxford: Blackwell. 60–71.
McKeon, Michael (2005) *The Secret History of Domesticity: Public, Private, and the Division of Knowledge*. Baltimore: Johns Hopkins University Press.
Moore, Lisa L. (1997) *Dangerous Intimacies: Toward a Sapphic History of the British Novel*. Durham and London: Duke University Press.
Nünning, Ansgar (2000) "Toward a Cultural and Historical Narratology: A Survey of

Diachronic Approaches, Concepts, and Research Projects." *Anglistentag 1999 Mainz: Proceedings.* Ed. Bernhard Reitz and Sigrid Rieuwerts. Trier: Wissenschaftlicher Verlag. 345–73.

Nussbaum, Felicity (1989) *The Autobiographical Subject: Gender and Ideology in Eighteenth-Century England.* Baltimore: Johns Hopkins University Press.

Riccoboni, Marie-Jeanne (1983) *Lettres de Milady Juliette Catesby à Milady Henriette Campley, son amie* [1759]. Paris: Desjonquères.

Richardson, Samuel (1985) *Clarissa, or, The History of a Young Lady* [1747–48]. Harmondsworth, England: Penguin.

Roof, Judith (1995) Ed. *Sexuality and Narrative.* Double Issue of *Modern Fiction Studies* 41.3–4: 429–698.

——— (1996) *Come As You Are: Sexuality and Narrative.* New York: Columbia University Press.

Rousseau, Jean-Jacques (1997) *Julie, or the New Heloise: Letters of Two Lovers Who Live in a Small Town at the Foot of the Alps* [1762]. Trans. Philip Stewart and Jean Vaché. Hanover and London: University Press of New England.

Sheridan, Frances (1995) *Memoirs of Miss Sidney Bidulph* [1761]. Oxford: Oxford University Press.

Sternlieb, Lisa (1999) "*Jane Eyre*: 'Hazarding Confidences.'" *Nineteenth-Century Literature* 53.4: 452–79.

Sturges, Robert S. (2005) *Dialogue and Deviance: Male-Male Desire in the Dialogue Genre.* New York: Palgrave Macmillan.

Walen, Denise (2002) "Constructions of Female Homoerotics in Early Modern Drama." *Theatre Journal* 54.3: 411–30.

Watt, Ian (1957) *The Rise of the Novel: Studies in Defoe, Richardson, and Fielding.* Berkeley: University of California Press.

AMIT MARCUS

Narrators, Narratees, and Mimetic Desire

Girard's thesis of mimetic desire (also called "triangular" or "metaphysical" desire)[1] has aroused much theoretical interest among literary scholars, who have expanded and expounded his theory, while at the same time criticizing its universal pretensions and its blurring of differences between different types of desire (e.g., male vs. female, heterosexual vs. homosexual).[2] Literary interpretations that apply Girard's ideas from his work *Deceit, Desire, and the Novel* (1965) to fictional narratives focus on the dynamics of mimetic desire and rivalry between two (or more) characters on the story level: the desiring subject, the mediator (or rival), and the desired object.

In this essay, I wish to examine the relations between *story* and *narration*[3] in connection with the triangular structure of desire and to demonstrate how mimetic rivalry can function between narrators and narratees. I claim that narration may affect mimetic desire in contradictory ways: on the one hand, narration may reinforce and perpetuate mimetic desire, both through

---

1. The terms "mimetic desire" and "triangular desire" are clearly equivalents, since the structure of mimetic desire—desiring subject-mediator-desired object—is triangular. The term "metaphysical desire" originates in Girard's claim that "[a]s the role of the metaphysical grows greater in desire, that of the *physical* diminishes in importance. As the mediator grows nearer, passion becomes more intense and the object is emptied of its concrete value" (1965: 85).

2. See, for instance, Dee (1999), Klarer (1991), Kofman (1980), Moi (1982), Morón Arroyo (1978), Sedgwick (1985).

3. My distinction between "story" and "narration" is based on Rimmon-Kenan, made "in the spirit of Genette's distinction between 'histoire,' 'récit' and 'narration' (1972: 71–6)" (2001: 3).

the re-experiencing of past events and through the mimicry of the mediator while relating the story; on the other hand, narration may clash with mimetic desire. In this case, the relations between narrator and narratee represent a possible world in which mimetic desire no longer exists. I conclude with remarks on the possible contribution of Girard's notion of metaphysical desire to narratology, specifically to the analysis of the interconnections between autodiegetic narrators, their narratees, and the main character(s) in their story.

Two qualifications for the argument are required at this preliminary stage: first, since mimetic desire can obtain only between subjects or characters that are structured as subjects, it can operate on the level of narration only if both the narrator and the narratee are personalized. In other words, my line of reasoning is applicable only for narratives in which the narrator and the narratee are also characters in the story or, at the very least, have some human properties such as gender, social status, or a system of beliefs. Thus the type of narratee under consideration differs significantly from the theoretical construct that Gerald Prince terms "a degree-zero narratee," which has neither personality nor any particular experience of the world (1973: 181–82, 1985; see also Piwowarczyk 1976).

Secondly, mimetic desire can exist on the level of narration insofar as there is a story at that level or mimetic desire motivates the narration and the narrator's appeal to a narratee (this point will be clarified in my interpretations of specific narratives). In such stories, there are significant similarities and contrasts between the theme of mimetic desire in the story and the narrator-narratee relation (see Chatman 1978: 259). Hence in discussing narration, I do not refer to the minimal function of any narrator to recount events and situations, which Genette names "the properly *narrative function*" (1980: 255). Instead, mimetic desire on the level of narration is closely related to another function of the narrator, which Genette calls "the *function of communication*" (256) and which echoes Jakobson's phatic and conative functions (1960: 357). In the narratives that I shall discuss, "the absent presence of the receiver becomes the dominant (obsessive) element of the discourse" (Genette 1980: 256).

GIRARD'S NOTION OF MIMETIC DESIRE

Girard sharply distinguishes between his notion of mimetic desire and the notion of desire in the romantic literary tradition. The romantic conception presents desire as spontaneous, that is, as a direct, linear connection between the desiring subject and the desired object (1965: 16–17, 29–39, 269). By contrast, according to Girard's triadic model, the subject does not desire the object in and for itself, but the desire is mediated by another subject who possesses, or pursues, this object. This other subject, *the mediator,* is at the same time admired by the desiring subject as a model, in extreme cases even as a human God (61), and despised as an obstacle in achieving the object. The desiring subject fallaciously presents his[4] own desire as both logically and chronologically original and the desire of the mediator as derivative, i.e., as emanating from the desiring subject's desire.

Girard believes that metaphysical desire is in principle insatiable: each time the desiring subject succeeds in achieving the desired object, he becomes disappointed and frustrated because he realizes that it is not really what he has coveted. The reason for this constant disappointment is that the subject cannot overcome his initial loss of self-respect and self-assurance caused by the painful recognition that he is not divine, namely, that he is not self-sufficient. In his attempt to compensate for this lack, the subject believes that he can achieve self-sufficiency if he is able to have the objects that his mediator possesses. The obsession of the desiring subject with obtaining objects turns him into a slave of his unrealizable desire.

The most crucial distinction within the category of metaphysical desire is between *external* and *internal* mediation. External mediators are spiritually, socially, and intellectually distant from the subject who imitates them and desires the same objects to such an extent that they do not inhabit the same world and therefore cannot engage in rivalry. For instance, Amadís de Gaula is the external mediator of Don Quixote, since the real knight and his zealous follower inhabit separate worlds and are spiritually and socially distant from each other.[5] By contrast, the desiring subject and his internal mediator in Dostoevsky's novels inhabit the same world, are closely related spiritually and are often members of the same family.[6] The great spiritual distance that

---

4. I avoid using "he or she" when referring to the desiring subject and his rival for two reasons. First, although Girard's theory purports to be universal and valid for both sexes, the great majority of the examples of mimetic desire that he provides are novels written by male authors and featuring male rivals and a woman as the "desired object." Second, the novels discussed in this essay comprise, even more so than those chosen by Girard, almost exclusively male characters. Yet unlike Girard and like most of his feminist critics, I do not assume that male and female desire necessarily fit into the same structure.

5. Amadís de Gaula was, according to the four-volume narrative written by Garci Rodríguez de Montalvo, the illegitimate child of King Perión of Gaul and Elisena of England and was raised by the knight Gandales. Unlike Amadís, Don Quixote, originally named Alonso Quixano, was a country gentleman who lived in an unnamed section of La Mancha with his niece and a housekeeper.

6. For instance, Andrei Versilov and his illegitimate son Arkadi Dolgoruky (the narrator)

characterizes external mediation tallies with an emotional distance, hence external mediation does not produce rivalry. By contrast, internal mediation generates rivalry between the desiring subject and his mediator, which becomes more passionate and destructive as the distance between them is reduced (8–9, 85–88). Another significant difference between external and internal mediation is that the subject of the first type openly admits his desire, whereas the subject of the second type makes great attempts to conceal it, since he believes that if his mediator knows what his desire is, the mediator will prevent him from achieving it.

Girard further claims that all great novels[7] show the futility of mimetic desire by transcending the obsession from which it has sprung (Girard 1965: 300). This final phase of moral recognition, which resembles *anagnorisis* in tragedies, provides novels with a sense of closure that liberates both the hero and his creator from the agony of delusions: "When he renounces the deceptive divinity of pride, the hero frees himself from slavery and finally grasps the truth about his unhappiness. There is no distinction between this renunciation and the creative renunciation. It is a victory over metaphysical desire that transforms a romantic writer into a true novelist" (307).

Narration as the perpetuation of triangular desire challenges Girard's claim that every great novel ends with the surmounting of desire, that is, with the conversion of the desiring subject, who recognizes that his desire is destructive.[8] Conversion is a historical convention that was prominent in nineteenth-century novels, which constitute the hard core of Girard's analysis; this convention was increasingly subverted by novels from the twentieth century. In the novels and novellas that will be analyzed in this essay—Günter Grass's *Cat and Mouse* (*Katz und Maus*), Jean Genet's *The Thief's Journal* (*Journal du voleur*), and Albert Camus' *The Fall* (*La chute*)—there is either no conversion at all or only a partial conversion (in the case of *La chute*, it is misleadingly presented as a complete conversion).

The issue of conversion is only one manifestation of the way in which Girard's choice to focus on a specific corpus of novels rather than another has affected his theoretical insights. Most of the novels that he discusses, written by Cervantes, Flaubert, Stendhal, Proust, and Dostoevsky, feature an external (extra-heterodiegetic) narrator who does not participate in the story

in Dostoevsky's *A Raw Youth* both fall in love with Katerina Nikolaevna Akhmatova, the widow of an army officer. It turns out that Arkadi's love for Akhmatova is an imitation of his father's, whom he at the same time venerates and detests.

    7. Girard has been justly criticized for confusing descriptive and normative categories (see Moi 1982: 23).

    8. Girard never defines the term "conversion," but its religious undertones are clear (see 1965: esp. 293–94).

and is not personally involved in the events. This non-personalized narrator is detached from the mimetic desire that dominates fictional characters. Proust's *A la recherche du temps perdu* is of course an exception, but even in this case, Girard does not distinguish between story and narration when discussing mimetic desire. In other words, he does not distinguish between the internal focalization of Marcel as character and the external, retrospective, and self-reflexive focalization of Marcel as narrator. By contrast, I wish to concentrate on narratives in which the narrator is both the main character (or one of the two main characters) in the story and the "desiring subject." These narratives foreground several ways in which narration can be associated with triangular desire.

Not many novels answer the three criteria which govern my inquiry: having a personalized narrator, a personalized narratee, and a story on the level of narration (or a relationship between a narrator and a narratee that directly addresses the issue of desire). The three fictional narratives that will be discussed in what follows were chosen because they dramatize the ambivalent relations between the narrator and the narratee—admiration and hostility, attraction and repulsion—which are inherent in mimetic desire. Each of these narratives manifests a specific type of mediation and desire on the level of narration, which is intricately connected to the level of the story.

Although Girard's *Deceit, Desire, and the Novel* is a well-known work, it has not received as much attention from literary scholars as have other theories of desire, in particular that of Jacques Lacan. Girard's Catholicism, his partly unjustified reputation as a political reactionary, and what is perceived by some as the reductiveness of his theory—which is accused of boiling down all cultural and historical phenomena into one underlying structure—have stood in the way of a more precise examination of his ideas (see Golsan 1993: 111–24). This essay is an opportunity to promote interest in Girard's insights and their great explanatory power.

I wish to emphasize at the outset the strengths of a Girardian analysis in comparison with an analysis based on Lacan's theory of desire. According to Lacan, desire emerges from the primary splitting of the ego and the inevitable failure of the subject to return to a fictive originary state—signified by the Real—of undisturbed unity with the (m)other (see Fryer 2004: 92–94). Genet's narrative is especially amenable to this type of explanation owing to the salient motif of the absent mother (e.g. 21–22), which a Girardian reading does not account for, but the other two narratives can at the most generate speculations about the infantile source of lack and desire. Girard's argument that desire necessarily fails because there is always another rival whose being cannot be completely appropriated proves more productive in these cases.

Moreover, Eve Kosofsky Sedgwick's interpretation of Girard (1985: esp. 21–25), which emphasizes the concealed homosocial relations between the desiring subject and his rival in Girard's structure of triangular desire, is particularly illuminating for narratives that highlight the ambivalent relations of admiration and hostility between male characters.[9]

CAT AND MOUSE

The mimetic rivalry between Pilenz—the narrating character[10]—and Mahlke is the major theme of Günter Grass's novella *Cat and Mouse* (1961). Pilenz belongs to a group of adolescents who mimic each other in an uncomplicated way. Their social interaction never develops into real competition or rivalry and helps to retain the unity of their small community. When Mahlke, Pilenz's idiosyncratic schoolmate (on the story level) and his narratee on the level of narration, joins the group, his unique appearance and conduct at the same time attract and repel Pilenz. Mahlke seems to belong to the group in certain respects but transgresses its borders in others; this feels threatening to Pilenz, because it signifies instability and undermines his ostensibly secure world.[11] Pilenz admires Mahlke for his apparent self-sufficiency as well as

---

9. A thorough examination of the points of convergence and divergence between the Lacanian and the Girardian conceptions of desire is far beyond the scope of this essay. This territory has been covered in part by Meloni (2002). Nonetheless, I wish to raise some ideas about this issue. Lacan's theoretical assumptions are based on Freud's, whereas Girard, though influenced by Freud, is critical of psychoanalysis. However, both Lacan and Girard have analyzed desire as insatiable, marking a lack in being that can never be filled. Accordingly, each of them concludes that the subject will never achieve complete satisfaction (Braunstein [2003]; Ragland-Sullivan [1995]). Lacan's model of desire, like Girard's, is based on intersubjectivity, that is, on a triadic structure (Meloni [2002]; Grigg [1991: 110]). Yet Girard takes a negative view of metaphysical desire and argues that it should be surmounted, whereas for Lacan desire is a necessary condition for the creation of the imaginary and the symbolic registers, hence also for the generation of representation and meaning and for the structuration of the subject (Sullivan [1995]).

10. In using the term "narrating character," I presuppose that there is at least a minimal psychological continuity between the autodiegetic narrator as narrator and as character, even if this continuity is replete with ruptures, splits, and fissures. Although classical narratologists such as Genette and Rimmon-Kenan supposed that their distinctions and classifications are devoid of psychological assumptions, it seems that they too presuppose such continuity in the very terms "homodiegetic" and "autodiegetic" narrators (see Genette [1980: 245]; Rimmon-Kenan [2001: 96–97]).

11. For a more detailed study of narratives featuring an individual whose idiosyncrasy and refusal to conform subverts the norms of the group, see Marcus (2008). However, whereas the essay in question focuses on the discursive aspects of such narratives, Mahlke challenges Pilenz and his friends by his behavior and his disproportioned body rather than by an exceptional discourse.

for his charisma, resoluteness, and unconventional behavior (Grass 1961: 24–26).[12]

Although Mahlke participates in certain communal activities, he remains an outsider whose inability or unwillingness to conform seems to challenge the norms of the group, its solidarity, and cohesiveness. For example, he does not take part in the communal sexual intercourse with Tulla, Pilenz's cousin, when the other boys vie with one another in order to prove their masculinity to themselves and to the other members of the group. It transpires that this abstinence is caused neither by Mahlke's impotence nor by his putative homosexuality, but stems from his self-assured virility that does not require proof (32–35).

Mahlke's extraordinary spiritual qualities are supplemented by his exceptional physical traits, above all his huge Adam's apple and his enormous penis, whose size presumably—so the text implies—corresponds to its fertility (33–34). The homosexual undertones of Pilenz's description of Mahlke turn him into an implicit source of libidinal desire that is rejected and denied.[13] As a typical case of mimetic rivalry, this admiration is mingled with hostility,[14] which is demonstrated not only in Pilenz's responsibility for Mahlke's probable death, but in other deeds as well. For instance, there is the repeated symbolic erasing of Mahlke's name and image: first, Pilenz erases the grotesque image of Mahlke-as-Christ, which was drawn on the blackboard by a classmate (38), and some years later, Pilenz with an ax destroys the words "Stabat Mater dolorosa" that Mahlke engraved on a board of the latrine of the Nazi Labor Service camp, thereby erasing Mahlke's name as well (109). Another deed that presumably manifests Pilenz's hostility towards Mahlke is the story of the cat and the mouse that is incessantly repeated throughout the novella in a number of variations and gives it its title: the cat is a real cat (but also, symbolically, the predator that chases Mahlke), whereas the "mouse" is Mahlke's exceptionally huge Adam's apple (and symbolically, Mahlke as prey). The most significant question of the plot, which remains undecided, is whether Pilenz alone enticed the cat to jump on the "mouse" when Mahlke

---

12. All references to specific pages in this essay refer to the original edition, unless otherwise indicated.

13. Girard believes that homosexuality is derived from heterosexuality: "Proustian homosexuality, for example, can be defined as a gradual transferring of erotic value which in 'normal' Don Juanism remains attached to the object itself" (1965: 47). See also Golsan (1993: 26); Moi (1982: esp. 28–30); Sedgwick (1989: 16–17, 21–25). Although Pilenz denies being sexually attracted to Mahlke, his fascination with Mahlke's genitalia certainly suggests that his adoration is not purely spiritual.

14. Ryan (1977) claims that Pilenz's ambivalent relationship with Mahlke is politically significant, as implied by the narrating character: Pilenz collaborates with the Nazi regime, whereas Mahlke shows signs of resistance (but also of resignation).

was lying asleep on the grass, whether one of his friends did this, or whether the cat jumped on the "mouse" of its own free will.

Pilenz's use of "wir" ("we") when narrating the story excludes Mahlke from the group to which Pilenz belongs, thereby increasing the distance between them while at the same time portraying Mahlke as a manifestation of *das Unheimliche* (the uncanny), whose idiosyncrasies prevent him from becoming an integral part of any human community.[15] This exclusion is one way in which the narrating character conceals his metaphysical desire not only from others, but also from himself, in order to pacify his conscience and deny his guilt (see Girard 1965: 10, 153–61). In other words, the use of the first-person plural is a camouflage which Pilenz uses to create the impression that his interest in Mahlke did not exceed the interest of his friends and that he was not solely responsible for Mahlke's end—an impression which is incompatible with the details of his story. Mahlke's mimetic rivalry with Pilenz illustrates Girard's claim about "the inverse relationship between the strength of desire and the importance of the object" (86): metaphysical desire which focuses on the mediator increases at the expense of the significance of the physical object that he possesses. Girard argues that the final stage in this evolution is the complete disappearance of the object. In *Cat and Mouse*, the objects of the mediator play a significant role, but they constantly replace one another, thereby revealing that none of them has a noteworthy intrinsic value.[16] The pompoms, the screwdriver, the military medal are all treated by Pilenz as sanctified objects not because of their essential properties, but simply because they are associated with the mediator:

Wenn Mahlke gesagt hätte: "Mach das und das!," ich hätte das und noch mehr gemacht. Mahlke sagte aber nichts . . . und als er die Puscheln als

---

15. The idiosyncrasy of Mahlke's character and Pilenz's responsibility for his probable death make Grass's novella relevant to a later major book by Girard, *Violence and the Sacred* (1977). In this work, Girard describes sacrificial violence as the remedy for unrestrained violence and total chaos in civil society: instead of fighting among themselves, mimetic rivals channel their hostility to an exceptionally vulnerable individual (or group), an outcast in their community. The sacrificial process can succeed only if the violence is in fact (or is at least presented as) *unanimous*, that is, if the whole community participates in the persecution, or at least accepts it passively (see also Golsan [1993: 29–84]). Like any scapegoat, Mahlke bears *victimary signs* which differentiate him from the rest of his community. However, unlike the typical sacrificial process described by Girard, Pilenz has *exclusive* responsibility for Mahlke's death and attempts either to repudiate his responsibility or to lay the blame on his classmates while at the same time confessing the deed.

16. Hilliard (2001: 425–30) contends that the objects used by Mahlke could be arranged in accordance with Roman Jakobson's definition of the poetic function as the projection of the principle of equivalence from the axis of selection into the axis of combination.

Mode einführte, war ich der erste, der die Mode mitmachte und Puscheln am Hals trug. Trug auch eine Zeitlang, aber nur zu Hause, einen Schraubenzieher am Schnürsenkel.... Und hätte Mahlke nach der Rede des U-Boot-Kommandanten zu mir gesagt: "Pilenz, klau ihm das Ding mit dem Drussel!," ich hätte das Ding mit dem schwarzweißroten Band vom Haken gelangt und für Dich aufgehoben. (1963: 81)

If Mahlke had said: "Do this and that," I would have done this and that and then some. But Mahlke said nothing.... When he introduced the pompom vogue, I was the first to take it up and wear pompoms on my neck. For a while, though only at home, I even wore a screwdriver on a shoelace... and if after the submarine captain's speech Mahlke had said to me: "Pilenz. Go swipe that business on the ribbon," I would have taken medal and ribbon off the hook and kept it for you. (1964: 74)

There is more than one way for the desiring subject to possess the desired object. When he wishes to conceal his desire from his rival and from others (perhaps also from himself), or when he is too much of a coward to face his rival directly and not shrewd enough to manipulate him, he may compromise the achievement of his desire by continually observing the desired object, which becomes sanctified in his view, regardless of its intrinsic value. This is a compromise, because while the object is not completely under his control, it nonetheless feeds his desire and gives him the illusion of gaining full control at some point in the future. Pilenz's desire for Mahlke is a case in point. Although he mimics Mahlke's behavior, Pilenz (perhaps unconsciously) knows that wearing a screwdriver on his neck is too transparent an impersonation. His solution is to fix his gaze on the screwdriver, possessing it merely with his eyes, and to wear it on his neck only when he is at home and nobody sees him. Similarly, Pilenz asks Mahlke if he (Pilenz) could touch the medal that the latter has stolen from a former pupil who had won it during the war (82), but when later Mahlke wins such a medal as a mark of distinction for his feats and asks Pilenz to keep it while he stays in his hiding place in the minesweeper, Pilenz refuses to take the desired object (136). His refusal demonstrates his wish to conceal his desire from himself and from others (he would not like to be viewed as someone who overtly mimics Mahlke) and indicates the transfer of his desire from the object to the rival/mediator (Pilenz does not deem the medal so important).

According to Girard, in the most intense and violent cases of internal mediation "the object is only a means of reaching the mediator. The desire is aimed at the mediator's *being*" (1965: 53).[17] The desiring subject deludes himself that if he succeeds in absorbing the being of the mediator, he will consequently become self-sufficient. Since these attempts are doomed to failure, the desiring subject must seek another solution to his feeling of existential worthlessness. One radical solution is to murder the mediator (or to cause his death indirectly). The desiring subject believes that if his rival—now the obstacle that thwarts his desire—no longer exists, he will be able to restore his self-assurance and self-fulfillment (85). The subject's mistake is that he ascribes the cause of, and the responsibility for, his feelings of inferiority to the other rather than to himself. An inverse solution is committing suicide, thus renouncing desire once and for all: "Desiring one's own nothingness is desiring oneself at the weakest point of his humanity, desiring to be mortal, desiring to be dead" (275). As the most extreme manifestations of the existential states of sadism and masochism (176–92, 287–92), the desperate acts of murder and suicide are "dialectical reverses" that arise from the same psychological source (184).

In *Katz und Maus*, murder—or at least causing the mediator's death—happens on the level of the story (Pilenz persuades Mahlke to hide in a sunken barge and deceptively steals the can opener from him, thus leaving him inside the barge without any food), while committing suicide is symbolically enacted on the level of the narration. Indeed, a compulsion of repetition that prevents the teller from continuing with his life is an exemplary manifestation of the death principle.[18] Paradoxically, this masochistic longing for

17. Girard distinguishes between two forms of internal mediation: "exogamic," or extrafamilial, and "endogamic," or intrafamilial (1961: 42). In exogamic internal mediation, metaphysical desire dominates the relations of subjects who inhabit the same world and are relatively close to each other spiritually and socially, but it does not penetrate the most intimate circle of the family. By contrast, in endogamic internal mediation, metaphysical desire takes over the relations between members of the same family and is hence more emotionally intense and more prone to becoming dangerously violent. *Cat and Mouse* demonstrates that endogamic metaphysical desire is not in all cases the more violent of the two. Familial relations are almost absent from Grass's novella: Pilenz lives with his family, but he is completely absorbed by his relations with his classmates; his parents do not interest him at all, and the death of his brother at war is briefly mentioned as an event that had no emotional effect on him at the time (122, 137). I suggest replacing Girard's categories of "exogamic" versus "endogamic" mediation with softer categories that avoid dichotomies and can give a better account for cultural differences, such as the significance of family relations for the desiring subject.

18. See Freud's *Beyond the Pleasure Principle* (1961), esp. 30–32, and also Rimmon-Kenan (1987: 177–78). Rimmon-Kenan interprets Pilenz's narration not as suicide, but as killing Mahlke yet again. Both interpretations (mine and Rimmon-Kenan's) presuppose that Pilenz is indeed responsible for killing, or at least attempting to kill, Mahlke. This assumption is challenged by Hilliard, who claims that Pilenz as narrator attempts "to give himself an importance that he did not in fact have, as a character at the time" by confessing crimes that

one's own (symbolic) death is achieved through the narration by the amplification of metaphysical desire and the accentuation of the prominent role of the mediator as an obstacle. The deceased Mahlke thwarts Pilenz's desire as he persists in haunting Pilenz after his death: guilt best preserves metaphysical desire and does not allow the perpetrator of the crime to forget his rival. This persistence of desire is also signaled by Pilenz's appeal to Mahlke in his role of narratee in at least 23 paragraphs and sentences, especially at the beginning and the end of some chapters (e.g., the beginning of chapter two and the end of chapter three). This strategy draws attention to Mahlke's role as mediator of Pilenz's metaphysical desire. The narrating character knows well that Mahlke cannot respond to his call, yet he insists on attempting to communicate with Mahlke as if the latter could reappear through the power of words. These hopeless attempts merely perpetuate Pilenz's confession of his guilt and prevent him from achieving contrition and atoning for his sin.

Pilenz feels compelled to tell the story in order to repudiate his guilt (7, 84), but the repetitive scene of the cat and the mouse and the lack of closure at the end of the narrative[19] attest to the failure of this attempt. Furthermore, the narrating character intends to tell only Mahlke's story (21, 99), but as the narrative unfolds, it becomes clear that this story is inseparable from Pilenz's, that is, that the life and death of his rival and of himself have become intermingled. Pilenz feels that Mahlke dominates his emotions and dictates his actions to such an extent that it is no longer clear who writes the story (98). Not only did the mediator's death fail to restore the subject's self-assurance; the atrocious deed has made this goal forever unachievable.

Thus narration can reinforce and perpetuate mimetic desire through re-experiencing and re-enacting. However, narration can also *be* mimetic desire, in the sense that it is motivated by the will to mimic the mediator and his desires. The conception of narration *as* mimetic desire contributes to Girard's argument against the romantic idea of spontaneous, unmediated desire: the desire to tell one's own story is—or can be—mediated, not only by external mediators from whom the desiring subject is socially and spiritually distanced, but also by internal mediators, indeed the same ones who inhabit the story-world.

---

he has not really committed (2001: 432).

19. In her analysis of the normative and functional aspects of the mediation gap between the author and reader in literary communication, Yacobi (1987) distinguishes between the perspectives of the narrator and reader on the lack of closure in *Cat and Mouse*. From Pilenz's perspective, "the uncertainty that surrounds the end is existential and in keeping with the openness and chaos of reality"; by contrast, the reader, who considers the text as a fictional creation of Grass, views this lack of closure as "one option out of many, chosen for a purpose of his own, and fictionally *motivated* (realized, justified, camouflaged) by reference to the narrator's 'constraints of reality'" (362).

Grass's novella obliquely and intricately displays triangular desire as the motivation for narration through an analogy between swimming and narrating.[20] After Mahlke learns to swim and to dive, these activities become his favorite habits. On one occasion, Pilenz swims after Mahlke in a manner that is presented not only as aimed at reaching a goal, but also—and more significantly—as mimicking his rival. These events are intertwined with the act of the narration, which is of course posterior to them, and the two acts—swimming and narration—are portrayed as analogous:

> Während ich schwamm und während ich schreibe, versuchte und versuche ich an Tulla Pokriefke zu denken, denn ich wollte und will nicht immer an Mahlke denken. Deswegen schwamm ich in Rückenlage, deswegen schreibe ich: Schwamm in Rückenlage . . . war aber, als ich die zweite Sandbank hinter mir hatte, weggewischt, kein Punkt Splitter Loch mehr . . . [Ich] schwamm Mahlke entgegen, schreibe in Deine Richtung: Ich schwamm in Brustlage und beeilte mich nicht. (1963: 79)

> As I swam and as I write, I tried and I try to think of Tulla Pokriefke, for I didn't and still don't want to think of Mahlke. That's why I swam back stroke . . . but when I had the second sandbank behind me, she was gone, thorn and dimple had passed the vanishing point . . . [I was] swimming toward Mahlke, and it is toward you that I write: I swam breast stroke and I didn't hurry. (1964: 72)

This paragraph not only metaleptically blends past and present, story and narration, but also indirectly applies mimetic desire to narration: if Pilenz mimics Mahlke by swimming after him, and if swimming is like narrating, then it makes sense that narrating is another form of mimicry. Once again, not only does Mahlke come back to life in Pilenz's memory: Pilenz writes through Mahlke, in the sense that their story lives have become irrevocably enmeshed.

I wish to end this section with a short discussion of two paragraphs from the novel that highlight the connection between the appeal to the mediator

---

20. Frye (1993) draws an interesting analogy between Pilenz's narration and the functions of Mahlke's body, particularly his digestive system. For the analogies between the process of narration and the events of the story, see also Hilliard (2001) and Rimmon-Kenan (1987). My use of "motivation" in interpretations of fictional narratives should be distinguished from its use by Russian Formalists as a literary device that could be given a compositional, a realistic, or an artistic *raison d'être*. My own employment of the term is based on its use in psychology and the philosophy of psychology as the reason and the initiation for a particular behavior as well as the direction, intensity and persistence of such behavior (see, e.g., Mook [1996: 4]).

(i.e., Mahlke) as narratee and the perpetuation of mimetic desire. The first paragraph relates directly to the analogy between swimming and narrating:

> Ich schwimme langsam in Brustlage, sehe weg, zu, vorbei . . . sehe, bevor meine Hände den Rost fassen, Dich, seit gut fünfzehn Jahren: Dich! Schwimme, fasse den Rost, sehe Dich: der Große Mahlke hockt unbewegt im Schatten, die Schallplatte im Keller hängt und ist in immer dieselbe Stelle verliebt, leiert aus, Möwen streichen ab; und Du hast den Artikel mit dem Band am Hals. (1963: 82)

> I swim slowly, breast stroke, look away, look beyond . . . and before my hands grip the rust, I see you, as I've been seeing you for a good fifteen years: You! I swim, I grip the rust, I see You: the Great Mahlke sits impassive in the shadow, the phonograph record in the cellar catches, in love with a certain passage which it repeats till its breath fails; the gulls fly off; and there you are with the ribbon and *it* on your neck. (1964: 74)

The text blurs the difference between seeing as a physical act that presupposes the presence of the seen object (in this case, Mahlke's body swimming) and "seeing" metaphorically, that is, the re-presentation of the once seen object in imagination. Pilenz's external gaze during the actual swimming turns inwards, as his memory evokes the moments in which he mimicked the movements of his rival; his direct appeal to Mahlke as narratee accords with this blurring of differences between past and present, presence and absence, since the desiring subject (i.e., Pilenz) considers these differences insignificant as long as his desire persists. Just like Mahlke, Pilenz repeats the same record; unlike Mahlke, however, his repetition does not bring him any happiness.

The second paragraph displays the repetition compulsion of the narrating character in a completely different context:

> Laß uns noch einmal zu dritt und immer wieder das Sakrament feiern: Du kniest, ich stehe hinter trockener Haut. Dein Schweiß erweitert Poren. Auf belegter Zunge lädt Hochwürden die Hostie ab. Eben noch reimten wir uns alle drei auf dasselbe Wort, da läßt ein Mechanismus Deine Zunge einfahren. (1963: 126)

> Let us all three celebrate the sacrament, once more and forever: You kneel, I stand behind dry skin. Sweat distends your pores. The reverend father deposits the host on your coated tongue. All three of us have just ended on the same syllable, whereupon a mechanism pulls your tongue back in. (1964: 114)

The quoted lines describe Mahlke, Pilenz, and Father Guzevsky during communion; Pilenz addresses Mahlke and asks him to re-experience this Christian ceremony. Narration in general, and the direct appeal to Mahlke as narratee in particular, serve here once more to revive the dead. A peculiar analogy is created between transubstantiation, that is, the change of the substance of bread into Christ's body occurring during communion, and the "necromancy" of Mahlke by means of Pilenz's story. Pilenz will never let his adored rival go.

THE THIEF'S JOURNAL

Unlike the symmetrical relations between admiration and hostility towards the mediator in Grass's novel, Genet's autobiographical narrative *The Thief's Journal* (1949) represents the relations between these two aspects of mimetic desire as asymmetrical: the autodiegetic narrator's adoration of the mediators—male criminals, outcasts, thieves, and beggars whose body and spirit he desires—outstrips his antagonistic emotions towards them: Genet maintains that he has never felt any hate for his lovers (284).[21] His hostility and contempt, but also his feeling of inferiority and his wish to compensate for the life he could not have had—or have chosen to avoid—are directed at his anonymous readers, whom he chooses to address as the narratees of his story and whose anonymity serves well his goal to project on them his radical, although confused, criticism of the mainstream society of his period.

Genet adores the penises of his lovers like a pious Catholic adores the relic of a saint. The penis both embodies and symbolizes everything that he covets: masculinity, power, prowess, domination, and self-sufficiency (e.g., 24, 144). The greater the obstacle the lover poses to Genet, the more Genet comes to worship and is attracted to this lover. The lovers' self-admiration, indifference to other people's agony and pain, and ostentatious desire for their own body mark them as tough personalities who will not easily give other people access to their body and soul. Armand, Genet's most admired lover, demonstrates these qualities and is therefore idolized (194). His narcissistic desire for his own body is contagious, and his adoration by other men attracts Genet and poses a challenge to him (see Girard [1965: 96–99]).

Contrasting with these expressions of adoration, and at the same time inseparable from them, are Genet's manifestations of rivalry with his media-

21. Morón Arroyo justly criticizes Girard for having "a reductionist conception of the object of desire" (1978: 84) and proposes that mimetic desire may promote cooperation between subjects who desire the same object.

tors: treason and envy. Treason, like Girard's "murderous hostility," expresses the wish of the desiring subject to dispose of the mediator, thereby proving to him, and most of all to oneself, one's self-sufficiency. The narrating character contends that the willingness to act cruelly towards one's beloved, to violate his trust, and to break the bonds of love is the most lofty and beautiful act of eroticism (89–90, 181, 257–58). Envy is described by the narrating character as a form of eroticism that may lead to the worst treason—murder. Genet plans to murder both Stilitano and Robert, when the friendship between the two men, whom he loves, distances him from them (151–52).

Like many characters (and subjects) whose conduct is motivated by powerful metaphysical desire, Genet holds a romantic view that conceives of the self as separate from the world and attributes the source of all his desires to himself (see Girard 1965: 11). Although Genet is aware that his search for a Nietzschean moral solitude and self-assured pride is mediated by his models of masculinity, he believes that he can dispose of those models once he has attained his goal. However, moral solitude does not actually break the ties of eroticism; defying the beloved simultaneously reassures and reinforces his influence as a model. The following lines demonstrate this blind spot and draw an ironic light on the ideal of self-sufficiency:

> C'est peut-être leur solitude morale—à quoi j'aspire—qui me fait admirer les traîtres et les aimer. Ce goût de la solitude étant le signe de mon orgueil, et l'orgueil la manifestation de ma force, son usage, et la preuve de cette force. Car j'aurai brisé les liens les plus solides du monde: les liens de l'amour. Et quel amour ne me faut-il pas où je puiserai assez de vigueur pour le détruire! (1949: 48)

> It is perhaps their moral solitude—to which I aspire—that makes me admire traitors and love them—this taste for solitude being the sign of my pride, and pride the manifestation of my strength, the employment and proof of this strength. For I shall have broken the stoutest of bonds, the bonds of love. And I so need love from which to draw vigor enough to destroy it! (1967: 36)

Genet's autobiography is replete with paragraphs that seem to indicate that his worldview has been molded by the mimicry of and identification with his fellow thieves to such an extent that he completely rejects the values of normative society. Genet constantly associates morally negative concepts, such as evil (*le mal*), cruelty (*la cruauté*), and treason (*la trahison*) with morally positive concepts, such as moral perfection (*la perfection morale*), as well as with aesthetic and religious terms (especially poetry and sainthood).

The shocking conceit with which the narrative opens, in which Genet points out the close similarity between the fragility and the delicacy of flowers and the brutal insensitivity of convicts, acutely represents his goal to undermine moral and aesthetic dichotomies and to dissent from hegemonic values.[22]

Yet Genet also expresses his inability or unwillingness to detach himself entirely from the norms that he despises. He avoids committing a murder because he understands that murderers are unable to detach themselves from the murdered, whose specter forever haunts them. Thus Genet admits that an unreserved detachment from the prevalent moral norms—the replacement of the worship of God with the worship of Satan—is an unattainable fantasy (113, 224–25).

A similar oscillation can be detected in the inconsistency of the narrating character concerning his motivation for narration. From some paragraphs, one may conclude that he does not desire to communicate with the reader, since he claims that only in solitude can erotic love and devotion be sustained, and his narrative is this erotic song of solitude (106–7, 116). In Genet's dictum "Ce livre 'Journal du Voleur': poursuite de l'Impossible Nullité" (1949: 100) ("This book, *The Thief's Journal*, pursuit of the Impossible Nothingness," 1967: 77), I interpret impossible nothingness as poetic self-sufficiency. The journal attempts to achieve this nothingness (i.e., complete detachment from the ordinary world) by comprehending and justifying this regulative ideal, but it can be achieved only by an act of communication, which inherently thwarts the goal whose attainment it was intended to promote.

However, in another paragraph Genet says he wishes to use his past tribulations in order to teach the reader who he is at the time of the narration (75). In a more ambiguous passage, he claims that he would like to use his narrative for virtuous purposes ("à des fins de vertus," 65). This virtuous purpose is perhaps self-perfection, but it can also be a didactic aim of educating his readers to become better people by contributing to their understanding of society's outcasts, whom they rarely have the opportunity to know personally.

Genet's ambivalence concerning the norms of hegemonic society and the purpose of his narration is reflected in his address to his narratee—"the reader." Genet's portrayal of his readers is far from Prince's "degree-zero narratee": they do not have specific physical traits, but they certainly share a particular mentality in representing a conservative bourgeois, a thoughtless adherent to the conventional system of values. Needless to say, the

22. For Genet's imperative "to establish a contingent relationship between flowers and criminals" and to enforce his belief "in the dialectical reconciliation of opposites," see Reed (2005: 79–84).

actual reader may have nothing in common with "the reader," with Genet's anonymous narratee, and may repudiate the worldview attributed to him or her. Most addresses to the narratee throughout this narrative highlight the unbridgeable distance between the narrating character's moral values and emotional world on the one hand, and those of the narratee on the other. The criminal must be endowed with fervent creativity, courage, and determination in order to surmount the difficulties of being divorced from the normative world; it is implied that the narratee lacks all of these precious qualities: "Niant les vertus de votre monde, les criminels désespérément acceptent d'organiser un univers interdit. Ils acceptent d'y vivre. L'air y est nauséabond: ils savent le respirer. Mais—les criminels sont loin de vous—comme dans l'amour ils s'écartent et m'écartent du monde et de ses lois" (1949: 10). "Repudiating the virtues of your world, criminals hopelessly agree to organize a forbidden universe. They agree to live in it. The air there is nauseating: they can breathe it. But—criminals are remote from you—as in love, they turn away and turn me away from the world and its laws" (1967: 5). In his separate world, the criminal reminds the narratee of the suffering and the pain that the latter marginalizes and ignores (57–58).

By contrast, in other paragraphs the narrating character conveys his wish to be accepted and even revered by the conformist narratee, from whom he seems to be unable to detach himself (285). The act of narration itself (in all written narratives) reveals, and is motivated by, the wish to communicate with the narratee. A precondition for such communication is a minimal degree of comprehension, since the articulation of disputes and disagreements is meaningless unless it can be at least partly understood by the other party. In order to win the narratee's recognition, the narrator is willing to combine conventional forms of beauty (i.e., rhetorical devices of narration) with unconventional forms, which risk being incomprehensible or unacceptable (108). However, understanding cannot be achieved unless the horizons of the reader-narratee fuse with those of the narrating character: " . . . j'utiliserai les mots non afin qu'ils dépeignent mieux un événement ou son héros mais qu'ils vous instruisent sur moi-même. Pour me comprendre une complicité du lecteur sera nécessaire. Toutefois je l'avertirai dès que me fera mon lyrisme perdre pied" (1949: 17). "I shall not make use of words the better to depict an event or its hero, but so that they may tell you something about myself. In order to understand me, the reader's complicity will be necessary. Nevertheless, I shall warn him whenever my lyricism makes me lose my footing" (1967: 11).

The act of communication between a narrating character and a reader-narratee both reinforces and weakens Genet's triangular desire. On the one hand, the act of narration reproduces this desire by making him re-experience and reinterpret his passionate stories of love and rivalry, admiration and hostility; moreover, as previously noted, Genet often identifies the beauty of poetic creation with the world of treason, evil, and repudiation of moral norms. His narration praises the alternative world of counter-norms; it justifies and intensifies triangular desire by providing eroticism with a suitable poetic form. On the other hand, the narratee's world, which lacks the vehement contradictory emotions that characterize the world of evil and crime, puts an end to triangular desire.

The contradictory addresses of the narrating character to the narratee could therefore indicate his ambivalence about the possibility that desire might be annihilated. The imagined secure and serene world of the narratee can offer Genet salvation from extreme emotion, suffering, and pain, but at the same time, this world is dreary and devoid of the challenges and excitements that only a world based on mimetic desire can supply.[23]

I have already stressed that internal mimetic desire is characterized by the craving of the desiring subject to eliminate the distance between himself and the mediator by becoming the other or by subordinating the subject's will to his mediator's or vice versa. Conversely, in addressing the reader, Genet does not attempt to dissolve the reader's otherness. The distance between him and his narratee remains. Accordingly, Genet constantly employs the second-person—"votre monde," "vos moeurs" ("your world," "your morals")[24]—rather than the first-person plural.

Like Pilenz in Grass's novella, the narrating character in Genet's narrative (who identifies himself as the author)[25] derives his motivation for narration from mimetic desire. In the paragraph quoted below, he blurs the difference between writing a story (or being engaged in any other type of creative activity) and living (or experiencing) it: an author who writes about evil should experience it as a necessary part of his creation by mimicking the desires and

23. Reed (2005: 107–8) points out a similar ambivalence concerning Genet's relationship with Lucien, one of his lovers in non-fictional reality and one of the characters in *The Thief's Journal*.

24. Genet's address to the reader can be interpreted as directed either to a single reader or to readers in general. Both interpretations underscore the spiritual distance between the narrating character and his reader(s), the first by the formality of the address ("vous" versus "tu"), and the second by contrasting the individualist, outcast narrator with the conformist, homogeneous community of readers.

25. Although the narrating character of *The Thief's Journal* is named after the author, Genet's work does not accord unproblematically with Philippe Lejeune's "autobiographical pact" (see Lejeune (1989)), since Genet constantly reminds the reader that his creation is fictional and that it is therefore futile to separate the true from the false in his narrative. See Spear (1996) and Ubersfeld (1996).

the crimes of his heroes. Hence the criminals are his mediators not only in "the real world," but also in his creative activity. The story cannot be told unless it is an authentic dramatization of a (mediated) eroticized life:

> Créer n'est pas un jeu quelque pas frivole. Le créateur s'est engagé dans une aventure effrayante qui est d'assumer soi-même jusqu'au bout les périls risqués par ses créatures. On ne peut supposer une création n'ayant l'amour à l'origine. Comment mettre en face de soi aussi fort que soi, ce qu'on devra mépriser ou haïr. . . . "Prendre le poids du péché du monde" signifie très exactement: éprouver en puissance et en effets tous les péchés; avoir souscrit au mal. Tout créateur doit ainsi endosser—le mot serait faible—faire sien au point de le savoir être sa substance, circuler dans ses artères—le mal donné par lui, que librement choisissent les héros. (1949: 220–21)

> Creating is not a somewhat frivolous game. The creator has committed himself to the fearful adventure of taking upon himself, to the very end, the perils risked by his creatures. We cannot suppose a creation that does not spring from love. How can a man place before himself something strong as himself which he will have to scorn or hate? . . . "Taking upon himself the sins of the world" means exactly this: experiencing potentially and in their effects all sins; it means having subscribed to evil. Every creator must thus shoulder—the expression seems feeble—must make his own, to the point of knowing it to be his substance, circulating in his arteries, the evil given by him, which his heroes choose freely. (1967: 172–73)

Metaphysical desire, according to Genet's "credo," is a productive force, since it constitutes all types of valuable creation (religious as well as poetic), therefore it should be endorsed and encouraged rather than renounced.

THE FALL

Metaphysical desire is not as explicitly present in Albert Camus' *The Fall* (1956) as it is in the other two narratives that I have analyzed. It is not clear whether the narrating character who introduces himself under the pseudonym Jean-Baptiste Clamence and his anonymous addressee are mimetic rivals. Yet the story is centered on the loss of existential self-sufficiency, which Girard points out as the source of mimetic desire, and on the futile search for others who may compensate the unstable self for this loss. It is not in vain that Girard briefly refers to Camus' novella in *Deceit, Desire, and the Novel* as an "admirable and liberating work," which suggests that "a whole new career was probably opening up before him [Camus]" (1965: 271–72).

In a later essay, "Camus' *Stranger* Retried" (1978), Girard argues that Camus' *The Fall* "goes higher and deeper" (33) than his previous novel *L'Etranger* (*The Stranger*) and demonstrates Camus' transition from the preliminary romantic phase of his career, characterized by bad faith, to a mature phase, in which he espouses a more complex worldview. In Girard's words, "[t]he confession of Clamence does not lead to a new 'interpretation' of *L'Etranger* but to an act of transcendence; the perspective of this first novel is rejected" (21). Surprisingly, in this essay Girard does not interpret *The Fall* in relation to his theory of mimetic desire.

The central event of the narrative (both in importance and in its location in the text) is the fall of an unknown woman into the Seine. Clamence avoids jumping into the water to save the woman and does not even inform anybody of this incident (81–83). At the time of the fall, Clamence believes he has already arrived at the peak of his achievement, a perfect man both intellectually and morally: "je me trouvais un peu surhomme" (36). After some years of repression and denial, he re-experiences this fall as a traumatic event. From this point onward, his irreversible fall begins. His deceitful self-image collapses like a pack of cards. He reckons that his only rescue from a complete mental breakdown is to share his guilt with the rest of humanity. To achieve this end, he repeatedly tells his story to people previously unknown to him, and in the course of his narration he manipulates them into a position in which they will be compelled to admit that they are Clamence's accomplices.

At the outset, it seems that the narrator wishes to establish close contact with his interlocutor thanks to the latter's particularly interesting, sympathetic, or otherwise appealing character. However, this first impression turns out to be an affectation, a ruse intended to draw the narratee's attention. Clamence clarifies that his privileged interest in the narratee is temporary and that it stems not from any of the latter's unique qualities, but from the narrative situation. He views the narratee as a kind of object that is interchangeable with any other narratee who has similar traits (160–65). At the end of the account Clamence will proceed to court another narratee, whereas this one is to become another member, unimportant in himself, of humanity.

The narratees whom the narrating character addresses function as his mediators: in his attempt to restore his previous image, the narrator pretends at first to be as self-assured as he assumes his interlocutor to be, in order finally to demonstrate that belief in one's own perfection is spurious. Clamence's infinite repetition of his narration to replaceable addressees is the most extreme case of the process that Girard describes as the breaking up of the unity of the mediator into multiplicity (1965: 91). The closer the internal mediator is to the subject in his social status and intellectual faculties, the briefer is his reign. Hence the mediator loses any enduring significance conferred to him in particular: "Beginning with Proust, the mediator may be literally *anyone at all* and he may pop up *anywhere*" (92).

In Clamence's narration, both the mediator and the desire are almost devoid of any concrete content. The mediator is an abstract and reticent double, or a mirror image, of the desiring subject, who desires, not any material object that his mediator possesses, but rather his spirit—his pride, self-confidence, and self-respect. Therefore mimetic rivalry in Camus' work lacks dramatic passion and overt violence. In other words, it does not produce the intense ambiguity of high admiration and murderous hostility typical of metaphysical desire. Instead, aggression appears in the narrative in the much more palatable form of rhetorical devices, such as the formulation of highly provocative and disputable statements as rhetorical questions (e.g. 80, 140). The suspicion and hostility of the narrating character towards his narratee is expressed by his hardly perceptible transformations from the first-person singular (*je*) to the first-person plural (*nous*). To be sure, the aim of this rhetorical ruse is not to display fraternity, but to render his personal life-story—above all his guilt and his chastisement—inseparable from the life-story of the narratee (e.g. 54–55, 90–91, 134–35).[26] Yet although the "desiring subject" Clamence craves to dominate his "mediator," he is well aware that the narrative situation renders him entirely dependent on the willingness of the narratee to listen to him and to follow him wherever he goes.

Unlike Grass's novella, Camus' represents a compulsive and insatiable impulse to dispose of the mediator once he has been efficiently used, even more so than in Genet's narrative. Yet both *Cat and Mouse* and *The Fall* perpetuate mimetic desire and represent a structure of infinite mediation, which promises only further agony and guilt in a recurring act of narration and deprives the desiring subject of any prospects for a calmer and more stable future.[27]

---

26. For a thorough treatment of the narrator's rhetorical devices, see Brochier (1979), Marcus (2006), and Quillard (1991).

27. Infinite repetitious mimetic desire in Camus' narrative, like in Grass's, represents a form of suicide, namely, a cessation of lived experience. See also Solomon (2006: 200).

INTRA- AND EXTRA-SUBJECTIVE NARRATEES AS MEDIATORS OF MIMETIC DESIRE

Rimmon-Kenan defines the narratee as "the agent which is at the very least implicitly addressed by the narrator. (A narratee of this kind is always implied, even when the narrator becomes his own narratee)" (2001: 90). I wish to extend Rimmon-Kenan's contention and claim that a personalized, autodiegetic, and self-conscious narrator is prone to address him- or herself, at least implicitly, in the narrative. This type of narratee—whom I name *intra-subjective narratee*—tends to be the past self of the narrator, that is, the narrator as he used to be as a character during the time of the narrated events. The split between oneself as narrator and oneself as character and narratee is implied by autodiegetic self-conscious narration, since writing or telling a story about oneself creates a temporal and logical gap between the narrating self and the experiencing self and presupposes a narratee (see Marcus [2006: 87, note 15]).

The second type of narratee in these narratives is the *extra-subjective narratee*,[28] discussed elaborately in this essay, whose identity is (or at least seems to be) separate from the narrator's (e.g., Mahlke in *Katz und Maus* and the silent narratee in Camus' *La Chute*). The extra-subjective narratee in these narratives may be, to a lesser or greater degree, a projection of the intra-subjective narratee, that is, of the image of the (past) self of the narrator. Hence the labels "intra-subjective" and "extra-subjective" are employed with regards to the narrator, as the addressor on the level of narration. In the three narratives discussed in this essay, the intra-subjective narratee is never directly addressed, but only implicitly, first and foremost through the relations of similarity and contrast between the extra-subjective narratee and the narrator-as-character.

The concept of the intra-subjective narratee is extremely relevant for Girard's conception of metaphysical desire. As previously noted, Girard emphasizes that the greater the similarity between the subject and his mediator, the more severe the rivalry between them. Along this line of argument, it seems plausible to claim that *the greatest rivalry takes place between oneself and oneself-as-another, i.e., between the autodiegetic narrator and his past self as a character.*

For instance, Pilenz's greatest rival is perhaps not Mahlke, but his past self, which is closely similar to his self-as-narrator, yet not identical with it.

---

28. I thank Shlomith Rimmon-Kenan for suggesting the terms "intra-subjective" and "extra-subjective" narratees.

The narrating character, which is "the subject" in the *external* level of mimetic desire, splits into two in the *internal* level: he remains in the position of "the desiring subject" as narrator (in his present self), whereas as character (in his past self) he takes the position of "the mediator" or "the rival": Pilenz-as-narrator continues to desire everything that belongs to Mahlke and by doing this, he imitates the desire of himself as character; this desire is inherently insatiable, since Mahlke most probably no longer exists.

Pilenz as character *is* or *becomes* Mahlke, in the sense that his life is gradually reduced to the observation of Mahlke's life and the mimicry of his acts, and this prevents him from becoming an autonomous subject. At the same time, Pilenz is *not* Mahlke, in the sense that his imitation cannot be but partial and inauthentic. Hence there are both similarities and differences between Mahlke as the external narratee of the narrative and Pilenz-as-character, its intra-subjective narratee. Pilenz's wish in the story to annihilate Mahlke (falsely believing that he will become self-sufficient as soon as Mahlke disappears) becomes, on the level of narration, a wish to annihilate himself as character: for what is the aspiration to dispose of his guilt through writing his story (84) if not an impossible wish to detach his present self from his past? Pilenz's story is indeed "von Mahlke oder von Mahlke und mir, aber immer im Hinblick auf Mahlke," (21) ("about Mahlke, or Mahlke and me, but always with the emphasis on Mahlke," 1964: 21), since Pilenz actually lacks a separate self. Pilenz as narrator imitates the desire of his past self to possess Mahlke, but he can satisfy this desire only through the endless repetitions of his story.

The analogy between the extra-subjective narratee and the intra-subjective narratee as two types of rivals/mediators on the level of narration is even more emphatic and explicit in the case of *La Chute*. Clamence's narcissism may make the readers wonder whether the narratee exists as a real character or only as a projection of the narrator, "in which case the supposed dialogue collapses into a ceaseless self-engendering monologue" (Ellison 2007: 183). Certain characteristics of the narratee differentiate him from the narrator and make it difficult to psychologically identify the narratee with the narrator. Especially prominent is the silent refusal of the narratee to confess to the narrator, despite the latter's efforts to manipulate the narratee to do so (51, 70–71, 159). In this way the role-playing persists throughout the novella: the narrator narrates (and occasionally verifies the narratee's attention), and the narratee's reactions are mentioned by the narrator as part of their dialogue: he sometimes interrogates, responds, smiles, or protests, but never tells his own story. In this respect, the narratee can be identified not with Clamence as narrator but with Clamence's former self as character. Like the narratee,

Clamence as character is a Parisian, apparently self-assured, educated male lawyer; like the narratee, Clamence as character is incapable of self-reflection and does not feel the need to narrate his story, probably because both of them deem themselves complete, immaculate, and self-sufficient. Thus, unlike Mahlke, who cannot be identified with Pilenz-as-character, there is no way to differentiate Clamence's narratee from his past self. Clamence as narrator envies and despises both for their self-assured existence, which turns out to be spurious and instable.

By contrast, Genet's extra-subjective narratee (the reader), characterized as bourgeois and unadventurous, seems to have nothing in common with the nonconforming, impertinent intra-subjective narratee—Genet as character. The extra-subjective narratee suggests the possibility of eradicating metaphysical desire, whereas the intra-subjective narratee—in his fervent desire for the penis of his lovers—revives this desire. Genet's unwillingness to conform as narrator is demonstrated in his conscious efforts to efface himself as character and recreate himself constantly from his current position as narrator (75–76, 126), hence to possess and control his most intimate rival—his past self. Paradoxically, in his retrospective writing he cannot avoid the construction of an image of his past while destroying this image time after time.

Unlike the romantic conception of desire resisted by Girard, my model does not suppose a whole, unified, and coherent subject of desire, but rather splits this subject into two: the self is at the same time the self-as-another. Hence one can also be one's own rival, and both types of rivals (the intra-subjective and the extra-subjective narratees) can reflect each other and differ from one another to a lesser or greater degree.

CONCLUSION
Girard's Notion of Mimetic Desire and Narratology

Girard's *Deceit, Desire, and the Novel* is not a work of structural narratology, but an attempt to identify and define a *thematic* construction shared by all (great) novels, which differentiates them from the romantic way of thinking. Girard is often accused by his critics of reducing the narrative text to its extralinguistic references, because he insists that the language of the text signifies (but also distorts and conceals) human relationships in the actual world.[29] Nevertheless, the classical narratological distinction between story and narration, or more precisely, the implications of this distinction for the

---

29. See Golsan (1993: 111).

narrative transaction, contribute to the qualification and elaboration of Girard's thesis.

The relations between the narrator and the narratee in Günter Grass's novella *Cat and Mouse* both reflect and amplify the relations of mimetic desire between the two as characters in the story. As opposed to the straight analogy between metaphysical desire on the levels of story and narration in Grass's novella, the relations between the narrator and the narratees in Genet's autobiographical novel *The Thief's Journal* represent a possible world in which mimetic desire no longer exists. Hence Genet's narrative is more amenable than Grass's to the Girardian conception of conversion as a resolution of mimetic desire, although the possibility of conversion is negated as soon as it is suggested. Like *Cat and Mouse* and unlike *The Thief's Journal*, Albert Camus' *The Fall* demonstrates the perpetuation of mimetic desire by the endless repetition of the act of narration. While in the two other narratives mimetic desire only motivates the narration and the narrator's appeal to a narratee, without a story on that level, *The Fall* presents a story on the level of narration, which is woven into the story of the past life of the narrator.

Girard's argument that heroes of novels experience a conversion towards the end of the plot (as do the authors of those novels; see Golsan [1993: 111]) is influenced by his worldview, according to which one can pave the way to a balanced and stable integration of the self and the other only by resigning metaphysical desire: "To triumph over self-centeredness is to get away from oneself and make contact with others but in another sense it also implies a greater intimacy with oneself and a withdrawal from others" (298). However, this argument also stems from his inattentiveness to the act of communication within narratives between the narrator and the narratee, which in some cases reproduces and augments triangular desire. Modernist autodiegetic narration is particularly prone to exhibiting this type of enduring self-centeredness.

Not only does narratology illuminate and challenge Girard's thesis of metaphysical desire; conversely Girard's thesis—when it is extended to the level of narration—can contribute to narratology by helping to demonstrate some patterns of relations between the narrator and the narratee and by elucidating possible connections between story and narration.

In *Story and Situation* (1984: esp. 50–69), Ross Chambers argues that the relations of power and authority between the narrator and the narratee are motivated by the narrator's wish to control the conveyance of information on the one hand, and by the narratee's willingness to offer attention in exchange for information on the other hand. The essay highlights these relations in a different manner: if metaphysical desire is the basis of this relation, then narratorial authority is motivated by the anxiety that the loss of the narratee will cause unbearable pain to the narrator, whose mediator and rival will no longer provide him with the (fragile) existential security that he needs. The narrator's concealment, duplicity, and deception, emphasized in Chambers's argument as means of seducing the narratee and reinforcing the authority of the narrator, are intensified in the analyzed narratives, in which they function as a feature of internal mimetic desire.

Mimetic desire in autodiegetic narratives that have two (or more) types of narratees offers a complex network of possible analogies between the participants in the act of communication on the level of the narration (i.e., narrators and narratees) and the participants on the level of the story (i.e., characters, particularly narrators-as-characters). One should, however, beware of a reductive conclusion: not every narrative of this kind presents metaphysical desire between the narrator and the narratee. Although there are certain types of correlations between the structure of a narrative and its themes, such correlations are never necessary connections.[30]

---

30. I would like to thank Jan Alber, Monika Fludernik, and Jonathan Stavsky for their comments on earlier versions of this essay, and Moshe Ron for his preliminary comments on the subject.

REFERENCES

Braunstein, Nestor A. (2003) "Desire and Jouissance in the Teachings of Lacan." *The Cambridge Companion to Lacan.* Ed. Jean-Michel Rabaté. Cambridge: Cambridge University Press. 102–15.
Brochier, Jean-Jacques (1979) *Albert Camus: Philosophie pour classes terminales.* Paris: Balland.
Camus, Albert (1956) *La Chute: Récit.* Paris: Gallimard. English translation by Justin O'Brien: *The Fall.* London: Hamish Hamilton.
Chambers, Ross (1984) *Story and Situation: Narrative Seduction and the Power of Fiction.* Minneapolis: University of Minnesota Press.
Chatman, Seymour (1978) *Story and Discourse: Narrative Structure in Fiction and Film.* Ithaca and London: Cornell University Press.
Dee, Phyllis Susan (1999) "Female Sexuality and Triangular Desire in *Vanity Fair* and *The Mill on the Floss.*" *Papers on Language and Literature* 35.4: 391–416.
Ellison, David R. (2007) "Withheld Identity in *La Chute.*" *The Cambridge Companion to Camus.* Ed. Edward J. Hughes. Cambridge: Cambridge University Press.
Freud, Sigmund (1961) *Beyond the Pleasure Principle* [1920]. New York: Norton.
Frye, Lawrence (1993) "Günter Grass, *Katz und Maus*, and Gastro-narratology." *The Germanic Review* 68: 176–84.
Fryer, David Ross (2004) *The Intervention of the Other: Ethical Subjectivity in Levinas and Lacan.* New York: Other Press.
Genet, Jean (1949) *Journal du voleur.* Paris: Gallimard. English translation by Bernard Frechtman: *The Thief's Journal.* Harmondsworth, Penguin Books, 1967.
Genette, Gérard (1980) *Narrative Discourse: An Essay in Method.* Trans. J. E. Lewin. Ithaca, NY: Cornell University Press. Orig. published in French in 1972 as *Figures III.* Paris: Seuil.
Girard, René (1965) *Deceit, Desire, and the Novel: Self and Other in Literary Structure.* Trans. Yvonne Freccero. Baltimore: The Johns Hopkins Press. Orig. published in French in 1961 as *Mensonge romantique et vérité romanesque.*
―――― (1977) *Violence and the Sacred.* Trans. P. Gregory. Baltimore: The Johns Hopkins University Press. Orig. published in French in 1972 as *La Violence et le Sacré.*
―――― (1978) "Camus' *Stranger* Retried." *'To double business bound': Essays on Literature, Mimesis, and Anthropology.* Baltimore and London: The Johns Hopkins University Press. 9–35.
Golsan, Richard J. (1993) *René Girard and Myth: An Introduction.* New York and London: Garland.
Grass, Günter (1963) *Katz und Maus: Eine Novelle* [1961]. Darmstadt und Neuwied: Luchterhand. English translation by Ralph Manheim. New York: Signet Books, 1964.
Grigg, Russell (1991) "Signifier, Object, and the Transference." *Lacan and the Subject of Language.* Ed. Ellie Ragland-Sullivan and Mark Bracher. New York: Routledge. 100–15.
Hilliard, K. F. (2001) "Showing, Telling and Believing: Günter Grass's *Katz und Maus* and Narratology." *The Modern Language Review* 96.2: 420–36.
Jakobson, Roman (1960) "Closing Statement: Linguistics and Poetics." *Style and Language.* Ed. Thomas A. Sebeok. Cambridge, MA: MIT Press. 350–77.
Klarer, Mario (1991) "David Leavitt's 'Territory': René Girard's Homoerotic 'Trigonometry' and Julia Kristeva's 'Semiotic Chora.'" *Studies in Short Fiction* 28.1: 63–76.

Kofman, Sarah (1980) "The Narcissistic Woman: Freud and Girard." *Diacritics* 10: 36–46.
Lejeune, Philippe (1989) *On Autobiography*. Ed. Paul John Eakin. Trans. Katherine Leary. Minneapolis: University of Minnesota Press.
Marcus, Amit (2006) "Camus' *The Fall*: The Dynamics of Narrative Unreliability." *Style* 40.4: 314–33.
—— (2006) "Sameness and Selfhood in Agota Kristof's *The Notebook*." *Partial Answers* 6.2: 79–89.
—— (2008) "Dialogue and Authoritativeness in 'We' Fictional Narratives: A Bakhtinian Approach." *Partial Answers* 6.1: 135–61
Meloni, Mauricio (2002) "A Triangle of Thought: Girard, Freud, Lacan." *Journal of European Psychoanalysis* 14: 27–56.
Moi, Toril (1982) "The Missing Mother: The Oedipal Rivalries of René Girard." *Diacritics* 12.2: 21–31.
Mook, Douglas G. (1996) *Motivation: The Organization of Action*. 2nd ed. New York and London: W. W. Norton and Company.
Morón Arroyo, Ciriaco (1978) "Cooperative Mimesis: Don Quixote and Sancho Panza." *Diacritics* 8.1: 75–86.
Piwowarczyk, Mary Ann (1976) "The Narratee and the Situation of Enunciation: A Reconsideration of Prince's Theory." *Genre* 9.1: 161–77.
Prince, Gerald (1973) "Introduction a l'étude du narrataire." *Poétique* 14, 178–96.
—— (1985) "The Narratee Revisited." *Style* 19.3: 299–303.
Proust, Marcel (1999) *A la recherche du temps perdu*. Paris: Gallimard. Orig. published 1913–27.
Quillard, Geneviève (1991) "Mécanismes ironiques et code socioculturel dans *La Chute*." *Albert Camus* 14, *Le texte et ses langages*. Ed. Raymond Gay-Crosier. Paris: Lettres Modernes. 75–95.
Ragland-Sullivan, Ellie (1995) *Essays on the Pleasures of Death: From Freud to Lacan*. New York: Routledge.
Reed, Jeremy (2005) *Jean Genet: Born to Lose*. Creation Books.
Rimmon-Kenan, Shlomith (1987) "Narration as Repetition: The Case of Günter Grass's *Cat and Mouse*." *Discourse in Psychoanalysis and Literature*. Ed. Shlomith Rimmon-Kenan. London and New York: Methuen. 176–87.
—— (2001) *Narrative Fiction: Contemporary Poetics* [1983]. London and New York: Routledge.
Ryan, Judith (1977) "Resistance and Resignation: A Reinterpretation of Günter Grass's *Katz and Maus*." *The Germanic Review* 57: 148–65.
Sedgwick, Eve Kosofsky (1985) *Between Men: English Literature and Male Homosocial Desire*. New York: Columbia University Press.
Solomon, Robert C. (2006) *Dark Feelings, Grim Thoughts: Experience and Reflection in Camus and Sartre*. Oxford: Oxford University Press.
Spear, Thomas C. (1996) "Le 'Véritable' Jean Genet." *Europe* 808–809: 26–33.
Sullivan, Henry W. (1995) "*Homo sapiens or Homo desiderans*: The Role of Desire in Human Evolution." *Lacan and the Subject of Language*. Ed. Ellie Ragland-Sullivan and Mark Bracher. New York: Routledge. 36–48.
Ubersfeld, Anne (1996) "Écriture de la Maîtrise." *Europe* 808–809: 56–64.
Yacobi, Tamar (1987) "Narrative Structure and Fictional Mediation." *Poetics Today* 8.2: 335–72.

JARMILA MILDORF

Narratology and the Social Sciences

Social science disciplines such as sociology, psychology, anthropology, education, and so on have long had an interest in narrative as a human cognitive and discursive device for sense-making and for ordering one's life experiences. The underlying assumption is that narratives are "*social products* produced by people within the context of specific social, historical and cultural locations. They are related to the experience that people have of their lives, but they are not transparent carriers of that experience. Rather, they are interpretive devices, through which people represent themselves, both to themselves and to others" (Lawler 2002: 242; emphasis in original). These disciplines have consequently developed their own specific methodological tools for analyzing narrative, which can be broadly separated into thematic analysis, structural analysis, dialogic/performance analysis and visual analysis (Riessman 2008). Even though thematic analysis is only one of four possibilities according to Riessman's outline, it is my impression that much narrative research in the social sciences is still limited to an investigation into *what* is told, while the *how* (that is, the process of constructing and conveying what is told) is discussed in fairly general terms. Despite their focus on narrative, many social scientists seem to be largely unaware of (and perhaps not interested in?) what (literary) narratology has to offer. The question arises to what extent "classical" narratological concepts that have hitherto been mainly applied to literary narratives can also be successfully exported to other disciplines which have an interest in narrative. Fludernik (1996) contends in her book on "natural narratology" that narratology can learn from oral narratives and discourse analysis: "It will be argued that oral narratives (more precisely: narratives of spontaneous conversational storytelling) cognitively correlate with perceptual parameters of human experience and that these parameters remain in force even in more sophisticated written narratives, although the textual make-up of these stories changes drastically over time" (12). Conversely, one could ask whether studies of oral narratives may likewise benefit from the discussions conducted in narratology.

I seek to answer this question by exploring ways of combining sociolinguistic narrative analysis with narratological terms and concepts. My aim is to demonstrate that narratology can, if suitably adapted to social science requirements, add further insights into the particularly "narrative" features of oral narratives. First I provide an outline of various narrative approaches in the social sciences, drawing upon Lieblich, Tuval-Mashiach, and Zilber's (1998) distinction between *holistic-content, holistic-form, categorical-content* and *categorical-form* modes of reading narrative. This outline suggests that narrative research can vary significantly in its theoretical depth and methodological rigor, ranging from detailed turn-by-turn linguistic analyses (e.g. in discursive psychology) to more thematic or topic-oriented approaches. I then analyze two oral narratives from the Database of Personal Experience of Health and Illness (DIPEx, now: healthtalkonline.org) with a view to identifying possible points of convergence between narratology and social science brands of narrative research. More specifically, I borrow narratological terms such as *experiencing/narrating I, focalization* or *slant* and *filter,* and *double deixis* in you-narratives for my analysis, and I contend that frequently evoked concepts in the social science literature such as *social positioning, identity* (Giddens 1991), and the marking of *in-group* and *out-group* relations (Tajfel 1974) can be further illuminated if reconsidered through a narratological lens.

NARRATIVE AND SOCIAL SCIENCE RESEARCH METHODS
An Overview

Research methods in the social sciences can be located along a continuum ranging from "quantitative" to "qualitative" approaches. Quantitative research methods are normally applied if one's aim is to deal with a large amount of data, and if the main interest lies in measuring these data, comparing figures and percentages, and calculating the relations between variables. The question one asks is "How many?" rather than "In what way?" or "Why?" The instruments for this type of research are standardized so that, ideally, every test subject is given the same input and tests are repeatable.

The aim is to reach valid and reliable results. Typical methods include large-scale surveys and statistical measurements. By contrast, qualitative methods are used when questions of motivation, attitudes, or opinions are concerned. With qualitative methods, one can generate data on people's interactions and their relationships and functional positions in social organizations, institutions and systems, or, more generally, one can obtain data on cognitive, affective and behavioral aspects of people in given social contexts, e.g. their beliefs, attitudes, feelings, opinions and real vs. reported, planned or remembered actions. Today, multi-method approaches, which combine both quantitative and qualitative methodologies such as surveys and interviews, are very common in social science research and, more specifically, in health research (McDonald and Daly 1992; McKie 1996).

Narrative research is one of a number of methods in the qualitative methods camp. One key tool is narrative interviewing. In narrative interviews open-ended questions are used to elicit stories from the interviewee. This type of interview is common, for example, in life history research. Narrative interviews can have a topical focus, i.e. they concentrate on specific events and on what happened when and why, but more often they are cultural interviews in the sense that they try to unravel norms, values and beliefs of a certain group or society (Rubin and Rubin 2005: 9–10). While the narrative interview is a method to elicit answers from respondents, the data thus generated can be analyzed from different vantage points, as explained below.

Oral narratives pose a series of questions in terms of possible analytical approaches but these questions can be summarized, by and large, in the following questions identified by Riessman (1993: 25):

1. How is talk transformed into a written text and how are narrative segments determined?
2. What aspects of the narrative constitute the basis for interpretation?
3. Who determines what the narrative means and are alternative readings possible?

Question one touches upon issues surrounding the transcription of interview material and the selection of narrative data. The second part of this question borders on considerations of form: what, in structural terms, constitutes a narrative? Narrativity plays a central role here. Questions two and three refer to the interpretation process: what is of interest in a narrative, i.e. what in particular does a researcher wish to investigate? And, finally, what is the analyst's role and to what extent does his or her interpretive focus influence research findings?

The answers to these questions depend largely on the conceptual frame one works in and are therefore also influenced by the specific discipline within which a researcher undertakes narrative analysis. However, it is possible to sketch a general outline of the types of narrative analysis currently available to scholars. Lieblich, Tuval-Mashiach and Zilber (1998: 12–14) propose the following model for the classification and organization of the narrative analysis of life stories, which is based on four cornerstones:

HOLISTIC-CONTENT   HOLISTIC-FORM

CATEGORICAL-CONTENT   CATEGORICAL-FORM

Even though this matrix was devised for life history research, the categories of *content* vs. *form* on the one hand and *categorical* vs. *holistic* on the other are applicable to any type of narrative analysis. The *holistic-content* approach, as its name suggests, looks at the content of a life story in its entirety. Even if only parts of the narrative are focused upon, e.g. the beginning or the ending, they are always interpreted holistically with regard to the entire narrative. The reconstruction of a life story can also involve using archival data and visual material. In the *holistic-form* approach, broad structural categories come under closer scrutiny. Thus one can look at genre allocations of life stories: for instance, does a story develop as a tragedy or as a comedy, or can one analyze in more detail how the plot develops throughout the life course? Are there turning points, for example, or a climax? On the *holistic-form* side, social science research has brought forth sociolinguistic narrative analysis in the Labovian tradition, which delineates the overall shape of oral narratives in terms of Labov's diamond diagram with *abstract, orientation, turning point, complicating action,* and *coda* (Labov and Waletzky 1967; Labov 1982). Another key concept is "evaluation," which explains why a narrative is told in the first place, for example because the related events are particularly exciting, important, dangerous, funny or, more generally, worth telling. Structurally, evaluation is marked through deviance from the overall "narrative syntax." This can be seen, for example, in a shift of tenses, modality, etc.

Since sociolinguistic narrative analysis also attends to features of narrative syntax one can also place it within the *categorical-form* area. The *categorical-form* mode focuses on a more detailed linguistic analysis of narratives, comments, utterances, etc. Analysts might look at metaphors used by the speaker or at the distribution of active/passive constructions, and the like. One type of research that is clearly located in the *categorical-form* axiom is the conversation-analytic approach practiced in discursive psychology, for example, where data are carefully transcribed including phonetic detail and prosodic features such as intonation patterns and pauses. These data are then analyzed on a turn-by-turn basis in order to trace the locally determined unfolding of the conversation. Discursive strategies and markers, such as backchannels, repairs, hedges, boosters, interruptions, tag questions, etc., come under closer scrutiny in this line of research. The *categorical-content* approach, by contrast, is equated with what is otherwise known as "content analysis," i.e. the extraction, classification and collection of separate utterances under the heading of predefined categories (Grbich 1999). Categories can be fairly broad or narrow, depending on one's research angle and detail of analysis. Data are coded for larger thematic features. The analysis can range from quasi-statistical forms where the frequency and length of discussion of recurring themes is measured, to more qualitative accounts marked by careful reading and the contextualization of data.

As Rentz (1999) demonstrates in her survey of case studies conducted in the area of professional communication, social science studies themselves often take a narrative form by presenting either the research activities or the explored phenomena, or both, as stories. Case studies frequently make use of narrative methods since narrative "is particularly critical to the making of experiential knowledge" (Rentz 1999: 54). Thus case studies invite the interpretations of readers and allow them to read the data against their own "folk knowledge" and life experiences. However, pieces of narrative research can vary significantly in their theoretical depth and methodological rigor, as we saw. I must add the caveat here that I consider it perfectly legitimate that researchers resort to different types of narrative analysis, depending on the data at hand and on the purpose and aim of the research. To adopt an argument used by social science researchers, the research questions ultimately determine the methods one uses (Frankfort-Nachmias and Nachmias 2008; May 2001; Silverman and Marvasti 2008). Further aspects to bear in mind in this context are disciplinary traditions as well as the audience the research is targeted at. For example, it may be counterproductive to present a detailed conversation-analytical account of doctor-patient interaction to medical practitioners as they may be uncomfortable with the linguistic terminology and may therefore not consider the analysis helpful for their own practical purposes. However, I think that discussions of narrative materials could sometimes benefit from closer linguistic and especially narratological analyses.

Over the last few decades narratology, by definition the prime discipline of narrative analysis, has branched out into a wide array of "post-classical" narratologies (Heinen and Sommer 2009; Herman 1999a; Nünning and Nünning 2002) that have borrowed concepts from psychology, sociology, anthropology, history, cognitive science, artificial intelligence, discourse linguistics, and other fields. In the past, attempts have also been made to build bridges between narratology and social science disciplines. Herman's (1999b) concept of "socionarratology," for example, takes into account narrative features, contextual factors, and the cognitive dimension in narrative production. Tannen (1989, 1997) demonstrates that spoken discourse is by no means less linguistically complex than literary discourse and that in fact oral narratives can display more effective strategies for creating involvement. Some scholars have also attempted to apply narratological concepts to non-literary narratives. For example, a recent collection of essays looks at the roles and functions of narrative in real-life contexts such as journalism, medicine, natural sciences, psychology, law, religion, economics, politics, and so on (Klein and Martínez 2009).[1] Potter (1996), a discursive psychologist, dedicates a section of his book on the discursive construction of reality to focalization in conversational narratives (163–65), arguing that focalization assigns to the listener the role of perceiver and endows the speaker with the authority of a "witness" (see also Atkinson 1990). Potter concludes his excursion into narratology by saying that "a more systematic study of the kinds of focalization that occur in everyday talk and news interview talk could be particularly revealing" (173). Another feature that is generally considered to be mainly "literary" is free indirect discourse. However, scholars like Polanyi (1984), Fludernik (1993), and Tommola (2003) have pointed out that certain forms of free indirect discourse can also occur in spoken language. Despite such efforts to encourage interdisciplinary approaches, however, a more consistent and systematic exploration of potential areas of cross-fertilization between narratology and other narrative approaches is still missing in the field. It is time to begin to close the gap. Before I move on to my analyses, let me provide some information concerning the narratives presented in this essay.

DATA

The two narratives were selected from the Database of Personal Experience of Health and Illness (DIPEx), which has changed its name to healthtalkonline.org and can be accessed online. DIPEx is a registered charity, whose aim

  1. One point in this volume I criticize is the fact that, even though it addresses narratives in real life ("*Wirklichkeitserzählungen*"), none of the contributions attends to spontaneous conversational storytelling, which, to my mind, can be considered the most typical kind of storytelling in comparison to the ones presented in the book.

is to make people's experiences with over one hundred common illnesses available to other patients but also to function as a teaching resource for health care professionals. The database contains excerpts from interviews conducted with patients as well as general information about a wide range of conditions. The first website was launched as a pilot site in 2001, and DIPEx has been expanding its online information base ever since. The team behind DIPEx consists of medical practitioners and social scientists working in the area of health and illness. The data for the website are generated in in-depth interviews conducted with patients in their homes or in other locations if they prefer not to be interviewed at home. All interviews are fully transcribed and coded for general themes and topics. Prior to publication on the website, the respondents read the transcripts and decide whether they wish some of the material to be excluded from publication. Copyright is then passed on to the DIPEx team.

While I was not able to access complete transcripts of the interviews because of financial limitations, I was kindly permitted to use the materials that are available on the actual DIPEx website. A few words are therefore in order concerning the narratives I use. First of all, the narratives are presented out of context in that only parts of the interview in which they emerged are available online. Second, the narratives have already been preselected according to the thematic criteria applied by the DIPEx research team. In other words, a certain bias may have been introduced by arranging the narrative materials in specific ways, and since I am not part of the research team I may be less aware of such a bias. Third, the materials on the website are tidied up in the sense that transcripts have been made more readable for a larger readership. Hence, one does not find a close phonetic transcription of the interviews. However, a minimum of description of the oral nature of these data is maintained in the notation of pauses and breaks in speech, for example. Unlike with other transcripts, the transformation from the oral to the written medium was not an issue for my analysis, since the DIPEx website also makes recordings of the presented excerpts available. In other words, prosodic features and other phonetic particularities can be and were double checked. My use of line breaks in the narratives follows Labov and Waletzky's (1967) typology of narrative clauses. I have not added transcription conventions other than the ones already used by the DIPEx team to ensure readability. Furthermore, I would like to add that, for my purposes, a holistic rather than a turn-by-turn presentation of the narratives is perfectly sufficient. While a conversation-analytic approach would require a more fully elaborated transcript with both speakers' (that is, the respondent's and interviewer's) turns, the sociolinguistic narrative approach coupled with narratological considerations does not necessarily require such detail. The narratives selected must be considered case studies, and I do not claim general applicability or validity for the results I present. The purpose of this paper is to open vistas to what, in my view, is a promising new line of research along the boundaries of narratology and the social sciences.

FAMILY STORIES AND PERSONAL IDENTITY

In an earlier article on focalization and double deixis in oral narratives (Mildorf 2006), I concentrate especially on the formation of professional identity in contrast to personal identity in the narrative discourse of general practitioners. However, society contains a great variety of groups one can belong to. Besides professional groups, friends and family also play a significant role in our lives and determine our identity. Sarangi (2006) maintains that "[f]amily is conceptualized as a social institution that mediates the individual and the social, with identifiable structures, functions, and hierarchies" (403). Family structures in turn are largely based on narratives, as Langellier and Peterson (2004) argue, and these narratives establish members' in-group and out-group status and thus define who belongs to a family and who does not: "What we commonly call 'the family' is not a single, naturally occurring phenomenon but variations in small group cultures produced in embodied, situated, and material performances such as family storytelling. Family storytelling is a multileveled strategic discourse carried out in diverse situations by multiple participants who order personal and group identities as family" (113). A problem arises when personal stories potentially threaten family unity because of a discrepancy between feelings of loyalty on the one hand and misgivings about other members of the group on the other. Let us have a closer look at the following interview narrative related by a 52-year-old man suffering from epilepsy. The narrative recounts his second seizure and the reaction of his family.

Narrative 1

1. When the second time it came round,
2. when I had the second fit which wasn't very long afterwards,
3. and they decided that "yeah you've got epilepsy,"
4. my grandmother, my grandparents, my grandmother particularly was really distraught, sobbing.

5. And basically my parents were supportive
6. but um, they kept the,
7. it's like they kept the lid on things.
8. Um, yeah they didn't want,
9. there was a degree of shame if you like,
10. not, I don't mean that unkindly on them,
11. I think they meant well
12. and they were very supportive to me.
13. But they didn't want to go round saying "Excuse me but my son's an epileptic,"
14. and they would much rather I suppose naturally talk about success rather than what was certainly perceived as a failure.

This narrative can be divided into two larger parts: the actual narrative ranging from lines 1 to 7, and a lengthy evaluation from line 8 onwards, which resumes and elaborates the key point of the narrative, namely that the family were not willing to discuss the narrator's illness openly ("they kept the lid on things," line 7). The narrative begins by anchoring the story world temporally in lines 1 and 2: "When the second time it came round, when I had the second fit which wasn't very long afterwards." While the first line gives a rather vague image of the incident because of the replacement of "the fit" with the third-person pronoun "it" and the somewhat unusual verb phrase "came round," the second line specifies what happened by explicitly mentioning "the fit" and by tying the incident back to the narrator's first seizure alluded to in the relative clause "which wasn't very long afterwards." The following narrative clause in line 3, which entails the complicating action of the story, depicts a crucial point in the illness narrative: the labeling of the illness as "epilepsy." Labeling plays an important role in medical consultations since giving a label to a physical condition turns this condition into a definite disease or problem and thus establishes it as a fact (Maynard 1988).

What is also noteworthy here is the use of direct speech or what Tannen (1989) calls "constructed dialogue," i.e. a seemingly verbatim rendition of a speech situation which, however, cannot be taken to be an accurate reflection of the original speech situation but is rather a version (re)constructed in the current conversational context: "'yeah, you've got epilepsy?'" As in literary narrative, direct speech is used to enliven a scene and to create in the listener a sense of vicinity to the characters in the scene. In this particular example, the use of direct speech gives additional weight to the labeling of the narrator's disease, which is also reinforced by the affirmative interjection "yeah." The revelation of the diagnosis is dramatized and the characters in this "drama" come to life, as it were. More importantly, however, the direct speech here also assumes a distancing function that works in two ways. On the one hand, the narrator as experiencing self distances himself from the doctors who passed the diagnosis by making them stand out as distinct characters or actors in his illness narrative (*"they* decided that . . ."). On the other hand, the narrator also distances himself from his ill persona and refuses identification with the label of "epilepsy" by reconstructing the diagnosis in direct speech and by thus presenting himself as second-person "you" rather than "I." The address form implies that the label was imposed on the experiencing self from the outside and has not been fully incorporated yet (compare with "and they decided that I had epilepsy" or even "and they decided that I've got epilepsy"). A similar strategy is used in line 13, where the identification, and hence acknowledgment, of the illness through labeling is again presented in direct speech: "'Excuse me but my son's an epileptic.'" This time, however, labeling the disease is precisely what does not happen, what the narrator's family "didn't want to go round saying." The constructed speech in this context thus has an almost sarcastic quality, especially since it contains the apologetic phrase "excuse me" and the generic category "an epileptic."

Criticism of the family's attitude towards the narrator's problem is the central topic of the narrative, and the family's behavior constitutes large parts of the plot. What is interesting, however, is the fact that the narrator repeatedly tries to tone down his criticism and that he uses a number of linguistic strategies in order not to come across as someone who is unjustifiably disappointed with his family. To use Tannen's (2006) term, the narrative is "rekeyed" in the sense that the overall tenor changes. In line 4 the narrator depicts the distress felt by his grandparents and especially his grandmother (see the self-correction from "my grandparents" to "my grandmother") and emphasizes this through the adverb "really" as well as the additional action verb "sobbing." The continuous form of the verb implies that this expression of the grandmother's distress must have been lengthy and ongoing. Line 5 focuses on the parents and describes them as "supportive." The adverb "basically," however, already anticipates some contrasting action, which is then introduced through the coordinator "but" in the following line: "but um, they kept the, it's like they kept the lid on things" (lines 6–7). The container metaphor evoked in the expression "they kept the lid on things" suggests that the parents regarded the narrator's illness as something that must be contained or suppressed. More precisely, the metaphor expresses what the narrator as experiencing self thought his parents did and felt. The hesitation marker "um" used at this point (lines 6 and 8), the speech cut-off in line 6, and the use of the modifier "it's like" in line 7 after "they kept the" before the phrase "they kept the lid on things" is completed—these all indicate a high level of self-monitoring and point towards the interaction work the narrator is doing as the narrating self, i.e. from his present-day perspective. In Jahn's (1996, 1999) terminology we could say that the narrator occupies *focus-1*, i.e. he offers the "lens" through which the story world is perceived. In his model of vision, Jahn distinguishes between two types of focus which he then applies to the concept of focalization: *focus-1* is "the burning point of an eye's lens, usually located in a person's head," while *focus-2* is "the area of attention which the eye focuses on to obtain maximum sharpness" (Jahn 1999: 88). In the narrative at hand, the speaker can be said to occupy *focus-1* in the sense explained above, as well as *focus-2* since he focuses on himself in relationship to his parents in his narrative. What I wish to suggest here is that even in oral storytelling one ought not to presuppose a simple co-referentiality between the storyteller and the person expressed in the first-person pronoun "I." Instead, it can be useful to differentiate between various narrative personae and functional roles a narrator may assume.

Rather than presenting the behavior of his parents straightaway as an absolute fact, the narrator reformulates it in terms of his own retrospective perception or focalizer position ("it's like") and thus mitigates the potentially critical stance conveyed in the metaphoric phrase. This mitigating strategy is repeated in another clause cut off in line 8 ("Um, yeah they didn't want"), which is then resumed in line 13 ("But they didn't want to go round saying . . .") with a range of excuses and justifications of the parents' behavior placed in between (lines 11–12: "I think they meant well and they were very supportive"). Furthermore, hedges are employed to deflect the impression of the narrator as unduly critical: "I don't mean that unkindly on them" (line 10); "a degree of shame" (line 9). The conditional clause "if you like" (line 9) indirectly negotiates the word choice of the noun "shame" and has the additional phatic function of establishing rapport between storyteller and listener (in the sense of "I am lacking a better word at this point but you know what I mean").

Chatman's (1986) distinction between filter and slant can also be useful for the analysis of this narrative. While the events at the time of the diagnosis and the family's reaction are "filtered through" the narrator's eyes both on the level of the experiencing and the narrating self, the critical judgment that is implicitly passed can be reframed as the "slant" the narrator takes on the events in retrospect. This slant, however, becomes more ambivalent through the excusatory tone introduced because of the interview situation. When talking to the interviewer the narrator feels obliged to maintain face as the understanding son of the family despite his probable disappointment about the reaction of his parents. The division of the narrator's position into slant and filter can be further observed in the final line of the narrative, in which the narrator speculates on reasons why his parents did not want to discuss his illness openly: "and they would much rather I suppose naturally talk about success rather than what was certainly perceived as a failure" (line 14). The most striking aspect here is the free indirect discourse (FID) in "they would much rather . . . talk about success," which blends the narrator's voice with the alleged thoughts/motives of his parents. One might object here that the clause is in fact an example of direct discourse, which is immediately dependent on the inquit formula "I suppose." I would reject such a reading because of the parenthetical insertion of "I suppose," which marks the putative verb phrase phonetically and thus lifts it out of the surrounding syntactical construction, no longer warranting its function as a real inquit formula. Typical features of FID in this example include the omission of the reporting clause ("they thought" or "they said" or "they felt"), the change from first-person to third-person pronoun use ("we would rather" to " "they would rather"), tense backshift of the modal verb "would," and the use of features of spoken language such as the combination of the quantifier "much" with the adverb "rather" (see also Leech and Short 1981: 325ff.). Since the verb is a modal verb, the backshift is not evident from the linguistic form alone as modals typically do not change when they are in past tense. However, the context with past tense in the preceding and following clause strongly suggests that the modal must also be set in the past here. It is important to bear in mind that the narrative does not represent what the parents actually said or thought but what their son assumes they may have said or thought. In other words, the clause containing FID is used to convey hypothetical thought or speech.

FID is said to be limited to literary narrative because it enables the narrator to access the minds of characters in the story world, a phenomenon that is supposed to be impossible in real life. In this narrative we see that even conversational storytellers can make use of FID if they present the thoughts, feelings, or motives of other people. That this form of access to other people's minds is unusual and hence needs to be explained or justified in oral narratives (while it is a perfectly legitimate form in literary narrative), can be seen in the insertion of the above-mentioned verb phrase "I suppose," which identifies the speaker's statement as his conjecture rather than an observable and verifiable fact. The parents' reasoning, which could easily come under attack if understood as a sign of lack of courage and acceptance of the son's predicament, is thus again mitigated and presented in a defensive manner. This verbal defense of the parents culminates in the passive construction used at the end of the narrative: "what was certainly perceived as a failure" (line 14). The adverb "certainly" again frames the presented feelings in terms of what the narrator "believes to be true" rather than what "is true" (what Leech [1987: 107–110] calls "theoretical meaning"). More importantly, however, the "experiencers" or "originators" of these feelings are completely blotted out. In other words, the perception of the narrator's illness as "failure" is not explicitly attributed to anyone. One could interpret the relative clause as referring to the perception of others ("what other people perceived as a failure"), in which case the parents' behavior would imply shame and lack of courage. One could also read the clause as indicating the parents' own perception ("what they perceived as a failure"), which would even magnify their sense of shame. Both interpretations are problematic in the context of family storytelling as they suggest criticism of one's parents and thus pose a potential threat to family unity.

Tajfel (1978) demonstrates that denigration of members of the out-group is necessary for the definition and demarcation of one's in-group. If family members are criticized, they are indirectly placed on a par with out-group members and the boundaries between groups become blurred. For this reason, criticism needs to be toned down by means of a defensive slant on the narrative expressed in numerous linguistic and narrative strategies. Chatman's distinction between filter and slant proves useful as it helps explain a discrepancy in this oral narrative: while the slant the narrator offers on the story world is defensive of the narrator's parents and ostensibly presents them in a positive light, the narrator's function as filter grants the listener an insight into the minds of the parents, which implicitly conveys a sense of disappointment and criticism. On a more global narrative level, the switch between the experiencing self and narrating self positions, which entails a switch from the filter to the slant function of the narrator, mark a shift in the narrator's positioning. He moves from the position of son who confirms his membership in the family group to the position of ill person who feels excluded and stigmatized by people who do not inhabit the same domain of illness (in the sense of Donald's [1998: 23] "wellness-illness divide").

ILLNESS, IDENTITY, AND DEICTIC TRANSFERS

Let us now turn to another narratological concept that can be used for the study of oral narratives, *double deixis* (Herman 1994). The following narrative is a personal narrative of a 60-year old woman suffering from depression who recounts the way in which she managed to go back to a "normal" life by taking on a secretarial post. The narrative is particularly interesting for its use of double deixis. Herman (1994) lists five possible functions of second-person pronoun "you": generalized *you,* fictional reference, fictionalized (= horizontal) address, apostrophic (= vertical) address, and doubly deictic *you.* One can speak of double deixis when the relationship between the morpho-syntactic form of *you* and its textual functions is not entirely clear-cut and when *you* assumes more than one of the above-mentioned first four functions at the same time.

Narrative 2

1. One day she (my social worker) knocked on the door
2. and said, "We're going to start a MIND group, a sort of MIND group, would you be interested in joining us?"
3. So I got into that
4. and because of my secretarial skills I was immediately taken on as a secretary of the working group.
5. And, and that's how it went.
6. And again because you're . . . becoming friendly with the professionals as it were, [pause]
7. and [pause] at a point where you, you were starting to give something back, starting to help other people.
8. And that made me realize how important it was to help other people.
9. And I think that gives you an uplift doesn't it.
10. And that's really what happened,
11. that's, that's how I got back into normality.

The narrative begins with a kind of mini-dramatization including constructed dialogue in line 2 and the metonymic image "knocked on the door" (line 1), which can be understood literally as the social worker knocking on the narrator's door and also figuratively as an image for the social worker's request. The complicating action from line 3 to 7 relates how the narrator became a secretary of the working group. This part of the plot then culminates in the resolution of the narrative (lines 8–11), the main point of which is the narrator's recognition of how important the job was for her well-being. In other words, the narrative describes a turning point in the narrator's life. As Rimmon-Kenan (2002) argues, the turning point structure in illness narratives "counteracts disruption" (18) and thus offers a sense of coherence to the ill person. However, this structure can also constitute a kind of "entrapment" in the sense that it suppresses the experience of chaos and can thus lead to a meaningless recycling of a culturally expected narrative type.

In narrative 2 the turning point in the narrator's life is presented in positive terms and thus matches the cultural expectation of the "getting better" plot line. Interestingly enough, the narrator switches from first-person to second-person narrative when she describes which aspects of her new job brought about the change in her life: "And again because you're . . . becoming friendly with the professionals as it were, [pause] and [pause] at a point where you, you were starting to give something back, starting to help other people" (lines 6–7). While the first instance of *you* still bears marks of generalized *you* since it is accompanied by the present tense (present progressive), the second *you* clearly indicates a replacement of the first-person pronoun with *you* which, however, still refers to the narrator as experiencing self. It is the narrator herself who started to help other people. The use of you-narrative creates a peculiar sense of self-distancing, as though the narrator were looking at herself from the outside of the narrated story world. One could also interpret the you-narrative in more positive terms as an inclusive move that enables the sick person to enter a dialogue with herself. At the same time, since the narrative was related in an interview, one can assume that there is also a residue of the vertical address function of "you" left. Put differently, the "you" can also be read as including the interviewer and thus it assumes the dialogic function of creating involvement by suggesting that, had the interviewer been in a similar situation, she may also have had a similar experience. The vertical address element is only minimal, however, since the recounted story is very specific and a distinct part of the narrator's life. In line 9, generalized *you* becomes more dominant again: "and I think that gives you an uplift doesn't it." While it was the narrator in particular who felt an uplift because of her changed situation, anyone in such a context may experience the same feeling. The simple present, which generalizes the statement, and the tag question, which has the phatic function of securing the listener's agreement with the statement made, support this interpretation. Only in line 8 does the narrator return to the first-person pronoun when she relates the point of her realizing what was important in her life, which also happens to be the turning point in her illness narrative.

What possible functions does the you-narrative in this particular story have? The fact that the narrative at this point is also marked by pauses points towards the narrator's thinking about how her job affected her life and thinking about how to frame this process in the interview. In a way, the narrator mentally (and then verbally) resumes her life, and the distance between the experiencing self in the past and the narrating self in the present is captured in the distancing *you*. As I said, it is almost as if the narrator entered a dialogue with herself at this point, thereby also supporting the memory work she is accomplishing in the interview. At the same time, *you* clearly lacks a sense of full identification if compared to *I*. One could therefore argue that the use of you-narrative here enacts the process of decentering or the narrator's shift of focus from herself as the ill person to others who also needed help. This reading is corroborated by another comment the narrator makes later in the interview: "And I do think that the idea that it was benefiting somebody else as well, that it wasn't just 'self.' Which is a good thing because you do turn in on yourself. And it made one sort of stop being focused on just oneself." This statement is highly interesting as it contains a deictic shift not only to second-person *you* but also to generic *one*, and moves the whole experience even further away from the narrator. It foregrounds the almost universal and indeed generic aspect of such turning point structures in illness narratives.

This example shows how deictic transfers in narratives can help elicit the dynamics of identity formation. In this narrative a move away from self-awareness typically expressed through the first-person pronoun "I" (Giddens 1991: 53) correlates with the narrator-protagonist's removal of focus from her sick persona to others on the intradiegetic level. This de-focusing is constructed as a beneficial process and as the prerequisite for change. The narrator's affirmative resolution, where she talks about "uplift" (line 9), "that's what really happened" (line 10), and "that's how I got back into normality" (line 11), underlines the positive tenor of the narrative. On the extradiegetic level the you-narrative places the listener in the peculiar position of someone who overhears the dialogue of the narrator with herself and at the same time in the position of an addressee who is invited to feel included in the narrated events. What we observe here is the kind of narrative work that forms the basis of our self-identities: "A person with a reasonably stable sense of self-identity has a feeling of biographical continuity which she is able to grasp reflexively and, to a greater or lesser degree, communicate to other people" (Giddens 1991: 54). Illness disrupts continuity but the turning point structure remedies this disruption by providing a new sense of continuity that centers on a "before" and "after." Ironically, then, the narrative strategy of deictic transfer that normally destabilizes a sense of narrative identity is used here to accomplish and to convey an even greater sense of identity lost and found. This stands in contrast to the first narrative in which the narrative strategies of focalization and FID compete with and subtly undermine some of the narrative's more explicit messages, which ultimately conveys a sense of ambivalence.

CONCLUSION

As we can see from these examples, further layers of complexity can be revealed in seemingly simple oral narratives by means of narratological analysis. While discourse linguistics has already made a significant contribution to a more systematic investigation of oral narratives, I argue that narratology can help elicit the particularly narrative features of oral narratives, which may lead to more finely-grained distinctions. Let us briefly reconsider the concepts I set out to investigate: identity, social positioning, in-group and out-group relations. Research on identity no longer assumes identity to be a monolithic conglomerate of essential features but rather a dynamic concept that is constantly and contextually (re)negotiated among interactants (de Fina, Schiffrin and Bamberg 2006).[2] If identities are partially negotiated through narratives, the question arises in what ways narratives can offer scope for identity formation. Social positioning as one facet of identity formation is a case in point. Hollway (1984), for example, states that "discourses make available positions for subjects to take up. These positions are in relation to other people" (236). Yet how do subjects "take up" positions? In narrative, positions can be made available through the characters that people the story world and also through the position of the narrator vis-à-vis the story world. One of the fallacies of narrative research in the social sciences to date, I would argue, is to assume that the storyteller equals the narrator and, if he or she is telling a personal story in the first person, also equals the character presented in the story. As my discussion has shown, narrators in and of oral stories can assume more complex positions, which can be captured if one adopts narratological terms such as *experiencing* and *narrating self* or *slant* and *filter*. Likewise, identities and group relations emerge in a process in which storytellers set themselves off from, identify with or in some other way relate to themselves as characters and to other characters in their storyworlds. Georgakopoulou (2005) demonstrates in her research on young Greek female adolescents' talk how, for example, stylization, i.e. the enactment of other people's (in this case, men's) voices in narratives, contributes to the constitution of her informants' "own gendered selves" (180). While the use of other characters' speech has been widely studied in discourse linguistics, the notion

---

2. Compare the contribution of Löschnigg in this volume.

that other people's "voices" may stand in for covert presentations of third-person consciousness has not featured prominently in the literature, one reason certainly being that this narrative phenomenon is not deemed possible in oral narratives.[3] And yet, such subtle phenomena do occur. The only problem is that very fine-tuned *narratological* sensors are required to discover them.

A lot more work needs to be done. First of all it would be desirable to analyze a large sample of oral narratives from a wide range of contexts to see if any common patterns emerge. For example, can certain narrative strategies be correlated with socio-demographic factors such as gender, age, social status, or professional group? To what extent can narrative strategies such as focalization, double deixis, or FID be linked to more general conversational strategies employed to establish rapport, to convince or persuade, to signal convergence or divergence, and so on? What these questions certainly demonstrate, however, is that scholars from various disciplines interested in narrative ought to collaborate more closely in order to arrive at more holistic approaches. After all, "the exploratory and experimental options of narrative are inextricably fused with our fleeting reality itself," as Brockmeier and Harré (2001) contend, and for this reason "one motive—perhaps even a leitmotif—of the study of narrative realities should be to investigate this opening-up quality of the discursive mind and to uncover the multifaceted forms of cultural discourse in which it takes place" (56).

---

3. It is nonetheless true that pragmatics is one linguistic area that has traditionally also considered the attribution of speaker meaning. More recent work that is particularly of interest here is relevance theory as put forward by Sperber and Wilson (see Wilson 2000: 419ff. for an overview). See also Mildorf (2008).

REFERENCES

Atkinson, Paul (1990) *The Ethnographic Imagination: The Textual Construction of Reality*. London: Routledge.
Brockmeier, Jens, and Rom Harré (2001) "Narrative: Problems and Promises of an Alternative Paradigm." *Narrative and Identity: Studies in Autobiography, Self and Culture*. Eds. Jens Brockmeier and Donal Carbaugh. Amsterdam: John Benjamins. 39–58.
Chatman, Seymour (1986) "Characters and Narrators: Filter, Center, Slant, and Interest-Focus." *Poetics Today* 7.2: 189–204.
de Fina, Anna, Deborah Schiffrin, and Michael Bamberg (2006) *Discourse and Identity*. Cambridge: Cambridge University Press.
DIPEx: Personal Experiences of Health and Illness (online database). Available at: http://www.DIPEx.org (last accessed: March 27, 2007). Now at http://www.healthtalkonline.org (accessed June 9, 2010)
Donald, Anne (1998) "The Words We Live In." *Narrative Based Medicine: Dialogue and Discourse in Clinical Practice*. Eds. Trisha Greenhalgh and Brian Hurwitz. London: BMJ Books. 17–26.
Fludernik, Monika (1993) *The Fictions of Language and the Languages of Fiction*. London: Routledge.
——— (1996) *Towards a 'Natural' Narratology*. London: Routledge.
Frankfort-Nachmias, Chava, and David Nachmias (2008) *Research Methods in the Social Sciences*. 7th ed. London/Melbourne/Auckland: Edward Arnold.
Georgakopoulou, Alexandra (2005) "Styling Men and Masculinities: Interactional and Identity Aspects at Work." *Language in Society* 34: 163–84.
Giddens, Anthony (1991) *Modernity and Self-Identity: Self and Society in the Late Modern Age*. Stanford, CA: Stanford University Press.
Grbich, Carol (1999) *Qualitative Research in Health: An Introduction*. London: Sage.
Heinen, Sandra, and Roy Sommer (2009) Eds. *Narratology in the Age of Cross-Disciplinary Narrative Research*. Berlin and New York: de Gruyter.
Herman, David (1994) "Textual *You* and Double Deixis in Edna O'Brien's *A Pagan Place*." *Style* 28.3: 378–410.
——— (1999a) Ed. Narratologies: New Perspectives on Narrative Analysis. Columbus: The Ohio State University Press.
——— (1999b) "Toward a Socionarratology: New Ways of Analyzing Natural-Language Narratives." *Narratologies: New Perspectives on Narrative Analysis*. Ed. David Herman. Columbus: The Ohio State University Press. 218–46.
Hollway, Wendy (1984) "Gender Difference and the Production of Subjectivity." *Changing the Subject: Psychology, Social Regulation, and Subjectivity*. Eds. Julian Henriques et al. London: Methuen. 227–63.
Jahn, Manfred (1996) "Windows of Focalization: Deconstructing and Reconstructing a Narratological Concept." *Style* 30.2: 241–68.
——— (1999) "More Aspects of Focalization: Refinements and Applications." *GRAAT: Revue des Groupes de Recherches Anglo-Américaines de L'Université François Rabelais de Tours 21*. Ed. John Pier. Tours: Publications des Groupes de Recherches Anglo-Américaines de l'Université François Rabelais de Tours. 85–110.

Klein, Christian, and Matías Martínez (2009) Eds. *Wirklichkeitserzählungen: Felder, Formen und Funktionen nicht-literarischen Erzählens*. Stuttgart and Weimar: Metzler.
Labov, William (1982) "Speech Actions and Reactions in Personal Narrative." *Analyzing Discourse: Text and Talk*. Ed. Deborah Tannen. Washington, D.C.: Georgetown University Press. 219–47.
Labov, William, and Joshua Waletzky (1967) "Narrative Analysis: Oral Versions of Personal Experience." *Essays on the Verbal and Visual Arts (Proceedings of the 1966 Annual Spring Meeting of the American Ethnological Society)*. Ed. June Helm. Seattle and London: University of Washington Press. 12–44.
Langellier, Kristin M., and Eric E. Peterson (2004) *Storytelling in Daily Life: Performing Narrative*. Philadelphia: Temple University Press.
Lawler, Steph (2002) "Narrative in Social Research." *Qualitative Research in Action* Ed. Tim May. London: Sage. 242–58.
Leech, Geoffrey N. (1987) *Meaning and the English Verb*. London: Longman.
Leech, Geoffrey N., and Michael H. Short (1981) *Style in Fiction: A Linguistic Introduction to English Fictional Prose*. London: Longman.
Lieblich, Amia, Rivka Tuval-Mashiach, and Tamar Zilber (1998) *Narrative Research. Reading, Analysis, and Interpretation*. Thousand Oaks/London/New Delhi: Sage.
May, Tim (2001) *Social Research: Issues, Methods and Process*. 3rd ed. Buckingham and Philadelphia: Open University Press.
Maynard, Douglas W. (1988) "Language, Interaction, and Social Problems." *Social Problems* 35.4: 311–34.
McDonald, Ian, and Jeanne Daly (1992) "Research Methods in Health Care—A Summing Up." *Researching Health Care: Designs, Dilemmas, Disciplines*. Eds. Jeanne Daly, Ian McDonald and Ewan Willis. London and New York: Routledge. 209–16.
McKie, Linda (1996) Ed. *Researching Women's Health: Methods and Process*. Wilts: Mark Allen.
Mildorf, Jarmila (2006) "Sociolinguistic Implications of Narratology: Focalization and 'Double Deixis' in Conversational Storytelling." *COLLeGIUM* 1: 42–59. Available at: http://www.helsinki.fi/collegium/e-series/volumes/volume_1/index.htm
—— (2008) "Thought Presentation and Constructed Dialogue in Oral Stories: Limits and Possibilities of a Cross-Disciplinary Narratology." *Narrative: Knowing, Living, Telling*. Eds. Matti Hyvärinen, Kai Mikkonen and Jarmila Mildorf. Special issue of *Partial Answers* 6.2: 279–300.
Nünning, Ansgar, and Vera Nünning (2002) Eds. *Neue Ansätze in der Erzähltheorie*. Trier: Wissenschaftlicher Verlag Trier.
Polanyi, Livia (1984) "Literary Complexity in Everyday Storytelling." *Spoken and Written Language: Exploring Orality and Literacy*. Ed. Deborah Tannen. Norwood, NJ: Ablex. 155–70.
Potter, Jonathan (1996) *Representing Reality: Discourse, Rhetoric and Social Construction*. London: Sage.
Rentz, Kathryn C. (1999) "What Can We Learn from a Sample of One?—The Role of Narrative in Case Study Research." *Narrative and Professional Communication* Eds. Jane M. Perkins and Nancy Blyler. Stamford: Ablex. 37–62.
Riessman, Catherine Kohler (1993) *Narrative Analysis*. Newbury Park/London/New Delhi: Sage.

——— (2008) *Narrative Methods for the Human Sciences*. Thousand Oaks/London/New Delhi: Sage.

Rimmon-Kenan, Shlomith (2002) "The Story of "I": Illness and Narrative Identity." *Narrative* 10.1: 9–27.

Rubin, Herbert, and Irene Rubin (2005) *Qualitative Interviewing: The Art of Hearing Data*. 2nd ed. Thousand Oaks/London/New Delhi: Sage.

Sarangi, Srikant (2006) "Editorial: Advances in Family Interaction Studies." *Text & Talk* 26.4–5: 403–5.

Silverman, David, and Amir Marvasti (2008) *Doing Qualitative Research: A Comprehensive Guide*. Thousand Oaks/London/New Delhi: Sage.

Tajfel, Henri (1978) *Differentiation Between Social Groups: Studies in the Social Psychology of Intergroup Relations*. London: Academic Press.

Tannen, Deborah (1989) *Talking Voices: Repetition, Dialogue, and Imagery in Conversational Discourse*. Cambridge: Cambridge University Press.

——— (1997) "Involvement as Dialogue: Linguistic Theory and the Relation Between Conversational and Literary Discourse." *Dialogue and Critical Discourse: Language, Culture, Critical Theory*. Ed. Michael S. Macovski. Oxford: Oxford University Press. 137–57.

——— (2006) "Intertextuality in Interaction: Reframing Family Arguments in Public and Private." *Text & Talk* 26.4–5: 597–617.

Tommola, Hannu (2003) "Conclusion: Aspects of Free Indirect Discourse and the Limits of Linguistic Analysis." *Linguistic and Literary Aspects of Free Indirect Discourse from a Typological Perspective*. Eds. Pekka Tammi and Hannu Tommola. Tampere: University of Tampere. 95–114.

Wilson, Deirdre (2000) "Metarepresentation in Linguistic Communication." *Metarepresentations: A Multidisciplinary Perspective*. Ed. Dan Sperber. Oxford: Oxford University Press. 411–48.

MARTIN LÖSCHNIGG

Postclassical Narratology and the Theory of Autobiography

> A self is probably the most impressive work of art we ever produce, surely the most intricate. (Bruner 2003: 14)

(0) INTRODUCTION

In the theory of autobiography, theoretical developments in literary studies are clearly reflected. From an earlier mimetic understanding of the genre as the representation of an autonomous and homogeneous self the pendulum swung to the deconstructionist view, dominant in the late 1970s and early 1980s. According to deconstructionist tenets, there can be no representation of self in language, but only an illusion of "self" generated by a purely textual subject. It was at this point that theorists like Michael Sprinker even went as far as to proclaim the "end of autobiography" (Sprinker 1980). Since the late 1980s, however, the pendulum seems to have come to a standstill at the center between the mimetic and deconstructionist extremes of amplitude, settled in a framework of constructivist (narrativist) theories of autobiography. Paul John Eakin (1992), Jerome Bruner (1991; 2003), and others have emphasized the role of narrative in the formation and maintenance of a sense of identity. They foreground, on the one hand, the creative (as opposed to the mimetic) function of autobiography with regard to individual identity, while, on the other hand, reviving the concept of autobiographical reference. At the same time, the framing of human experience in the form of narrative(s) has become the focus of interest in a range of disciplines beyond those immediately concerned with life-writing, and narratology has branched out to investigate the role of narrative in a variety of different fields.

In the following, I propose to show which models and categories of contemporary narratology may be relevant for a narratologically grounded discussion of autobiographical discourse. The aim of my essay is therefore not to add to the already vast body of narrative theory (including the theory of autobiography), but to bring to focus some recent theoretical developments which bear on autobiographical narrative(s). In particular, I shall point to the interfaces which exist between narrativist theories of autobiography and cognitive narratology and demonstrate how an analysis of autobiographical discourse may benefit from the synthesis of these disciplines. In my essay, I shall concentrate (1) on the discursive representation of the experiential in autobiography; (2) on narrativity and the self, i.e. the role of narrative in the formation of identity; (3) on the role of frames and scripts in the textual representation of memory; and, finally (4) on the fictionality of autobiography.

The question of the fictionality of autobiography requires some elucidation because in both fields, postclassical narratology and the theory of autobiography, the role of the fictional in (autobiographical) narrative has recently been redefined. In autobiographical theory in particular, the distinction between fact and fiction no longer seems to be the overriding concern that it was until relatively recently. This relaxation of the borders between truth and fiction is due not so much to the undermining of "facticity" in life-writing caused by the general post-structuralist mistrust of "truth" and "authenticity." Rather, the noted shift in perspective seems to correlate with an emphasis on narrativity as a vital factor in the construction of identity, i.e. a view that autobiography, in narrative terms, stages the drama of creating the autobiographer's identity. In this drama, as I shall explain under (4), fiction plays an important role. As regards postclassical narratology, narratologists like Monika Fludernik (1996) have suggested ways out of the fact/fiction divide by aligning narrativity with fictionality (cf. 4). Such a shift away from an emphasis on the referential clearly has its advantages, since it enables one to accommodate the variety of forms which has been characteristic of autobiographical writing especially since the second half of the twentieth century.[1]

(1) WRITING THE EXPERIENTIAL

In all forms of autobiographical discourse, the narrative rendering of individual experience and of a sense of identity is inextricably linked with basic

---

1. For the autobiographical in various media and cultural approaches to the autobiographical, see the essays in Kadar et al. (2005).

structural patterns. These emanate from what classical narratology has described as the dual aspect of the (fictional) autobiographer as experiencer and narrator. This duality has until now been investigated primarily with regard to plotlines and genres, to forms of focalization and to the problem of unreliable narration. I want to argue that, if one conceives of autobiography as a psychological activity which creates, rather than merely depicts, identity, retrospection and the double aspect of the self involve the construction not only of the experiencing, but also of the narrating self. These should therefore be viewed not in terms of the dichotomy sometimes suggested by structuralist accounts, but within larger frames of rendering the experiential.

On the textual level of autobiography, the continuity between experience and narrative is manifested in what Genette has termed homodiegesis, i.e. the rootedness of the narrative voice in the world of the narrative. In the case of factual autobiography, this rootedness rests on actual embodiment, and the ensuing "materiality" provides a criterion which in principle distinguishes it from other (especially fictional) forms of writing (cf. Smith/Watson 2005). Classical narratology has investigated homodiegesis primarily with regard to fictional narratives. It distinguishes between two aspects of the narrative instance, as it were, the self as character and the self as narrator, variously referred to as the "narrated" or "experiencing" self, on the one hand, and the "narrating self" or "narrating I," on the other. Valid as this distinction may be for the structural analysis of literary narratives, its application to autobiography seems problematic as it is prone to introduce a dichotomy which detracts from the continuity of (remembered) experience as emphasized by narrative psychology and recent theories of life-writing. Such continuity even applies to narratives of conversion. These are a common type of autobiography that seems to give absolute priority to the narrating self by establishing a superior standpoint in the present, namely that of a reformed wrongdoer who has gained an insight into some "higher" truth about himself. Yet even in conversion narratives a clear-cut division between narrator and experiencer cannot always be upheld, as emerges clearly, for instance, from the following passage in John Bunyan's spiritual autobiography *Grace Abounding to the Chief of Sinners* (1666):

> In **these** days, the thoughts of religion were very grievous to me; I could neither endure it my self, nor that any other should; so that, when I have seen some read in those books that concerned Christian piety, it would be as it were a prison to me. *Then I said unto God, Depart from me, for I desire not the knowledge of thy ways,* Job. 21.14, 15. I was **now** void of all good consideration; Heaven and Hell were both out of sight and minde; and as for

Saving and Damning, they were least in my thoughts. *O Lord, thou knowest my life, and my ways were not hid from thee.*

Yet this I well remember, that though I could my self sin with the greatest delight and ease, and also take pleasure in the vileness of my companions; yet even then, if I have at any time seen wicked things by those who professed goodness, it would make my spirit tremble. As once above all the rest, when I was in my height of vanity, yet hearing one to swear that was reckoned for a religious man, it had so great a stroke upon my spirit, that it made my heart to ake. (Bunyan 1962: 7; Bunyan's emphasis in italics; my emphasis in bold)

Here the super-ordinate perspective of the present, reformed narrator at first appears to be the only vantage point which enables the creation of meaning. Yet the reverberations of actual experience are emphasized in the narrative, e.g. by underlining the vividness of memories and by the use of proximal deictics (*"now"*), while the insertion (and identification) of the biblical quotations indicates an attempt at authenticating as well as re-living experience in the light of ulterior established authority. Rather than implying a dichotomy between "then" and "now," therefore, the temporal levels of narrator and experiencer in this passage are really made to interact, the result being a continuity of experience.

According to traditional views of the genre, the "I" in autobiography represents subject and object, *viz.* the past and present selves, and the privileged position of the present narrator is confirmed exactly because the past self is different from the present self. The autobiographer thus recounts not only what has happened to him/her at an earlier time, but above all how he/she has become himself/herself from the "other" which he/she was. The difference produced by autobiographical reflection is therefore twofold, comprising a difference in time as well as in identity. According to such views, the personal reference ("I") is ambivalent, since the narrator was a different person in the past from what he/she is now.[2] As we have seen from the above-cited example, however, a continuity of experience and of a sense of self applies even when the discourse seems at first to confer upon the autobiographer's self a sense of "otherness."

I should emphasize here that I am concerned with the conception of a structural aspect of homodiegetic narration and with its theoretical implications. As conceived in the terms of classical (structuralist) narratology, these

---

2. Cf. Laura Marcus: "Autobiography imports alterity into the self by the act of objectification which engenders it" (1994: 203).

implications would in fact amount to a division between narrator and experience on epistemological and ontological grounds, whereas I would argue for re-conceiving this structural aspect in terms of a continuum and of "writing the experiential." What I am not concerned with here is the extent to which autobiographies may explicitly reflect on differences between the writer's "then" and "now" on a meta-textual level.

Instead of emphasizing the duality of narrator and experiencer, it might be more appropriate to regard the autobiographical act as an experiential site, as a re-living of experience rather than as an attempt by a detached subject to interpret itself as object. This is because autobiography, as has been indicated at the beginning, may no longer be viewed in terms of a retrospective rendering of an already formed self, but should best be regarded as an act of identity-construction. Such identity-construction is decisively shaped by present motivations, desires and anxieties. Indeed, the actual writing of autobiography is a re-enactment of the (sub)conscious construction processes that have preceded it. The experiential in the sense of a psychological re-living and cognitive re-construction of experience is therefore really an element of the autobiographical act itself. Autobiographical narrative may therefore be conceived of in terms of the frames of experiencing and reflection provided by models of cognitive narratology.

One such model has been proposed by Monika Fludernik in her groundbreaking *Towards a 'Natural' Narratology* (1996). Fludernik's categories are derived from her analysis of spontaneous oral narrative, which she regards as prototypical of the narrative rendering of specifically human (or at least anthropomorphic) experience. The "natural" form of such a rendering is the first-person: "[In the oral mode] [. . .] the experientiality of story-experience [. . .] is aligned primarily with the first-person frame" (315). The concept of *experientiality* is basic to Fludernik's understanding of narrative. Roughly speaking, *experientiality* refers to an individualized rendering of experience as reflected in human consciousness. The continuity of experience and narration, which is also emphasized in recent theories of autobiography, is thus central to Fludernik's narratological model. One of her aims in *Towards a 'Natural' Narratology* is to radically revise conventional notions of narrativity. As opposed to traditional definitions of narrativity, which are based on plot, Fludernik rejects plot as a necessary component of narrativity. Instead she grounds narrativity in experientiality, emphasizing the presence of a "human (anthropomorphic) experiencer" as an indispensable precondition of experientiality (13). Human consciousness and its representation are of supreme importance in her model: "[Consciousness] both mediates narrativity and constitutes one of its signifiers" (374). Because of its emphasis on the "consciousness factor," Fludernik's model appears to be more suitable to the description of autobiographical narrative; it is able to reflect to the focus on the inner life of the subject typical of most autobiographies better than are traditional, event-centered concepts of narrativity. It is not only this foregrounding of consciousness, however, that makes Fludernik's model an ideal descriptor of autobiographies, but also the fact that autobiographies frequently focus on the specificity of the represented experience, which, according to Fludernik, is another criterion in defining narrativity (cf. 29).

Fludernik regards narrativity as resulting from the reader's integration of a text into the framework of real-life experience, a script that also includes frames of narrative mediation and of narrative genres (cf. also Fludernik 2003). In particular, she distinguishes between five cognitive frames which "relate to basic perspectives on human experience and its narrative mediation" (2003: 246) and which therefore become functional in narrative discourse: action, telling, experiencing, viewing, and reflecting. In the case of autobiography, frames of telling, experiencing, and reflecting are of special importance, and the distinction made in classical (structuralist) narratology between the narrating and experiencing selves of autodiegetic narrators can now very easily be re-formulated in these terms. I have shown elsewhere (Löschnigg 2006a: 84–86; 2006b) how an emphasis on either one or the other of these frames will determine the narrative profile of a text, and how fictional autobiographies (i.e. novels in the form of autobiography) in particular have tended to concentrate on rendering the experiential substance rather than the reflective process. In any case, a flexible model such as Fludernik's seems to be more adequate for a description of autobiographical narrative than the division implied by the teller vs. experiencer model of classical narratology. Moreover, Fludernik's experiential model of narrative connects with those approaches to autobiography which regard life-writing as the construction of individual identity in the medium of narrative, since both highlight the significance of individual experience and its reflective processing (or re-enactment) in the narrating consciousness.

(2) NARRATIVITY AND THE SELF

Different concepts of narrative and narrativity notwithstanding, it is generally agreed that autobiography is a "narrative" genre. If one looks at the historical range of autobiographical texts, however, one perceives a remarkable difference between, for instance, St. Augustine's narrative realism, on the one hand, and (post-)modernist texts such as Beckett's, on the other. The latter seem to reject narrative as a form reflecting an inherent order in life, and to suggest that the narrative form is really a liability from which the "I" has to free itself. Considering the protean nature of contemporary life-writing, and especially the tendency towards fragmentation and experiment in many twentieth-century autobiographies, one may start to wonder, as Paul John Eakin does, whether "narrative as a structure of reference [is] to be understood as a period-specific phenomenon, an outmoded literary convention that is to be identified as a vestige of a nineteenth-century historicist model of the subject?" (Eakin 1988b: 34). While Eakin still maintains that narrative is essential to the genre, other theoreticians have questioned this view. For instance, James Olney regards "autobiography [not as] a definition of the writer's self in the past, at the time of action, but in the present, at the time of writing" (1972: 44). Narrative, Olney seems to imply, is only of secondary importance, serving just as a vehicle for expressing the insights gained by the subject into his/her own existence.[3] Both Eakin and Olney use a definition of narrative that is based on plot or event-structure.

No doubt, some of the skepticism about the role of narrative in autobiography may ultimately be attributed to a questioning of traditional assumptions about the mimetic functions of life-writing. As has already been stated, recent theoretical positions on autobiography hold that the "I" which emerges from autobiographical discourse is not the faithful rendering of an autonomous and homogeneous self, but rather a self which has been construed in the narrative act. (In this respect, I find Olney's term "definition" in the passage cited above somewhat problematic, too.) Autobiography is a poietic rather than a mimetic genre, which also includes an element of the imaginary in the emerging "portrait" of the subject. The narrative act, it needs to be emphasized, acquires a vital role in the construction of a sense of identity. Indeed, the view that the narrative rendering of lived experience engenders such a sense of identity seems to be supported by psychological studies, which indicate that *dysnarrativia,* i.e. the inability to construct or understand stories, seriously impairs a sense of selfhood (cf. Bruner 2003: 86).

"Narrativized" understandings of identity focus on lived experience rather than on some quality which essentially "defines" a person, and on the capacity of narrative to impose order and coherence on what is otherwise a jumble of disconnected fragments of experiences and memories (see Mink 1978; Ricœur 1984–1988; Bruner 1991). The epistemological aspect of narrative, i.e. its functioning as a "cognitive instrument," is emphasized in particular by

---

3. Some theorists, e.g. Michel Beaujour, have distinguished between "autobiography" and the "autoportrait," the latter being characterized by its lack of a coherent narrative (1980: 348).

Bruner and Mink, while Ricœur leans towards an ontological understanding, according to which narrative discourse reflects a narrative order of experience as such. The assumption that our experience and memories are organized in the form of narratives, however, is common to all the theorists mentioned, and is inseparably linked in their thinking with the heuristic function of narrative when it comes to creating a sense of identity. Peter Brooks, referring to Rousseau's *The Confessions,* keeps insisting that narrative provides the only means by which the autobiographer has access to his/her identity:

> The question of identity [. . .] can be thought only in narrative terms, in the effort to tell a whole life, to plot its meaning by going back over it to record its perpetual flight forward, its slippage from the fixity of definition, [. . .] the contradictions encountered in the attempt to understand and present the self in all its truth provide a powerful narrative machine. Any time one goes over a moment of the past the machine can be relied on to produce more narrative—not only differing stories of the past, but future scenarios and narratives of writing itself. (1984: 33)

The narrative construction of self, it must be pointed out, is a continuous process which is pragmatic in the sense that it meets the needs of the situation encountered. In the theory of autobiography, the recognition of the pragmatic function of autobiographical narrative has given rise to approaches which regard autobiography as a "mode of cognition and perception" (Nalbantian 1994: 36) rather than as a literary genre. They see the writing of one's life as the re-enactment of a process of creating, rather than finding, a sense of identity, "not merely as the passive, transparent record of an already completed self but rather as an integral and often decisive phase of the drama of self-definition" (Eakin 1988a: 226). Since this process unfolds along narrative lines, particular emphasis has been placed upon narrative's capacity to create order: "[N]arrative plays a central, structuring [!] role in the formation and maintenance of our sense of identity" (Eakin 1999: 123). By structuring contingent experience, narrative enables us to grasp identity as the *telos* of a coherent story: "We achieve our personal identities and self-concept through the use of the narrative configuration, and make our existence into a whole by understanding it as an expression of a single unfolding and developing story" (Polkinghorne 1988: 150). The contiguity of experience is thus structured by language (and especially by narratives) into a series of verbalized events; according to Bruner, selfhood is a "kind of meta-event that gives coherence and continuity to the scramble of experience" (Bruner 2003: 73). Even if the narrative construction of the self is "more constrained by memory than fiction," it is indeed "uneasily constrained" (Bruner 2003: 65), the process fusing memory and the imagination. Seen in this light, the referential "truth-claim" of autobiography emerges as the result of a transferring of cognitive parameters onto an ontological plane.

The advent of postclassical narratology has undoubtedly helped to strengthen those views in the theory of autobiography which have emphasized the importance of narrative and of "narrativity" for the genre. Focusing as it does on the "question of how the human mind picks up patterns and enriches them with schematic information (from expectations and memories) into meaningful units" (Bamberg 2005: 218), cognitive narratology in particular should prove fruitful for the study of autobiographical discourse, as I shall try to show in the following section of this essay.

(3) MEMORY, SCRIPTS, AND SCHEMATA

The "cognitive turn in narratology" (Ibsch 1990) has yielded valuable insights into the workings of narratives as a readily available tool-kit in the "domain of human interaction" (Bruner 2003: 4). Cognitive narratology has become an interdisciplinary project in itself, drawing from and combining disciplines such as cognitive psychology, frame theory, linguistics, and the study of artificial intelligence (cf. Herman 2003a; Hogan 2004). In particular, the specific conditions of memory and their importance for the constitution of identity have become one of the central fields of cognitive and especially of narrative psychology. Humans retell memories according to pre-conceived notions about their functioning and the way in which they reach into the past.[4] In this process, as in the cognitive processing of immediate experience, narrative structures and schemata play a vital role: "[A]ll forms of memory are explicitly or implicitly based on retrospective narratives that seek to cross the unbridgeable gap between the time of narrating and the time of the events that will be narrated" (Müller-Funk 2003: 207). The significance of narrative for the content as well as the relevance of our memories underlines once more the importance of narrative as a means of creating meaning or a sense of identity. In this connection, it should be emphasized that one needs to consider the remembered past as being just as "real" as the autobiographer's present consciousness, since the contents of memory are determined by present motivations, desires, and anxieties (and also by internalized social, ethical, and moral norms or "frames").

  4. See Rubin (1986); Thompson et al. (1996); Schacter (1996).

In his classic psychological study *Remembering: A Study in Experimental and Social Psychology*, Frederick Bartlett describes the workings of memory as the organizing of past experience into anticipatory patterns for dealing with the present (cf. 1932: 201–14). In order to cope with present experience, memory thus references a considerable number of experiential repertoires. It engenders dynamic "scripts" as well as static "schemata," to use well-known terms from cognitive psychology.[5] Narrative shows a particular affinity to these processes, since its specific temporal structure is ideally suited to conveying the interaction of past and present consciousness underlying Bartlett's model of memory. The rendering of past events includes a consciousness, in the present, of their eventual outcome, which is why "[t]elling narratives is a certain way of reconciling emergent with prior knowledge" (Herman 1997: 1048). This insight seems to be particularly valid for autobiographical narration, since retrospection always includes a consciousness of what was not known at the time of the events referred to. The temporal structure of life-writing is therefore really a threefold one, comprising the autobiographer's past and present, and also that which is now the past, but what from an earlier point of view was the future,[6] i.e. that which the autobiographer could not have known at the time: "If subjects come into being through their relationship with narratives, then narratives are formed in time; [. . .] but the form of narrative time [. . .] does not flow in only one direction" (Williams 1995: 126).

This may be illustrated by passages such as the following. My example is taken from the chapter in John Stuart Mill's *Autobiography* (1873), in which he reviews his companionship with his future wife, Harriet Taylor, and the influence she was to prove on his life:

> At the present period, however, this influence was only one among many which were helping to shape the character of my future development: and even after it became, I may truly say, the presiding principle of my mental progress, it did not alter the path, but only made me move forward more boldly and at the same time more cautiously in the same course. The only actual revolution which has ever taken place in my modes of thinking, was already complete. My new tendencies had to be confirmed in some respects,

---

5. Dennis Mercadal defines "script" as "[a] description of how a sequence of events is expected to unfold [. . .] Scripts represent a sequence of events that take place in a time sequence" (1990: 255). "Schema" is defined as "[a] term used in psychology literature which refers to memory patterns that humans use to interpret current experiences" (ibid. 254). The term is used more or less synonymously in cognitive psychology with "cognitive frames."

6. See Ricœur (1984, ch. I, 1) on Book 11 of St. Augustine's *Confessions*.

moderated in others: but the only substantial changes that were yet to come, related to politics [. . .]. (1969: 114–15)

As can be seen, the narrative moves backwards in time from a super-ordinate vantage-point in the autobiographer's present to a "present period" in the past, continuing as a subtly graded alternation of anticipation and retrospection which oscillates between these two temporal levels. However, if autobiographical discourse is frequently characterized by chronological complexity, narrative provides the organizational strategies which ensure that this complexity can be dealt with by writers and readers. This is because narrative, as David Herman has shown, supports cognition by "enabl[ing] tellers and interpreters to establish spatiotemporal links between regions of experience and between objects contained in those regions" (2003: 169). It does so, first of all, through what Herman calls its "power [. . .] to chunk phenomenal reality into classifiable, knowable, and operable units" (174). Along the same lines, Charlotte Linde (1993) has emphasized that a life story is the result of segmenting operations which structure the continuity of experience into cognitively manageable blocks. Mill's *Autobiography*, with its clear-cut divisions between his childhood and youth subjected to a rationalist education, the sudden awakening to feeling, and his achievement of a balance between the two, which Mill claims to have accomplished in later life, may serve as a case in point.

Narrative further helps cognition, as Herman (2003) reminds us, by establishing causal connections and by providing a framework which enables the specific to be integrated into the typical and actual occurrences into expectations. The latter function has also been stressed by Jerome Bruner, for whom "narrative in all its forms is a dialectic between what was expected and what came to pass" (Bruner 2003: 15), and for whom "the 'suggestiveness' of a story lies [. . .] in the emblematic nature of its particulars, its relevance to a more inclusive narrative type" (1991: 7). As becomes evident from the example of Mill, much nineteenth-century autobiography is modeled on a *Bildungsroman* type of narrative, on the underlying belief that individual identity can be grasped in terms of organic development. Another such type, which has been of central importance in the history of autobiography, is the conversion narrative, while narratives of estrangement and fragmentation seem to have become the dominant pattern in contemporary autobiography (with the exception, of course, of the plethora of celebrity lives). This means that autobiography has come to be dominated by self-referential and literary modes of writing, a process which has raised anew the debate about the fictionality of the genre. In the following, I want to show how recent developments in narratology and in the theory of autobiography may shed new light on the referential and pragmatic aspects which have been in the center of that debate.

(4) THE FICTIONALITY OF AUTOBIOGRAPHY

Even before the post-structuralist demise of the autonomous subject, the reception of autobiography had been characterized by some complexity. On the one hand, readers expected autobiographers to provide "truthful" accounts of their lives, at least in the sense that the narrative was based on an effort to remember as accurately as possible what had happened. In other words: readers expected an account that was free from deliberate distortions and from too much self-fashioning. According to conventional understanding, autobiography rendered an intimate portrait of a person who signaled, by the very act of writing his/her life story, that this life was worth the reader's notice. Autobiographers such as Rousseau asserted the "honesty" of their narratives and the fact that they had consciously neither concealed nor added anything of importance. This frankness contributed much to the attraction autobiographies held for readers. On the other hand, such declarations of honesty could awaken a dormant skepticism on the reader's part. After all, autobiographies were written not least with an intention of impressing the reader, and declarations of "honesty" might serve to distract, as likely as not, from some hidden motive. In the case of Rousseau, this becomes evident when one realizes what amazing self-centeredness is unwittingly revealed in his *Confessions* (1781–89). As Rousseau insists on the accuracy of his recollections, he at the same time frankly admits to the gaps in his memory and indicates that some of these may actually have been filled by his imagination. For instance, this is how he writes about the happy times with Mme de Warens ("maman") at Les Charmettes:

> Nothing that happened to me during that delightful time, nothing that I did, said or thought all the while it lasted, has slipped from my memory. The period preceding it and following it recur to me at intervals; I recall them irregularly and confusedly; but I recall that time in its entirety, as if it existed still. My imagination, which in my youth always looked forward but now looks back, compensates me with these sweet memories for the hope I have lost forever. I no longer see anything in the future to attract me; only a return into the past can please me, and these vivid and precise returns into the periods of which I am speaking often give me moments of happiness in spite of my misfortunes. (1953: 215–16)

The suspicions aroused by this passage that Rousseau may project an unduly idyllic version of Les Charmettes are confirmed by the sequel, where it becomes evident that this pastoral serves to relieve, by means of contrast, the writer's present predicament, i.e. the conspiracy against him which he felt was brewing among those around him. As the result of several such passages, readers' attitudes towards the *Confessions* will typically fluctuate between trust and skepticism,[7] and this may well hold for autobiography in general. However, the genre's central paradigm, for most of its history, has nevertheless been that of the authenticity of the life and the authority of the autobiographer as the source of the narrative. Postmodern autobiography, on the other hand, relies on the tenets of post-structuralist theory which have eliminated the category of authorial intention from textual analysis. On the side of readers, the blend of skepticism and trust which shaped the reception of a text such as the *Confessions* has given way to a general mistrust of autobiography as a genre and to a *rapprochement* of "autobiography" and "fiction."

The question of fictionality, including the fictional element in autobiography, has been discussed extensively, and it would transcend the spatial limits of this essay to recapitulate this discussion here (for some key contributions to this discussion, cf. note 8). Suffice it to say that a pragmatic definition is now widely accepted which regards fiction as a specific form of communication that is subject to aesthetic norms rather than those which govern non-fiction texts, and by different contextual conventions, and which can therefore not be contested in the way non-fiction texts can. However, this understanding of fictionality does not allow for a clear-cut distinction between "factual" and "fictional" autobiography, especially if one considers that it is really the representation of inner states which is at the core of the genre. Neither does it provide guidelines for distinguishing "genuine" from "fake" autobiographies, since "fiction" does not equal "lying."[8]

While classical narratology concentrated almost exclusively on the analysis of literary narratives, recent narratological approaches have begun to investigate, in a systematic manner, the non-fictional domain, too. It may well be assumed that this extension of narratology's sphere of interest will benefit the study of autobiography, a genre which has increasingly come

---

7. It would thus be interesting to investigate the *Confessions* with a view to the dynamics of the primacy and recency effects as explained by the cognitive sciences: readers tend to cling to their intial interpretations of a given text (in this case, an interpretation determined by Rousseau's explicit declarations of honesty), until confronted with substantial textual evidence which contradicts this interpretation. It is at that point that the primacy effect will be overlaid by the recency effect, and textual data are integrated into a revised interpretive framework (cf. Zerweck 2002: 222–23).

8. On this issue, see Henrik Skov Nielsen's essay in the present volume.

to be situated along the borderlines of the factual and the fictional.⁹ The many examples of contemporary autobiography which actually investigate these borderlines, and which through formal experiment attempt to render a sense of estrangement and fragmentation on the part of the writer, have clearly called for a different reception than did straightforwardly chronological accounts such as Mill's. Theoretical approaches to autobiography should therefore focus on the text as a manifestation of the writer's present concerns rather than on abstract notions of "authenticity." Inconsistencies in life-stories should be analysed with a view to their function and significance for the subject rather than as violations of the "truth." In other words, one should distinguish perhaps not so much between "fiction" and "reality" as between different kinds of "reality": the lived and the narrated. This applies to a diachronic investigation of autobiography, too, in particular to an analysis of the correspondences between factual autobiography and the *Bildungsroman*. This relationship has been a complex one, since the novel has explored the domain of autobiography while at the same time fictional life-writing seems to have exerted a profound influence on its factual model. As Michael McKeon claimed, "authenticity began by being mimicked in the novel before being recuperated and interiorized by the autobiographers. The autobiographer could only become himself by imitating people who imagined what it was to be an autobiographer" (1987: 47). The question then is how genres such as the novel and autobiography combine to create traditions, or even world-pictures, and to negotiate frames of "self" and "other." To answer this question, one may want to refer to a central tenet of cognitive narratology, namely the tendency towards "naturalization" on the part of readers, i.e. their integration of texts into real-life frames or familiar generic frames. In the case of autobiographical narratives, the generic frame is that of the life-story, and the reception of autobiographical writing will therefore be determined ultimately by those cultural factors which shape prevailing views on narrative and the transparency (or opacity) of language with regard to the rendering of a life as lived.

Regarding autobiography neither as the mimetic depiction of a personality already formed, nor as a genre which conveys merely an illusion of the

---

9. The amphibious nature of autobiography was already highlighted by scholars such as Northrop Frye, for whom autobiography and the novel merged in a "series of insensible gradations" (1957: 307), and by Paul Ricœur, for whom autobiography is characterized by the *encroisement* of two primary modes of narrative, history and fiction (cf. Ricœur 1984–88). Similarly, Smith and Watson (2005) have pleaded for treating autobiography as a special case in that it presents a specific combination of factual and fictional narrative, while theorists such as e.g. Philippe Lejeune (1989) and Elizabeth Bruss (1976) have staunchly defended the distinction between autobiography and the novel.

self, but as the textual manifestation of a continuous process of identity-construction, suggests a way out of the impasse of "fact" *versus* "fiction." This is the case because reception may then focus not on the 'authenticity' of the life as narrated, but on the presence of the autobiographer and on the narrative construction, rather than re-construction, of the self.[10] The structuring of contingent experience which is an essential part of this process has been variously referred to as relying on "fictions" (Eakin 1988a) and "metaphor" (Olney 1972). As employed by Olney, the term metaphor denotes "all the world views and world pictures, models and hypotheses, myths and cosmologies" which humans use in order to give structure to the reality of existence, including their understanding and representation of self. And more often than not, one should add, these metaphors come in the form of narratives. If metaphors, according to Olney, "are that by which the lonely subjective consciousness gives order not only to itself but to as much of objective reality as it is capable of formalizing and controlling" (1972: 30), then it is narratives that constitute the basis which underlies this process.[11] If the narrativizing of experience in autobiography is thus enmeshed in other narratives, the fictional and the referential in autobiography no longer appear to be mutually exclusive. Underlining "the essential narrativity of human experience" (Eakin 1992: 87), Eakin and others have argued for re-introducing "reference" into the theory of autobiography. Yet this referent of autobiographical discourse, the subject, after its deconstructionist demise is no longer a pre-existing self, as these critics have shown themselves, but human experience as such. Experience, that is, may be conceived in narrative categories, which makes the text of an autobiography appear as a duplicate narrative structure, i.e. a narrative re-configuration of what has already been encoded, in narrative terms, at a first level. Similarly, in narratology, Fludernik's experientially-based model of narrative has aligned fictionality and narrativity, playing down the relevance of a distinction between fictional and non-fictional narratives. Fictionality is inherent in her definition of narrativity, since, as she claims, "the experience portrayed in narrative is typically non-historical (non-documentary, non-argumentational)" (1996: 39).

Emphasizing the narrativity of autobiography and the narrative construction of our sense of identity enables one to regard the fictional element in

---

10. In some ways, this has been anticipated by an understanding of autobiography which has emphasized consistency and the logics of development, regarding autobiographical "authenticity" as the result of coherence and "inner truth" rather than some kind of "referential truth" (cf. e.g. Pascal 1960).

11. The function of metaphor in Olney's theory of autobiography is thus similar to that of the emplotment of contingent events in historiography, as outlined by Hayden White and others (see White 1973; Mink 1978).

autobiography in a new light. Fictionality can now be seen as an integral element in the formation of identity. It does not need to be set in opposition to autobiographical "truth," as was proposed by early studies of autobiography, nor does it constitute the hallmark of all attempts at life-writing, as was claimed by the deconstructionists. Due to the selectivity of memory and the impact of psychological factors pertaining to the autobiographer's present, the "I" of an autobiography will always comprise a fictional element. Acknowledging this fictional element will free autobiography from the constraints of the confessional paradigm which has traditionally dominated the genre. The demands of telling the "truth" and of making this truth subject to verification contributed towards a reductive view of autobiography that relies on simplifying distinctions between the true" and the "false," the "authentic" and the "invented." In addition, since standards of authenticity are shaped by the cultural context, the confessional paradigm has tended to favor concepts of "self" which are based on dominant male and middle class norms, while at the same time undermining the truth-claim of autobiographies by marginalized groups, including women. Small wonder, therefore, that recent autobiographical writing, especially by women or members of ethno-cultural minorities, has avoided these generic constraints by rejecting the "autobiographical contract" which guarantees the non-fictional status of autobiography (cf. Lejeune 1989). These autobiographies resort to innovative strategies such as the explicit inclusion of fictional elements in order to express the uneasy cultural position of their subjects.

(5) CONCLUSION

According to Michael Sheringham, different positions on autobiography have usually depended on "prevailing views of narrative": "Any moves towards a rehabilitation of narrative's mimetic, heuristic or pragmatic functions are likely to support comparable shifts in the way autobiography is regarded" (1993: 23). Proceeding upon the assumption of a privileged relationship between autobiographical narrative and the investigation of mental processes, this article has tried to show which areas of analysis may profit from a synthesis of new developments in narratology, especially cognitive narratology, and recent theories of autobiography. The benefits of such a combined approach for describing central aspects of autobiographical discourse concern the rendering of experience, the importance of narrative in the creation of a sense of identity, and the significance of cognitive frames for the temporal structure of memory-based narration. As to the rendering of experience, I have argued that a new frame-oriented model of narrative will provide criteria for describing a life as (re-)lived upon a different and more flexible basis than that offered by the binary narrator-experiencer model of classical narratology. It also allows one to emphasize the continuity of narration and experience. With regard to the importance of narrative, I have tried to show how "narrativity" is a determinant of autobiography, independent of the actual textual shape of an individual work. In the third section of my essay I pointed out how cognitive narratology can help us grasp hold of the genre's temporal complexity. Discussing the structure of autobiography, I was able to identify two types of processes which come into play in memory-based narratives: processes of segmentation and processes of creating coherence. Finally, as I have tried to show in the last section of my essay, the question of fictionality in autobiography may now be approached in a more differentiated manner. If narratology cannot provide criteria to distinguish between "fact" and "fiction" in autobiographical writing, provided such a distinction can be made at all, it can provide the theoretical basis for describing the fictional as an integral element of life-writing. After all, to quote Graham Swift's novel *Waterland* (Swift 1983: 53), man is "the story-telling animal" and the fictional element which is inherent in this definition applies first and foremost to our own life-stories, too.

REFERENCES

Bamberg, Michael (2005) "Narrative Discourse and Identities." *Narratology Beyond Literary Criticism: Mediality, Disciplinarity.* Ed. Jan Christoph Meister in collaboration with Tom Kindt and Wilhelm Schernus. Berlin and New York: de Gruyter. 213–37.

Bartlett, Frederick (1932) *Remembering: A Study in Experimental and Social Psychology.* Cambridge: Cambridge University Press.

Beaujour, Michel (1980) *Miroirs d'encre: rhétorique de l'autoportrait.* Paris: Seuil.

Brooks, Peter (1984) *Reading for the Plot.* Oxford: Clarendon.

Bruner, Jerome (1991) "The Narrative Construction of Reality." *Critical Inquiry* 18: 1–21.

—— (2003) *Making Stories: Law, Literature, Life* [2002]. Cambridge, MA/London: Harvard University Press.

Bruss, Elizabeth (1976) *Autobiographical Acts: The Changing Situation of a Literary Genre.* Baltimore: Johns Hopkins University Press.

Bunyan, John (1962) *Grace Abounding to the Chief of Sinners* [1666]. Ed. Roger Sharrock. Oxford: Clarendon.

Canary, Robert H., and Henri Kosicki (1978) Eds. *The Writing of History.* Madison: University of Wisconsin Press.

Coelsch-Foisner, Sabine, and Wolfgang Görtschacher (2006) Eds. *Fiction and Autobiography: Modes and Models of Interaction.* Frankfurt am Main: Lang.

Eakin, Paul John (1988a) *Fictions in Autobiography: Studies in the Art of Self-Invention.* Princeton, NJ: Princeton University Press.
—— (1988b) "Narrative and Chronology as Structures of Reference and the New Model Autobiographer." *Studies in Autobiography.* Ed. James Olney. New York: Oxford University Press. 32–41.
—— (1989) Ed. *On Autobiography.* Minneapolis, MN: University of Minnesota Press.
—— (1992) *Touching the World. Reference in Autobiography.* Princeton: Princeton University Press.
—— (1999) *How Our Lives Become Stories: Making Selves.* Ithaca and London: Cornell University Press.
Echterhoff, Gerhard (2002) "Geschichten in der Psychologie: Die Erforschung narrativ geleiteter Informationsverarbeitung." *Erzähltheorie transgenerisch, intermedial, interdisziplinär.* Eds. Vera Nünning and Ansgar Nünning. Trier: Wissenschaftlicher Verlag Trier. 265–90.
Echterhoff, Gerhard, and Jürgen Straub (2004) "Narrative Psychologie." *Psychologie als Humanwissenschaft: Ein Handbuch.* Ed. Gerd Jüttemann. Göttingen: Vandenhoeck & Ruprecht. 102–33.
Fludernik, Monika (1996) *Towards a 'Natural' Narratology.* London, New York: Routledge.
—— (2003) "Natural Narratology and Cognitive Parameters." *Narrative Theory and the Cognitive Sciences.* Ed. David Herman. Stanford, CA: Center for the Study of Language and Information. 243–67.
Frye, Northrop (1957) *Anatomy of Criticism: Four Essays.* Princeton, NJ: Princeton University Press.
Herman, David (1997) "Scripts, Sequences and Stories: Elements of a Postclassical Narratology." *PMLA* 112: 1046–59.
—— (2003a) Ed. *Narrative Theory and the Cognitive Sciences.* Stanford, CA: Center for the Study of Language and Information.
—— (2003b) "Stories as a Tool for Thinking." *Narrative Theory and the Cognitive Sciences.* Ed. David Herman. Stanford, CA: Center for the Study of Language and Information. 163–91.
Hogan, Patrick Colm (2004) *Cognitive Science, Literature, and the Arts: A Guide for Humanists.* New York and London: Routledge.
Ibsch, Elrud (1990) "The Cognitive Turn in Narratology." *Poetics Today* 11.2: 411–18.
Jüttemann, Gerd (2004) Ed. *Psychologie als Humanwissenschaft: Ein Handbuch.* Göttingen: Vandenhoeck & Ruprecht.
Kadar, Marlene, et al. (2005) Eds. *Tracing the Autobiographical.* Waterloo, ON: Wilfrid Laurier University Press.
Lejeune, Philippe (1989) "The Autobiographical Pact." *On Autobiography.* Ed. Paul John Eakin. Minneapolis, MN: University of Minnesota Press. 3–30.
Linde, Charlotte (1993) *Life Stories: The Creation of Coherence.* New York and Oxford: Oxford University Press.
Löschnigg, Martin (2006a) *Die englische fiktionale Autobiographie. Erzähltheoretische Grundlagen und historische Prägnanzformen von den Anfängen bis zur Mitte des neunzehnten Jahrhunderts,* Trier: Wissenschaftlicher Verlag Trier.
—— (2006b) "Narratological Perspectives on 'Fiction and Autobiography.'" *Fiction*

and Autobiography: Modes and Models of Interaction. Eds. Sabine Coelsch-Foisner and Wolfgang Görtschacher. Frankfurt am Main: Lang. 1–11.
McKeon, Michael (1987) *The Origins of the English Novel, 1600–1740.* Baltimore: Johns Hopkins University Press.
Marcus, Laura (1994) *Auto/Biographical Discourses: Theory, Criticism, Practice.* Manchester and New York: Manchester University Press.
Meister, Jan Christoph, in collaboration with Tom Kindt and Wilhelm Schernus (2005) Ed. *Narratology Beyond Literary Criticism: Mediality, Disciplinarity.* Berlin and New York: de Gruyter.
Mercadal, Dennis (1990) *A Dictionary of Artificial Intelligence.* New York: Van Nostrand.
Mill, John Stuart (1969) *Autobiography* [1873]. Ed. Jack Stillinger. Boston: Houghton Mifflin.
Mink, Louis O. (1978) "Narrative Form as a Cognitive Instrument." *The Writing of History.* Eds. Robert H. Canary and Henri Kosicki. Madison: University of Wisconsin Press. 129–49.
Müller-Funk, Wolfgang (2003) "On a Narratology of Cultural and Collective Memory." *Journal of Narrative Theory* 33.2: 207–27.
Nalbantian, Suzanne (1994) *Aesthetic Autobiography: From Life to Art in Marcel Proust, James Joyce, Virginia Woolf and Anaïs Nin.* Houndsmills and London: Macmillan.
Nünning, Vera, and Ansgar Nünning (2002) Eds. *Erzähltheorie transgenerisch, intermedial, interdisziplinär.* Trier: Wissenschaftlicher Verlag Trier.
Olney, James (1972) *Metaphors of Self: The Meaning of Autobiography.* Princeton, NJ: Princeton University Press.
——— (1980) Ed. *Autobiography: Essays Theoretical and Critical.* Princeton, NJ: Princeton University Press.
——— (1988a) Ed. *Studies in Autobiography.* New York: Oxford University Press.
——— (1998b) *Memory and Narrative: The Weave of Life-Writing.* Chicago: University of Chicago Press.
Pascal, Roy (1960) *Design and Truth in Autobiography.* London: Routledge & Kegan Paul.
Phelan, James, and Peter J. Rabinowitz (2005) Eds. *A Companion to Narrative Theory.* Malden, MA: Blackwell.
Polkinghorne, Donald (1988) *Narrative Knowing and the Human Sciences.* Albany: State University of New York Press.
Ricœur, Paul (1984–88) *Time and Narrative.* 3 vols. Trans. Kathleen McLaughlin and David Pellauer. Chicago: University of Chicago Press.
Rousseau, Jean-Jacques (1953) *The Confessions of Jean-Jacques Rousseau* [1781–89]. Trans. J. M. Cohen. Harmondsworth: Penguin.
Rubin, David C. (1986) Ed. *Autobiographical Memory.* Cambridge and New York: Cambridge University Press.
Sarbin, T. R. (1986) Ed. *Narrative Psychology: The Storied Nature of Human Conduct.* New York: Praeger.
Schacter, Daniel (1996) *Searching for Memory: The Brain, the Mind, and the Past.* New York: Basic Books.
Sheringham, Michael (1993) *French Autobiography: Devices and Desires.* Oxford: Clarendon.

Smith, Sidonie, and Julia Watson (2005) "The Trouble with Autobiography: Cautionary Notes for Narrative Theorists." *A Companion to Narrative Theory*. Eds. James Phelan and Peter J. Rabinowitz. Malden, MA: Blackwell. 356–71.

Sprinker, Michael (1980) "Fictions of the Self: The End of Autobiography." *Autobiography: Essays Theoretical and Critical*. Ed. James Olney. Princeton, NJ: Princeton University Press. 321–42.

Swift, Graham (1983) *Waterland*. London: Picador.

Thompson, Charles, et al. (1996) *Autobiographical Memory: Remembering What and Remembering When*. Mahwah, NJ: Lawrence Erlbaum.

White, Hayden (1973) *Metahistory: The Historical Imagination in Nineteenth-Century Europe*. Baltimore and London: Johns Hopkins University Press.

Williams, Linda Ruth (1995) *Critical Desire: Psychoanalysis and the Literary Subject*. London: Edward Arnold.

Zerweck, Bruno (2002) "Der *cognitive turn* in der Erzähltheorie: Kognitive und 'Natürliche' Narratologie." *Erzähltheorie transgenerisch, intermedial, interdisziplinär*. Eds. Vera Nünning and Ansgar Nünning. Trier: Wissenschaftlicher Verlag Trier. 219–42.

HENRIK SKOV NIELSEN

Natural Authors, Unnatural Narration[1]

INTRODUCTION

Hardly anything is more familiar to literary scholars than fictional narrative. Yet this simple term contains a slight tension between the *invention* associated with fiction, from its root in the Latin *fictio*, and the *knowing* associated with narration and its root in the Latin *gnarus*. How can you invent what you know or know what you invent? In all standard models of narratology, the answer to this question has been to split the tasks and distinguish between the narrator who *knows* and the author who *invents*, and this is the case particularly in the framework of Gérard Genette.[2]

The present essay discusses whether this narratological model of the relationship between narrator and author has served to naturalize the understanding of fictional narratives and of fictionality in the sense that they are understood along the lines of everyday reports.[3] In its attempt to understand

---

1. I wish to thank Stefan Iversen and Rolf Reitan for their considerable contributions to this essay. Stefan Iversen's theses on the concept of experientiality and other topics, and Rolf Reitan's work on Genette's and Hamburger's concepts of narrators and narratives have both served as rich sources of inspiration.
2. See Walsh (2007: 72–74) and Genette (1980: 214).
3. An important context for the present article is the work of a research group formed by Brian Richardson, Jan Alber, Stefan Iversen, Rolf Reitan, Maria Mäkela, myself, and several others on what we call "unnatural narratology" (see www.unnaturalnarratology.com). The work of the group includes Brian Richardson's *Unnatural Voices* as well as five panels on unnatural narratology at the ISSN conferences in 2008, 2009, and 2010. A joint article by Alber,

fiction as a form of communication from a narrator,[4] narratology has rarely devoted much attention to the author. Although paratextually grounded approaches make important and necessary contributions to our understanding of fiction, they face problems when encountering works that are framed by ambiguous paratexts. This essay raises the question of the relationship between author and text by addressing some of these difficulties. It asks what such paratexts imply for the narrator-author distinction which supposedly exists in fiction and is absent in nonfiction. The texts used in this essay range from fictional to nonfictional writing, though I will focus particularly on James Frey's *A Million Little Pieces* (2003). The essay will discuss in detail what may be gained by giving more attention to the rhetorical resources of the actual author. As signaled by the title, the aim is to demonstrate that the real author has the ability to transcend communicational models and to employ techniques of fictionalization, regardless of whether the narrative is presented as fiction or not. It is argued that such techniques can more helpfully be explained by distinguishing between fiction and fictionality as well as between narration and communication than by assuming the existence of a narrator distinct from the author.

In classical structuralist narratology, the relationship between author and narrator was central for the distinction between fictional and nonfictional narratives. In fictional narratives there is a narrator who is not the same person as the author. In nonfictional narratives like autobiographies, on the other hand, there is no narrator other than the author.[5] This distinction is conventional and indispensable. It explains, for instance, why we must not arrest Bret Easton Ellis, assuming he is identical with the first-person narrator of *American Psycho* (1991), who is a serial killer.

However, the distinction between author and narrator is also problem-

---

Iversen, Nielsen, and Richardson, "Unnatural Narratives—Unnatural Narratology: Beyond Mimetic Models?" has just been published, and two anthologies on unnatural narratology are in progress. In the group we are concerned with radically anti-mimetic texts but also with unnatural features in conventionalized genres and forms like the realist novel. These features comprise narrative "omniscience," paralepsis, and what James Phelan refers to as redundant telling. We also deal with storyworlds that contain physical or logical impossibilities (Alber 2009). For my own part, I take a special interest in unnatural acts of narration by which I understand physically, logically, mnemonically, or psychologically impossible enunciations.

4. Ann Banfield also argues that "there have been numerous attempts to submit narrative to the communication paradigm by positing a narrator addressing a reader for every text" (1982: 10, 8–18).

5. See Genette (1993: 68–84), Lejeune (1975: 16ff), and Cohn (1999: 30 and 59). Hernadi probably puts it most concisely: "Fictional narratives demand, historical narratives preclude a distinction between the narrator and the implied author" (Hernadi, in Cohn 1999: 124).

atic. First, it tends, at least implicitly, to place an absolute barrier between fictional and nonfictional narratives, that is, between narratives with, and narratives without, a narrator other than the author. Second, it encounters difficulties when facing a range of limit cases where the question of fiction remains difficult to decide. These problems notwithstanding, the distinction is fundamental to most classical as well as postclassical narratologies: in nonfictional written narratives the communication is taken to proceed from author to reader, in fictional ones (also) from a narrator to a narratee.

These ideas have led narratologists to consider literary fictions as acts of communication and "reports" by narrators, and have resulted in a prevailing lack of interest in the author (Walsh 2007: 69). It almost seems as if Barthes's 1967 statement about the birth of the reader (at the cost of the death of the author) also holds true for the birth of narratology, baptized two years later by Todorov. Near the beginning of his essay, Barthes writes:

> As soon as a fact is *narrated* no longer with a view to acting directly on reality but intransitively, that is to say, finally outside of any function other than that of the very practice of the symbol itself, this disconnection appears, the voice loses its origin, the author enters into his own death, writing begins. (Barthes 2004: 125)

Accordingly, and perhaps even necessarily, when analyzing narrated facts in a novel, narratological analysis seems to have confirmed this disconnection between fictional text and real-world author.[6] Postclassical narratology has considered narratives in the light of a wide range of different contexts. It has invoked the reader, the importance of historical periods, gender issues, questions of ethics, ideology, and, perhaps more than anything, the workings of the human mind. But only rarely has it considered the author to be a relevant topic for narratology. It is a telling fact that *The Cambridge Companion to Narrative* (Herman 2007) has no chapter on the author. Additionally, the word "author" does not even appear in its glossary. Even in the comprehensive index, the entry "author" points the reader to "rhetorical approaches." I will follow this advice and approach the problem of the author by considering the tradition of rhetoric in narratology. I will first turn to James Phelan and then to Richard Walsh.

---

6. For a few concise and precise remarks about the role of the author in narratology, see Fludernik (2006: 23–25).

RHETORICAL APPROACHES

James Phelan has written a number of books on rhetoric and narration. In *Living to Tell about It* (2005), Phelan defines narrative as follows: "First, narrative itself can be fruitfully understood as a rhetorical act: somebody telling somebody else on some occasion and for some purpose(s) that something happened" (Phelan 2005: 18).[7] By implication: if nothing happened, or no one told it, there would be no narrative. A great strength of Phelan's book is the way in which he simultaneously approaches the standard cases, the exceptions to the rule, and the potential problems they create for his theory. Large parts of his book are devoted to problematic cases, and to cases that seem to contradict his definition. In his introduction, Phelan mentions a series of text examples in which the narrator narrates either what the narratee already knows ("My Last Duchess" by Robert Browning and "Barbie-Q" by Sandra Cisneros), or what the narrator himself could not know (*Angela's Ashes* by Frank McCourt and *The Great Gatsby* by F. Scott Fitzgerald, where something is narrated in great detail from an episode where the narrator himself was absent).[8] Phelan also mentions texts in which the narrator seems not to know a fact although the reader must infer that he actually knows it since at the time of narration he has come to the end of his story ("My Old Man" by Ernest Hemingway, e.g., is not permeated by the disillusionment experienced by the narrator at the end).[9] Phelan quotes several other examples, all of which seem to contradict his definition of narrative as a report from narrator to narratee.[10] He provides a brilliant analysis of these narratives and explains many of the peculiarities mentioned by "the author's need" (12) and the use of "disclosure functions":

> The motivation for redundant telling resides in the *author's need* to communicate information to the audience, and so we might use the longer phrase *redundant telling, necessary disclosure* to describe it. [. . .] communication in character narration occurs along at least two tracks—the narrator-narratee track, and the narrator-authorial audience track. Along the narrator-narratee track, the narrator acts as a reporter, interpreter and evaluator of the narrated for the narratee, and those actions are constrained by the narrative situation (a character narrator, for example, cannot enter the consciousness of another character); let us call these actions "narrator functions." Along

---

7. For variations of the same definition, see Phelan (1996: 8) and Phelan (2007: 3).
8. See also Phelan (1996: 106).
9. See also Phelan (1996: 103).
10. See also the excellent examples in Phelan (1996: chapter 5).

the narrator-authorial audience track, *the narrator unwittingly reports information of all kinds to the authorial audience* (the narrator does not know that an authorial audience exists); let us call this reporting "disclosure functions." (Phelan 2005: 12; my emphasis)

Phelan's explanations show why the above-mentioned example texts should not be considered as "mistakes" by their authors (as in fact they seldom are by readers), and why—although probably unreliable in other respects—the texts appear in the mentioned passages to present the story in an authoritative way even when it clashes with the knowledge of the narrator. A potential problem, however, to be discussed in the following, is that—while serving the author's need—the words are still described as "reports" from "the narrator." If all narration is report and communication (I use the two words synonymously, as Phelan seems to do)—then there must be a reporter. This explains why the author has come to stand outside the focus of narratology. In fictional narratives, the author does not tell the reader that something happened; the author invents the events. So in order to be able to view fictional narratives as reports, we must take an interest in the narrator instead. However, as soon as it becomes evident that the narrator is not reporting (when, for instance, he cannot know what is being recounted), the need for the author returns. Phelan responds to this problem by saying that the (implied) author has the narrator narrate to audiences and for purposes the narrator is unaware of. The general logic—one which is not specific to Phelan but common to all narratological models that equate communication and narration—is that if it is not the author who is reporting, then the narrator is doing it. And, conversely, if it is not the narrator who is reporting, then it must be the author.

In what follows, I will suggest that there is a simpler and less circular way of approaching the problem. My suggestion is that one does not have to consider all forms of narration as report and communication. Many narratologists have described narration—fictional and nonfictional, conversational and literary—under the umbrella of a unified theory, most often one based on oral storytelling. I am skeptical of this attempt and my skepticism boils down to the assumption that there is a crucial difference between narration and communication. Much, but not all, narration is communication. I will call that part of narration that is not communication "unnatural narration" because it deviates from the paradigm of natural, i.e., oral narratives.

After these remarks on narration vs. communication, I will briefly place the question of fiction vs. fictionality in the context of the ongoing discussion about fiction vs. nonfiction. At opposite corners of the debate, we find a separatist position associated with Dorrit Cohn and (especially the early) Philippe Lejeune, and a panfictionalist position often associated with Hayden White and more broadly with postmodernism and deconstruction.[11] The first position deals in tell-tale signposts of fictionality that will reveal to a reader whether a text is fiction or nonfiction. By contrast, I follow Walsh and Phelan (see below) and think of such signposts rather as techniques of fiction*alization* that can also be used in nonfictional texts. As opposed to the dominant belief of the second position that everything can be read as fiction and according to the same rules of interpretation, I believe that the reader is often guided in his or her interpretation by a number of features that invite different readings. Furthermore, I claim that readers do, in fact, react very differently depending on whether they think they are reading fiction or not. Phelan puts this idea as follows:

> The one theoretical generalization I would offer is that there is no one-to-one correspondence between any specific formal feature of a narrative and any effect, including the placement of a narrative along the fiction/nonfiction spectrum. [. . .] I do not believe [. . .] that we can make the distinction on the basis of techniques that are either sure markers of fiction or nonfiction or that appear exclusively in one. As soon as such techniques get identified, some narrative artists will use them for unanticipated effects. (Phelan 2005: 68)

Similarly, in the fortieth anniversary edition of Scholes and Kellogg's *The Nature of Narrative,* Phelan points out four "unresolved instabilities" in narrative theory. The first one concerns the study of unnatural narrative and refers to Brian Richardson.[12] The second concerns digital narratives and the fourth a paradigm shift to questions of space and time. Interestingly, the third unresolved instability is about the question of fiction vs. nonfiction:

> In my rhetorical view, preserving the borders [between fiction and nonfiction] has the major advantage of helping us account for the differences in the ways we respond to particular narratives, even as the debate calls attention to various kinds of border-crossing—of technique, of character, of place, and so on. (Phelan, Scholes and Kellogg 2006: 335)

11. For a good, short survey of the position from its roots in Saussurian linguistics to theorists like Eagleton, Hillis Miller and Norris, see Ryan (1997: 173ff).

12. In *Unnatural Voices,* Brian Richardson demonstrates through careful readings of an impressive range of narratives how postmodern (as well as many earlier) narratives prove resistant to mimetic approaches. This paper was partly inspired by Richardson's arguments about misguided mimetic generalizations.

To put it bluntly, the advantage is that the borderline works, the disadvantage is that it does not exist—a slightly paradoxical description, but one I would actually subscribe to myself.

In *The Rhetoric of Fictionality,* Richard Walsh also addresses this problem and offers the following solution:

> By speaking of the quality of fictionality, I am framing the argument at one remove from the generic distinction between fiction and nonfiction per se, but fictionality is certainly an attribute of all fictions in that sense since it is applicable to all narratives deemed fictional (as distinct from false). [. . .] Of course it is the case that most fictions do in fact exhibit characteristics indicative of their fictional status [. . .] but these are neither necessary nor sufficient conditions of fictionality. [. . .] Even within the terms of the familiar, modern fictional contract, though, fictionality has no determinate relation to features of the text itself. [. . .] Fictionality is the product of a narrative's frame of presentation, of the various possible elements of what Gérard Genette has described as the paratext (1997). [. . .] And the distinction is categorical [. . .] because the interpretative operations applicable to a narrative text are globally transformed, one way or the other, by the extrinsic matter of the contextual frame within which it is received. (Walsh 2007: 44–45)

Taking his point of departure from a position close to Phelan's, Walsh argues that fictionality cannot be determined by text-internal evidence, and I agree with this argument.[13] However, while Walsh stresses the *globally* transforming power of the frame, I would like to add that fictionality may also be *local*. In fact, in other places, especially in his introduction, Walsh seems to acknowledge this fact, since it must be the reason why fictionality as a rhetorical strategy is sometimes also apparent in nonfictional narratives:

> Not that fictionality should be equated simply with "fiction," as a category or genre of narrative: it is a communicative strategy, and as such it is apparent on some scale within many nonfictional narratives, in forms ranging from something like an ironic aside, through various forms of conjecture or imaginative supplementation, to full-blown counterfactual narrative examples. (Walsh 2007: 7)

In the useful distinction between fiction and fictionality, the global and the local seem to me equally important. Frame and paratext may produce a form

---

13. See also Löschnigg (1999) and Fludernik (2001).

of fictionality that invites certain interpretative operations towards the narrative as a whole. Using any of a range of techniques of fictionality (including omniscience, free indirect discourse, simultaneous narration, imaginative supplementation, and counterfactual narrative) will locally produce fictionality that similarly invites certain interpretative operations at least towards parts of the narrative—without necessarily turning the *whole* narrative into a fictional text. I will argue this in detail below in the context of the case of James Frey.

So far I have argued that there can be fictionality without fiction and narration without communication. Ann Banfield's book *Unspeakable Sentences* (1982) has greatly influenced my thinking about fictional narratives. I will just briefly indicate a few differences between us regarding some points on which she and I seem to agree. We both reject the assumption of much communication theory that every sentence has a speaker and every text a narrator (Banfield 1982: 11). However, Banfield holds "represented speech and thought" (free indirect discourse) to be an "exclusively literary style" (68), a view few would agree with today. For Banfield, narration (in a narrow sense as a translation of Benveniste's *histoire* and Hamburger's *fiktionales Erzählen* [142]) has no addressee (171), and is globally made up of sentences of non-communication (242). In contrast to her, I stress that non-communication does not only appear in narrative fiction and, conversely, that not all narrative fiction is non-communicative.

The following sections pursue some of the questions raised when paratextual information makes it difficult to determine which interpretative operations a narrative invites.

DETERMINING FICTION

In "Postmodernism and the Doctrine of Panfictionality," Marie-Laure Ryan mentions a crisis regarding the distinction between fiction and nonfiction (1997: 165). She argues against the theory of panfictionality, understood in the sense of the fictionality of all discourse (177). Opposing views that regard fiction and nonfiction as indistinguishable, Ryan proposes that "[t]he possibility of hybridization does not necessarily mean that the two categories are inherently indeterminate: the many shades of gray on the spectrum from black to white do not turn black and white into the same color (165)." In describing features of fictional text, Ryan takes her point of departure in a view that is very similar to Phelan's:

According to a widely accepted model, which I endorse in its broad lines, fictional communication presupposes a layered situation, in which an author addresses a real or "authorial" audience through a narrator addressing an imaginary or narratorial audience. [. . .] It [fictional communication] makes no claim to external truth, but rather, guarantees its own truth. (167)[14]

Ryan then presents some dominant panfictionalist positions (175–79), and convincingly counters them with arguments like the following: "But even if one concedes the unavoidable artificiality of representation, the thesis of universal fictionality rests on a faulty syllogism: all fictions are artifices. All representations are artifices. Hence, all representations are fictions (180)."

In place of panfictionality, Ryan offers a model and a taxonomy that draw different conclusions from the acknowledged lack of clear borderlines:

If we maintain the distinction, what, then, is the literary-theoretical significance of the current destabilization of the borderline between fiction and nonfiction? I would suggest that the contribution of postmodern writing practice to the system of genres is not to have merged fiction and nonfiction into one category, but on the contrary to have introduced a third species in the taxonomy. The system now comprises: (1) Those texts that overtly say "I am true," asking the reader to accept this claim as a criterion of validity. (Biographies, historiography, traditional journalism, scientific discourse.) (2) Those texts that send a mixed message: I am not true but I pretend that I am. (Prototypes: *Madame Bovary, War and Peace, Jane Eyre, Buddenbrooks*). (3) Texts that say "I am not true" through overt makers, and inhibit participation in a textual world. ([. . .] *The French Lieutenant's Woman, The Unnamable* etc.). (181)

While I am completely sympathetic to Ryan in her case against panfictionality, I think that this triad tends to overemphasize the importance of or challenge posed by metafiction, or what Ryan here refers to as postmodern writing practice. To me, there is a clear distinction in the taxonomy between nonfiction (category 1) and fiction (whether metafictive or not [categories 2 and 3]). Although I see Ryan's point, I am skeptical about the description of the second category. In my opinion, the books mentioned can all be placed on either side of the border because they do not really send a mixed message. It is simply not possible for a text to send the message "I am not true but I

---

14. For an even more elaborate account of the truth value of fiction and possible worlds, see Ryan (1991: 13–47).

pretend that I am," insofar as true texts do not normally send the message that they are not true.[15] Therefore, any text that sends the message that it is not true does not pretend to be true. For the same reason, no one would mistakenly take any of the examples mentioned in category 2 to belong to any of the genres mentioned in category 1.

Based on Ryan's refutation of panfictionalism and her article in general, I want to argue in the following that a more profound challenge to the distinction between fiction and nonfiction comes from texts that present themselves as *neither* fiction *nor* nonfiction (I will call these texts "underdetermined") and from texts that present themselves—in some cases at different times, in others at the same time—as *both* fiction *and* nonfiction (and hence can be called "overdetermined"). This leads me to modify Ryan's taxonomy into one of my own invention:

(1) Fictional texts (prototypes: *Madame Bovary, War and Peace, The French Lieutenant's Woman, The Unnamable*, etc.).
(2) Underdetermined texts (prototypes: *Les Mots* by Sartre, *A Million Little Pieces* by Frey, etc.). For other examples like Knut Hamsun's *Hunger,* see Cohn (1999: 34).
(3) Overdetermined texts (prototypes: *Fils, Lunar Park*, etc.).
(4) Nonfictional texts (biographies, historiography, traditional journalism, scientific discourse)

In my view, the majority of written narratives can easily be characterized as either fictional or nonfictional because paratexts, styles, techniques, and so forth, all point in the same direction. A minority of sometimes highly interesting and controversial texts, however, display ambiguous, deceptive, missing, or self-contradictory paratexts. This can happen in a multitude of ways, and it is not my intention here to make an inventory of these. Instead, I will simplify the matter and differentiate between only two categories of problematic cases. The first category ("underdetermined") contains texts with paratexts that send no clear message (*A Million Little Pieces* by James Frey will be the main example in this category). The second category ("overdetermined") contains texts with paratexts that send mixed or mutually exclusive messages.

It is tempting to insert a fifth category in the middle, to include fiction disguised as nonfiction and vice versa. This category would then include texts that are wholly or partly true, but present themselves as fiction, and texts that are wholly or partly fiction, but attest to the opposite, and possibly also

---

15. Ryan seems to acknowledge this herself when she writes a little earlier: "But novels rarely read like the nonfictional genres they are supposed to imitate" (169).

pseudo-autobiography and pseudo-history. However, it would not be easy to come up with examples because all fiction makes some reference to the real world, and since non-accurate parts in nonfiction normally compromise their veracity instead of turning it into fiction (Walsh 2007: 45). In the following discussion of the famous controversy about James Frey, questions like these will also be raised. I do not think of the four categories as separate boxes, but rather as forming a continuum with many shades of gray, to reuse Ryan's expression. Far from turning fiction into nonfiction or vice versa, texts in categories 2 and 3 are placed in a middle region, drawing on resources from both categories 1 and 4. Likewise, I think that any attempt to place absolute boundaries between the categories is doomed to failure. Even underdetermined and overdetermined narratives are not always as different as could be expected. In fact, an underdetermined text may occasionally change its status to an overdetermined text if new paratextual information is added.[16]

In the following, I will inquire into the question of what problematic paratexts do to the narrator-author distinction supposedly present in fiction and absent in nonfiction.

JAMES FREY'S *A MILLION LITTLE PIECES* AS AN UNDERDETERMINED TEXT[17]

To represent the possible cases of underdetermined and overdetermined texts, I have chosen *A Million Little Pieces* (2003) by James Frey and *Lunar Park*

---

16. Underdetermined texts can become overdetermined when text-external contradictory contracts are signed—for example, in interviews at different times or by the publisher. Scandals are more likely to occur in cases of underdetermination than overdetermination, especially when an underdetermined text is first read as nonfiction and then as fiction, like Frey's, but also when a text about, say, incest, is first read as fiction, then as nonfiction. Some underdetermined texts will easily lend themselves to being read according to more than one contract established outside the text.

17. I do not devote attention to Frey's book and the discussions that followed it because the book is especially complex or transgressive or because it is a perfect example of an underdetermined work. My interest has to do with the fact that the case is very instructive; also, the book can be read as fiction, nonfiction, or both at the same time. The settlement in the case even puts an exact date on the change, January 26, 2006, when Frey admitted inaccuracies and Oprah Winfrey withdrew her support for the book. Only readers who had bought the book before that date were eligible for refunds. There is no denying that the book tried to pass as nonfiction—I will say more about that later—and that it could be called a hoax. At a purely paratextual level, however, the first editions of the book were designed and published in ways that allowed it to be read, first as nonfiction, then as fiction. And although it is very clear that the book cannot unambiguously be described as nonfiction, it is equally clear that it is not "pure" fiction. On a paratextual level, the book was underdetermined, and on a descriptive level it remains difficult to clearly determine it as belonging to one or the other category.

(2005) by Bret Easton Ellis. The two works mirror each other: the former was published as nonfiction, but turned out to be a rather inaccurate representation of the experiences of its author; the latter was published as fiction, but is in many (though definitely not all) respects accurate in its facts and information about the author. In *Lunar Park*, then, the real author seems to be *too much* a part of the story for it to be clearly fictional, and in *A Million Little Pieces* the real author seems *not sufficiently* to be a part of the story for it to be clearly nonfictional. Whereas *Lunar Park* did not provoke any controversy, discussions of *A Million Little Pieces* were heated, to put it mildly. Since Frey's book, as well as the discussions surrounding it, are illuminating for arguments about narrators and authors, I will first concentrate on Frey's case. *Lunar Park* will be discussed by way of comparison.

A Million Little Pieces is about a very heavy substance abuser and how he overcomes his addiction. In September 2005, it was promoted by Oprah Winfrey on her talk show and was her book of the month. It was also at the top of the *New York Times* nonfiction paperback bestseller list for many weeks. Then, in the beginning of 2006, it was "exposed" as fraud by the website *The Smoking Gun,* which renamed it "A Million Little Lies." Frey appeared on several talk shows, including Larry King's; at the end of this show Oprah Winfrey called in to reconfirm her support for him. Later on, he was a guest on Oprah's show again, on which occasion she withdrew her support and accused him of betrayal. Many other readers also reacted to the exposure with outrage.[18] A poll at abebooks.com revealed that a significant "67.3% [said they] felt *betrayed* by Frey, and that a memoir should not contain fictional information"[19] (emphasis in the original). Here are a few telling quotes:

> I was under the impression this was a real life experience. I've read more than half of this book and don't know if I want to even finish it now. I want to know what is real in this book.

> A memoir should be accurate. What's the point of reading a non-fiction book if it's fiction? (ibid.)

These statements clearly suggest that the difference between fiction and nonfiction matters to real readers. Most readers seem to have different rules and expectations for fictional narratives than they do for nonfictional narratives.

---

18. See Lanser (2005: 209) for similar famous incidents causing outrage.
19. See http://www.abebooks.com/docs/Community/Featured/james-frey-poll.shtml.

Hence, lawsuits were filed, and Frey's publisher finally made the following offer:

> NEW YORK (Reuters)—Random House is offering refunds to readers who bought James Frey's drug and alcohol memoir "A Million Little Pieces" directly from the publisher, following accusations the author exaggerated his story.[20]

Navigating between fiction and truth, Reuters uses the word "exaggerated." On the one hand, this lexeme only makes sense with reference to what really happened in Frey's life. On the other hand, the word highlights the fact that this is not *exactly* the truth but an exaggerated version of it. As incidental as the usage of this word may seem, it is significant that *The Smoking Gun* investigates the case from the same basic assumption of reference with a difference. In every instance in which *The Smoking Gun* wants to prove that Frey deviates from reality in his representation of different incidents, it starts by showing how many details are *true,* in order to show that they are investigating the right incident:

> However, based on Frey's own statements in a TSG interview, there can be little, if any, doubt that the incident described in the Granville police report is the same one fictionalized in Frey's book.[21]

The controversy and the lawsuit surrounding *A Million Little Pieces* raises problems of central importance to our issue here, i.e., the question of the importance of deceptive or problematic paratextual information concerning the fiction/nonfiction distinction and the narrator/author distinction. At least two very basic questions can be asked: is *A Million Little Pieces* paratextually determined as either fiction or nonfiction? And if so, what does this determination entail, and by what rules is it governed? Turning to the first, seemingly easy, question, let me quote from the final settlement:

> A. Factual and Procedural Background
> This action arises out of the publication and marketing of the book *A Million Little Pieces* by James Frey (the "Book"). The Book, which was published by defendant Random House, Inc. in 2003, is based on Frey's experiences during a stay at a drug rehabilitation center and his subsequent

---

20. See http://www.harrisonfordweb.com/forums/showthread.php?t=5388.
21. See http://www.thesmokinggun.com/jamesfrey/0104061jamesfrey4.html.

recovery from drug addiction. After its publication, the Book gained critical success, and in the Fall of 2005, it was chosen as a featured selection of the Oprah Winfrey Book Club. The back cover classified the Book as "memoir/literature."[22]

Whereas the later Anchor Books edition is tagged as claimed here, neither the first nor the following paperback edition used that label. It is doubtful that the book was "classified" at all when first published. The first edition bears no generic markers on the front cover. On the back cover it has no statements by the publisher or author, but instead two blurbs by Bret Easton Ellis and Pat Conroy. Ellis calls it "a heartbreaking memoir" but also mentions, curiously, its "poetic honesty." Conroy makes no generic reference, but instead compares it to a major work of fiction: "James Frey has written the *War and Peace* of addiction." Although the design and front and back cover have all been changed for the paperback edition, this still carries no generic markers. The settlement goes on to refer to the lawsuits:

> All of these lawsuits focus on (1) the author's alleged embellishments in the Book; (2) the labeling of the Book as a "memoir"; and (3) various other ways in which the Book was advertised, publicized, and marketed.[23]

Point (3) seems to touch on something essential: although not exactly labeled as such, the book was distributed, advertised and sold in the guise of a memoir. The paratext is not restricted to the book cover. James Frey sticks to a double defense strategy not completely unlike Freud's kettle argument. He claims, first, that a memoir is not unambiguously nonfiction, and, second, that, even if regarded as nonfiction, it does not necessarily have to be entirely accurate. This is apparent from his comments on Larry King's talk show. Frey comments on the ambiguous fictional status of memoirs as follows:

> [. . .] the genre of memoir is one that's very new and the boundaries of it had not been established yet. [. . .]
> Yes. Again, I don't think it's fair to classify this "Million Little Pieces" as fiction at all. It's a memoir. A very small portion is in dispute. [. . .]
> I couldn't have written it if I hadn't been through a lot of the things I talk about. You know, it's a memoir. [. . .] I don't think it should be held up and scrutinized the way a perfect non-fiction document would be or a newspaper article.[24]

22. See http://www.amlpsettlement.com/pdfs/Final_Approval_of_Settlement.pdf.
23. See http://www.amlpsettlement.com/pdfs/Final_Approval_of_Settlement.pdf.
24. See http://transcripts.cnn.com/TRANSCRIPTS/0601/11/lk1.01.html.

Frey argues that his book is neither completely fictional nor completely nonfictional. His publisher, Nan Talese, backs him up on this point on Oprah Winfrey's show:

> A novel is something different than a memoir. And a memoir is different from an autobiography. A memoir is an author's remembrance of a certain period in his life. Now, the responsibility, as far as I am concerned, is does it strike me as valid? Does it strike me as authentic? I mean, I'm sent things all the time and I think they're not real. I don't think they're authentic. I don't think they're good. I don't believe them. In this instance, I absolutely believed what I read.[25]

Nan Talese thus places memoirs in the overlap between fictional novels and nonfictional autobiographies. In his interview with King, Frey comments on the accuracy of a memoir if regarded as nonfiction as follows:

> KING: But it is supposed to be factual events. The memoir is a form of biography.
> FREY: Yes. Memoir is within the genre of non-fiction. I don't think it's necessarily appropriate to say I've conned anyone. The book is 432 pages long. The total page count of disputed events is 18, which is less than five percent of the total book. You know, that falls comfortably within the realm of what's appropriate for a memoir. [. . .]
> KING: But you will agree, if you went into a bookstore and it said memoirs, you would think non-fiction?
> FREY: Yes. I mean, it's a classification of non-fiction. Some people think it's creative non-fiction. It's generally recognized that the writer of a memoir is retailing a subjective story. That it's one person's event. I mean, I still stand by the essential truths of the book.[26]

I am not the one to decide whether memoirs must be nonfictional or whether it is appropriate for certain forms of nonfiction to be slightly, somewhat, considerably, or even necessarily incorrect. What *is* clear is that *A Million Little Pieces* was read as nonfiction, and that many readers found its inaccuracies (regarding a train accident, a prison sentence, and several other central issues) highly disturbing. More interesting still is the fact that in the many discussions surrounding the controversy surprisingly little attention was given

---

25. See http://www.oprah.com/tows/slide/200601/20060126/slide_20060126_350_115.jhtml.
26. See http://transcripts.cnn.com/TRANSCRIPTS/0601/11/lk1.01.html.

to the actual wordings in the book. It can be argued—and was argued—that the paratext of Frey's book did not determine the fictional status of the narrative. Irrespective of whether we think of the paratext as underdetermined or deceptive, the narrative *techniques* used by Frey are frequently fictionalization techniques. Frey himself gives one obvious example:

> [. . .] One of the things I think is interesting is there are 200 pages of recreated conversations in the book, but people haven't been questioning those because, in that area, it's understood that it's a memoir, it's a recreation, it's my subjective recreation of my own life.[27]

It is very easy to realize that the represented events differ from what actually happened: the book does nothing to disguise this. Despite the narrator's supposedly imperfect memory, the book is made up of page- and chapter-long dialogues and exact renderings of speech. Even more significantly, the whole book is narrated in the present tense. The present tense here is clearly not the historical present or simply an interior monologue, but rather corresponds to what Cohn calls the "fictional present" (1999: 106), a form Cohn limits to fictional narratives.

In chapter 6 of *The Distinction of Fiction,* Cohn describes a "mounting trend in modernist first-person fiction to cast a distinctively narrative (not monologic) discourse in the present tense from first to last" (1999: 97). Cohn rejects both the historical present and the interior monologue as satisfactory explanations for the phenomenon, and takes as her main example a passage from Coetzee's *Waiting for the Barbarians* (1980), containing the words that form the title of her chapter 6, "I doze and wake." Cohn comments on this as follows:

> But the introspective instance that most strongly resists the interior monologue reading is no doubt the one that reads: "I doze and wake, drifting from one formless dream to another." Here semantic incongruence combines with the formal feature that most forcefully counteracts the impression of an unrolling mental quotation in this passage as a whole: the pace of its discourse is not consistently synchronized with the pace of the events it conveys [. . .]. (103)

A Million Little Pieces contains numerous passages that could not be said, written, or even thought while the depicted events happened. There are

---

27. See http://transcripts.cnn.com/TRANSCRIPTS/0601/11/lk1.01.html.

descriptions in the present tense of being alone, sometimes overwhelmingly consumed by "the fury" (Frey 2003: 203 et passim). There are also passages that report how the narrator is falling asleep:

> [. . .] I climb into bed [. . .] I haven't slept in forty hours. I'm still smiling [. . .]. My hand drops. Still. Eyes close. Smiling. (169) [. . .]
> The two men on the couches next to me are both sound asleep. [. . .] I fade in and out. The TV is narcotic. In and out. In. Out. In. Out. (286)

It is obvious that everything Cohn said about "I doze and wake" and the use of the present tense in first-person fiction also applies here. Insofar as "out" describes a state of mind, of not being conscious, it cannot possibly be reported at the same time. The techniques used in the extract dissociate the words from the narrator's account. The words of the narrative in *A Million Little Pieces* are unnatural, in the sense that they are not modeled on natural narrative, i.e., everyday conversational storytelling. The book uses many techniques of fictionalization, but, as Frey mentioned, readers did not realize them. This was probably due to the fact that the text only uses techniques that have already been conventionalized in first-person narration.

Let us now contrast the case of Frey's (underdetermined) *A Million Little Pieces* with that of Bret Easton Ellis's (overdetermined) *Lunar Park*. After this comparison, I will consider the possible consequences of non-communicative narration.

BRET EASTON ELLIS'S *LUNAR PARK* AS AN OVERDETERMINED TEXT

Lunar Park is an example of autofiction in the sense of Serge Doubrovsky: it is a novel labeled as fiction whose protagonist has the same name as the author.[28] Furthermore, there is no doubt that much of what is said about the first-person narrator, who is called Bret Easton Ellis, holds true for the author as well. The book begins with a description of Ellis's career as a writer, blended with short analyses of his prose and the opening lines of his earlier

---

28. Coined by Doubrovsky (1977: back cover et passim), "autofiction" designates books specifically defined as novels, with the protagonist, author, and narrator sharing the same name. Later on, Genette (without even mentioning Doubrovsky) expands the term to denote any long or short fictional narrative in which the author and one of the characters have the same name (Genette 1993: 68–84). For more on metalepsis and fictionality see McHale (1987) and several articles in Pier and Schaeffer (2005).

works, such as *Less than Zero* (1985) and *The Rules of Attraction* (1987). In the first chapter, Ellis also talks about his promotion tours, his relationship to his publisher, the scandal following *American Psycho*, his friendship with Jay McInerney, and so forth (2005: 3–40). All of this is well known to readers who have followed Ellis's career and read his books.

However, there are also numerous elements that are not in accordance with the biography of the real author. In the book, Ellis has spent years at Camden College (a college many fictional characters from earlier Ellis books went to), and he is married to one Jayne Dennis (a fictional character who nonetheless has her own website[29]). Moreover, the events gradually turn into a Hamlet-gone-Stephen King-plot. Among other things, we are confronted with a haunted house that changes its appearance, ghosts, a living bird doll, and unexplained disappearances. At one point, Ellis and his son Robby are almost swallowed by a monster (316). Also, the fictional character Patrick Bateman from *American Psycho*, who reappears in Ellis's novel *Glamorama*, turns up in *Lunar Park*, too, and begins (maybe as a copycat-killer incarnation) to copy the murders from *American Psycho*. And Terby, the bird doll, a rather uncanny and disturbing element, gradually turns into a murderous creature (376). Interestingly, spelled backward, the name of the doll contains a question that might be addressed to the book's narrator and/or its author: "TERBY"—"YBRET"—"*Why, Bret?*" (344).

Lunar Park blends reality and fiction in a rather fascinating way. Since the fictional parts are so obviously fictional, the novel is clearly not an example of embellished nonfiction. However, it is worth noting that it also contains true information about the author's life. It therefore seems reductive to see the book as pure fiction. Overdetermined autofictions urge readers to read them as fictional and nonfictional at the same time.[30]

29. See http://www.jaynedennis.com/home.html. Interestingly, the book has a website, too: http://www.randomhouse.com/kvpa/eastonellis/.

30. See the remarks on Lanser below and my forthcoming article "What's in a Name? Double Exposures in *Lunar Park*." In the article, I argue that autofictions bear numerous structural resemblances to double exposures in the visual medium. The photographic technique of "double exposure" merges temporally or spatially distinct figures. Similarly, autofictions superimpose an image of the real author over an image of characters in a fictional world. In the textual form of double exposure, the reader's knowledge about the author (from interviews, biographies, the media, and so on) contributes to his or her view of the author in the literary work and vice versa: exaggerations, fictional inventions, and narrative fantasies in the work contribute to rumors and imaginations about the author. In any autofiction, then, the reader sees the sum of two pictures or two narratives superimposed over each other and haunting each other. Because *Lunar Park* demands to be read as both fiction and nonfiction, the novel can be viewed as a form of double exposure: the (nonfictional) story about the author is superimposed on the (fictional) story about the character. The effect is formally quite different

NATURAL AUTHORS

In the contractual language of Lejeune's *Le pacte autobiographique*, *Lunar Park* signs two mutually exclusive contracts. The two contracts give the reader two contradictory messages: (1) "you must read this with *Interesselosigkeit* in the Kantian sense" (or, alternatively, "you won't be able to find out what actually happened") and (2) "you cannot read this with *Interesselosigkeit*" (or, alternatively, "you must try to find out what really happened"). Frey claimed to have signed neither of the two contracts, the contract for fictional narratives or the one for nonfictional narratives. To my mind, contractual thinking urges readers to make a choice between regarding *A Million Little Pieces* as narrated by a lying author, or, alternatively, regarding it as narrated by a reliable narrator. In an illuminating article on the ways in which we link texts and authors, Susan Lanser argues that readers do not always react as instructed by theory. Lanser begins by stating that "[a]s the history of literary reception has made dramatically evident, there is simply no way to resolve these questions [of fictionality and truthfulness] from the text itself" (Lanser 2005: 206). Her opening example is a piece by Ann Beattie in *The New Yorker*, which remains equivocally attached to its author. The reader will hesitate between attaching the "I" of the prose text to the author and attaching it to a narrator distinct from the author. Beattie's text is exemplary of the way literary discourse works rather than an exception to it: "The 'I' that characterizes literary discourse, in other words, is always potentially severed from *and* potentially tethered to the author's 'I'" (210–211). Lanser argues that readers make connections between the author and the "I" of a narrative—even if the "I" is a fictional character—and that these connections are much stronger than narrative theory has hitherto claimed. Lanser is interested in both ambiguously and clearly fictional narratives. She argues that "[. . .] readers *routinely* 'vacillate' and 'oscillate' and even double the speaking voice against the logic of both structure and stricture" (207; emphasis in the original). Later on, she says the following about fiction: "yet readers may ignore the technical boundaries of fictional voice, in effect *doubling* the 'I' so that the narrator's words sometimes belong to the author *as well as* to the narrating character and sometimes do not" (216). In both cases, Lanser uses the word "double/doubling" for the activity of the reader. In narratives designated as fiction this is something the reader tends to do—"against theory," as it were.

---

from the reference to real historical events or places in fictional works where the principle of minimal departure applies.

When Walsh addresses the relationship between fictive and nonfictive discourse in *The Rhetoric of Fictionality,* he also connects it to questions about narrators and authors. Rather than drawing ontological boundary lines, Walsh draws on the relevance theory of Dan Sperber and Deirdre Wilson. He points out that this paradigm has a very useful feature:

> [. . .] a pragmatic theory of fictionality does not require detachment of fictive discourse from real-world context. [. . .] Fictionality is neither a boundary between worlds, nor a frame dissociating the author from the discourse, but a contextual assumption by the reader [. . .]. (36)

Discussing the consequences of a pragmatic approach for the concept of the narrator, Walsh writes that "[. . .] the narrator [. . .] functions primarily to establish a representational frame within which the narrative discourse may be read as report rather than invention" (69). Following this insight, I would like to dissociate report and invention to highlight that invention is also a resource of fictionality available to the actual author. This strategy will typically (but not always) result in a work of fiction. This insight sheds new light on some of the questions that texts like *A Million Little Pieces* pose to narrative theory. Due to its ambiguous generic affiliation, *A Million Little Pieces* can serve as a triple test case:

(1) If it is read as fiction, it will come across as authoritative, because it looks like many other fictional first-person narratives, using simultaneous narration and other techniques of fictionalization. It does not break any contemporary norms, and it does not mark the "narrator" as unreliable according to current conventions for fictional first-person narratives. It is also worth noting that readers are used to fictional first-person narratives that reliably recount information which exceeds what a real person can remember. However, in Frey's case, the author does nothing to pretend that a narrator is speaking to someone. As a person in the narrative, "the narrator" makes referential statements in his interactions with other characters, but the text never suggests that the narrator is—during or after the events—narrating the narrative to an addressee. The narrative is obviously the creation of the author, rather than something the character says, thinks, or even knows. If we read this text as fiction, we assume that the author has created a world that we should trust. In this case, the act of communication takes place between the author and the reader.

(2) On the other hand, if the narrative is read as nonfiction, we may question the accuracy of the narrative, and perhaps even investigate the facts, as did *The Smoking Gun.* There is, then, no narrator other than the author him-

self. We might argue that James Frey is the narrator in the sense of Lejeune's formula: "narrator = author." The author then clearly uses techniques of fictionalization to get his story across, but this need not change the readers' view that what they are reading is essentially a true, an exaggerated or possibly even untrue story about the life of the author. In this case, the act of communication takes place between the author and the reader as well.

(3) Whereas overdetermined narratives arguably urge readers to read them as both fictional and nonfictional, underdetermined narratives seem to invite different readings at different times. Notwithstanding, in Frey as well as in Ellis, a third reading with a double vision—as proposed by Lanser—is possible. In fact, any reading that sees the book as being purely referential or purely non-referential will miss something. A reading of *Lunar Park* as pure fiction will have to play down some of its most essential messages about addiction and how to overcome it, not to mention the many striking similarities between character and author, including the name. Similarly, a reading of *A Million Little Pieces* that does not take into account its techniques of fictionalization and its (re)invention of dialogues and events will miss some of the premises that are actually visible in the narrative itself. If the reader assumes that there is an equivocal attachment between the textual "I" and the real author, then the narrative is read as true communication from author to reader about the author's life (maybe telling important things about this life even as it occasionally deviates from biographical truth) *as well as* a form of fictional communication from author to reader about the life of a heavy substance abuser. The author shares the name and the first-person pronoun with this abuser, but not all of his experiences.

It is important to note that the differences between the three reading strategies one could adopt towards *A Million Little Pieces* do not include differences as to whether a concept of a narrator is needed to describe the narrative. In each case, the communication is from author to reader. One could decide to read the narrative as fiction and *a posteriori* assume the existence of a narrator, but it is not possible to verify the existence of a narrator by means of intratextual features and to then determine the status of the narrative as fiction. Whether we read the book as fiction or not, and whether we assume the existence of a narrator or not, we cannot find realistic explanations for the passages describing things of which the character is unaware. Nor will we be able to explain the conversations and renderings of dialogues that no narrator, character, or author could possibly remember. In short: deciding pro or contra fiction or pro or contra narrator will not really prove helpful in explaining the techniques and style used in the bulk of the book.

UNNATURAL NARRATION

I have argued that underdetermined and overdetermined narratives pose a problem to any theory that acknowledges distinctions between fiction and nonfiction but grounds the decision in paratextual information. I also pointed to the potential problems in explaining the narration of something a narrator could not know or need not tell. Third, I tried to demonstrate that the concepts of author and narrator have been used to mutually explain an absence of communication in the other and therefore to avoid the problem of narration without communication. The lesson from *A Million Little Pieces* is threefold: first, the narrative is openly fiction*alized;* second, this fact does not automatically turn the book into pure fiction; and, third, the fictionalization cannot helpfully be explained by assuming the existence of a narrator other than the author. In fact, any rhetorical approach that takes narration to be report will—among other problems—encounter a major difficulty in *A Million Little Pieces*. The narrative cannot be communication from the author, since he is not now experiencing what is narrated; nor can it be communication from a narrator, since he is not now narrating what is experienced. I will conclude by suggesting that there is a way of approaching these problems that is more helpful than trying to decide the text's fictional status, or assuming a narrator between the author and the narrative. This suggestion is simply that not all narration is report and communication.

As a beginning, let us note that relevance theory, as put forward by Walsh, is compatible with Lanser's idea of double vision and equivocal attachment. Some narratives will prompt assumptions of fictionality and nonfiction alike. Such a narrative was designed—whether intentionally or not—by the author. Let us then reconsider Phelan's suggestion that narrative "can be fruitfully understood as a rhetorical act: somebody telling somebody else on some occasion and for some purpose(s) that something happened" (2005: 18). It is reasonable to argue that a negation of any segment on the right side of the equation may not lead to a negation of *narrative,* but more precisely to a negation of *communication.* In my opinion, Phelan's formula is accurate—necessary as well as sufficient—as a definition of (conscious human) communication, but it is not a definition of narrative. What he really defines is not narrative, but conscious human communication. I want to argue instead that non-communication is a resource of fictionality available to the real author. Frey, like any other author, can opt for or against any technique of fictionality—one of these being non-communicational narration.

If we maintain the difference between fiction and fictionality, we find that invention and non-communication can be described as resources of fictionality, even though they do not belong exclusively to fiction. As argued above, fictionality is also a local quality of a narrative. Not all nonfiction refrains from techniques of fictionality, and not all fiction employs such techniques. This being said, it seems to me that to describe non-communication (in the very inclusive form of all sorts of narration that transcend Phelan's formula of somebody telling somebody else that something happened) as a resource of fictionality available to the author is an economical way of describing a very distinctive feature in much fiction.

Let me return briefly to the example of falling asleep: "I fade in and out. The TV is narcotic. In and out. In. Out. In. Out" (Frey 2003: 286). Irrespective of the global status of the narrative as fiction, this is not communication.[31] The reasons include the fact that there is no one to tell, and no one with a conscious mind able to do the telling. In fictionalized narrative neither of the two parties necessary for communication (sender and receiver) needs to be present. It can be argued that some form of communication may also exist between, say, neurons or bacteria, and obviously between animals, without it necessarily entailing a "purpose" or a report "that something happened." However, I have never encountered a definition of communication that did not include two parties in the form of a sender and a receiver. To what extent they need a shared cognitive environment, a channel, a message, a purpose, and so forth is beside the point I am making here: if nothing happened or no one recounted it, or if it is not told to anyone, there could still be narration but not communication.[32]

While the narrative in texts of this nature can *globally* be considered a form of communication from author to reader, this global narrative may include local non-communication rather than a report from an unwitting narrator. It may, for example, include narration that is unnatural, in the simple sense that it transcends the norms of everyday conversation and communication, and in the sense that it is without sender or receiver, without narrator or narratee. While much attention has been given to oral language as a prototype for literary and written narrative (Fludernik 1996), it should be noted that written narrative lends itself more easily to non-communication, for the simple reason that it is more detachable from the enunciator of an utterance in time and space than is spoken language. Communicational models face

---

31. The comical qualities of this passage when read aloud reveal that this is a curious form of narration. The words form, quite literally "unspeakable sentences."

32. In this respect my proposal is very similar to Monika Fludernik's suggestions in *Towards a 'Natural' Narratology*, where she defines narrativity as centering on experientiality (1996: 26) and as always implying the consciousness of a protagonist (30). For Fludernik "no teller is necessary" (26) for narrativity.

difficulties with regard to some narratives. By understanding all narratives (fictional and nonfictional, fictionalized and nonfictionalized alike) along the lines of a communication model, we run the risk of modeling the subject after the model, instead of vice versa (Richardson 2006: 139ff.).

The concept of the narrator can be a helpful tool for the interpretation of a text. Many narratives firmly attach words, thoughts, and opinions to narrators which are quite different from their authors. It therefore makes sense to talk about narrators. It is perfectly possible to refer to James Frey as the narrator of *A Million Little Pieces,* and to Bret Easton Ellis as the narrator of *Lunar Park*. However, this does not solve questions raised by the non-report of the author in fictionalized narratives. Since narrators as "agents" do not invent, they cannot help to explain passages that are—inside fiction itself— obviously invented and not reported. Putting all parts of a fiction "in the mouth" of a narrator brings with it a double problem in fictionalized narratives since it tends to deprive them of their distinctive fictionality without really explaining what the positing of a narrator was meant to explain: the absence of report in the author's narrative.

Having said that the author uses unnatural narration as part of the global communication of the narrative to the reader, the question is with what terms to best describe that type of narration. What is the relation between authorial communication and unnatural narration? Turning back to Phelan's account of disclosure functions and narrator functions one could say that in unnatural narration, the disclosure functions proceed not along the narrator-authorial audience track but the author-authorial audience track as the author, in the interest of disclosure, violates the limits of narratorial communication. Compared to the description quoted above with the two tracks consisting of the narrator-narratee track and the narrator-authorial audience track, this seems to me a welcome addition. I much prefer the description that the author violates the limits of narratorial communication over the description that the narrator unwittingly reports information since I believe that there is no report at the local level and at the level of the character-narrator. In this respect, then, Phelan's model and my own model converge. And this convergence reinforces the idea that the author and not the narrator is necessary to explain the specific phenomena discussed.

The global communication from author to reader exists in *any* written narrative whether natural or unnatural, mimetic or non-mimetic, fictional or nonfictional. This description hardly captures the specificity of the mentioned passage in the "fictional present" and the consequences of using techniques of fictionality and unnatural narration. To do this, I believe, we have to disentangle the words from a narrator. The author violates the limits of narratorial communication, but also of real-world discourse. It is a moment of fictional invention (whether the narrative is globally a fiction or not), not a moment of report by the character-narrator. Attributing the words to the author is correct but only in the sense that he is producing a fictionalized passage in a way that is not reducible to naturally recurring oral discourse.

The real author may or may not choose to construct the narrative in such a way that a narrator addresses a narratee. And having chosen to construct a narrator, the author may or may not limit the narration to telling what this narrator would be likely to know. The unnatural features of non-communication (no one telling anyone on any occasion and for any reason about any events) are neither necessary nor sufficient features ontologically or generically in fiction, but they *are* features of fictionality.

My proposal has the advantage of acknowledging the ability of authors to employ such features of their choosing, as well as their ability to transcend normal communication and the rules governing conversation or storytelling from narrator to narratee. This ability to go beyond communicational models is paradoxically, yet completely logically, possessed by no narrator understood within the framework of the very same communicational model.[33]

It seems important to acknowledge that the explanatory power of communicational models is great, but limited in relation to the sum of all narratives. Some narratives are natural, others are not. If we analyze all narratives according to the same model, we oversimplify matters. It would seem that an important task for narrative theory is to develop models that account for the specific properties of storyworlds, of experientiality, and of representations and narratives that resist description and understanding based on linguistic understandings of natural, oral communication.

As I have shown, narration cannot always be understood according to the rules of communicational discourse. Furthermore, this fact ties narration more closely to its flesh-and-blood author. Far from being deprived of responsibility, this author is responsible for all his/her choices, including the possible choice of techniques of fictionalization and of non-communicative passages or whole narratives. To realize the full potential of authors, we should "employ" rather than "imply" them.

---

33. In this article I have limited myself to claiming that there are features of fictionality that the concept of the narrator will obscure rather than explain. In a broader context there is no denying that I also agree with Walsh on his more general point that "[. . .] the narrator is always either a character who narrates, or the author" (Walsh 2007: 78).

REFERENCES

Alber, Jan (2009) "Impossible Storyworlds—and What to Do with Them." *Storyworlds: A Journal of Narrative Studies* 1.1: 79–96.
Alber, Jan, Stefan Iversen, Henrik Skov Nielsen, and Brian Richardson (2010) "Unnatural Narratology: Beyond Mimetic Models." *Narrative* 18.2: 113–26.
Banfield, Ann (1982) *Unspeakable Sentences: Narration and Representation in the Language of Fiction*. Boston: Routledge & Kegan Paul.
Barthes, Roland (2004) "The Death of the Author [1967]." *Authorship. From Plato to the Postmodern: A Reader*. Ed. Sean Burke. Edinburgh: Edinburgh University Press. 125–30.
Cohn, Dorrit (1999) *The Distinction of Fiction*. Baltimore: Johns Hopkins University Press.
Doubrovsky, Serge (1977) *Fils*. Paris: Éditions Galilées.
Ellis, Bret Easton (2005) *Lunar Park*. New York: Vintage.
Fludernik, Monika (1996) *Towards a 'Natural' Narratology*. London: Routledge.
——— (2001) "Fiction vs. Non-Fiction: Narratological Diffentiations." *Erzählen und Erzähltheorie im 20. Jahrhundert. Festschrift für Wilhelm Füger*. Ed. Jörg Helbig. Heidelberg: Winter. 85–103.
——— (2006) *Einführung in die Erzähltheorie*. Darmstadt: Wissenschaftliche Buchgesellschaft.
Frey, James (2003) *A Million Little Pieces*. New York: Random House.
Genette, Gérard (1980) *Narrative Discourse* [1972]. New York: Cornell University Press.
——— (1988) *Narrative Discourse Revisited* [1983]. New York: Cornell University Press.
——— (1993) *Fiction & Diction* [1991]. Ithaca and London: Cornell University Press.
——— (1997) *Paratexts: Thresholds of Interpretation* [1987]. Cambridge: Cambridge University Press.
Herman, David (2007) Ed. *The Cambridge Companion to Narrative*. Cambridge: Cambridge University Press.
Lanser, Susan (2005) "The 'I' of the Beholder: Equivocal Attachments and the Limits of Structuralist Narratology." *A Companion to Narrative Theory*. Eds. James Phelan and Peter Rabinowitz. Malden: Blackwell. 206–19.
Lejeune, Philippe (1975) *Le pacte autobiographique*. Paris: Seuil.
Löschnigg, Martin (1999) "Narratological Categories and the (Non-)Distinction Between Factual and Fictional Narratives." *Recent Trends in Narratological Research. Papers from the Narratological Round-Table ESSE4—September 1997—Debrecen, Hungary, and Other Contributions*. Ed. John Pier. Tours: Université François Rabelais. 31–48.
McHale, Brian (1987) *Postmodernist Fiction*. New York: Methuen.
Nielsen, Henrik Skov (forthcoming) "What's in a Name? Double Exposures in *Lunar Park*." *Bret Easton Ellis*. Ed. Naomi Mandel. London and New York: Continuum.
Phelan, James (1996) *Narrative as Rhetoric: Technique, Audiences, Ethics, Ideology*. Columbus: The Ohio State University Press.
——— (2005) *Living to Tell About It: A Rhetoric and Ethics of Character Narration*. Ithaca and London: Cornell University Press.
——— (2007) *Experiencing Fiction: Judgments, Progressions, and the Rhetorical Theory of Narrative*. Columbus: The Ohio State University Press.

Phelan, James, and Peter Rabinowitz (2005) Eds. *A Companion to Narrative Theory.* Malden: Blackwell.

Phelan, James, Robert Scholes, and Robert Kellogg (2006) *The Nature of Narrative.* 2nd ed. New York: Oxford University Press.

Pier, John, and Jean-Marie Schaeffer (2005) Eds. *Entorses au pacte de la représentation.* Paris: École des Hautes Études en Sciences Sociales.

Richardson, Brian (2006) *Unnatural Voices: Extreme Narration in Modern and Contemporary Fiction.* Columbus: The Ohio State University Press.

Ryan, Marie-Laure (1991) *Possible Worlds, Artificial Intelligence, and Narrative Theory.* Bloomington: Indiana University Press.

——— (1997) "Postmodernism and the Doctrine of Panfictionality." *Narrative* 5.2: 165–87.

Walsh, Richard (2007) *The Rhetoric of Fictionality: Narrative Theory and the Idea of Fiction.* Columbus: The Ohio State University Press.

Contributors

JAN ALBER is assistant professor in the English Department at the University of Freiburg (Germany), where he teaches English literature and film. He is the author of a critical monograph entitled *Narrating the Prison: Role and Representation in Charles Dickens' Novels, Twentieth-Century Fiction, and Film* (Cambria Press, 2007) and the editor/co-editor of collections such as *Stones of Law, Bricks of Shame: Narrating Imprisonment in the Victorian Age* (University of Toronto Press, 2009), *Unnatural Narratology* (de Gruyter, forthcoming), and *Why Study Literature?* (Aarhus University Press, forthcoming). Alber has also authored and co-authored articles that were published or are forthcoming in such international journals as *Dickens Studies Annual, The Journal of Popular Culture, Narrative, Short Story Criticism, Storyworlds,* and *Style*. In 2007, he received a scholarship from the German Research Foundation (DFG) which allowed him to spend a year at The Ohio State University doing research under the auspices of Project Narrative. His new research project focuses on unnatural (i.e., physically or logically impossible) scenarios and events in fiction and drama.

MONIKA FLUDERNIK is professor of English literature at the University of Freiburg, Germany. She is the author of *The Fictions of Language and the Languages of Fiction* (Routledge, 1993), *Towards a 'Natural' Narratology* (Routledge, 1996), which was awarded the Perkins Prize by the Society for the Study of Narrative Literature (SSNL), *Echoes and Mirrorings: Gabriel Josipovici's Creative Oeuvre* (Lang, 2000), and *An Introduction to Narratology* (Routledge, 2009). She has edited special issues on second-person fiction (*Style* 28.3, 1994), on "Language and Literature" (*EJES* 2.2, 1998), on "Metaphor and Beyond: New Cognitive Developments" (with Donald and Margaret Freeman, *Poetics Today* 20.3, 1999), and on German narratology (with Uri Margolin, *Style* 48.2–3, 2004). Further publications include collections of essays (e.g., *Hybridity and Postcolonialism: Twentieth-Century Indian Literature,*

1998; *Diaspora and Multiculturalism: Common Traditions and New Developments*, 2003; and *In the Grip of the Law: Trials, Prisons and the Space Between*, with Greta Olson, 2004). Her articles include papers on expatriate Indian literature in English, British aesthetics in the eighteenth century, and narratological questions. Work in progress concerns prison settings and prison metaphors in English literature and the development of narrative structure in English literature between 1250 and 1750.

DAVID HERMAN teaches in the English Department at The Ohio State University. The editor of the *Frontiers of Narrative* book series and the journal *Storyworlds*, he has published a number of studies on interdisciplinary narrative theory, narrative and mind, storytelling across media, modern and postmodern fiction, and other topics.

SUSAN S. LANSER is professor of English, Comparative Literature, and Women's and Gender Studies at Brandeis University. She is the author of *The Narrative Act: Point of View in Prose Fiction* (1981) and *Fictions of Authority: Women Writers and Narrative Voice* (1992), and the co-editor of *Women Critics 1660–1820: An Anthology* (1995) and *Letters Written in France* (2001). Lanser has published numerous articles in journals such as *Style, Eighteenth-Century Studies, Feminist Studies, Textual Practice, Semeia, Eighteenth-Century Life*, the *Journal of Homosexuality*, the *Journal of American Folklore*, and *Novel* and in books including *The Faces of Anonymity, Reconsidering the Bluestockings, Blackwell Companion to Narrative Theory*, and *Singlewomen in the European Past*. Her research interests include narrative theory, the novel, eighteenth-century cultural studies, the history of gender and sexuality, and the French Revolution. Lanser is currently completing a book entitled *The Sexuality of History: Sapphic Subjects and the Making of Modernity*.

MARTIN LÖSCHNIGG studied English and German literature and linguistics at the Universities of Graz (Austria) and Aberdeen (UK). He is currently associate professor of English, chair of the Section on the New Literatures in English, and deputy director of the Centre for Canadian Studies at Graz University. Löschnigg was a visiting scholar at the Free University of Berlin and at Harvard University in 1995 and 1996, and a visiting associate professor of English at the University of Minnesota in Minneapolis in autumn 2005. His main research interests are narrative theory, autobiography, the English novel, the literature of war, and Canadian literature. Löschnigg has published on the literature of the First World War (*Der Erste Weltkrieg in deutscher und englischer Dichtung* [1994] and *Intimate Enemies—English and German Literary Reactions to the Great War 1914–1918*, edited with Franz K. Stanzel [1993]), on fictional autobiographies (*Die englische fiktionale Autobiographie: Erzähltheoretische Grundlagen und historische Prägnanzformen von den Anfängen bis zur Mitte des neunzehnten Jahrhunderts* [2006]), and on Canadian literature with Maria Löschnigg (*Kurze Geschichte der kanadischen Literatur* [2001] and *Migration and Fiction: Narratives of Migration in Contemporary Canadian Literature* [2009]).

AMIT MARCUS studied comparative literature and philosophy at The Hebrew University of Jerusalem. He is the author of *Self-Deception in Literature and Philosophy* (Wissenschaftlicher Verlag Trier, 2007) and of several articles which were published in international journals such as the *Journal of Literary Semantics, Mosaic, Narrative, Partial Answers,* and *Style.* The main focus in his research so far has been on unreliable narration and fictional "we" narratives. He was granted a scholarship from the Minerva Foundation for the years 2006–2008 at the universities of Freiburg and Giessen, and recently received another scholarship from the Humboldt foundation for the years 2010–2012 at the University of Freiburg.

JARMILA MILDORF completed her PhD in sociolinguistics at the University of Aberdeen (Scotland) and now teaches English literature and language at the University of Paderborn (Germany). She is the author of *Storying Domestic Violence: Constructions and Stereotypes of Abuse in the Discourse of General Practitioners* (University of Nebraska Press, 2007) and she has co-edited a volume on *Magic, Science, Technology, and Literature* (2006) as well as a special issue of the journal *Partial Answers* on *Narrative: Knowing, Living, Telling* (2008). Mildorf has also published articles in collections and journals such as *The Sociology of Health and Illness, The Journal of Gender Studies, Narrative Inquiry,* and *COLLeGIUM.* Her research interests are narrative, gender studies, language and literature, and medical humanities.

HENRIK SKOV NIELSEN is professor in the Scandinavian Institute at the University of Aarhus (Denmark). He is the author of articles and books in Danish on narratology and literary theory, including his dissertation on digression and first-person narrative fiction, *Tertium datur—On Literature or on What Is Not.* His publications in English include articles on Bret Easton Ellis, Edgar Allan Poe, psychoanalysis, and extreme narration, including an article on first-person narrative fiction in *Narrative* 12.2 (2004). A recent article, "Colonised Thinking" on the US influence on the humanities in Europe was published in the *Oxford Literary Review* (2008). He is the editor of a series of anthologies on literary theory, and is currently working on a narratological research project on the relation between authors and narrators.

ALAN PALMER is an independent scholar living in London and an honorary research fellow in the Department of Linguistics and English Language at Lancaster University. His book *Fictional Minds* (University of Nebraska Press, 2004) was a co-winner of the MLA Prize for Independent Scholars and also a co-winner of the Perkins Prize (awarded by the Society for the Study of Narrative Literature). His new book, *Social Minds in the Novel,* will be published by The Ohio State University Press. He has contributed essays to the journals *Narrative, Style* and *Semiotica,* as well as chapters to *Narrative Theory and the Cognitive Sciences* (ed. David Herman), *Narratology beyond Literary Criticism* (ed. Jan Christoph Meister), *Introduction to Cognitive Cultural Studies* (ed. Lisa Zunshine), *Contemporary Stylistics* (eds. Marina Lambrou and Peter Stockwell), and *The Emergence of Mind: Representations of Consciousness in Narrative Discourse in English, 700 to the Present* (ed. David Herman). His chief areas of interest are narratology, cognitive poetics and cognitive approaches to literature, the cognitive sciences and the study of consciousness, the nineteenth-century novel, modernism, and the history of country and western music.

RICHARD WALSH is senior lecturer in English and Related Literature at the University of York, where he teaches primarily narrative theory, early film, and American literature. His first book, *Novel Arguments: Reading Innovative American Fiction* (Cambridge University Press, 1995), argued for the positive rhetorical force of nonrealist narrative modes, and opened up a line of inquiry that defined his subsequent research in the field of narrative theory. Beginning with "Who Is the Narrator?" (*Poetics Today,* 1997) and culminating in *The Rhetoric of Fictionality: Narrative Theory and the Idea of Fiction* (The Ohio State University Press, 2007), Walsh proposes a fundamental reconceptualization of the role of fictionality in narrative, and in doing so challenges many of the core assumptions of narrative theory. His current research is concerned with narrative in its broadest interdisciplinary contexts, using the concept of emergence as a way to negotiate between its ubiquity and its limitations. He is the leader of the Fictionality Research Group, and director of Narrative Research in York's Centre for Modern Studies.

WERNER WOLF is professor and chair of English and General Literature at the University of Graz (Austria). His main areas of research are literary theory (concerning aesthetic illusion, narratology, and metafiction in particular), functions of literature, eighteenth- to twenty-first-century English fiction, eighteenth- and twentieth-century drama, metareference in various arts, as well as intermediality studies. His publications include, besides numerous essays, *Ästhetische Illusion und Illusionsdurchbrechung in der Erzählkunst (Aesthetic Illusion and the Breaking of Illusion in Narrative,* 1993) and *The Musicalization of Fiction: A Study in the Theory and History of Intermediality* (1999). He is also co-editor of volumes 1, 3, 5, and 11 (forthcoming) in the book series "Word and Music Studies" (published by Rodopi), and has co-edited *Framing Borders in Literature and Other Media* (2006) and *Description in Literature and Other Media* (2007), both in the "Studies in Intermediality" series at Rodopi. Wolf is currently directing a project funded by the Austrian Science Foundation (FWF) on "Metareference in the Media," which hosted several conferences. Two proceeding volumes (also in the series "Studies in Intermidiality") were also edited by Wolf: *Metareference across Media: Theory and Case Studies* (2009) and *The Metareferential Turn in Contemporary Arts and Media: Forms, Functions, Attempts at Explanation* (forthcoming).

Author Index

2001: A Space Odyssee (Kubrick), 170
Absalom, Absalom! (Faulkner), 107
L'académie des dames ou la philosophie dans le boudoir du Grand Siècle (Chorier), 191, 193, 197
Aczel, Richard, 54n14
Adolphs, Ralph, 152
Aelred, 202
Alber, Jan, 14, 14n15, 17-18, 21, 275n3
L'Alcibiade fanciullo a scola (Rocco), 202
American Psycho (Ellis), 276, 292
Aretino, Pietro, 189-92
Arabian Nights, 38, 42-43
Aristotle, 195
Armstrong, Nancy, 188
Auerbach, Erich, 186
Austen, Jane, 200
The Autobiographical Subject (Nussbaum), 189n4
Autobiography (Mill), 264-65

Bach, Michaela, 164
Bakhtin, Mikhail, 8, 15, 52-54, 56, 94, 100, 187, 189-90, 193

Bal, Mieke, 13, 44, 105, 105n1, 116, 119-22
Balzac, Honoré de, 41
Bamberg, Michael, 13, 263
Banfield, Ann, 14, 114, 117, 123, 276n4, 282
Barrin, Jean, 191
Barry, Sebastian, 122
Barthes, Roland, 2, 166n9, 277
Bartlett, Frederick, 264
Beaujour, Michel, 261n3
A Beautiful Mind (Howard), 173, 173n19
Behn, Aphra, 202
The Belle of Belfast City (Reid), 122, 122n13
Belinda (Edgeworth), 199
Benveniste, Émile, 282
Beyond the Pleasure Principle (Jenseits des Lustprinzips) (Freud), 215n18
Billy Liar (Schlesinger), 51
Black, David A., 168
The Blair Witch Project (Myrick and Sánchez), 46
Blake, William, 17, 138-58
"The Bloody Chamber" (Carter), 108
Booth, Wayne C., 9-11, 17, 115, 166-67, 169n13, 177, 181

Author Index

Boothe, Brigitte, 13
Bordwell, David, 47n9, 163
The Bourne Identity (Liman), 171
Branigan, Edward, 47n9, 174
Bremond, Claude, 2
Bridget Jones Diary (Fielding), 201
Brooks, Peter, 262
Bruder, Gail A., 146
Bruner, Jerome, 255, 261–63, 265
Bruss, Elizabeth, 268n9
Bunyan, John, 257–58

The Cabinet of Dr. Caligari (Wiene), 171
The Cambridge Companion to Narrative (Herman), 277
Camus, Albert, 18, 209, 224–27, 230
"Camus' *Stranger* Retried" (Girard), 225
The Canterbury Tales (Chaucer), 61–62
Carter, Angela, 108, 110
Carter, Elizabeth, 196
Cat and Mouse (*Katz und Maus*) (Grass), 18, 209, 211–19, 223, 226–30
Cervantes, Miguel de, 209
Chafe, Wallace, 13
Chambers, Ross, 230–31
Chaucer, Geoffrey, 61–62
Chatman, Seymour, 2, 14, 17, 21, 105, 107, 109–11, 113–16, 118–20, 120n11, 126, 128–30, 163, 164n3, 168–69, 171–72, 244, 246
Chomsky, Noam, 109, 129
Chorier, Nicolas, 191
Cicero, 201
Cinderella, 109–10, 123
Cité des dames (Pisan), 189
Citizen Kane (Welles), 49
Clarissa (Richardson), 191, 197–200, 202
Cleland, John, 193, 199n9
A Clockwork Orange (Kubrick), 170–71
Coetzee, J. M., 290

Cohn, Dorrit, 46, 116, 276n5, 280, 290–91
Coincidence and Counterfactuality: Plotting Time and Space in Narrative Fiction (Dannenberg), 187
Come As You Are: Sexuality and Narrative (Roof), 7, 187
Coming to Terms (Chatman), 118–19
Confessions (St. Augustine), 264n6
The Confessions (Rousseau), 262, 266–67, 267n7
Conrad, Joseph, 63, 70, 78
The Coquette (Foster), 196
The Countryman and the Cinematograph (Paul), 124
Currie, Mark, 77n28, 164

Dällenbach, Lucien, 59
Dangerous Intimacies: Toward a Sapphic History of the British Novel (Moore), 187, 188n3
Dannenberg, Hilary, 187
Daphnis and Chloe (Longus), 66
"The Dead" (Joyce), 158n14
Death of a Salesman (Miller), 123
Deceit, Desire, and the Novel (Girard), 206, 210, 225, 229
Defoe, Daniel, 62
Dennett, Daniel C., 166–67, 169, 181
Dialogues of the Courtesans (Lucian), 189
Dickens, Charles, 108, 174
Diderot, Denis, 192, 199, 202
The Distinction of Fiction (Cohn), 290
Doležel, Lubomír, 12
Dostoevsky, 54, 208, 208n6, 209
Doubrovsky, Serge, 291, 291n28
Duchan, Judith F., 146

Eakin, Paul John, 255, 261–62, 269
L'école des filles, ou la philosophie des dames [*The School of Venus*] (Millot), 191n6
Edgar, David, 123

Edgeworth, Maria, 199
Edwards, Derek, 152
Edzard, Christine, 174
Erlich, Victor, 106
Eichenbaum, Boris, 106
Eliot, George, 84, 101
Ellis, Bret Easton, 276, 286, 288, 291–92, 295, 298
The Emergence of Mind (Herman), 13
Emmott, Catherine, 146, 148–49
Entertaining Strangers (Edgar), 123

The Fall (*La chute*) (Camus), 18, 209, 224–26, 227, 228, 230
Famous Last Words (Findley), 107
Farwell, Marylin, 187
Faulkner, William, 107
Fenwick, Eliza, 191, 196
Ferenz, Volker, 172–73
Fictional Minds (Palmer), 83, 85
Fielding, Helen, 201
Fielding, Henry, 117n7
Field, Todd, 158n14
Fight Club (Fincher), 174n20
Fina, Anna de, 13, 250
Findley, Timothy, 107
Fludernik, Monika, 5, 11, 13–16, 19, 22, 22n18, 45, 51n10, 107, 111n4, 186, 234, 239, 256, 259–60, 269, 277n6, 297, 297n32
Fonte, Moderata, 189
Forster, E. M., 15, 106–7
Foster, Hannah, 196
Frank, Joseph, 70
Frankenstein (Shelley), 44, 70–73, 202
Freeman, Mark, 13
The French Lieutenant's Woman (Fowles), 46, 283–84
Freud, Sigmund, 196, 211n9, 215n18, 288
Frey, James, 20, 276, 282, 284–91, 293–98
Friedemann, Käte, 112
Frow, John, 53n12
Frye, Lawrence, 217n20

Frye, Northrop, 268n9
Fury (Lang), 170

Gallagher, Philip J., 143–44, 146, 148
Gaiman, Neil, 124
Gates, Henry Louis, 8
Gaut, Berys, 164, 166, 169n13
Genet, Jean, 18, 209–10, 219–24, 226, 229–30
Genette, Gérard, 2, 8, 9, 13, 16, 21, 37–42, 44–46, 48, 55, 59, 61, 78, 106–7, 111n4, 114–15, 117–23, 128–29, 206n3, 207, 211n10, 257, 275, 276n5, 281, 291n28
Georgakopoulou, Alexandra, 13
Gibson, Andrew, 2, 3, 15, 58, 77–78
Girard, René, 15, 18, 21, 206–31
Gleckner, Robert F., 142, 142n4
Goethe, Johann Wolfgang von, 114, 202
Goffman, Erving, 61, 61n11
Goldmann, Lucien, 187
Grace Abounding to the Chief of Sinners (Bunyan), 257
Grass, Günter, 18, 209, 211–13, 215–17, 219, 223, 226, 230
Greenberg, Mark L., 142
Greimas, A. J., 2, 187
Grice, H. P., 175
Griffiths, Paul E., 152

Hale, Dorothy M., 8
Hamburger, Käte, 112, 157n13, 275n1, 282
Harré, Rom, 154, 251
Haywood, Eliza, 191, 193–94
Heart of Darkness (Conrad), 39n3, 63–64, 70–71
Heinze, Rüdiger, 14
Helbig, Jörg, 9, 174n20
Hemingway, Ernest, 151, 169, 278
Herman, David, 1–6, 6n7, 8, 11, 13, 17–19, 22n18, 23, 79, 87, 166, 239, 246–47, 264–65
Herman, Luc, 5

Hernadi, Paul, 276n5
Heterosexual Plots and Lesbian Narratives (Farwell), 187
Hewitt, Lynne E., 146
Hilliard, Kevin, 213n16, 215n18, 217n20
"Hills like White Elephants" (Hemingway), 151
Hitchcock, Alfred, 52, 165, 172
Homer, 39, 41
Hornby, Richard, 67
Hutcheon, Linda, 59, 108, 108n3, 110
Huxley, Aldous, 65–66

The Importance of Being Earnest (Wilde), 62–63
The Ingenious Hidalgo Don Quixote of La Mancha (Cervantes), 208, 208n5

Jahn, Manfred, 9, 9n10, 11, 11n13, 22n18, 46n7, 121, 121n12, 164, 169n13, 244
James, Henry, 15, 115
Jakobson, Roman, 68, 207, 213n16
Jameson, Fredric, 187
Jane Eyre (Brontë), 188, 200–201, 203, 283
Jerslev, Anne, 180
Johnson, Mark, 138
Joyce, James, 107, 158n14
Julie, ou la nouvelle Héloïse (Rousseau), 191, 197, 198–99

Keen, Suzanne, 157n13
Kellogg, Robert, 280
"The Killers" (Hemingway), 169
Kindt, Tom, 10n12, 167
Korte, Barbara, 107
Kubrick, Stanley, 165

Laas, Eva, 163n2, 173n19

Labov, William, 13, 237, 240
Lacan, Jacques, 210, 211n9
Laclos, Pierre Choderlos de, 202
Lakoff, George, 138
Lämmert, Eberhard, 2
Lang, Fritz, 165, 168
Langenhove, Luk van, 154
Lanser, Susan, 2, 7, 18, 53n13, 293, 295–96
Larroux, Guy, 64, 64n16
Die Leiden des jungen Werthers (Goethe), 202
Lejeune, Philippe, 223n25, 268n9, 270, 276n5, 280, 293, 295
Less than Zero (Ellis), 292
Lettres de Milady Juliette Catesby à Milady Henriette Campley, son amie (Riccoboni), 191, 195–97, 199–200
Levinson, Jerrold, 163n2, 164n4, 167, 169n13
Levinson, Marjorie, 186
Les liaisons dangereuses (Laclos), 202
Lieblich, Amia, 235, 237
The Life and Strange Surprising Adventures of Robinson Crusoe (Defoe), 62, 65n17, 189
Linde, Charlotte, 265
Little Children (Field), 158
Living to Tell about It (Phelan), 278
Lodge, David, 15
Longus, 66
Lost Highway (Lynch), 18, 165, 175–81
Love Letters between a Nobleman and His Sister (Behn), 202
Lucian, 189
Lukács, Georg, 187
Lunar Park (Ellis), 20, 284, 285–86, 291–93, 295, 298
Lynch, David, 18, 165, 175, 181
Lysis (Plato), 202

Mandeville, Bernard, 191n6
Marcus, Sharon, 187, 201
The Masqueraders; or, Fatal Curiosity (Haywood), 191, 193–95, 197

McHale, Brian, 14, 186, 291n20
McKeon, Michael, 188, 268
Melmoth the Wanderer (Maturin), 49–50
Memoirs of a Woman of Pleasure (Cleland), 193, 197, 199
Memoirs of Miss Sidney Bidulph (Sheridan), 191, 195–97, 200
Mercadal, Dennis, 264n5
Il merito delle donne (Fonte), 189
Metropolis (Lang), 171, 171n16
Mezei, Kathy, 7
Middlemarch (Eliot), 84–104, 201
Mill, John Stuart, 264–65, 268
A Million Little Pieces (Frey), 20, 276, 284–91, 293–98
Mimesis (Auerbach), 186–87
Mink, Louis O., 261–62, 269n11
Mitchell, W. J. T., 142n4, 144, 144n7
Moby-Dick (Melville), 49
Montaigne, Michel de, 195
Moore, Lisa, 187, 188n3
Morón Arroyo, Ciriaco, 219n21
Mrs. Dalloway (Woolf), 169, 173n19
Müller, Günther, 118
Müller, Hans-Harald, 167
Müller-Funk, Wolfgang, 263
"The Murders in the Rue Morgue" (Poe), 68–69

Narrative Discourse (Genette), 37, 38n2, 39, 207
Narrative Discourse Revisited (Genette), 40
Narrative Fiction: Contemporary Poetics (Rimmon-Kenan), 2
Narratologies: New Perspectives on Narrative Analysis (Herman), 1–2
Nathan, Daniel O., 165, 168n11
The Nature of Narrative (Scholes and Kellogg), 280
Le neveu de Rameau (Diderot), 202
Nielsen, Henrik Skov, 14, 20
Nietzsche, Friedrich, 151, 220
Nobody's Fault and *Little Dorrit's Story* (Edzard), 174

Nocturnes for the King of Naples (White), 8
Notes from Underground (Dostoevsky), 54
Nünning, Ansgar, 5–6, 13, 22, 119, 187
Nussbaum, Felicity, 189n4

Odyssey (Homer), 38
Olney, James, 261, 269, 269n11
Olson, Greta, 173n18
Once upon a Time in the West (Leone), 51

Page, Ruth, 7
Pallavicino, Ferrante, 191n6
Palmer, Alan, 12, 15–16, 22, 165, 166–67, 169, 175, 177, 181
Pamela (Richardson), 188, 199
Patron, Sylvie, 123
Pascal, Roy, 52
Paul, R.W., 124
Pavel, Thomas, 2
Le Père Goriot (Balzac), 41
Perkins Gilman, Charlotte, 201
Persuasion (Austen), 99
Petsch, Robert, 112
Petzold, Jochen, 22
Pfister, Manfred, 113
Phelan, James, 9–11, 15n17, 17, 181, 276n3, 277–82, 296–98
Phillips, Michael, 140
Philosophie dans le boudoir (Sade), 191, 193
Pier, John, 291n20
Pisan, Christine de, 189
Plato 16, 36, 38–39, 41, 45–47, 55, 109, 189, 201–2
Poe, Edgar Allan, 68
Point Counter Point (Huxley), 65–66
The Political Unconscious: Narrative as a Socially Symbolic Act (Jameson), 187
Potter, Jonathan, 239

Pratt, Marie-Louise 175
"Preface" (Shelley), 73
Pride and Prejudice (Austen), 200
Prince, Gerald, 2, 114n5, 207, 221
Proust, Marcel, 209–10, 212n13, 226

Rabinowitz, Peter, 9–10, 154n12
Ragionamenti (Aretino), 189
A Raw Youth (Dostoyevsky), 209n6
Reed, Jeremy, 221n22, 223n23
À la recherche du temps perdu (Proust), 210
Reid, Christina, 122
La religieuse (Diderot), 192, 199
Remembering: A Study in Experimental and Social Psychology (Bartlett), 264
Rentz, Kathryn C., 238
La retorica delle puttane (Pallavicino), 191n6
Le rêve d'Alembert (Diderot), 202
The Rhetoric of Fictionality (Walsh), 10n12, 15, 123, 281, 294
Ricardou, Jean, 59–60
Riccoboni, Marie-Jeanne, 191, 195
Richardson, Alan, 137
Richardson, Brian, 8, 14, 39n4, 46n7, 47n8, 275n3, 280, 280n12
Richardson, Samuel, 191, 197–99
Ricoeur, Paul, 108, 261–62, 268n9
Riessman, Catherine Kohler, 234, 236
Rimmon-Kenan, Shlomith, 2, 21, 77, 81, 119, 206n3, 211n10, 215n18, 227, 247
The Rise of the Novel (Watt), 187
Rocco, Antonio, 202
Romeo and Juliet (Shakespeare), 65
Ronen, Ruth, 12
Roof, Judith, 7, 187
Rousseau, Jean-Jacques 191, 197–98, 262, 266–67, 267n7
The Rules of Attraction (Ellis), 292
Ryan, Judith, 212n14
Ryan, Marie-Laure, 9, 12, 42–43, 125, 282–85

Sade, Donatien Alphonse François, Marquis de, 193
Sandman (Gaiman), 124
Saussure, Ferdinand de, 11, 146
Schaeffer, Jean-Marie, 291n20
Schmid, Wolf, 111n4
Schneider, Ralf, 11, 22
Scholes, Robert, 280
Searle, John, 40n5, 156
Secresy, or The Ruin on the Rock (Fenwick), 191, 196–97
The Secret Life of Walter Mitty (McLeod), 51
Sedgwick, Eve Kosofsky, 211
Segal, Erwin M., 147
Sense and Sensibility (Austen), 200
Shakespeare, William, 65, 67
Shaw, George Bernard, 128
Shelley, Mary, 44, 70, 202
Shelley, Percy Bysshe, 73
Sheridan, Frances, 191, 195
Sheringham, Michael, 270
Shklovsky, Victor, 4, 106–7, 113
Sir Charles Grandison (Richardson), 199
Smith, Barbara Herrnstein, 17, 109–10, 123, 128–29
Smith, Murray, 175, 177n24
Smith, Sidonie, and Julia Watson, 257, 268n9
The Smoking Gun, 286–87, 294
Songs of Innocence and Experience (Blake), 139, 142, 142n4
Spielhagen, Friedrich, 112
Sperber, Dan, 251n3, 294
Sprinker, Michael, 255
Stage Fright (Hitchcock), 172
Stanzel, Franz Karl, 2, 8, 16, 21, 37, 44, 46, 105–6, 111–19, 121, 126–30
Stearns, Carol, 152
Stearns, Peter, 152
Steen, Francis, 137
Sternberg, Meir, 2
Sternlieb, Lisa, 201
Stoppard, Tom, 122
Story and Discourse (Chatman), 2, 107, 109, 118–19

Story and Situation (Chambers), 230–31
The Stranger (*L'étranger*) (Camus), 225
The Steward of Christendom (Barry), 122, 122n13
Sturges, Robert, 201–2
Swift, Graham, 271

Tajfel, Henri, 246
Talese, Nan, 289
Talmy, Leonard, 138
The Taming of the Shrew (Shakespeare), 67
Tannen, Deborah, 13, 239, 242–43
The Temptations of Big Bear (Wiebe), 107
A Theory of Narrative (*Theorie des Erzählens*) (Stanzel), 45
The Thief's Journal (*Journal du voleur*) (Genet), 18, 209, 219–24, 226–27, 229–30
Thomson-Jones, Katherine, 164
Todorov, Tzvetan, 2, 2n2, 177n25, 277
Tom Jones (Fielding), 40, 123
To the Lighthouse (Woolf), 151
Towards a 'Natural' Narratology (Fludernik), 116, 126, 259, 297n32
Travesties (Stoppard), 122
Tristram Shandy (Sterne), 107, 113
Turner, Mark, 137–39, 146
Tuval-Mashiach, Rivka, 235, 237

Ulysses (Joyce), 39, 42, 107
Unnatural Voices (Richardson), 275n3, 280n12
Unspeakable Sentences (Banfield), 14, 282
The Usual Suspects (Singer), 172

Vénus dans le cloître, ou, La religieuse en chemise: entretiens curieux (Barrin), 191–92, 197
Vertigo (Hitchcock), 52n11

Vervaeck, Bart, 5
Veyne, Paul, 108
Vieux Carré (Williams), 123
Violence and the Sacred (*La violence et le sacré*) (Girard), 213n15
The Virgin Unmask'd: or, Female Dialogues Betwixt an Elderly Maiden Lady and her Niece (Mandeville), 191n6

Waiting for the Barbarians (Coetzee), 290
Walsh, Richard, 10n12, 14–17, 22, 109–10, 123–25, 127, 130, 169n14, 277, 280–81, 294, 296, 299n25
Warhol, Robyn, 7
Waterland (Swift), 271
Watt, Ian, 187
Werth, Paul, 146
White, Edmund, 8
White, Hayden, 109, 114n5, 269n11, 280
The Whores Rhetorick: Calculated to the Meridian of London (Pallavicino), 191n6
Wiebe, Rudy, 107
Wilde, Oscar, 62–63
Williams, Linda Ruth, 264
Williams, Tennessee, 123
Wilson, Deirdre, 251n3, 294
Wilson, George, 164
Winfrey, Oprah, 285n17, 286, 289
Wolf, Werner, 9, 13–16, 22, 116
Woolf, Virginia, 83n1, 151, 169, 173n19

Yacobi, Tamar, 216n19
"The Yellow Wallpaper" (Perkins Gilman), 201
You Only Live Once (Lang), 168

Zilber, Tamar, 235, 237
Zunshine, Lisa, 12, 22n18, 165

Subject Index

act: cognitive, 51; communicative, 35, 42-43, 150, 175; discursive, 48; fictive, 46; linguistic, 46; narrative, 35, 38, 42-44, 261; narrational, 115, 119, 128, 154; of fictive representation, 41; of imitation, 41; of narration, 38, 40, 41, 113-14, 116, 128, 140, 148, 222-23, 226, 230; of narrative representation, 16, 36, 48, 55
action(s), 95, 106-7, 153, 155, 171, 192, 216, 236, 242-43, 247. *See also* event and *Geschehen*
action movie, 165n7
adaptation, 108n3, 158n14, 174
agency, 16, 36-37, 46-47, 55
anachrony (Genette), 107
anagnorisis, 209
analepsis, 62, 108. *See also* flashback
anti-illusionism (Wolf), 13-14
anti-mimeticism, 14-15
attribution theory, 97, 99-100
audience: authorial, 7, 10, 177, 298
author: death of (Barthes), 277; implied, 10, 10n12, 13-14, 14n14, 17, 47n9, 119, 123, 166-67, 169n13, 181, 267n5, 279; real, 10, 114, 166, 276, 286, 292-94, 292n30, 299

autobiographical pact/contract (Lejeune), 233, 270, 293
autobiography, 3-4, 9, 19-20, 73, 189, 189n4, 219, 220, 223, 223n35, 230, 255-71, 276; fictionality of, 266-70; nineteenth-century, 265; postmodern, 267
autofiction, 291, 291n28, 292, 292n30

beginning/ending, 11, 237

captions, 168, 170, 171
canon, 39, 39n4, 108, 150, 199
categorical vs. holistic, 235, 237
character(s), 7, 10, 12, 18, 36, 41, 46, 49, 50-53, 55, 73, 87, 91, 97-99, 108, 108n3, 113, 115-16, 118-26, 130, 140, 149-51, 154, 156, 159, 167, 174, 174n19, 175, 179, 181, 188, 192, 199, 206-7, 208n4, 210-11, 220, 225, 227-31, 242-43, 245, 250, 291n28, 292, 292n30, 294-95; character-narrator, 168, 171-72, 172n17, 299; character perspective, 44-45; narrating char-

acter, 49, 53, 211, 211n10, 212n14, 213, 216, 218, 220–26, 228; town as character, 84–85. *See also* protagonist
characterization, 16, 49, 55, 83
chronotope (Bahktin), 191, 192
close-up, 120–22, 126, 178n26
closure, 198–99, 209; lack of, 192, 216, 216n19
coding, 61–63, 65, 67, 74–75
cognitive: approach, 12, 17, 22, 83, 158, 166; functioning, 84, 94, 97; narrative, 97–98, 101–3; revolution, 137; terms, 56, 85
communicative functions (Jakobson), 207; conative, 207; phatic, 207, 244, 248; poetic, 68, 213n16
communicative model, 15, 35, 39–41, 44–45, 47, 55; in film, 47n9
configuration (Ricoeur), 108
conflict, 94, 101, 144n6, 146
consciousness, 13, 83, 85, 93, 95, 116, 126, 130, 140, 145, 251, 259–60, 263–64, 269, 297n32; center of consciousness (James), 115–16; continuing-consciousness frame (Palmer), 166–67, 169, 175, 177, 181; narrative and consciousness, 155–57
content (vs. form), 18, 48, 65, 74, 79, 155–56, 186–88, 191n6, 198, 202–3, 226, 235, 237, 263; manifest, 193
conversation analysis, 13
credits: opening credits, 170; final credits, 170
culturalist approach, 58, 78
cut, 168, 170, 178n26

death principle (Freud), 215
decoding, 74
deictic center, 116, 123, 146n8
deictic shift theory, 146–47
deictic transfer, 249
descriptivity, 60
desire, 176, 179, 202, 207, 210, 211n9, 212; desired object/object of desire, 195, 206, 208, 208n4, 214, 218, 219n21; desiring subject, 206, 206n1, 208–11, 214–16, 218, 219n21, 220, 223, 226–28; gay, 202; lesbian, 18, 188, 190, 193, 195, 198, 200–202; mimetic/triangular/metaphysical (Girard), 206–10, 206n1, 213–18, 219, 220, 222–24, 226, 227–31; theory of (Lacan), 210
dialogic, 53–54, 56, 234; sapphic, 186–205
dialogue, 18, 54, 89, 126, 129, 189–93, 228, 248–49, 290, 295; constructed dialogue (Tannen), 242, 247; male-male, 201; pederastic, 202
diégèse (Genette), 39, 39n3, 40–41. *See also* diegetic universe and storyworld
diegesis (vs. mimesis) (Plato), 16, 36, 38–47, 49–51, 52n11, 53, 55. *See also* telling
diegetic universe (vs. screen universe) (Souriau), 39, 40, 85. See also *diégèse* and storyworld
direct thought, 85. *See also* interior monologue
direct speech, 89, 242–43
discourse (Foucault), 53, 282; autobiographical, 19, 256, 261, 263, 265, 269–70; character, 46; direct (Cohn), 46, 245; double-voiced (Bakhtin), 52, 54; face-to-face, 138, 146; filmic, 36–37, 47; neo-colonial, 8; oral, 50, 299; practices, 139, 150, 152, 154; real-world, 20, 299; representational, 48–50
discourse analysis, 13, 235
discourse environment, 157
discursive event, 35
discursive subject, 48–49, 52, 55
discursive rhythm, 91
double deixis (Herman), 19, 235, 241, 246, 247, 251
drama, 9, 16, 21, 37, 46, 65, 67, 105, 113–15, 121–24, 126–28

Subject Index 317

duration (Genette), 118n9

emplotment (White), 269n11
empty center (Banfield), 117
Erzählzeit (Müller) (narrating or discourse time), 118, 118n9, 192
erzählte Zeit (Müller) (narrated or story time), 118, 118n9, 192
ethical judgments, 10
evaluation, 72, 116, 237, 242
event, 6n7, 14, 38–41, 46, 49, 89, 107–9, 111n4, 113, 119–20, 129, 138n1, 143, 144n6, 146–52, 155–57, 158n14, 175, 177n25, 188, 192, 197, 199, 200, 207, 210, 217, 217n20, 222, 225, 227, 236–37, 244, 249, 260–64, 279, 290, 292, 294–95, 299; heterosexual, 194. *See also* action(s) and *Geschehen*
experiencing I (vs. narrating I), 19, 147–48, 155. *See also* experiencing self
experiencing self (vs. narrating self), 227, 243, 246, 248–49, 257. *See also* experiencing I
experientiality (Fludernik), 19, 22, 117, 129, 256–57, 259–60, 264, 269, 275n1, 297n32, 299

fabula (vs. *syuzhet*), 47n9, 105n1, 106, 110, 124, 158. See also *Geschichte, histoire,* and story
family storytelling, 241, 243, 246
feminism, 53n13, 59, 59n2, 108, 208n4; proto-feminism, 189, 201
fictive, 35, 38n2, 40–46, 48, 210, 294
fictivity, 157
fiction: as a form of communication, 276, 298; etymological root of, 275; vs. nonfiction, 276–77, 279–80, 284, 287, 296; fictional present (Cohn), 290, 298 (*see also* present-tense narration and simultaneous narration)

fictionality, 19–21, 37, 41–42, 45–47, 47n9, 55, 124, 256, 265, 267, 269–70, 282, 291n28, 294, 296–99, 299n33; signposts of (Cohn), 280
fictionalization: techniques of, 20, 276, 280, 290–91, 294–96, 299
filter (Chatman) (vs. slant), 19, 107, 119, 120n11, 130, 155, 188, 192, 200, 235, 244–46, 250
fiktionales Erzählen (Hamburger), 282
filmic composition device (FCD) (Jahn), 164, 169n13
filmmaker: hypothetical (Alber), 167–77, 179, 180–81; implied, 17, 164, 166–67, 169, 175, 177, 181; real, 166–67, 175
flashback, 125, 129, 172, 179. *See also* analepsis
focalization (Bal), 13, 44, 105, 105n1, 120–22
focalization (Genette), 9n10, 13, 16, 19, 36–37, 44, 51n10, 51–53, 56, 83–84, 87, 93–94, 97, 105–9, 111, 114–15, 117–22, 117n7, 125, 127–30, 210, 235, 239, 241, 244, 249, 251, 257; ambient (Jahn), 121, 121n12; external (Genette), 117n7, 119, 128–29, 169; external in film, 120–21, 169, 174; heterogeneous, 93–94; homogeneous, 93; hypothetical (Herman), 87; internal (Genette), 44, 51, 53, 114, 117n7, 122, 128, 130, 155, 210; internal in film, 120–21, 173–74, 174n19, 174n20; intermental (Palmer), 84, 93; intramental (Palmer), 93; multiple, 93; single, 93–94; strict (Jahn), 121, 121n12; weak (Jahn), 121, 121n12; zero (Genette), 115, 118n7, 120, 122, 128–29
focalizer, 93–94, 120, 122, 244; in film, 173, 174n19, 174n20
folk psychology, 164, 164n6, 181
folk theory of discourse, 151
foreshadowing, 63, 65–66, 69, 70,

71n22, 73–75, 75n27, 77. See also
  prolepsis
form (vs. content), 186–88, 192, 203, 237
frame (cognitive), 11, 11n13, 22, 59–69,
  71–72, 74–75, 77–78, 116–17, 120,
  124–26, 128, 147, 149, 168, 175,
  237, 246, 256–57, 259–60, 263,
  264n5, 270–71. See also schemata
frame narrative, 61–73, 78
frame theory, 59–60, 61n10; contextual
  (Emmot), 146, 148, 263
free indirect discourse, 36–37, 51–52,
  56, 97, 120–22, 158n14, 239, 245,
  249, 251, 282
free indirect thought, 85, 97

gender, 2, 4, 7–8, 11, 15, 18, 21, 59n2,
  188–89, 192, 200–202, 207, 251,
  277
genre, 53n12, 61–62, 65–67, 65n17,
  74, 116, 118n8, 147, 153, 156,
  189, 191, 237, 255, 257–59, 265,
  267–68, 270–71, 276n3, 284; narrative, 8–9, 9n10, 20–21, 115, 260
genre conventions, 109–10, 122
genre distinction (Goethe), 114
Geschehen (Schmid), 107. See also event
Geschichte (Schmid), 107. See also
  fabula, *histoire*, and story
Gricean Cooperative Principle, 175
group minds (Palmer), 84, 89

health and illness, 19, 239–41, 246–49
heteroglossia (Bahktin), 8, 190
heterosexual masterplot/heteronormativity, 7–8, 187, 200, 212n13
high-angle shot, 121
histoire (Benveniste) (vs. *discours*), 105,
  282. See also *fabula*, *Geschichte*,
  and story
historical present tense, 143, 148,
  155–56, 290
historical writing, 108. See also historiography

historicism, 186, 203
historiography, 9, 109, 269n11, 284. See
  also historical writing
hypothetical intentionalism, 17, 164,
  166–67, 169–70, 179, 181

ideology, 2, 5, 8, 53–55, 119, 277
identity, 13–14, 19, 22, 40, 53, 55,
  100–101, 103, 172, 176, 179, 227,
  235, 241, 246, 249–50, 255–60; in
  autobiography, 262–63, 265, 270
immediacy, 115, 127–28, 168
indirect speech, 40n5
in-group/out-group relations, 19, 235,
  241, 246, 250
instance: narrating, 35, 37–39, 46–52,
  55, 114; rhetorical model of, 36
intentional stance, 166–67, 169, 181
intentional fallacy, 166n9
interior monologue, 46–47, 116,
  120–22, 290. See also direct thought
intermediality, 60, 66, 75, 78
interpretation, 45, 48, 49, 62, 110, 139,
  159, 164–66, 168n11, 175, 178,
  181, 236, 280, 298
intertitles, 168, 170–71, 171n16

labeling, 242–43
langue (vs. *parole*) (Saussure), 6
lesbianism, 187, 199. See also sapphic
life history research, 236–37
low-angle shot, 120
low-key illumination, 176n22

mediacy (Stanzel), 15–17, 21, 37,
  39–40, 44, 46, 105–6, 111–18,
  125–30, 168. See also *Mittelbarkeit*
mediator (Girard), 16, 18–19, 206–9,
  213–17, 219–20, 223–28, 231. See
  also rival
medium, 8, 16–17, 36–37, 42, 46,
  46n7, 50, 60, 70, 74, 106–7,
  110–13, 116, 119–20, 122, 124–28,

Subject Index   319

139, 142n4, 158, 167, 169, 240, 260, 292n30
memoir, 286–90
memory, 19–20, 51, 122, 155, 174, 192, 217–18, 249, 256, 262–66, 270–71, 290
memory play, 47n8, 122n13
mental model, 145, 146n8, 147
metalepsis, 48, 78, 148n10, 217, 291n1
metafiction, 14, 66, 283
metaphor, 5, 16, 36–37, 42–43, 48, 50–51, 55–56, 84, 129–30, 203, 218, 237, 243–44, 269, 269n11; cinematic, 170–71, 171n15, 178n26, 179n27
meta-referentiality, 60
metonymy, 64n15, 87, 247
mind-narrative nexus, 140, 155, 158–59
mirroring, 66, 72, 75
mimesis (vs. diegesis) (Plato), 16, 36, 38, 41, 44–49, 51, 55, 130, 255. *See also* showing
mimetic rivalry (Girard), 206, 211–13, 219, 226–27
mimicry, 207, 217, 220, 228
mise en abyme, 16, 59–60, 63–69, 73, 75, 77, 78n29
mise en cadre, 16, 59–60, 63–75, 77–79, 78n29
mise en reflet/mise en série, 68–69, 75, 77–78
Mittelbarkeit (Stanzel), 111–12, 116. See also mediacy
mode (Stanzel), 106; teller mode, 45, 115, 117, 260; reflector mode, 45–46, 106, 114–19, 117n7, 118n8, 128, 169
Modernism, 107, 230, 260
modes of reading narrative, 235, 237
montage, 123
mood (Genette), 37
multiperspectivism, 94n2

narratee, 7, 10, 18–19, 188, 193, 197, 199, 199n9, 200–202, 206–7,
210–11, 216, 218–19, 221–23, 225–31, 277–78, 297–99; extradiegetic, 202; extra-subjective, 227–29; intra-subjective, 227–29; personalized, 210
narrating character, 49, 53, 211, 211n10, 212n14, 213, 216, 218, 220–26, 223n24, 223n25, 228, 293
narrating I (vs. experiencing I), 19, 147–48, 155, 235, 257. *See also* narrating self
narrating self (vs. experiencing self), 227, 244, 246, 249–50, 257. *See also* narrating I
narration, 194, 202, 206, 207, 210, 218, 229–31; act of, 222, 230; as mimetic desire, 216–17; authorial (Stanzel), 10n12, 44, 115–16, 119, 121, 123, 128, 168; autodiegetic (Genette), 38, 230; cinematic, 163–81; covert (Chatman) (vs. overt), 114–16, 126, 128, 168–69, 251; dynamic of, 197; extradiegetic (Genette), 39–41, 39n3, 40n5, 46, 48, 55, 68, 78, 114, 123; etymological root of, 275; first-person (Stanzel), 38, 44–45, 53, 108, 115–16, 128, 156, 291; homodiegetic (Genette) (vs. heterodiegetic), 41, 46, 48, 55, 118n8, 189, 258; heterodiegetic (Genette) (vs. homodiegetic), 38–41, 48, 55, 84, 194–95, 201; intradiegetic (Genette), 38–39, 46, 48, 55, 78, 188, 197, 202; motivation for, 217, 221, 223; of historical fiction, 40; overt (Chatman) (vs. covert), 46, 115–16, 126, 128, 168; simultaneous (Cohn), 282, 294 (*see also* fictional present and present-tense narration); third-person, 38, 157n13, 158n14; unreliable, 120, 257; unreliable in film, 171–74
narration (Genette), 206, 206n3
narrative: as report, 279; as sense-making device, 234; conversational, 13, 239; embedded, 49, 102; first-

person, 44, 113, 115, 117n7, 118n8, 128, 294; history of, 190; 'natural' (oral), 239n1, 279; reflector-mode, 114–16, 117n7, 128, 169; rhetorical definition of, 278, 296; second-person, 19, 248; syntax, 237; third-person, 169; unnatural, 14, 14n15, 17, 175, 275n3, 279–80, 291, 297–99

narrative clauses (Labov and Waletzky), 240

narrative discourse (vs. story), 7, 13–14, 16–19, 36–40, 47–49, 53, 71, 85, 88, 105–11, 111n4, 114–19, 122, 124, 126–29, 139–40, 146, 148, 151–53, 157–58, 164, 192, 241, 260, 262, 294; different definitions of, 105. See also *syuzhet/sujet*

narrative interviewing, 236

narrative levels, 35, 37–39, 41–46, 59, 71, 77–78, 85, 105–7, 111, 114; extradiegetic level (Genette), 39, 46, 68, 168, 249; intradiegetic/diegetic level (Genette), 39, 67–68, 78, 249; metadiegetic level (Genette), 38; hypodiegetic level (Bal), 64, 66–68, 71–73, 78

narrative mediation, 105–6, 112–13, 115–18, 120, 122–30, 260; external/internal, 208–9, 214–16; action (Fludernik), 126; experiencing (Fludernik), 126; reflecting (Fludernik), 126; telling (Fludernik), 126; viewing (Fludernik), 126

narrative report, 105

narrative representation, 9, 15–16, 35–37, 48, 55, 124

narrative situation (Stanzel), 106, 113, 116, 128, 225–26 (*see also* typological circle); authorial, 44, 117n7, 128; figural, 44–45, 115–17, 117n7, 121; first-person, 44, 117n7, 118n8

narrative structure: same-sex; woman-to-woman, 190

narrative transmission, 17, 35–41, 44–45, 48, 51, 55, 107, 110–11, 113–14, 119, 125–26, 128

narrative turn, 3

narrativity, 9, 16, 19, 60, 114, 150, 236, 256, 259–60, 263, 269, 271, 297n32; different definitions of, 105

narrativization (Fludernik), 269

narratologies: postclassical, 6–8, 11, 23, 277

narratology, 2n2; classical (structuralist), 1–4, 5–6, 6n7, 11, 58, 146, 267, 271, 276–77; cognitive, 9n9, 11–12, 14, 22n19, 139, 158, 263, 270; deconstructive, 3, 58; diachronic, 13 (*see also* historical); feminist, 7; historical, 6, 186 (*see also* diachronic); 'natural,' 58, 234–35; neoclassical (Wolf), 79; postclassical, 1–6, 11–12, 14, 16, 21–23, 58, 158–59, 238, 256, 263, 277; second phase of, 4–5, 15–23, 158–59; postcolonial, 8; postmodernist, 14–15; queer, 7, 18; rhetorical, 9–11, 35–56, 278–82; socionarratology, 239; transmedial, 8–9, 17, 19, 158; unnatural, 14–15, 17, 275n3, 280

narrator, 105–7, 112–16, 118, 122–23, 124–26, 128, 143–44, 151, 153–54, 156–57, 202, 207, 210, 225, 227–31, 244–50, 257–58, 275, 276, 279, 294, 298–99; autodiegetic, 207, 211n10, 219, 227, 230–31, 260; cinematic, 9, 17, 107, 115, 118, 128, 163–65, 168–69, 169n13, 172n17, 173n19, 181; covert vs. overt (Chatman), 116, 126, 128, 168; dramatic (Jahn), 9; engaging (Warhol), 7; external (extra-heterodiegetic), 209–10; first-person (Stanzel), 108, 276, 291; heterodiegetic (Genette) (vs. homodiegetic), 10n12, 41, 84, 38–39, 168, 169n14, 194, 200, 209; homodiegetic (Genette) (vs. heterodiegetic), 10n12, 38–41, 46, 55, 118n8, 169n14, 189, 211n10, 258; homodiegetic personalized, 210; omniscient, 38, 108, 117n7; personalized (Stanzel),

210; voice-over, 9, 121, 126, 128, 158n14, 168, 171, 174n20
narratorial persona, 114
naturalization (Culler/Fludernik), 268, 275
no-mediation thesis (Walsh), 17, 123–24, 130
no-narrator theory (Banfield), 114, 123, 126–27. *See also* non-communication
non-communication, 282, 296–97, 299. *See also* no-narrator theory
non-diegetic inserts, 168, 168n12, 170
non-diegetic music and sound, 168, 168n12, 170, 176
non-natural, 61
novel, 209–10, 229; courtship, 188, 193, 200; dialogue, 115; domestic 193, 199, 201; epistolary, 195, 197; Gothic, 44n6, 49, 73; history of, 203; Modernist, 107; realist, 276n3; postmodernist, 14; Victorian, 187–88, 201

omniscience, 45, 180, 276n3, 282
oral narratives, 19, 235–37, 239, 241, 245–46, 250–51, 259, 279. *See also* oral storytelling
oral storytelling (see also oral narratives), 244, 279
overdetermined texts (Nielsen), 284, 291–92, 295–96

painting, 9, 21, 63, 67, 73–75, 78–79, 126, 145
panfictionalism, 284
paratexts, 61–62, 66–67, 75; in film, 170; in written texts, 276, 281–82, 284–85, 287–88, 290, 296
parole (vs. *langue*) (Saussure), 6
person (Stanzel), 35, 37–41, 44–45
perspective (Stanzel), 106, 113; limited, 45; external, 45
phoneme/phone dichotomy, 109

picture frame, 61–62, 75
plot, 7, 65, 84, 100, 104, 105n1, 106–8, 110–11, 111n4, 119, 122–27, 129, 188, 191–92, 194–201, 203, 212, 230, 237, 243, 247–48, 257, 259, 261, 292; dynamic of, 197
point of view, 106, 117n7, 118–19, 121, 129
point-of-view (POV) shot, 51, 174
polychrony, 148
polyphony, 54
porn film, 165n7
pornography, 188, 190–93, 200
positioning, 19, 154–55; social, 235, 250
possible-worlds theory, 2, 12, 59
postcolonialism, 11, 59, 78–79
postmodernism, 79, 123, 280
postmodernity, 21
pragmatics, 6, 12–13, 251n3
present-tense narration (Cohn), 38, 40. *See also* fictional present and simultaneous narration
prolepsis, 62. *See also* foreshadowing
protagonist, 18, 51, 106, 116, 121, 171, 249, 291. *See also* character
psychoanalysis, 3–4, 18, 21, 211n9
psychonarration, 85, 122. *See also* thought report

qualia, 17, 156. *See also* what it's like
queer, 3–4, 7–8, 11, 18, 21, 188, 192, 199n9, 200

rapport, 244, 251
reader: implied, 10; real, 286
reader-response theory, 18, 78
realism, 187, 191, 260
récit (Genette), 115, 206n3
recursiveness, 36, 42, 44, 55
relevance theory, 251n3, 294, 296
remediation, 111, 144, 158n14
remedialization, 110–11, 125–28
repetition compulsion (Freud), 218, 230

ressentiment, 151
rhetorical model, 10, 35-36, 40n5, 46
rival (Girard), 206, 208, 213-19, 223-29. *See also* mediator
Russian formalism, 2n2, 4, 106

sapphic, 197-98, 200-201; dialogic, 18, 188, 190, 201; dialogue, 191, 196, 200; form, 189, 202; literary history, 187; narration/narrative, 189-92, 197; narrative layer, 189; (narrative) structure, 191-92, 196, 199, 202. *See also* lesbianism
schemata (cognitive), 11, 20, 61, 163, 263-64, 264n5. *See also* frame
screen universe (Souriau), 39
script (cognitive), 11, 11n13, 19, 20, 256, 264, 264n5
self vs. other, 268
setting, 63, 65, 70, 108, 110, 123
sexuality: history of, 188, 190, 203
shot-reverse shot, 120, 122
showing (vs. telling), 62-63, 65, 69, 74-75, 116, 163, 169. *See also* mimesis
signifying (Gates), 8
slant (vs. filter) (Chatman), 107, 235, 244-46, 250
social science research methods: qualitative, 235; quantitative, 235
social sciences, 234-35, 238-39, 241, 250
sociolinguistic narrative analysis, 235, 237
soliloquy, 121-22
speech act, 154, 192; indirect, 40n5; theory, 3, 12, 109
stack, 42-43
story/discourse dichotomy, 13-14, 16-19, 106-7, 109, 119, 127
story (vs. narrative discourse), 7-9, 18, 36-38, 43, 49, 62-64, 66, 69-73, 83, 85, 87, 102, 105-15, 118-19, 121, 123-25, 127-29, 146-47, 151, 154, 158, 163, 171-72, 187-91, 194, 196-97, 200, 206-7, 206n3, 209-13, 215-17, 219, 223-31, 262, 265-66, 278-79, 286, 295. *See also fabula, histoire,* and *Geschichte*
story (vs. plot) (Forster), 106-7
storyworld (Herman), 39-41, 85, 87, 98, 119, 130, 138n1, 139, 146-47, 146n8, 148n10, 149, 150-51, 155-57, 158n14, 159, 216, 242, 244-46, 248, 250, 276n3, 299. *See also diégèse* and diegetic universe
syuzhet/sujet (vs. *fabula*), 106, 110, 124. *See also* narrative discourse

telling (vs. showing), 36-37, 62, 65, 69, 75, 113, 115-118, 193, 126-28, 130, 148, 155. *See also* diegesis
tense (Genette), 107, 115
text world theory, 146
theory of mind, 97-99
thought, 83, 90, 98; intermental (Palmer), 16, 83-86, 88-102, 104; intramental (Palmer), 16, 83-84, 91-97, 99-103
thought report, 85, 89, 158n14. *See also* psychonarration
temporality 123, 191
transmediality, 9, 60, 67, 75
typological circle (Stanzel), 45. *See also* narrative situations

uncanny (*das Unheimliche*) (Freud), 213, 292
uncanny (Todorov), 177n25
underreading (vs. overreading), 143; underdetermined texts (Nielsen), 284-91, 295-96
unnatural, 14-15, 175, 291, 297; historical development of, 14n15
unnatural narration, 296-99
unreliability, 13-14, 173n18, 173n19, 195; cinematic, 120, 171-74, 181

vocalization, 37
voice (Genette), 13–16, 21, 35–37, 41, 44, 47–56, 107, 115, 118–19, 128–30, 189, 192–93, 197, 199, 257; as idiom, 36, 44, 44n6, 48–56; as instance, 36–37, 48–49, 52–56; as interpellation, 36, 52–56

we-narration, 8, 213, 226

what it's like, 140, 156–57. See also *qualia*
wipe, 168

you-narrative, 235, 248–49

zoom, 52n11, 120, 122

THEORY AND INTERPRETATION OF NARRATIVE
JAMES PHELAN AND PETER J. RABINOWITZ, SERIES EDITORS

Because the series editors believe that the most significant work in narrative studies today contributes both to our knowledge of specific narratives and to our understanding of narrative in general, studies in the series typically offer interpretations of individual narratives and address significant theoretical issues underlying those interpretations. The series does not privilege one critical perspective but is open to work from any strong theoretical position.

Towards the Ethics of Form in Fiction: Narratives of Cultural Remission
  Leona Toker

Techniques for Living: Fiction and Theory in the Work of Christine Brooke-Rose
  Karen R. Lawrence

Tabloid, Inc.: Crimes, Newspapers, Narratives
  V. Penelope Pelizzon and Nancy M. West

Narrative Means, Lyric Ends: Temporality in the Nineteenth-Century British Long Poem
  Monique R. Morgan

Understanding Nationalism: On Narrative, Cognitive Science, and Identity
  Patrick Colm Hogan

Joseph Conrad: Voice, Sequence, History, Genre
  Edited by Jakob Lothe, Jeremy Hawthorn, James Phelan

The Rhetoric of Fictionality: Narrative Theory and the Idea of Fiction
  Richard Walsh

Experiencing Fiction: Judgments, Progressions, and the Rhetorical Theory of Narrative
  James Phelan

Unnatural Voices: Extreme Narration in Modern and Contemporary Fiction
  Brian Richardson

Narrative Causalities
  Emma Kafalenos

Why We Read Fiction: Theory of Mind and the Novel
  Lisa Zunshine

I Know That You Know That I Know: Narrating Subjects from Moll Flanders *to* Marnie
  George Butte

Bloodscripts: Writing the Violent Subject
  Elana Gomel

Surprised by Shame: Dostoevsky's Liars and Narrative Exposure
  Deborah A. Martinsen

Having a Good Cry: Effeminate Feelings and Pop-Culture Forms
  Robyn R. Warhol

Politics, Persuasion, and Pragmatism: A Rhetoric of Feminist Utopian Fiction
  Ellen Peel

Telling Tales: Gender and Narrative Form in Victorian Literature and Culture
  Elizabeth Langland

Narrative Dynamics: Essays on Time, Plot, Closure, and Frames
  Edited by Brian Richardson

Breaking the Frame: Metalepsis and the Construction of the Subject
  Debra Malina

Invisible Author: Last Essays
  Christine Brooke-Rose

Ordinary Pleasures: Couples, Conversation, and Comedy
  Kay Young

Narratologies: New Perspectives on Narrative Analysis
  Edited by David Herman

Before Reading: Narrative Conventions and the Politics of Interpretation
  Peter J. Rabinowitz

Matters of Fact: Reading Nonfiction over the Edge
  Daniel W. Lehman

The Progress of Romance: Literary Historiography and the Gothic Novel
  David H. Richter

A Glance Beyond Doubt: Narration, Representation, Subjectivity
  Shlomith Rimmon-Kenan

Narrative as Rhetoric: Technique, Audiences, Ethics, Ideology
  James Phelan

Misreading Jane Eyre: A Postformalist Paradigm
  Jerome Beaty

Psychological Politics of the American Dream: The Commodification of Subjectivity in Twentieth-Century American Literature
  Lois Tyson

Understanding Narrative
  Edited by James Phelan and Peter J. Rabinowitz

Framing Anna Karenina: *Tolstoy, the Woman Question, and the Victorian Novel*
  Amy Mandelker

Gendered Interventions: Narrative Discourse in the Victorian Novel
  Robyn R. Warhol

Reading People, Reading Plots: Character, Progression, and the Interpretation of Narrative
  James Phelan

www.ingramcontent.com/pod-product-compliance
Lightning Source LLC
Chambersburg PA
CBHW021846300426
44115CB00005B/38